T0180920

Lecture Notes in Artificial Intelligence 12090

Subseries of Lecture Notes in Computer Science

Series Editors

Randy Goebel
University of Alberta, Edmonton, Canada
Yuzuru Tanaka
Hokkaido University, Sapporo, Japan
Wolfgang Wahlster
DFKI and Saarland University, Saarbrücken, Germany

Founding Editor

Jörg Siekmann
DFKI and Saarland University, Saarbrücken, Germany

More information about this series at http://www.springer.com/series/1244

Andreas Holzinger · Randy Goebel ·
Michael Mengel · Heimo Müller (Eds.)

Artificial Intelligence and Machine Learning for Digital Pathology

State-of-the-Art and Future Challenges

 Springer

Editors
Andreas Holzinger (iD)
Medical University of Graz
Graz, Austria

University of Alberta
Edmonton, AB, Canada

Michael Mengel
University of Alberta
Edmonton, AB, Canada

Randy Goebel
University of Alberta
Edmonton, AB, Canada

Heimo Müller
Medical University of Graz
Graz, Austria

ISSN 0302-9743 ISSN 1611-3349 (electronic)
Lecture Notes in Artificial Intelligence
ISBN 978-3-030-50401-4 ISBN 978-3-030-50402-1 (eBook)
https://doi.org/10.1007/978-3-030-50402-1

LNCS Sublibrary: SL7 – Artificial Intelligence

This Springer imprint is published by the registered company Springer Nature Switzerland AG
The registered company address is: Gewerbestrasse 11, 6330 Cham, Switzerland

Preface

The work of pathologists is interesting for fundamental research in Artificial Intelligence (AI) and Machine Learning (ML) for several reasons: 1) digital pathology is not just the transformation of the classical microscopic analysis to a digital visualization, it is a disruptive innovation that will markedly change health care in the next few years; 2) much information is hidden in arbitrarily high dimensional spaces of heterogenous data sources (images, patient records, *omics data), which is not accessible to a human, and consequently we need AI/ML to generate a novel kind of information; and 3) pathologists are able to learn from very few examples and to transfer previously learned knowledge quickly to new tasks. This implies developing software which can learn from experience and can adapt to the context, similarly as we humans do. A major issue is to foster transparency, re-traceability, and explainability, to explain why a machine decision has been made and to understand the underlying explanatory factors.

ML requires access to large training data sets that cover the spectrum of a variety of human diseases in different organ systems very well. Training data sets must meet quality and regulatory criteria and be well annotated for ML at patient-, sample-, and image-level. Currently, only relatively small data sets are available, which could already demonstrate proof of concept at the first level. For enabling the future broad application of AI in digital pathology, orders of magnitudes of larger training data sets are required. Here biobanks play a central role providing large collections of high-quality, well-annotated samples and data. The main biobanking-related challenges to solve are: finding the best biobank containing "fit-for-purpose" samples, providing quality related meta-data, gaining rapid access to standardized medical data and annotations, and scanning the biobank samples (slides) in an acceptable time period, including efficient management, established and standardized procedures, as well as regulations of the carrier organization and national law. Finally, we thank each and everybody who contributed to the success of this volume and we dedicate this volume to a great pioneer in this field, Professor Kurt Zatloukal, on the occasion of his 60th birthday.

April 2020

Andreas Holzinger
Randy Goebel
Michael Mengel
Heimo Müller

Organization

Scientific Committee

Peter Bankhead	University of Edinburgh, UK
Jaesik Choi	Ulsan National Institute of Science and Technology (UNIST), South Korea
Toby Cornish	University of Colorado, USA
Thomas J. Fuchs	Memorial Sloan Kettering Cancer Center, USA
David Andrew Gutman	University School of Medicine, Atlanta, USA
Randy Goebel	University of Alberta, Canada
Anant Madabhushi	Case Western Reserve University, USA
Craig Mermel	Google AI, USA
Jose M. Oramas	KU Leuven, Belgium
Liron Pantanowitz	University of Pittsburgh Schools of Health Sciences (UPMC), USA
Christin Seifert	University of Twente, The Netherlands
Klaus-Robert Müller	TU Berlin, Germany, and Korea University, South Korea
Nasir M. Rajpoot	University of Warwick, UK
Kurt Zatloukal	Medical University Graz, Austria
Jianlong Zhou	Sydney University of Technology, Australia

Contents

About the Editors

Andreas Holzinger is lead of the Human-Centered AI Group at the Medical University Graz and since 2016 he is Visiting Professor for machine learning in health informatics at Vienna University of Technology. Currently, he serves as Visiting Professor for explainable AI at the xAI Lab of the University of Alberta, Edmonton, Canada. Andreas obtained a PhD in Cognitive Science from Graz University in 1998 and his second PhD in Computer Science from TU Graz in 2003. Andreas is internationally well known for his pioneer work on interactive machine learning with a human-in-the-loop. He is in the advisory board of the strategy "AI Made in Germany 2030" of the German Government and in the advisory board of the "AI Mission Austria 2030", he serves as consultant for the Canadian, USA, UK, Swiss, French, Italian, and Dutch governments, for the German Excellence Initiative, and as national expert in the European Commission. He serves as Austrian Representative for AI in IFIP TC 12 and in 2019 was elected as ordinary member into the European Academy of Sciences in the field of explainable AI.

Randy Goebel is head of the explainable AI Lab at the Alberta Machine Intelligence Institute, and also Vice President of Research and Professor of Computer Science at the Faculty of Sciences of the University of Alberta. Randy obtained a PhD in Computer Science from the University of British Columbia in 1985. Randy's theoretical work on abduction, hypothetical reasoning, and belief revision is internationally well known, and his recent application of practical belief revision and constraint programming to scheduling, layout, and Web mining is now having industrial impact. Randy has previously held faculty appointments at the University of Waterloo, Multimedia University (Malaysia), Hokkaido University (Japan), the University of Tokyo (Japan), and he is actively involved in academic and industrial collaborative research projects in Canada, Japan, China, and the German Research Center for Artificial Intelligence in Saarbrücken, Germany.

Michael Mengel is Chair/Professor, Clinical Department Head, and Medical Director for Laboratory Medicine and Pathology at the Division of Anatomical Pathology of the University of Alberta. Dr. Mengel also works with the Alberta Public Laboratories in Edmonton, Canada. As a sub-specialized Transplantation and Renal Pathologist, Dr. Mengel is engaged in various international sub-specialty societies related to nephropathology and organ transplantation. Dr. Mengel studied medicine at the Semmelweiss University in Budapest, Hungary, before going on to specialize in pathology and further in transplantation pathology and nephropathology. Dr. Mengel has published widely in his field and his current work is focused on applying molecular AI techniques to biopsy specimens, with the aim to increase diagnostic precision in organ transplantation. Dr. Mengel is president of the Canadian Society of transplantation and board member of the Renal Pathology Society.

Heimo Müller studied Mathematics in Graz and Vienna, Austria concluding with a thesis on data space semantics. He worked on data visualisation at JOANNEUM RESEARCH, participated as national expert in ISO/IEC JTC1 SC24 and SC29, and was document editor in SC24/WG7. He was a Marie Curie fellow at the Vrije Universiteit Amsterdam, The Netherlands, and the Founding Head of the Information Design program of the University of Applied Sciences FH Joanneum. He developed an interactive data exploration system for clinical data and was part of the FET flagship project IT Future of Medicine responsible for ICT aspects of the medical platform. He participated in several EC funded projects (Biomedbridges, BBMRI-LPC, ESGI, BioShare, CORBEL, B3Africa, ADOPT) and is currently heavily involved in EOSC-Life (European Science Cloud for Life Science), EJP-RD (European Joint Programming on Rare Diseases), and IMI Conception (Medication Safety in Pregnancy). Heimo Müller is the PI of the BIBBOX, an open source platform for data sharing developed by the BBMRI-ERIC common service IT and the H2020 project B3Africa.

Expectations of Artificial Intelligence for Pathology

Peter Regitnig[1(✉)] [ID], Heimo Müller[1,2], and Andreas Holzinger[2] [ID]

[1] Diagnostic and Research Institute of Pathology, Medical University of Graz,
Neue Stiftingtalstraße 6, 8036 Graz, Austria
`peter.regitnig@medunigraz.at`
[2] Institute for Medical Informatics, Statistics and Documentation, Medical
University of Graz, Auenbruggerplatz 2/V, 8036 Graz, Austria

Abstract. Within the last ten years, essential steps have been made
to bring artificial intelligence (AI) successfully into the field of pathology. However, most pathologists are still far away from using AI in daily
pathology practice. If one leaves the pathology annihilation model, this
paper focuses on tasks, which could be solved, and which could be done
better by AI, or image-based algorithms, compared to a human expert.
In particular, this paper focuses on the needs and demands of surgical
pathologists; examples include: Finding small tumour deposits within
lymph nodes, detection and grading of cancer, quantification of positive tumour cells in immunohistochemistry, pre-check of Papanicolaou-
stained gynaecological cytology in cervical cancer screening, text feature
extraction, text interpretation for tumour-coding error prevention and
AI in the next-generation virtual autopsy. However, in order to make
substantial progress in both fields it is important to intensify the cooperation between medical AI experts and pathologists.

Keywords: Artificial Intelligence · Medical AI · Machine learning ·
Digital pathology · Practical implementations of AI

1 Introduction and Motivation

1.1 What Is the Difference Between Artificial Intelligence (AI), Machine Learning (ML) and Deep Learning (DL)?

A very short answer is $DL \subset ML \subset AI$. For the sake of simplicity, we will
use the term AI exclusively in this paper because of the common usage these
days. We refer with this term to data-driven machine learning algorithms and, of
course, deep learning approaches. The latter represent a currently particularly
popular and successful family of learning algorithms [1]. To give the reader a
good introduction, we will nevertheless briefly explain these terms.

Artificial Intelligence (AI) deals with the automation of intelligent behaviour
with the long-term goal of reaching general intelligence ("strong AI"). This is

© Springer Nature Switzerland AG 2020
A. Holzinger et al. (Eds.): AI & ML for Digital Pathology, LNAI 12090, pp. 1–15, 2020.
https://doi.org/10.1007/978-3-030-50402-1_1

the reason why AI cannot be clearly defined because a precise definition of intelligence is lacking [22]. AI had always a close connection to cognitive science and is indeed a very old scientific field going back to the early work of Alan Turing [54]. After extremely high expectations to the classical logic-based AI between 1950 and 1980 the success was relatively low, resulting in a so-called "AI-winter". From 2010 on, AI regained much interest due to practical success of statistical machine learning and especially the family of deep learning algorithms [23].

Machine Learning (ML) deals with the design, development and evaluation of algorithms that can learn from data, to gain knowledge from experience and improve their learning behaviour over time. Most of all it allows to infer unknowns and to make predictions to support decision making. One challenge is to discover relevant structural and/or temporal patterns ("knowledge") in data, which is often hidden in arbitrarily high dimensional spaces, thus not accessible to a human expert [21]. Although ML is well defined, demonstrates much practical success, and is seen as the fastest growing technical field in computer science - ML is often summarized under the vague term AI. This may be understandable if we look at the challenges, which include sensemaking, context understanding, and decision making under uncertainty. We have to be fair to say that ML is the technical field that deals with the design, development and evaluation of algorithms, while AI covers also philosophical, social, ethical and juridical aspects, encompasses the underlying scientific theories of human learning vs. machine learning, and also explainability [20] and causability [24] which includes trust, fairness and ethical responsible decision making. Consequently, "Medical AI" is quite an acceptable term for the application of AI to study and pursue the effective use of ML for scientific problem solving and decision making motivated by efforts to safe and improve human health.

Deep Learning (DL) is one methodological family of ML based on, among others, artificial neural networks, deep belief networks, recurrent neural networks, etc. To give a precise example of a feed forward ANN: the multilayer perceptron [56], which is a very simple mathematical function mapping a set of input data to output data. The concept behind such ML models is representation learning, i.e. introducing other representations that are expressed in terms of simpler representations. Despite of the simplicity one huge shortcoming of these approaches is that due to their size they quickly become non-traceable, i.e. it becomes difficult to retrace and to understand why a certain result has been achieved. This makes the field of explainable AI a necessity [14].

AI, ML, DL, or however we call it, may help to solve certain problems, particularly in areas where humans have limited capacities (e.g. in high dimensional spaces, large numbers, big data, etc.). However, we must acknowledge that the problem-solving capacity of the human mind is still unbeaten in certain aspects (e.g. in the lower dimensions, when having little data, complex problems, etc. [42]). Consequently, it is sometimes desired to keep the human-in-the-loop [19], but it is indispensable to keep the doctor-in-control. For all these reasons integrated solutions are urgently needed in the future [25].

1.2 Is Pathology an Uncomplicated Medical Speciality?

In 2015 Levenson et al. [29] published a paper about pigeons, which differentiated between benign breast samples and malignant breast samples.

The excitement in popular media and also within the pathology community was enormous. Newsflashes about this paper were as follows: "Pigeons spot cancer as well as human experts", "Pigeons to replace pathologists in diagnosing benign from malignant tumours", and the most aggressive within these headlines came from NBC News: "Bird brain? Pigeons make good pathologists, study finds".

Of course, such headlines make a pathologist frustrated and lead to increased aversions to all innovations in this field, despite that this was also critically discussed; for example [15] acknowledged that algorithms fall short of matching some basic human vision capabilities, i.e. when humans look at images they can interpret scenes and predict within seconds what is likely to happen after the picture is taken away ("object dynamic prediction").

By looking at the pictures used in the study by Levenson et al. (2015), one feature is quite apparent, namely that benign samples were less cellular and showed less blue areas compared to the malignant samples. If one takes this single, but very typical characteristic as a diagnostic feature, many breast samples would be misdiagnosed within a few days, but at least for a pigeon, it makes a reasonable success rate. Nevertheless, this work highlighted a phenomenon that even small neuronal networks (the "pigeon brain") have enough cognitive potential to differentiate between pictures which show less blue and which show bluer, the latter is often coupled to malignancy due to its higher cellularity. Compared to AI generally and neuronal networks particularly, this has something in common: we are also not able to ask a pigeon *why* a certain characteristic it recognised to differentiate between benign and malignant and so we are not able to recognise in most neuronal network architectures, i.e. which features were the most weighted. Although there are already some methods of explainable AI [46] to overcome these problems, in many clinical situations, AI is still kind of black box – lacking interpretability by the human expert. Current pathology text-books contain hundreds of pages per organ and around 10 to 20 typical morphological features per entity. Moreover, if all the requirements and challenges a pathologist faces day by day [26], it is evident that in the near future not a single neuronal network will be able to recognise all the details which clinicians need for further therapy and to show contextual understanding. On specific questions, however, support by AI can be expected, but for the next years it is rather sure that pathologists will be neither replaced by pigeons nor by AI. That does not mean that the workflows might be optimized and that integrated solutions appropriately designed to support effective human-AI interaction will be beneficial to reduce time-pressure, enhance quality, and enable interpretability which would also bring huge benefits in the education and training of pathologists, which are urgently needed.

2   Glossary

Pathology: Discipline in medicine, which diagnoses diseases from tissue, which is obtained by biopsy or surgical procedure. Pathology uses many biomedical techniques, and the two mainly used are microscopy and immunohistochemistry.

Immunohistochemistry: is a biomedical technique to microscopically visualize highly specific certain proteins to determine tissue-typical protein expression for differential diagnosis or treatment decisions.

Breast Cancer: A malignant neoplasm or tumour evolves from the breast gland tissue and which is capable of spreading in local lymph nodes, i.e. lymph node metastasis or via blood vessels in distant organs, i.e. distant metastasis.

Malignant Melanoma: A malignant neoplasm evolves from pigment cells of skin or mucosa and which can spread to lymph nodes or in distant organs.

Lymph Node Metastases: Deposits of malignant tumour cells in regional lymph nodes. Lymph node metastases are crucial prognostic information, because it is often coupled to a systemic tumour disease and indicating later appearing distant metastases.

Sentinel Lymph Node: A specific lymph node, which is the first in a region of a nearby malignant tumour. Sentinel lymph nodes indicate whether other regional lymph nodes might contain metastases, too. Instead of full lymph-node dissection nowadays only the Sentinel lymph node is surgically removed to diminish adverse effects, like lymphoedema.

TNM System: A system describing the extent of a malignant tumour. T stands for local tumour extend, N for lymph node metastases, M for distant metastases. Each cancer patient is staged for the tumour extend at the time of diagnosis to provide prognostic information, which influences the further treatment.

Tumour Grading: A system describing the maturation or similarity of a malignant tumour compared to its normal-tissue counterpart. Grading is a morphological evaluation of architecture of the tumour and its cytological cell features. It ranges from Grade 1 (i.e. well-differentiated) to Grade 3 (i.e. poorly differentiated). Grading also gives important information for prognosis and thus further treatment decision.

Gleason Grading: Tumour grading in prostate cancer facilitates a particular form of Grading, mainly focusing on the architecture of neoplastic glands. This pattern recognition is 5-tired and based on synoptic drawings. For example, Gleason grade 1 is defined as uniform, well circled, evenly distributed glands; grade 4 contains cribriform, i.e. sieve-like structures and grade 5 has solid or single cells unevenly distributed.

Papanicolaou Test: Epithelial cells from the cervix uteri are stained with the Papanicolaou technique and microscopically evaluated for atypical cells. The Pap-test is the most efficient cervical cancer preventive test over the last decades. Nowadays, it is replaced or preceded by the more sensitive HPV test, which focuses on the underlying HPV infection.

3 State-of-the-Art

3.1 The Position of AI in Pathology Today?

Within the last ten years, significant steps have been made to make AI relevant in the field of pathology. Nevertheless, we are currently far away from using AI in daily pathology practice. Scanning and storage of whole slides became quite affordable, but the applications for using AI are still in the field of basic research and highly diverse. During the last decade, machine learning got applicable on whole slide images, and thus AI is also called the third revolution in pathology, after the invention of immunohistochemistry and next-generation sequencing [5, 32, 38, 45].

When one compares the development of AI in pathology to the development of self-driving cars, we see a very long time passing by between the first cars which had adaptive cruise controls in the 1950ies; and even nowadays an autopilot is not standard, as we would have expected some years ago. One reason for that is the fatality-risk of an error caused by the autonomous car; although errors by *human* drivers result in enormous death rates. For example in the US there were in 2014 over 6.1 million reported collisions, 94% attributed to driver error [41]. Consequently, autonomous vehicles have a huge potential to dramatically reduce the contribution of driver error and negligence as the cause of vehicle collisions.

The same is true for a diagnostic error in pathology, where misdiagnosis leads to under- or overtreatment. Even for the non-medical community, it might be evident that chemotherapy for a non-cancer patient is fatal. Therefore in both systems, certainty and reliability are the essential features to be reached and to be tested.

Who really thinks that driving a car is as complex as pathology has no idea how complicated biological tissues can be. The learning curve of a pathologist in training looks like this: To become a good pathologist, it takes about 5 to 6 years to study general medicine, after that 2 to 6 years of residency (depending on national regulations) and after that, another 4 to 10 years to become a good pathologist with a broad knowledge about all possible diseases and differential diagnosis. Becoming an expert in a field, e.g. gynecopathology or neuropathology, takes even more years. General pathologists knowing "everything" do unfortunately not exist anymore compared to 20–30 years ago, because medical knowledge increased so dramatically and the organ-specialisation went in parallel with specialisation in other medical fields. Coming back to the comparison with automatic car-driving: Acquiring a driving license takes a few weeks, probably this comparison of learning times makes it more evident that interpreting morphology in biological tissues is a huge task.

Medical AI will also have great potential to support successfully, but will be similarly or even more dependent on the solution of ethical and legal problems [47].

3.2 Where Could Pathologists Need Support by AI?

Beside the limitations mentioned above, some applications are useful due to their highly specific scope. AI will support the daily work of pathologists within the next few years. Here are some of these summarised as good practice examples.

Finding Small Tumour Deposits Within Lymph Nodes. For cancer therapy, it is crucial to recognise lymph node metastases (see Fig. 1). Some of these are big enough to be seen by naked eye or on radiological imaging, but some require a thorough work-up of the tissue by step sectioning in 200 μm distance or less, resulting in 15 to 20 levels on glass slides for a single lymph node, the so-called sentinel-lymph-node evaluation. This procedure is most often required in breast cancer or malignant melanoma [13,36], but it is also used in other tumour entities nowadays [6].

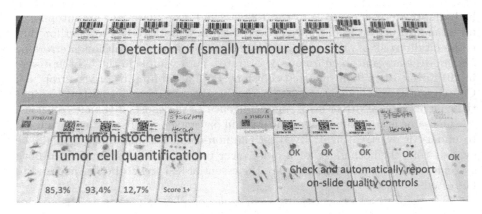

Fig. 1. Glass slides of three pathology cases of breast cancer samples. Upper row: Sentinel lymph node sections immunohistochemically stained with anti-keratin. Lower row: Haematoxylin and Eosin (yellow labels) and immunohistochemically stained (white labels) sections of breast cancer biopsies illustrating potentially supportive quantification of immuno-stained tumour cells, on-slide controls and detection of tumour deposits in lymph nodes. (Color figure online)

This evaluation is laborious, and error-prone due to highly repetitive images seen and a low number of recognisable events, or better said a low number of small tumour deposits. It is a good example where AI can bring pathology to the next level in daily routine work. Applications for metastasis detection in lymph nodes were published in recent years already [2,30].

The main task for AI in this field should be the detection of (small) tumour cells aggregates as a screening method before the stained slides of a case will be seen by a human pathologist. However, the final decision about a metastasis or an artefact should stay in the hands of humans, unless real good trained image recognition software will be able to do the same task equal or better with very high specificity. A high number of cases is needed to train and further to prove the software in a validation study. The first level to reach is a high sensitivity of detection, which can reduce the work-load of pathologists.

Detection and Grading of Cancer. One of the main tasks in pathology is the detection of cancer in tissues removed by biopsy or surgery. The first big question is whether a patient has a tumour or not. In radiological imaging, inflammatory changes often mimic neoplastic growth and thus have to be diagnosed microscopically by pathologists in a certain way.

Within neoplasms, pathologists differentiate between benign, premalignant and malignant and do a further refinement of the tumours, called tumour typing. For malignant tumours, this is done according to the WHO tumour typing [8]. Furthermore, all malignant tumour types are categorized according to the likelihood of their normal tissue counterpart. This is the so-called Grading, where mostly architectural and cytological details are considered. Grading ranges from well-differentiated (G1) to poorly differentiated (G3) and in some instances undifferentiated (G4) exists, too. For each neoplasm, a specific definition of the tumour grades exists. In most tumour types, the grading definitions and microscopical appearance cannot be transferred from one to the other. Tumour-typing and Grading are two of the hallmarks for tumour prognostication and do have direct influence to further treatment decisions. For example, well-differentiated (G1) malignant tumours do have a favourable prognosis and therefore need lees often chemotherapy treatment compared to poorly differentiated (G3) tumours.

Thus, AI has a full limitation when trying to generalize in these fields. However, in recent years, good examples of tumour detection algorithms, particularly using deep learning approaches, and it's specific Gleason grading [10,11] have been achieved in prostate cancer [3,28,35,43,57].

In breast cancer, counting of mitotic figures is essential besides tubule formation and pleomorphism of nuclei for grading. However, mitotic counting is time-consuming and error-prone. Recently, a method to automatically detect mitotic figures in breast cancer tissue sections based on convolutional neural networks was published [51]. These are good examples that machine learning for a particular type of tumour can be reached successfully in a distinct question, but compared to the number of tumour types, it is still a tiny application. Cancers occur in most types of cells; compared with the 300 or so different types of cells in the human body, we can recognize 200 different types of human cancers [31] and countless variants. It must be recognized that each tumour is highly individual and has distinct biological and thus also morphological features.

Quantification of Positive Tumour Cells in Immunohistochemistry. Another example of support in pathology will be the exact quantification of positive tumour cells in immunohistochemistry. In daily pathology practice, counting is too time-consuming and seen in the light of relevance not feasible. Therefore, real counting is most times replaced by estimation in a semi-quantitative manner or counted in a fraction of cells. It has been shown that quantification is also possible by relative simple morphometry [12,53], but the limitation is to differentiate tissue types, like malignant and normal epithelial structures or differentiation between invasive and non-invasive tumour cells and surrounding stromal tissue. Machine learning can achieve such a tissue-type differentiation in advance of the final quantification. However, one may never forget, that even such technically sophisticated procedure might only produce pseudo-precision because most tumours show an intra-tumour heterogeneity, which is typical for biological structures.

Checking of On-Slide Quality Controls. Regarding immunohistochemistry, another application of artificial intelligence could be checking of on-slide quality controls. To follow the accuracy of immunohistochemistry additional tissue pieces or cultured cell-lines are placed and stained on the same glass slide as the patient's tissue and are visually checked in the microscope for true positive-, negative-staining and staining intensity in the expected cell types. Such measurements over several runs and several days could be achieved by image similarity measurements, as already shown for histopathology [16].

Pre-check of Papaniculaou-Stained Gynaecological Cytology in Cervical Cancer Screening. An exciting application for machine learning for microscopy could be a pre-check of Papanicolaou stained gynaecological cytology. The Pap-test is used to detect atypical epithelial cells, which are a precursor of cervical cancer (see Fig. 2). The cells are obtained from the cervix uteri in a non-invasive way. After that directly placed on a glass slide or in a liquid for further processing and staining. Specialised trained biomedical technicians and doctors search for atypical cells, an event occurring in around 1–3 % of cases and seen only in a small fraction of all cells on the glass-slide. On each glass slide, around 20.000 epithelial cells have to be inspected and in a positive case around 10–1000 with a wide variation can be found. Such numbers make it evident that the detection rate is only reaching 50–70%. Based on classical morphometry image analysis, several companies worked already on this topic [4,7,9,27].

Since a few years, machine learning algorithms have been implemented in this field, e.g. DeepPap where the authors implemented a deep convolutional network [58], or the work of [49], where the authors applied a Mask Regional Convolutional Neural Network (Mask R-CNN) to cervical cancer screening using pap smear histological slides. A current review [55] indicated that there are still weaknesses in the available techniques, resulting in low accuracy of classification in some classes of cells and that a shortcoming is that most of the existing algorithms work either on single or on multiple cervical smear images.

However, not only screening for atypical cells could be an application, but also the first level of assessment could be done by a AI system, namely to count how many cells are within a PAP smear and if there are endocervical cells are present or not. All these features are important for interpreting the adequacy of a Pap smear, which underlines the repetitiveness and certainty of a given cell-sample. In the second level of assessment, algorithms could highlight atypical cells among thousands of normal cells within one Pap smear.

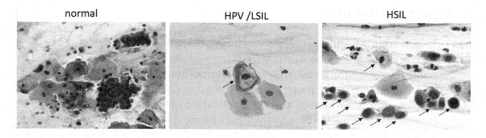

Fig. 2. Papanicolaou-stained cells from the cervix uteri in different appearances: left: different types of normal cells (squamous and glandular epithelial cells and some erythrocytes); middle: one atypical cell of HPV infection (cell with a halo in the cytoplasm, Koilocyte), which is named low grade squamous intraepithelial lesion (LSIL); right shows several squamous cells with high grade atypia, which is named high grade squamous intraepithelial lesion (HSIL). LSIL and HSIL are precursor lesions of invasive cervical cancer.

Text Feature Extraction. A completely different field of medical AI is not connected to images but is connected to pathology-reports, which pathologists typically tend to make like an essay [37, 44, 50]. There are manifold useful applications here, e.g. AI can help to structure or extract specific text parts from routine pathology reports for further scientific purposes. Especially all the reports could be better used for any scientific purpose if it would be easier to search for different disease entities. This could increase the value of millions of biospecimens which are currently stored in pathology archives or biobanks [33, 34].

Text Interpretation and Coding Error Prevention. Another possibility for text-interpreting software could be the preventive error correction. Nowadays errors can occur in classifications during a hard-working day, for example within the TNM system or the tumour grading system. Software running in the background of laboratory information systems might be able to highlight an error of misconduct instantly. For example, instead of well-differentiated, invasive breast carcinoma (NST), G2 it should immediately highlight that "well differentiated" and G2 is incompatible. As a training set thousands, if not millions of already written reports could be taken to learn what is correct and what is outside of this reasonable conduct.

Medical AI in Next-Generation Autopsy. An autopsy is a long and historical field of pathology tasks. Also, in this field, new imaging techniques can be observed. CT or MRI imaging is already used in virtual autopsies and by using such a technique, image analysis comes into the field again. For example, machine learning provides new opportunities for investigating minimal tumour burden and therapy resistance in cancer patients and can lead to an enhanced or augmented autopsy [39,40].

4   Open Problems

In conclusion some specific problems hindering the progress of digital pathology and machine learning can be summarized:

User interfaces are far away from being ergonomic, thus usability engineering [18] is for future Human-AI more necessary than ever. A wise way would be the integration of digital pathology and AI applications together within the laboratory information systems (LIS). On the other hand, a decoupling of such systems is desirable in order to make legal aspects manageable, such as liability via medical device laws. This requires standardized interfaces and thus enables a modular extension of existing workflows via "AI-Apps". It would also be necessary that measurements would be directly transferred back to the LIS. Such advantages in ergonomics would make the acceptance enormously high and enable trustworthy AI integration.

Nowadays, several proprietary image formats exist among scanner vendors. A single image format like DICOM [17,52,59], which is in development for pathology whole slide images, is necessary for the widespread use and also for consultation purposes between different institutions and standardised exchange of data with neuronal network algorithms. Also, software licensing has to be rethought by vendors. It will be impossible for pathology institutes to purchase several software systems for a wide range of diagnostic reasons and different tissue-specific applications. A way out of this could be a pay-per-case model. A technical issue which might be solved within the next years is the large image file sizes, but technical advances could solve compression and also storage issues. By the way, simple greyscale images, still provide much information for pathologists due to structural preservation.

Finally, the most important and probably obvious problem is that there is too little interaction between AI scientists on the one side and pathologists on the other side. Imagine an AI scientist developing a self-driving car without knowing how to drive a car, which is pretty impossible. Currently, we are in the situation that AI scientists sometimes produce fascinating morphology-interpretation software, but they typically lack knowledge about morphology or the clinical value about image and text interpretation. On the other hand, pathologists, although often very much interested in this topic, lack time, due to shortage of personal and increasing specialisation of organ-specific pathology with sometimes overwhelming daily work-load.

5   Future Outlook

Nowadays, we face an innovative and exciting technique, which will surely find its way in the pathology departments. Some of the advantages are set in the framing of whole slide imaging and digital pathology in a strict sense: By scanning all the thousands of slides in a pathology lab, there will be not so much lost or broken slides anymore. It is expected that there is less time wasting for organisation of cases by bringing together all slides. A tremendous advantage in digital pathology is quick access to archived slides of one patient for comparison of older slides to the actual slides and also to get quicker access to second opinions worldwide [48].

Residential teaching can facilitate typical cases, which will be stored and collected digitally and could be shared worldwide. Measurements of tumour sizes or distances to resection margins will be more objective compared to classical microscopy.

Furthermore, new AI applications will support and improve the quantification, especially in immunohistochemistry, and it might prevent pathologists from typical text-errors. Moreover, the hope exists that machine learning will bring a lot of new insights in tumour prognostication because certain morphological features could be highlighted by unsupervised machine learning only, which humans would hardly recognise at all.

In the author's view, the intensified cooperation between AI scientists and pathologists would bring enormous progress, and we hope that AI will support the next generation of pathologists like computers support pilots in a plane today. Due to the enormous complexity of biology and pathology of tissues, pathologists will not be replaced by AI in the near future, however, such thoughts increase fear and might interfere with further progress.

Acknowledgements. The authors declare that there are no conflicts of interests and the work does not raise any ethical issues. Parts of this work has been funded by the Austrian Science Fund (FWF), Project: P-32554 "A reference model of explainable Artificial Intelligence for the Medical Domain", and by the European Union's Horizon 2020 research and innovation program under grant agreements No 824087 "EOSC-Life" and No 826078 "Feature Cloud". We thank the anonymous reviewers for their critical but helpful comments.

References

1. Arvaniti, E., et al.: Automated gleason grading of prostate cancer tissue microarrays via deep learning. Sci. Rep. **8**(1), 1–11 (2018). https://doi.org/10.1038/s41598-018-30535-1
2. Bandi, P., et al.: From detection of individual metastases to classification of lymph node status at the patient level: the camelyon17 challenge. IEEE Trans. Med. Imaging **38**(2), 550–560 (2018). https://doi.org/10.1109/TMI.2018.2867350
3. Bulten, W., et al.: Automated deep-learning system for gleason grading of prostate cancer using biopsies: a diagnostic study. Lancet Oncol. (2020). https://doi.org/10.1016/S1470-2045(19)30739-9

4. Cengel, K.A., et al.: Effectiveness of the surepath liquid-based pap test in automated screening and in detection of hsil. Diagn. Cytopathol. **29**(5), 250–255 (2003). https://doi.org/10.1002/dc.10373
5. Chang, H.Y., et al.: Artificial intelligence in pathology. J. Pathol. Transl. Med. **53**(1), 1–12 (2019). https://doi.org/10.4132/jptm.2018.12.16
6. Cibula, D., McCluggage, W.G.: Sentinel lymph node (SLN) concept in cervical cancer: current limitations and unanswered questions. Gynecol. Oncol. **152**(1), 202–207 (2019). https://doi.org/10.1016/j.ygyno.2018.10.007
7. Duggan, M.A., Brasher, P.: Paired comparison of manual and automated pap test screening using the papnet system. Diagn. Cytopathol. **17**(4), 248–254 (1997)
8. Ellis, I., et al.: The 2019 who classification of tumours of the breast. Histopathology (2020). https://doi.org/10.1111/his.14091
9. Elsheikh, T.M., Austin, R.M., Chhieng, D.F., Miller, F.S., Moriarty, A.T., Renshaw, A.A.: American society of cytopathology workload recommendations for automated pap test screening: developed by the productivity and quality assurance in the era of automated screening task force. Diagn. Cytopathol. **41**(2), 174–178 (2013). https://doi.org/10.1002/dc.22817
10. Epstein, J.I., Amin, M.B., Reuter, V.E., Humphrey, P.A.: The 2014 international society of urological pathology (ISUP) consensus conference on gleason grading of prostatic carcinoma: definition of grading patterns and proposal for a new grading system. Am. J. Surg. Pathol. **40**(2), 244–252 (2017). https://doi.org/10.1097/PAS.0000000000000530
11. Epstein, J.I., Amin, M.B., Reuter, V.E., Humphrey, P.A.: Contemporary gleason grading of prostatic carcinoma: an update with discussion on practical issues to implement the 2014 international society of urological pathology (isup) consensus conference on gleason grading of prostatic carcinoma. Am. J. Surg. Pathol. **41**(4), e1–e7 (2017). https://doi.org/10.1097/pas.0000000000000820
12. Fulawka, L., Halon, A.: Proliferation index evaluation in breast cancer using imagej and immunoratio applications. Anticancer Res. **36**(8), 3965–3972 (2016)
13. Garcia-Etienne, C.A., et al.: Management of the axilla in patients with breast cancer and positive sentinel lymph node biopsy: an evidence-based update in a european breast center. Eur. J. Surg. Oncol. **46**(1), 15–23 (2020). https://doi.org/10.1016/j.ejso.2019.08.013
14. Goebel, R., et al.: Explainable AI: the New 42? In: Holzinger, A., Kieseberg, P., Tjoa, A.M., Weippl, E. (eds.) CD-MAKE 2018. LNCS, vol. 11015, pp. 295–303. Springer, Cham (2018). https://doi.org/10.1007/978-3-319-99740-7_21
15. Granter, S.R., Beck, A.H., Papke, D.J.: Alphago, deep learning, and the future of the human microscopist. Arch. Pathol. Lab. Med. **141**(5), 619–621 (2017). https://doi.org/10.5858/arpa.2016-0471-ED
16. Hegde, N., et al.: Similar image search for histopathology: smily. NPJ Digit. Med. **2**(1), 1–9 (2019). https://doi.org/10.1038/s41746-019-0131-z
17. Herrmann, M.D., et al.: Implementing the DICOM standard for digital pathology. Journal of pathology informatics **9**, 37 (2018)
18. Holzinger, A.: Usability engineering methods for software developers. Commun. ACM **48**(1), 71–74 (2005). https://doi.org/10.1145/1039539.1039541
19. Holzinger, A.: Interactive machine learning for health informatics: when do we need the human-in-the-loop? Brain Inform. **3**(2), 119–131 (2016). https://doi.org/10.1007/s40708-016-0042-6
20. Holzinger, A.: From machine learning to explainable AI. In: 2018 World Symposium on Digital Intelligence for Systems and Machines (IEEE DISA), pp. 55–66. IEEE (2018). https://doi.org/10.1109/DISA.2018.8490530

21. Holzinger, A.: Introduction to machine learning and knowledge extraction (make). Mach. Learn. Knowl. Extr. **1**(1), 1–20 (2019). https://doi.org/10.3390/make1010001
22. Holzinger, A., Kickmeier-Rust, M., Müller, H.: KANDINSKY patterns as IQ-test for machine learning. In: Holzinger, A., Kieseberg, P., Tjoa, A.M., Weippl, E. (eds.) CD-MAKE 2019. LNCS, vol. 11713, pp. 1–14. Springer, Cham (2019). https://doi.org/10.1007/978-3-030-29726-8_1
23. Holzinger, A., Kieseberg, P., Weippl, E., Tjoa, A.M.: Current advances, trends and challenges of machine learning and knowledge extraction: from machine learning to explainable AI. In: Holzinger, A., Kieseberg, P., Tjoa, A.M., Weippl, E. (eds.) CD-MAKE 2018. LNCS, vol. 11015, pp. 1–8. Springer, Cham (2018). https://doi.org/10.1007/978-3-319-99740-7_1
24. Holzinger, A., Langs, G., Denk, H., Zatloukal, K., Müller, H.: Causability and explainability of artificial intelligence in medicine. WIRES Data Min. Knowl. **9**(4), e1312 (2019). https://doi.org/10.1002/widm.1312
25. Holzinger, A., et al.: Machine learning and knowledge extraction in digital pathology needs an integrative approach. In: Holzinger, A., Goebel, R., Ferri, M., Palade, V. (eds.) Towards Integrative Machine Learning and Knowledge Extraction. LNCS (LNAI), vol. 10344, pp. 13–50. Springer, Cham (2017). https://doi.org/10.1007/978-3-319-69775-8_2
26. Kargl, M., Regitnig, P., Mueller, H., Holzinger, A.: TOWARDS A BETTER UNDERSTANDING OF THE WORKFLOWS: MODELING PATHOLOGY PROCESSES IN VIEW OF FUTURE AI INTEGRATION. In: Springer LNCS, vol. 12090, p. 16. Springer, Cham (2020). https://doi.org/10.1007/978-3-030-50402-1_7
27. Keyhani-Rofagha, S., Palma, T., O'Toole, R.V.: Automated screening for quality control using PAPNET: a study of 638 negative Pap smears. Diagn. Cytopathol. **14**(4), 316–320 (1996)
28. Kott, O., et al.: Development of a deep learning algorithm for the histopathologic diagnosis and gleason grading of prostate cancer biopsies: a pilot study. Eur. Urol. Focus (2020). https://doi.org/10.1016/j.euf.2019.11.003
29. Levenson, R.M., Krupinski, E.A., Navarro, V.M., Wasserman, E.A.: Pigeons (Columba livia) as trainable observers of pathology and radiology breast cancer images. PLoS ONE **10**(11), e0141357 (2015). https://doi.org/10.1371/journal.pone.0141357
30. Liu, Y., et al.: Artificial intelligence-based breast cancer nodal metastasis detection: insights into the black box for pathologists. Arch. Pathol. Lab. Med. **143**(7), 859–868 (2019). https://doi.org/10.5858/arpa.2018-0147-OA
31. Lodish, H., Berk, A., Zipursky, S., Matsudaira, P., Baltimore, D., Darnell, J.: Tumor cells and the onset of cancer. In: Molecular Cell Biology, 4th ed. Freeman, New York (2000)
32. Madabhushi, A., Lee, G.: Image analysis and machine learning in digital pathology: challenges and opportunities. Med. Image Anal. **33**, 170–175 (2016). https://doi.org/10.1016/j.media.2016.06.037
33. Müller, H., Dagher, G., Loibner, M., Stumptner, C., Kungl, P., Zatloukal, K.: Biobanks for life sciences and personalized medicine: importance of standardization, biosafety, biosecurity, and data management. Curr. Opin. Biotechnol. **65**, 45–51 (2020)
34. Müller, H., et al.: State-of-the-art and future challenges in the integration of biobank catalogues. In: Holzinger, A., Röcker, C., Ziefle, M. (eds.) Smart Health. LNCS, vol. 8700, pp. 261–273. Springer, Cham (2015). https://doi.org/10.1007/978-3-319-16226-3_11

35. Nagpal, K., et al.: Development and validation of a deep learning algorithm for improving gleason scoring of prostate cancer. Nat. Digit. Med. (NPJ) **2**(1), 1–10 (2019). https://doi.org/10.1038/s41746-019-0112-2

36. Nakamura, Y.: The role and necessity of sentinel lymph node biopsy for invasive melanoma. Front. Med. **6**(231), 1–7 (2019). https://doi.org/10.3389/fmed.2019.00231

37. Napolitano, G., Marshall, A., Hamilton, P., Gavin, A.T.: Machine learning classification of surgical pathology reports and chunk recognition for information extraction noise reduction. Artif. Intell. Med. **70**, 77–83 (2016). https://doi.org/10.1016/j.artmed.2016.06.001

38. Niazi, M.K., Parwani, A.V., Gurcan, M.N.: Digital pathology and artificial intelligence. Lancet Oncol. **20**(5), e253–e261 (2019). https://doi.org/10.1016/S1470-2045(19)30154-8

39. O'Sullivan, S., Holzinger, A., Wichmann, D., Saldiva, P.H.N., Sajid, M.I., Zatloukal, K.: Virtual autopsy: machine learning and AI provide new opportunities for investigating minimal tumor burden and therapy resistance by cancer patients. Autops. Case Rep. **8**(1), e2018003 (2018). https://doi.org/10.4322/acr.2018.003

40. O'Sullivan, S., Holzinger, A., Zatloukal, K., Saldiva, P., Sajid, M.I., Dominic, W.: Machine learning enhanced virtual autopsy. Autops. Case Rep. **7**(4), 3–7 (2017). https://doi.org/10.4322/acr.2017.037

41. Paden, B., Cap, M., Yong, S.Z., Yershov, D., Frazzoli, E.: A survey of motion planning and control techniques for self-driving urban vehicles. IEEE Trans. Intell. Veh. **1**(1), 33–55 (2016). https://doi.org/10.1109/TIV.2016.2578706

42. Pohn, B., Kargl, M., Reihs, R., Holzinger, A., Zatloukal, K., Müller, H.: Towards a deeper understanding of how a pathologist makes a diagnosis: Visualization of the diagnostic process in histopathology. In: IEEE Symposium on Computers and Communications (ISCC). IEEE (2019). https://doi.org/10.1109/ISCC47284.2019.8969598

43. Poojitha, U.P., Sharma, S.L.: Hybrid unified deep learning network for highly precise gleason grading of prostate cancer. In: 41st Annual International Conference of the IEEE Engineering in Medicine and Biology Society (EMBC), pp. 899–903. IEEE (2019). https://doi.org/10.1109/EMBC.2019.8856912

44. Reihs, R., Pohn, B., Zatloukal, K., Holzinger, A., Müller, H.: NLP for the generation of training data sets for ontology-guided weakly-supervised machine learning in digital pathology. In: 2019 IEEE Symposium on Computers and Communications (ISCC), pp. 1072–1076. IEEE (2019)

45. Salto-Tellez, M., Maxwell, P., Hamilton, P.: Artificial intelligence–the third revolution in pathology. Histopathology **74**(3), 372–376 (2019). https://doi.org/10.1111/his.13760

46. Samek, W., Montavon, G., Vedaldi, A., Hansen, L.K., Müller, K.-R. (eds.): Explainable AI: Interpreting, Explaining and Visualizing Deep Learning. LNCS (LNAI), vol. 11700. Springer, Cham (2019). https://doi.org/10.1007/978-3-030-28954-6

47. Schneeberger, D., Stoeger, K., Holzinger, A.: The European legal framework for medical AI. In: International Cross-Domain Conference for Machine Learning and Knowledge Extraction, Fourth IFIP TC 5, TC 12, WG 8.4, WG 8.9, WG 12.9 International Cross-Domain Conference, CD-MAKE 2020, Proceedings, p. in print. Springer, Cham (2020). https://doi.org/10.1007/978-3-030-29726-8

48. Smeulders, A., Van Ginneken, A.: An analysis of pathology knowledge and decision making for the development of artificial intelligence-based consulting systems. Anal. Quant. Cytol. Histol. **11**(3), 154–165 (1989)

49. Sompawong, N., et al.: Automated pap smear cervical cancer screening using deep learning. In: 41st Annual International Conference of the IEEE Engineering in Medicine and Biology Society (EMBC). IEEE (2019). https://doi.org/10.1109/EMBC.2019.8856369

50. Tang, R., et al.: Machine learning to parse breast pathology reports in Chinese. Breast Cancer Res. Treat. **169**(2), 243–250 (2018). https://doi.org/10.1007/s10549-018-4668-3

51. Tellez, D., et al.: Whole-slide mitosis detection in H&E breast histology using PHH3 as a reference to train distilled stain-invariant convolutional networks. IEEE Trans. Med. Imaging **37**(9), 2126–2136 (2018). https://doi.org/10.1109/TMI.2018.2820199

52. Tuominen, V.J., Isola, J.: Linking whole-slide microscope images with DICOM by using JPEG2000 interactive protocol. J. Digit. Imaging **23**(4), 454–462 (2010). https://doi.org/10.1007/s10278-009-9200-1

53. Tuominen, V.J., Ruotoistenmäki, S., Viitanen, A., Jumppanen, M., Isola, J.: Immunoratio: a publicly available web application for quantitative image analysis of estrogen receptor (ER), progesterone receptor (PR), and Ki-67. Breast Cancer Res. **12**(4), 1–12 (2010). https://doi.org/10.1186/bcr2615

54. Turing, A.M.: Computing machinery and intelligence. Mind **59**(236), 433–460 (1950). https://doi.org/10.1093/mind/LIX.236.433

55. William, W., Ware, A., Basaza-Ejiri, A.H., Obungoloch, J.: A review of image analysis and machine learning techniques for automated cervical cancer screening from pap-smear images. Comput. Methods Programs Biomed. **164**, 15–22 (2018). https://doi.org/10.1016/j.cmpb.2018.05.034

56. Yan, H., Jiang, Y., Zheng, J., Peng, C., Li, Q.: A multilayer perceptron-based medical decision support system for heart disease diagnosis. Expert Syst. Appl. **30**(2), 272–281 (2006). https://doi.org/10.1016/j.eswa.2005.07.022

57. Yang, Q., et al.: Epithelium segmentation and automated gleason grading of prostate cancer via deep learning in label-free multiphoton microscopic images. J. Biophotonics **13**(2), e201900203 (2019). https://doi.org/10.1002/jbio.201900203

58. Zhang, L., Lu, L., Nogues, I., Summers, R.M., Liu, S., Yao, J.: Deeppap: deep convolutional networks for cervical cell classification. IEEE J. Biomed. Health Inf. **21**(6), 1633–1643 (2017). https://doi.org/10.1109/JBHI.2017.2705583

59. Zwoenitzer, R., Kalinski, T., Hofmann, H., Roessner, A., Bernarding, J.: Digital pathology: DICOM-conform draft, testbed, and first results. Comput. Methods Programs Biomed. **87**(3), 181–188 (2007). https://doi.org/10.1016/j.cmpb.2007.05.010

Interpretable Deep Neural Network to Predict Estrogen Receptor Status from Haematoxylin-Eosin Images

Philipp Seegerer[1], Alexander Binder[2(✉)], René Saitenmacher[1],
Michael Bockmayr[3,6], Maximilian Alber[3], Philipp Jurmeister[3],
Frederick Klauschen[3], and Klaus-Robert Müller[1,4,5]

[1] Machine Learning Group, Technical University Berlin, Berlin, Germany
[2] Singapore University of Technology and Design (SUTD), Singapore, Singapore
alexander_binder@stud.edu.sg
[3] Institute of Pathology, Charité University Hospital, Berlin, Germany
[4] Department of Brain and Cognitive Engineering, Korea University, Seoul, Korea
[5] Max-Planck-Institute for Informatics, Campus E1 4, Saarbrücken, Germany
[6] Department of Pediatric Hematology and Oncology, University Medical Center
Hamburg-Eppendorf, Hamburg, Germany

Abstract. The eligibility for hormone therapy to treat breast cancer largely depends on the tumor's estrogen receptor (ER) status. Recent studies show that the ER status correlates with morphological features found in Haematoxylin-Eosin (HE) slides. Thus, HE analysis might be sufficient for patients for whom the classifier confidently predicts the ER status and thereby obviate the need for additional examination, such as immunohistochemical (IHC) staining. Several prior works are limited by either the use of engineered features, multi-stage models that use features unspecific to HE images or a lack of explainability. To address these limitations, this work proposes an end-to-end neural network ensemble that shows state-of-the-art performance. We demonstrate that the approach also translates to the prediction of the cancer grade. Moreover, subsets can be selected from the test data for which the model can detect a positive ER status with a precision of 94% while classifying 13% of the patients. To compensate for the reduced interpretability of the model that comes along with end-to-end training, this work applies Layer-wise Relevance Propagation (LRP) to determine the relevant parts of the images a posteriori, commonly visualized as a heatmap overlayed with the input image. We found that nuclear and stromal morphology and lymphocyte infiltration play an important role in the classification of the ER status. This demonstrates that interpretable machine learning can be a vital tool for validating and generating hypotheses about morphological biomarkers.

Keywords: Digital pathology · Deep learning · Explainable AI

© Springer Nature Switzerland AG 2020
A. Holzinger et al. (Eds.): AI & ML for Digital Pathology, LNAI 12090, pp. 16–37, 2020.
https://doi.org/10.1007/978-3-030-50402-1_2

1   Introduction and Motivation

Determining the estrogen receptor (ER) status of a tumor is of high clinical importance for the management of breast cancer patients because it specifies the eligibility for hormone therapy. So far, the gold standard for determining the ER status is immunohistochemical (IHC) staining. However, recent work shows that the ER status also correlates with morphological features found in Haematoxylin-Eosin (HE) slides even though these features are hardly apparent to pathologists [10, 32, 36]. This would make an additional IHC staining unnecessary if the ER status can already be determined from the HE stain with high confidence and therefore save both time and budget in clinical routine. Furthermore, it can provide a valuable "second opinion" in assessing the ER status, especially if one considers that up to 20% of IHC-based ER and progesterone status assessments might be inaccurate [14]. Nevertheless, it remains unclear what features are used by the learning machine to determine the ER status; analysis was so far limited to low-resolution heatmaps that indicated certain importance of stromal regions [36].

To address this, our work presents a novel end-to-end deep neural network (DNN) ensemble trained on pooled random patches that shows competitive performance compared with prior work [10, 32, 36] for the prediction of the ER status and pathological cancer grade in terms of area under the ROC curve (AUC). Based on the validation data, a minimum classifier confidence can be chosen below which a sample is rejected from the classification; by doing so, the model reaches a high precision (94%) while still classifying a considerable amount (13%) of patients. For these patients, in principle no additional staining would be needed.

A disadvantage of deep end-to-end learning can be the lack of interpretability of the model. We try to alleviate this issue by analyzing relevance heatmaps of model predictions. This showed that the model mostly relies on stromal texture and nuclear features to identify ER-positive samples and demonstrate how explanation methods can be used to not only verify machine learning models but also to validate and generate biomedical hypotheses. Moreover, by using these explanation methods one can validate whether a trained model relies on unstable features, such as discussed in [26].

2   Glossary

Breast Cancer Grading: Morphological assessment of a breast cancer that measures the degree of differentiation. It consists of the evaluation of the percentage of tubuli formation, the degree of nuclear pleomorphism and the number of mitoses. These three morphological features are assigned a score in a semi-quantitative way and then combined to an aggregated cancer grade score, that can be 1, 2 or 3 [12].

End-to-End Learning: Opposed to the classical pattern recognition pipeline, where features are usually chosen by the developer and only the classifier is learned, end-to-end learning means that everything from the input data to the classifier output, i.e. including the features, is learned from the data. A very successful instance of end-to-end learning are deep neural networks.

Estrogen Receptor Status: This is an important parameter for prognosis and the prediction of therapy response in breast cancer. A lack of ER receptor is correlated with a higher rate of recurrence and shorter survival as well as a decreased probability of responding to endocrine therapy [30].

Immunohistochemical Staining: The different immunohistochemical stains allow the detection and localization of chemical compounds, e.g. proteins, by binding marked antibodies to them. Amongst others, there are stains to detect hormone receptors, such as the estrogen and progesterone receptors.

Model Explanation and Interpretability: Montavon et al. (2017) define interpretation as a "mapping of an abstract concept (e.g. a predicted class) into a domain that the human can make sense of.", such as images or text [29]. An explanation is then "the collection of features of the interpretable domain, that have contributed for a given example to produce a decision (e.g. classification or regression)." A common explanation for image data are heatmaps that visualize which pixels were relevant for the model output. Furthermore, they divide interpretability into two subgroups: post-hoc interpretability that aims at analysing a given trained model and interpretability incorporated into the model (sometimes called ante-hoc interpretability [17]).

Nested Crossvalidation: A method for model selection and performance evaluation of a machine learning model, that makes optimal use of the available data and is therefore suitable for small datasets.

3   State of the Art

3.1   Prediction of ER Status Using DNNs

Recently, several studies applied DNNs to the classification of ER status from HE images. Rawat et al. (2018) constructed spatial maps of engineered features that describe nuclear morphology from HE images [32]. These features are then classified by a DNN into ER+ and ER− with an AUC of 0.72. The approach requires prior segmentation of the nuclei and manual feature engineering. This adds to the complexity of the method but on the other hand the results are better interpretable. Furthermore, the method was developed on a relatively small sample (57 train and 56 test samples).

Couture, Williams et al. (2018) trained an ensemble of calibrated SVMs on intermediate VGG16 features to predict patch-wise scores for the ER status and other quantities such as the tumor grade [10]. These scores were then aggregated into quantiles and classified by another SVM to get the final patient-wise prediction. This yielded 84% accuracy, 88% sensitivity and 76% specificity. A possible limitation of this work is that it is not an end-to-end model, i.e. that the used features are not necessarily well-suited for HE images. Moreover, even though the sample size is significantly larger than in [32] (571 train and 288 test samples), it is still small enough that the estimation of the performance on unseen data might be heavily perturbed if only a single hold-out set is used for evaluation.

Recently, Shamai et al. (2019) presented a ResNet model that was trained to predict the ER status from tissue microarray (TMA) samples [36], similar to our work. The model was trained on two cohorts of 20600 HE TMAs of 5356 patients in total. This resulted in an AUC of 0.84 and 0.88, for the two cohorts respectively, that decreased to 0.73 and 0.84 when only one TMA image per patient was used. Furthermore, they report a balanced accuracy of 77% and 82% for both cohorts, respectively. Even though the authors showed response maps of the classifier indicating relevant parts of the input image by overlaying the final feature maps with the image, these response maps were in a lower spatial resolution as the input image.

3.2 Post-hoc Model Explanation

A variety of methods have been developed to explain the output of neural network classifiers [2], with applications including histopathology [7,13,25]. For image data, many of these methods aim to produce explanation heatmaps that indicate the "importance" of each pixel, such that the user can see which structures the model considered relevant. For instance, Smilkov et al. (2017) developed a method called SmoothGrad that averages gradient maps of several noisy versions of an input image [37]. Selvaraju et al. (2017) presented GradCAM that aims to project the activations of the last feature extraction layer of a DNN back to the image space [35]. Bach, Binder et al. (2015) proposed Layer-wise Relevance Propagation (LRP), that decomposes the classifier output in a layer-by-layer fashion to propagate the output signal back to the input space [4]. In the PatternNet and PatternLRP approaches proposed by [22], explanations are learned from the data by optimizing a quality criterion that is based on the observation that an input signal is composed of an informative signal and uninformative noise.

4   Methods

4.1   Data and Preprocessing

The data are taken from TCGA "BRCA" project [1]. From the whole-slide HE images, a board-certified pathologist selected representative regions of interest (ROIs) of $2000 \times 2000\,\mathrm{px}$. The ROIs were preprocessed using the method by [38] to account for the variability in staining. In total, 702 cases had labels for the ER status. The classes were imbalanced with 176 (25%) ER$-$ and 526 (75%) ER$+$ samples. For grading, we used the annotations by [8] where 469 cases were available from which 53 had grade 1, 219 grade 2 and 197 grade 3. We combined grade 1 and 2 to a class "low grade" resulting in 272 (58%) low-grade and 197 (42%) high-grade samples.

---

[1] Available at https://portal.gdc.cancer.gov/projects/TCGA-BRCA/.

4.2   Training and Evaluation

We designed an ensemble of DNNs for ER status prediction that is trained end-to-end. The core of the model is a ResNet18 [16] that was truncated after the third (out of four) residual block. This allowed benefitting from transfer learning but at the same time limited the number of parameters to reduce overfitting (see Table 3). After the final residual block, the feature maps were spatially averaged to yield a 256-d feature vector. For each ROI, multiple small patches (size 64×64 px) were processed individually by this feature extraction part of the DNN in order to regularize by limiting the context size. The resulting feature vectors were then fused by averaging over the patches to yield a combined representation of the entire image. This averaged feature was then fed to a dense layer with two output dimensions and softmax activation. Before the processing, each ROI was downsampled to half resolution since this performed consistently better than full resolution (see Table 3). The patches were sampled with uniform probability since more sophisticated, novel sampling strategies did not exhibit a significant performance gain (see Sect. 5). The model was trained using the Adam optimizer [23] with a learning rate of 10^{-4} and a cross entropy loss where each class was weighted proportional to the inverse of its frequency in the training data (weights are normalized such that they sum to 1).

Different strategies of random patch sampling have been explored in this paper. The first one is a simple uniform sampling where all patch locations are sampled with equal probability. Secondly, the complement of the red channel ("1 - red") in RGB space was used to undersample regions with high stromal tissue content. The third sampling strategy is intended to focus on nuclei by focusing on the Haematoxylin channel (computed using the method by [38]). Areas with high Haematoxylin content therefore were sampled more frequently.

Model selection and performance evaluation are performed by stratified nested crossvalidation (CV) [39]. This procedure and the terminology used in this paper are sketched in Fig. 1. In the outer CV loop, the dataset was randomly partitioned into five folds with class stratification, i.e. each of the folds had approximately the same number of positive and negative samples, respectively. Then, 4 of these folds were combined (called "development" fold in this paper) and used for training and validation in the inner CV procedure. The remaining fold (called "test" fold) was used to estimate the generalization performance of the models trained in the inner CV procedure. This procedure was repeated five times such that each fold served as a test fold once. In the inner CV loop, the respective development fold was further split randomly into five folds with stratification. Each fold was once excluded from the training and used for validation and early stopping (called "validation" fold). The remaining 4 folds were combined to a "training" fold and used to learn the weights and biases of the model. The mean validation performance over the five inner splits was used as estimate of the performance for this particular outer split. This quantity was used for model selection, i.e. to rank different hyperparameter settings.

After five-fold inner CV for hyperparameter tuning, the final classifier was obtained by forming an ensemble of the five individual models by averaging their output probabilities. This ensembling not only reduces the variance of the estimator [15] but also does not require resource-intensive retraining and no additional validation data for early stopping. Both outer and inner splits were the same for all experiments to facilitate comparison.

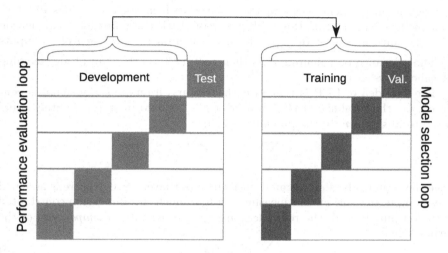

Fig. 1. Illustration of the nested CV procedure for model selection and performance evaluation. *See text for details.*

The performance on unseen data is estimated by averaging the test performances over five outer splits, that are not used for training or model selection. Following [32], we used AUC (averaged over inner folds) as model selection metric because of its applicability to imbalanced data [9]. To evaluate the final performance, we report ROC curves, balanced accuracy, precision and accuracy.

4.3 Visual Explanation of ER Status Predictions

Layer-Wise Relevance Propagation. [4] A feedforward DNN processes an input signal x^0 by propagating it through a sequence of layers and hence computes a mapping $f(x^0)$. In each layer l, the signal is recombined by a linear projection parametrized by weights W and biases b^2 and usually passed through a non-linear activation function σ:

$$x^{l+1} = \sigma(W^l x^l + b^l) = \sigma(z^l) \ , \tag{1}$$

where z denotes the preactivation of the layer. By doing so, the network extracts features from the input signal, that grow more and more abstract and complex after each layer. For a classification task, the feature of the last layer is usually

---

[2] Note that this formulation includes both fully-connected and convolutional layers.

the output of a fully-connected layer and converted into probabilities via the softmax function.

LRP aims at computing a score for every input dimension, which denotes the contribution of the input dimension to the classification result [4]. The output signal $r^L := f(\boldsymbol{x}^0)$ is distributed backwards through the network, using the same topology as in gradient backpropagation, yet with message functions different from the gradient. During this backward pass, LRP computes for every neuron x_j^{l+1} relevance messages $R_{x_i^l \leftarrow x_j^{l+1}}$ from the neuron x_j^{l+1} to each of its inputs x_i^l. The relevance of a neuron x_i^l is then computed as the sum of all incoming relevance messages.

The key idea of LRP is that in each decomposition step, the signal is conserved, i.e. the total signal r^{l+1} in a layer $l + 1$ should be approximately equal to the total signal r^l in the previous layer l:

$$\sum_i r_i^l \approx \sum_j r_j^{l+1} \ . \tag{2}$$

Once the signal is backpropagated until the input layer $l = 0$, a score is assigned to each input dimension that measures by how much this dimension contributed to the output. Indeed, the relevances are an approximate *decomposition* of the output signal:

$$\sum_i r_i^0 \approx f(\boldsymbol{x}^0) \ , \tag{3}$$

which directly follows from Eq. 2. This quantity—termed *relevance*—can hence be interpreted as the "importance" of this dimension for the predicted output. For images, the input relevances can be conveniently visualized as a heatmap.

The conservation property is ensured by applying specific decomposition rules, that determine how the relevance of a layer is distributed to the neurons in the previous layer, as described in the following section.

z**-rule:** The basic intuition is that a neuron i in layer l receives a share of the relevance of each connected neuron j in the following layer $l + 1$ and this share should be proportional to its relative contribution to the input of j:

$$r_i^l = \sum_j \frac{z_i^l}{\sum_k z_k^l} r_j^{l+1} \ . \tag{4}$$

Note that this rule is commonly not directly used in practice but serves as basis for further, improved rules, as described below.

ϵ**-rule:** Equation 4 is ill-defined for $\sum_k z_k^l = 0$ and therefore, a small positive constant ϵ can be added to the denominator that relaxes the conservation property but enhances numerical stability:

$$r_i^l = \sum_j \frac{z_i^l}{\sum_k z_k^l + \epsilon \ \text{sign}(\sum_k z_k^l)} r_j^{l+1} \ . \tag{5}$$

$\alpha\beta$**-rule:** Positive relevance indicates that a neuron increased the output score; negative relevance means decrease. In some applications, positive and negative relevance should be interpreted differently. In order to weight them separately, this rule thus introduces two parameters α and β:

$$r_i^l = \sum_j \left(\alpha \frac{\max(0, z_i^l)}{\sum_k \max(0, z_k^l)} + \beta \frac{\min(0, z_i^l)}{\sum_k \min(0, z_k^l)} \right) r_j^{l+1}. \tag{6}$$

Both parameters are related by $\alpha + \beta = 1$ to ensure relevance conservation. Common choices are $(\alpha = 1, \beta = 0)$ and $(\alpha = 2, \beta = -1)$.

$|z|$-**rule:** Modern DNNs often apply batch normalization [20]. Hui et Binder (2019) demonstrated that other LRP rules often perform poorly for batch normalization layers and devised a sign-invariant alternative that should be used instead [19]:

$$r_i^l = \sum_j \frac{\left| w_{ij}^l x_i^l \right|}{\left| w_{ij}^l x_i^l \right| + \left| b_j^l \right| + \epsilon} r_j^{l+1}. \tag{7}$$

For further methods, applications and implementation details of LRP, we refer to [1, 11, 26, 28].

Application to ER Status Predictions. In order to elucidate which features were used by the model to classify a tumor sample into ER+ and ER−, we applied LRP to create relevance heatmaps. In particular, we applied the ϵ-rule ($\epsilon = 0.1$) to dense layers and the $|z|$-rule proposed by [19] to Batch Normalization layers. To convolutional layers, the $\alpha\beta$-rule ($\alpha = 1$, $\beta = 0$) was applied. In order to create heatmaps for an ROI, the LRP-decomposition was restricted to the logit of the highest scoring class by clamping the respective other logit to zero. Relevances were summed over color channels.

We chose to overlap patches by striding with half the patch size in order to average out potential border effects and translation dependence of the prediction, as recommended by [29]. To distinguish between positive and negative predictions in the final heatmap tile, the sign of the relevances of predicted negative patches was flipped before averaging. For visualization, relevances were clipped at the 0.995 quantile of the averaged heatmap tile; by doing so, extremely high relevance values did not influence the colormap substantially. This normalization process was performed for negative and positive relevances separately. In this paper, we restrict the heatmap analysis to a single CV fold.

Furthermore, visualizations were computed using SmoothGrad [35]. The magnitude of the gradient was averaged over 15 samples and sign-flipped for ER−predictions for visualization purposes, similar to above. For visualization we clipped the relevances at the 0.98 quantile to achieve a similar appearance as the LRP heatmaps.

5   Experiments

5.1   Hyperparameter Tuning and Performance Evaluation

For the ER status, we tuned the following hyperparameters on the validation sets: learning rate, image resolution, depth of the network and sampling method

Table 1. AUC (in %) for ER status and cancer grade for validation and testing for our end-to-end method and the method by [10] ("SVM") for all outer folds.

Fold	Val. (ER)		Test (ER)		Val. (Grade)		Test (Grade)	
	SVM	Our	SVM	Our	SVM	Our	SVM	Our
0	79.4	82.6	81.1	73.0	74.7	78.0	81.8	84.8
1	79.7	80.1	72.5	80.8	77.0	80.3	71.9	74.2
2	78.5	80.7	76.1	79.6	76.9	80.6	72.6	71.5
3	78.5	80.8	75.4	75.9	71.6	77.4	78.6	86.5
4	73.5	78.0	86.7	92.0	76.1	81.4	70.0	76.2
Avg.	77.9	80.5	78.4	80.3	75.2	79.5	75.0	78.6

Table 2. Comparison of the mean AUCs (in %) of the individual models (each trained on one inner fold) to the AUC (in %) of an ensemble of them for all outer folds.

Fold	Mean AUC (individual)	Ensemble AUC
0	72.5	73.0
1	78.6	80.8
2	77.4	79.6
3	73.3	75.9
4	89.2	92.0

(see Table 3 for results from hyperparameter tuning following the procedure described in Sect. 4.2). The validation and test results for our end-to-end method and a state-of-the-art method [10] for both ER status and cancer grade are summarized in Table 1.

No significant difference between the different sampling methods (uniform, "1 - red" and Haematoxylin oversampling) could be observed (see Table 3). Hence, we chose to remove this hyperparameter from the model selection and constantly used uniform sampling instead because it has the fewest assumptions and is therefore not prone to introducing any bias.

After determining hyperparameters during model selection, the final performance was estimated by averaging the test performance over all outer splits. As expected, the ensemble performed better than the individual models on average (see Table 2). This yielded an AUC of 0.80 (see Table 1), balanced accuracy of 73%, precision of 72% and accuracy of 79%. The AUC is thus substantially higher than in [32].

In order to test whether the benefit of end-to-end learning translates to other clinically relevant variables, we trained the same architecture to predict the pathological cancer grade. As before, we applied stratified nested CV. Without additional hyperparameter optimization, i.e. using the same configuration as for the ER status, the model achieved an average test AUC of 0.79 (see Table 1) and a balanced accuracy of 72%. This could be further increased to an AUC 0.81 and balanced accuracy of 73% by hyperparameter optimization (see Table 3).

5.2   Comparison to a State-of-the-Art Method

We applied the method by [10] ("SVM") to our dataset with the following minor modifications: Instead of 800×800 px patches with 400 px overlap, we used 600×600 px with 300 px overlap since the downscaled images only had a size of 1000×1000 px. Furthermore, we used standard Platt scaling [31] instead of isotropic regression for the calibration of the first SVM. We found that balancing the classes during training deteriorates the validation performance and thus, we did not apply any reweighting (see Table 3). Apart from that, the method was applied as described in [10].

A comparison showed an improvement by our method compared to the SVM method in all folds during validation (see Table 1). Similarly to our method, half resolution yielded a higher AUC than full resolution. Furthermore, the SVM method performed better with VGG16 features as in [10] compared to the truncated ResNet features (see Table 3). Our method performed better not only in the validation but also in the test phase, where the SVM method scored on average an AUC of 0.78 (see Table 1), balanced accuracy of 70%, precision of 70% and accuracy of 78%. The ROC curves of the two methods are compared in Fig. 2.

We compared different resolutions for the prediction of the grade, for each of which the end-to-end method was superior in terms of AUC, even by a larger margin than for the ER status prediction (see Table 3). As for the ER status, half resolution performed best. Using the same hyperparameters as for the ER status, the SVM method scored an AUC of 0.75 (see Table 1) and a balanced accuracy of 70% on the test set which is outperformed by our end-to-end approach.

5.3   Variance over the Splits

We observed that the test AUC varied significantly between the different outer CV splits (see Table 1). Thus, the test performance computed on a single outer split is an unreliable estimate of the true generalization performance. Even more concerning is the fact that this variance can be substantial: In our experiments, the test AUC ranged from 0.73 to 0.92 (see Table 1). Hence, if the evaluation relied on a single train-test split only, the real-world performance could have been severely over- or underestimated. Figure 2 shows the ROC curves for the different outer splits to demonstrate this variance.

Interestingly, the outer fold with the best mean validation performance (fold 0) has the worst test performance. This means that the test set of fold 0 is particularly hard (i.e. harder than average) to classify; vice versa, its train and validation sets are particularly easy since they are disjoint from the test set. This leads to an overly optimistic validation performance in fold 0 (and to a overly pessimistic validation performance in all the other folds) whereas the

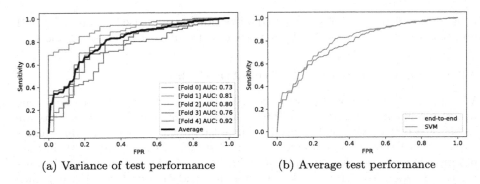

(a) Variance of test performance   (b) Average test performance

Fig. 2. (a): ROC curves for all outer test sets for our method. (b): Average test ROC curves comparing our end-to-end method to the SVM method by [10].

test performance in fold 0 is overly pessimistic. Similarly, the fold with the worst validation performance (fold 4) shows the best test performance.

5.4 Rejection Option

The clinical relevance of HE-based determination of the ER status largely depends on the amount of patients that are classified correctly with high confidence[3] because these patients would not require additional examination e.g. by IHC stains. On the other hand, cases that cannot be classified confidently should be rejected by the classifier and undergo additional examination, such as IHC staining.

Therefore, we investigated whether a threshold on the classifier output ("confidence") can be chosen on the validation data such that a reasonable amount of test data can be classified with high confidence, similar to [10] and [21]. To this end, the ER+ precision of the model, i.e. the ratio of true ER+ patients of all patients classified as ER+, as well as the ratio of non-rejected samples, i.e. patients classified as ER+, were plotted against the confidence threshold (see Fig. 3). For the validation data, we averaged over the inner splits.

The confidence threshold was chosen based on the validation data for each outer split individually such that the precision was maximized while classifying more than 10% of the cases. These thresholds are shown as vertical lines in Fig. 3. Introducing this rejection option resulted in a precision of 97% and 94% for validation and test data, respectively, and a ratio of non-rejected samples of 20% and 13%, respectively (averaged over the outer folds).

---

[3] The output of a DNN typically does not represent the true confidence of the model in terms of probability since it is not properly calibrated. However, here, we stick with the term "confidence" to denote the output probability of the highest scoring class as it is commonly used that way in the literature.

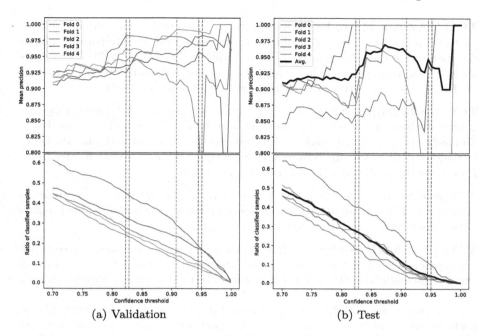

(a) Validation   (b) Test

Fig. 3. Precision and ratio of classified (not rejected) samples when introducing a rejection option. Confidence thresholds (depicted as vertical lines) are chosen on the validation data for each fold individually.

5.5   Visual Explanation

The resulting LRP heatmaps for classifying the ER status were inspected visually. From this, the following findings are deduced:

- Stroma is an important indicator for the model for ER+. This is in line with previous findings that suggest that stromal morphology correlates with survival [5] and the ER status [36]. Nevertheless, we consider this a potential issue of the learned predictor (see Sect. 6).
- Lymphocyte infiltration is an indicator for ER−. This is plausible because it has been reported in the literature that increased lymphocytic infiltration correlates with decreased ER activity [24,27].
- A high nuclear grade (prominent nucleoli, nuclear pleomorphism), i.e. poor differentiation, and mitoses are an indicator for ER−, in line with [27].
- The model responds to cells arranged in an "indian file"-like pattern. This pattern is typically observed in infiltrating lobular carcinoma, a histological subtype of breast cancer that correlates with a positive ER status [3].

Exemplary heatmaps are shown in Fig. 4, where red indicates evidence for ER+, blue for ER− and green is neutral (for more examples, see Fig. 6). In the following, we discuss these example cases in more detail.

TCGA-A2-A0CR (see Fig. 4(a)): Cancer cells aligned in an "indian file"-like pattern are evidence for ER+. This pattern is typical for infiltrating lobular carcinoma that more frequently is ER+. Additionally, stroma and the low-grade nuclear morphology are evidence for ER+. Lymphocyte infiltration is evidence for ER−. It is correctly predicted ER+ with confidence of 0.989.

TCGA-E2-A1LL (see Fig. 4(b)): This tumor features a bad differentiation and a high nuclear grade and thus, nuclear morphology is an indicator for ER−. Similarly, mitoses are correlated with uncontrolled tumor growth and are hence evidence for ER−. The small ratio of stromal tissue is however evidence for ER+. It is correctly predicted ER− with confidence 0.923.

TCGA-E2-A158 (see Fig. 4(c)): The large portion of stroma in this tumor is evidence for ER+; lymphocytes are evidence for ER−. The model falsely predicts ER+, albeit with a relatively low confidence of 0.834.

TCGA-C8-A12P (see Fig. 4(d)): This is a tumor with a medium degree of differentiation. The large number of lymphocytes is evidence for ER−. Even though the stroma indicates ER+, the model correctly predicts ER− with confidence 0.804.

A comparison of LRP heatmaps to SmoothGrad heatmaps showed that these findings are consistent with a differently motivated explanation method (see Fig. 5) and not a special finding of LRP. However, note that the SmoothGrad heatmaps come along with a significantly higher computational effort compared to LRP because they require an average over multiple gradient maps.

6   Discussion

It is common knowledge in machine learning that training models end-to-end is beneficial because not only the classifier but also the features are adapted specifically to the task at hand [6]. We demonstrated that this also holds for the classification of ER status and cancer grade from HE images even though our sample was relatively small: The end-to-end method compared favorably with recent prior DNN-based methods.

The high variance of the test performance between different outer folds shows that it can be misleading to rely on the performance on a single outer fold only to estimate generalization performance because it can be biased either too pessimistically (e.g. as in fold 0) or too optimistically (e.g. fold 4) and this bias can be substantial. This is due to the high variance with which the generalization performance is estimated that arises from the relatively modest sample size. This dilemma can be solved by averaging the test performances over the different outer splits which gives a more reliable estimate because the averaging reduces the variance of the estimator [15]. We argue that, while this might be irrelevant in general computer vision where usually large labeled datasets are available,

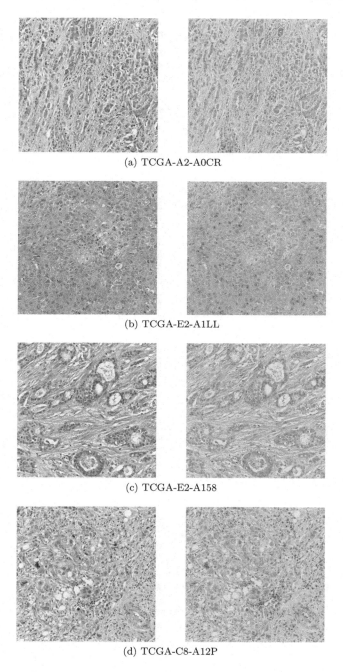

(a) TCGA-A2-A0CR

(b) TCGA-E2-A1LL

(c) TCGA-E2-A158

(d) TCGA-C8-A12P

Fig. 4. Examplary images and LRP-heatmaps (overlayed on image) for the detection of ER status. (a) Cell patterns typical for lobular breast carcinoma indicate ER+ (red). Lymphocyte infiltration indicates ER− (blue). (b) High nuclear and mitotic grade and lymphocyte infiltration indicate ER−. (c) Stromal patterns indicate ER+. (d) Lymphocyte infiltration indicates ER−. (Color figure online)

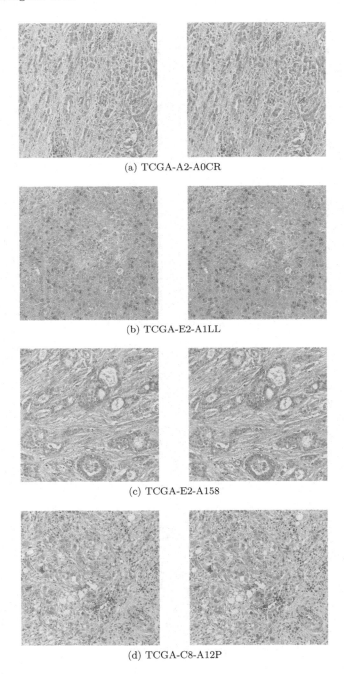

(a) TCGA-A2-A0CR

(b) TCGA-E2-A1LL

(c) TCGA-E2-A158

(d) TCGA-C8-A12P

Fig. 5. Comparison of LRP - (left) and SmoothGrad (right) heatmaps (overlayed on image), analogous to Fig. 4. This highlights similar features for both methods. (Color figure online)

in many medical image analysis tasks this variance is a serious problem because the datasets are much smaller. Furthermore, especially in the medical domain it is highly relevant to reliably estimate the performance of a machine learning model. Thus, we hope to focus the attention of the field to methodically sound model tuning and evaluation procedures, such as nested CV, even if this comes along with a considerably higher computational burden. We claim that in the context of machine learning applied to medicine, a reliable performance estimation should always have priority over finding an optimal hyperparameter setting because otherwise, trust of medical professionals and patients in learning machines can easily be undermined.

As shown in Table 1, the predictor has a competitive prediction performance. This is even more remarkable as the total sample size is 702 samples only, whereas a larger study [36] which reported AUCs of 0.73 and 0.84 was able to employ a sample size of 5356 patients. Visual explanation revealed several morphological features that the model considered relevant for classification: stromal features, lymphocyte infiltration, high nuclear grade and cell arrangement correlated with a specific histological subtype.

However, we would like to express doubts whether the stroma structure used as evidence for ER+ is a causal feature, despite work supporting this view like [5] and [36], that showed that the ER status could be learned from the stroma to a certain extent. In a larger study, this observation could be validated by inspecting a larger patient dataset, for which we are unable to obtain sufficient samples from the used TCGA dataset. While this hypothesis cannot be ascertained at this stage, this raised concern demonstrates the value of explanation methods for the development of machine learning models, in particular for features such as ER status which are not easily recognized by a human expert from HE stains. This is fundamentally different to many problems in the natural image domain, where the correctness of a prediction can be verified at a glance by non-experts.

An argument for the latter is the reliable selection of high-confidence predictions that results in high precision. Nevertheless, this study shows that explainable AI can be a tool to investigate models for ER status prediction and should be combined with domain knowledge for verification. This is especially important because the prediction of the ER status from HE images has a relatively modest classification performance [10, 32, 36] and hence could be more prone to a confusion of correlation and causation.

Table 3. Additional validation AUCs (in %) for ER status and cancer grade. (**ER**) SVM method by [10]: full resolution, truncated ResNet18 ("ResNet3L") as feature extractor and class balancing. Our method: full resolution, ResNet18 as model and different sampling methods (Haematoxylin and complement of red channel). (**Grade**) SVM method: quarter and full resolution. Our method: additional hyperparameter tuning. For comparison, the results of the final models are shown (see Table 1).

ER

Fold	SVM				Our				
	Full Res.	ResNet3L	balanced	Final	Full res.	ResNet18	Haem.	1-red	Final
0	70.6	74.9	76.5	79.4	78.7	79.8	82.1	82.6	82.6
1	69.1	72.7	74.5	79.7	74.9	78.5	81.3	80.1	80.1
2	69.1	73.7	73.0	78.5	74.1	80.4	81.5	82.6	80.7
3	72.7	73.5	73.0	78.5	73.5	79.5	80.1	81.9	80.8
4	69.1	70.7	69.7	73.5	69.7	75.9	75.9	75.1	78.0
Avg.	70.1	73.1	73.3	77.9	74.2	78.8	80.2	80.5	80.5

Grade

Fold	SVM			Our	
	Quarter res.	Full res.	Final	Tuned	Final
0	69.6	68.4	74.7	80.5	78.0
1	75.4	73.9	77.0	83.0	80.3
2	76.8	70.6	76.9	82.5	80.6
3	73.6	69.9	71.6	83.5	77.4
4	75.1	75.5	76.1	84.7	81.4
Avg.	74.1	71.7	75.2	82.8	79.5

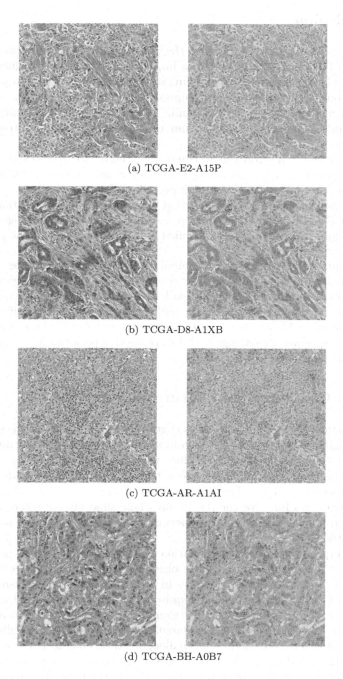

(a) TCGA-E2-A15P

(b) TCGA-D8-A1XB

(c) TCGA-AR-A1AI

(d) TCGA-BH-A0B7

Fig. 6. Additional images and LRP-heatmaps (overlayed on image). (Color figure online)

7   Conclusion

This work presents a method to learn the prediction of the ER status of breast cancer from HE images, a task that is important for patient stratification but usually not visually apparent to the human observer. In contrast to prior work that relied on engineered or generic representations, this method uses features that are learned from the data at hand. This is achieved by training a DNN ensemble end-to-end on pooled random patches which shows state-of-the-art performance.

We show how CV naturally gives rise to an ensemble to avoid costly retraining after model selection. By introducing a rejection class, a considerable amount of test samples can be classified with high precision. Furthermore, we demonstrate the importance of robust model selection and performance evaluation, in this case nested CV, in the context of deep learning-based medical image analysis. Moreover, the architecture can be applied out-of-the-box to e.g. the prediction of cancer grade.

After training the model, we computed explanation heatmaps to better understand the model intrinsics. This revealed a number of biologically plausible features that are used by the model to predict the ER status: stromal and nuclear morphology, lymphocytic infiltration and disease-specific cell patterns. Explainable AI can thus be an important tool to verify hypotheses about biomarkers, especially in settings with low predictive performance as in the case of ER status prediction.

8   Open Challenges and Future Work

More sophisticated sampling strategies that oversample specific tissue structures had a negligible effect in this paper compared to naive uniform sampling. We hypothesize that this is due to the fact that the dataset consists of expert-selected ROIs; uniformly sampling from these ROIs is thus already likely to yield an informative patch. Thus, future work should investigate whether those sampling strategies improve the results on whole-slide images where it is more important to focus the attention to relevant parts of the data than for training on preselected ROIs.

The interpretation of the explanation heatmaps in this study is done by visual inspection. To leverage a more objective evaluation, the overlap of the relevance scores with specific structures in the tissue should be measured quantitatively [13]. However, this would require an expensive pixel-level annotation of e.g. cancer cells, lymphocytes and stroma, and is thus left for future work.

Moreover, the goodness of the explanation heatmaps should ideally be measured quantitatively [33]. This is a challenging task and no consensus on the best evaluation method has been reached yet. However, approximations to this problem exist, e.g. by destroying the information in the image based on the pixel relevances [34] and—after a possible retraining the model [18]—reevaluating the model. These evaluation methods will further help to establish trust in the interpretability methods themselves and can hence be an important ingredient in the path to applying artificial intelligence in a clinical setting.

References

1. Alber, M.: Software and application patterns for explanation methods. In: Samek, W., Montavon, G., Vedaldi, A., Hansen, L.K., Müller, K.-R. (eds.) Explainable AI: Interpreting, Explaining and Visualizing Deep Learning. LNCS (LNAI), vol. 11700, pp. 399–433. Springer, Cham (2019). https://doi.org/10.1007/978-3-030-28954-6_22
2. Alber, M., et al.: Innvestigate neural networks!. J. Mach. Learn. Res. **20**(93), 1–8 (2019)
3. Arpino, G., Bardou, V.J., Clark, G.M., Elledge, R.M.: Infiltrating lobular carcinoma of the breast: tumor characteristics and clinical outcome. Breast Cancer Res. **6**(3), R149 (2004). https://doi.org/10.1186/bcr767
4. Bach, S., Binder, A., Montavon, G., Klauschen, F., Müller, K.R., Samek, W.: On pixel-wise explanations for non-linear classifier decisions by layer-wise relevance propagation. PLoS ONE **10**(7), e0130140 (2015)
5. Beck, A.H., et al.: Systematic analysis of breast cancer morphology uncovers stromal features associated with survival. Sci. Transl. Med. **3**(108), 108ra113–108ra113 (2011)
6. Bengio, Y., Courville, A., Vincent, P.: Representation learning: a review and new perspectives. IEEE Trans. Pattern Anal. Mach. Intell. **35**(8), 1798–1828 (2013)
7. Binder, A., et al.: Towards computational fluorescence microscopy: machine learning-based integrated prediction of morphological and molecular tumor profiles. arXiv preprint arXiv:1805.11178 (2018)
8. Budczies, J., et al.: Classical pathology and mutational load of breast cancer-integration of two worlds. J. Pathol. Clin. Res. **1**(4), 225–238 (2015)
9. Cortes, C., Mohri, M.: AUC optimization vs. error rate minimization. In: Advances in Neural Information Processing Systems, pp. 313–320 (2004)
10. Couture, H.D., et al.: Image analysis with deep learning to predict breast cancer grade, ER status, histologic subtype, and intrinsic subtype. NPJ Breast Cancer **4**, 30 (2018)
11. Dombrowski, A.K., Alber, M., Anders, C., Ackermann, M., Müller, K.R., Kessel, P.: Explanations can be manipulated and geometry is to blame. In: Advances in Neural Information Processing Systems, pp. 13567–13578 (2019)
12. Elston, C.W., Ellis, I.O.: Pathological prognostic factors in breast cancer. i. The value of histological grade in breast cancer: experience from a large study with long-term follow-up. Histopathology **19**(5), 403–410 (1991)
13. Hägele, M., et al.: Resolving challenges in deep learning-based analyses of histopathological images using explanation methods. Sci. Rep. **10**(1), 1–12 (2020)
14. Hammond, M.E.H., et al.: American society of clinical oncology/college of american pathologists guideline recommendations for immunohistochemical testing of estrogen and progesterone receptors in breast cancer (unabridged version). Archiv. Pathol. Lab. Med. **134**(7), e48–e72 (2010)
15. Hastie, T., Tibshirani, R., Friedman, J.: The Elements of Statistical Learning: Data Mining, Inference, and Prediction, 2nd edn. Springer, Heidelberg (2009). https://doi.org/10.1007/978-0-387-84858-7

16. He, K., Zhang, X., Ren, S., Sun, J.: Deep residual learning for image recognition. In: Proceedings of the IEEE Conference on Computer Vision and Pattern Recognition, pp. 770–778 (2016)
17. Holzinger, A., Langs, G., Denk, H., Zatloukal, K., Müller, H.: Causability and explainabilty of artificial intelligence in medicine. Wiley Interdisc. Rev. Data Min. Knowl. Discov. **9**(4), e1312 (2019)
18. Hooker, S., Erhan, D., Kindermans, P.J., Kim, B.: Evaluating feature importance estimates. arXiv preprint arXiv:1806.10758 (2018)
19. Hui, L.Y.W., Binder, A.: BatchNorm decomposition for deep neural network interpretation. In: Rojas, I., Joya, G., Catala, A. (eds.) IWANN 2019. LNCS, vol. 11507, pp. 280–291. Springer, Cham (2019). https://doi.org/10.1007/978-3-030-20518-8_24
20. Ioffe, S., Szegedy, C.: Batch normalization: accelerating deep network training by reducing internal covariate shift. arXiv preprint arXiv:1502.03167 (2015)
21. Jurmeister, P., et al.: Machine learning analysis of DNA methylation profiles distinguishes primary lung squamous cell carcinomas from head and neck metastases. Sci. Transl. Med. **11**(509), eaaw8513 (2019). 11 September 2019, https://doi.org/10.1126/scitranslmed.aaw8513
22. Kindermans, P.J., et al.: Learning how to explain neural networks: PatternNet and PatternAttribution. arXiv preprint arXiv:1705.05598 (2017)
23. Kingma, D.P., Ba, J.: Adam: a method for stochastic optimization. arXiv preprint arXiv:1412.6980 (2014)
24. Klauschen, F., et al.: Scoring of tumor-infiltrating lymphocytes: From visual estimation to machine learning. Semin. Cancer Biol. **52**, 151–157 (2018)
25. Korbar, B., et al.: Looking under the hood: deep neural network visualization to interpret whole-slide image analysis outcomes for colorectal polyps. In: IEEE Conference on Computer Vision and Pattern Recognition Workshops (CVPR), pp. 821–827 (2017)
26. Lapuschkin, S., Wäldchen, S., Binder, A., Montavon, G., Samek, W., Müller, K.R.: Unmasking clever hans predictors and assessing what machines really learn. Nat. Commun. **10**(1), 1096 (2019)
27. Millis, R.R.: Correlation of hormone receptors with pathological features in human breast cancer. Cancer **46**(S12), 2869–2871 (1980). https://doi.org/10.1002/1097-0142(19801215)46:12+⟨2869::AID-CNCR2820461426⟩3.0.CO;2-Q
28. Montavon, G., Binder, A., Lapuschkin, S., Samek, W., Müller, K.-R.: Layer-wise relevance propagation: an overview. In: Samek, W., Montavon, G., Vedaldi, A., Hansen, L.K., Müller, K.-R. (eds.) Explainable AI: Interpreting, Explaining and Visualizing Deep Learning. LNCS (LNAI), vol. 11700, pp. 193–209. Springer, Cham (2019). https://doi.org/10.1007/978-3-030-28954-6_10
29. Montavon, G., Samek, W., Müller, K.R.: Methods for interpreting and understanding deep neural networks. Digit. Signal Proc. **73**, 1–15 (2018)
30. Osborne, C.K., Yochmowitz, M.G., Knight III, W.A., McGuire, W.L.: The value of estrogen and progesterone receptors in the treatment of breast cancer. Cancer **46**(S12), 2884–2888 (1980)
31. Platt, J.: Probabilistic outputs for support vector machines and comparisons to regularized likelihood methods. Adv. Large Margin Classif. **10**(3), 61–74 (1999)
32. Rawat, R.R., Ruderman, D., Macklin, P., Rimm, D.L., Agus, D.B.: Correlating nuclear morphometric patterns with estrogen receptor status in breast cancer pathologic specimens. NPJ Breast Cancer **4**, 32 (2018)

33. Samek, W., Montavon, G., Vedaldi, A., Hansen, L.K., Müller, K.-R. (eds.): Explainable AI: Interpreting, Explaining and Visualizing Deep Learning. LNCS (LNAI), vol. 11700. Springer, Cham (2019). https://doi.org/10.1007/978-3-030-28954-6
34. Samek, W., Binder, A., Montavon, G., Lapuschkin, S., Müller, K.R.: Evaluating the visualization of what a deep neural network has learned. IEEE Trans. Neural Netw. Learn. Syst. **28**(11), 2660–2673 (2016)
35. Selvaraju, R.R., Cogswell, M., Das, A., Vedantam, R., Parikh, D., Batra, D.: Grad-CAM: visual explanations from deep networks via gradient-based localization. In: Proceedings of the IEEE International Conference on Computer Vision, pp. 618–626 (2017)
36. Shamai, G., Binenbaum, Y., Slossberg, R., Duek, I., Gil, Z., Kimmel, R.: Artificial intelligence algorithms to assess hormonal status from tissue microarrays in patients with breast cancer. JAMA Netw. Open **2**(7), e197700–e197700 (2019)
37. Smilkov, D., Thorat, N., Kim, B., Viégas, F., Wattenberg, M.: SmoothGrad: removing noise by adding noise. arXiv preprint arXiv:1706.03825 (2017)
38. Vahadane, A., et al.: Structure-preserving color normalization and sparse stain separation for histological images. IEEE Trans. Med. Imaging **35**(8), 1962–1971 (2016)
39. Varma, S., Simon, R.: Bias in error estimation when using cross-validation for model selection. BMC Bioinformatics **7**(1), 91 (2006)

Supporting the Donation of Health Records to Biobanks for Medical Research

Horst Pichler and Johann Eder[✉]

Department of Informatics-Systems, Alpen-Adria University Klagenfurt,
Klagenfurt, Austria
{horst.pichler,johann.eder}@aau.at

Abstract. Biobanks are infrastructures for medical research providing biological material together with data describing these materials and their donors. Annotating biological samples with health related data of the donors is cumbersome, in particular when these data are produced by several independent data sources. We argue that the value of the samples stored in a biobank increases with a more wholesome availability of medical data of the donors and thus we argue for a system encouraging individuals to complement the donation of biological material with the donation of data. We explore the requirements for a system managing the donation of data as a first step for the design of a donation management system for biobanks.

1 Introduction

Biobanks are infrastructures for medical research collecting and storing biological material together with data describing these materials and providing both for (medical) research projects [15,17,22,24]. The annotation of the biological samples with quality-controlled data about the donor considerably increases the usefulness of biological material collected in biobanks. Complementing the donation of biological material with donation of personal data is a strong desideratum, in particular when data originates from several health care providers. Health care data consists of various types of information, like doctoral notes and hospital reports describing symptoms and diagnoses, as well as detailed information about medication, lab results, and imaging data. It is the mission of biobanks, to make all these resources available to promote and advance research [38].

Biobanks usually store and link data to describe samples and donors. While the administration of data derived from the stored biological material was in the focus of many developments, the administration of data of the donor of this biological material is considerably limited in many biobanks. Donor related

This work has been supported by the Austrian Bundesministerium für Bildung, Wissenschaft und Forschung within the project bbmri.at (GZ 10.470/0016-II/3/2013 and 10.470/0010-V/3c/2018).

© Springer Nature Switzerland AG 2020
A. Holzinger et al. (Eds.): AI & ML for Digital Pathology, LNAI 12090, pp. 38–55, 2020.
https://doi.org/10.1007/978-3-030-50402-1_3

data comes typically from data acquisition in the course of medical studies, from routine health care provisions, or from data collection in the creation of cohort biobanks. However, we observed that the collected data in a biobank is stems mainly from the hosting institution of the biobank and rarely includes data from other health care providers. A particular deficiency often bemoaned is missing follow-up information, when the follow up-treatment or treatments of other ailments is performed in other health care institutions.

However, gathering health care data in order to retrace the medical history of a donor is a rather ambitious goal demanding to address enormous challenges:

- Completeness and quality: required parts of medical documentation may not be available any more, or donors don't remember or deliver wrong information (e.g. childhood diseases, prior medication).
- Transformation: unreadability of handwritten documents, transformation errors when transcribing data from documents; furthermore the diversity of formats and technologies regarding health care data, makes it very difficult to provide unified transformation, mapping, and search interfaces,
- Interpretation: problems to give meaning to data, as it probably relates to undocumented or unknown proprietary semantics, which requires input of the original author to translate and interpret it; even worse, the semantics of data produced by one data provider may evolve over time leading to heterogeneity between and within data sources.
- Distribution and technical heterogeneity: the required information is usually stored in the databases of hospitals and other health service providers, thus it is distributed over multiple organizational units, each running different systems with diverse technologies and different interface technologies.
- Access: BBMRI.at-associated biobanks reported that they have often only very marginal information about the donors and their medical history mainly because of organizational and legal reasons but also because of technical barriers.
- Laws and regulations: and last, but definitely not least, access to and use of health-related personal data is regarded extremely sensitive and therefore very restricted, often prohibited, heavily regulated by laws and regulations, as well as corporate ethical rules and guidelines.

In summary, due to semantic, organizational and technical challenges, as well as critical ethical, legal and societal issues, gathering high quality health care data of patients for medical research, in particular for annotating samples in biobanks, is a rather difficult endeavour.

In this paper we discuss and present the requirements for data donation management, analyzing the demands, motivation, and constraints of all the stakeholders, and the technical challenges of integrating data coming from multiple heterogeneous sources. We discuss in particular an exploratory case study of the situation in Austria, where a federated national health record infrastructure, ELGA (Elektronische Gesundheitsakte) [3] is being established, which can serve as mediator for the access to health records.

2   A Motivating Scenario

The following example shows the value of a complete set of health care records collected over time stemming from various health care providers:

Interactions between drugs administered concurrently [32] *may cause severe adverse drug reactions inducing excessive responses* [25,28] *and even fatal effects. For example,* [36] *lists 12 (out of 31) cases of fatal rhabdomyolysis implied by the withdrawal of cerivastatin, prior to a combined administration of cerivastatin–gemfibrozil. Furthermore, drug-drug-interactions (DDIs) can also significantly change toxicities. For example, the combined administration of pravastatin (lipid-lowering agent) and paroxetine (antidepressant) may increase blood glucose levels unexpectedly, while for each of the drugs administered alone, these effects have not been reported* [37]. *The combinatorial expectation, that the risk of adverse DDIs increases exponentially for each additional administered drug has been shown in several studies* [30,39].

By linking and querying donor, sample, and distributed health care data repositories a researcher could test such a hypothesis by starting an inquiry at a biobank for the existence of blood samples, frozen, of male or female patients, aged 40 and above, diagnosed with M62.82 Rhabdomyolysis (ICD10-code), where cerivastatin and gemfibrozil was prescribed up to two years before the diagnosis, and blood counts and therapy descriptions are available. Additionally, the usage of data mining and other computer-aided analytical tools on detailed high-quality health care data has the potential to greatly improve the quality of research results and may show new relations between diseases, diagnoses, therapies, and medications otherwise overlooked or even impossible to achieve.

Figure 1 shows different actors and the data flow to and from biobanks. (1) A biobank *collects* samples along with sample data, donor data, and data derived from research studies, which is usually stored in various specialized *(i) Sample, Donor and Research Data Repositories.* Therefore, the focus of this paper is on *(2) gathering* high quality patient health care data of donors produced in prior treatments and therapies by various health care providers, to be stored in a *(ii) Medical Health Care Data Repository.*

Donor data from (i) and patient data from (ii) must be *(3) linked* for further use and stored in a *(iii) Linked Data Repository.* Before submitting a research proposal, a researcher will perform a *(4) search* for the required material and data. Later, when the researcher is conducting her study, she will request the donor-related linked data, which will be *(5) transferred* to her, preferably in a standard format permitting computerized processing and analysis. The cycle is concluded when the researcher hands study-related data and results (like lab report values, diagnoses, demographics, results of questionnaires, and so on) over to the biobank, which is again a *(1) collection* step.

This example shows in a nutshell the significantly added value of the resources provided by biobanks, if the biological material is associated with more complete data about a person. Besides offering additional data like in the example above, integrating data from various sources directly increases also the quality of those data, which currently solely rely on the patient's memory (e.g. childhood

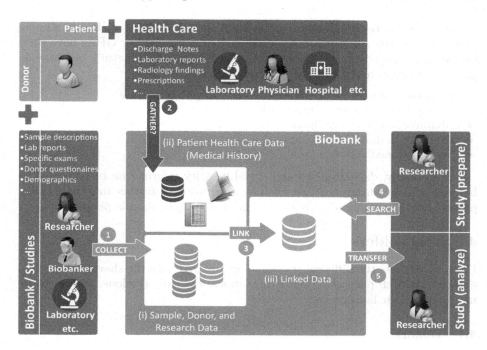

Fig. 1. Data flow between different actors in biobanks.

diseases). An additional promising source of information is currently also the proliferation of devices collecting various physical parameters, from number of steps per day to sleeping habits, which are a source of measured data (as opposed to answers to questions in questionnaires collecting life style data), which only recently also attracted researchers [23].

3 ELGA - A Prototypical Mediator of Health Records

The Austrian Electronic Health Record (ELektronische GesundheitsAkte, short ELGA) [3] gathers, connects, and distributes health data of patients from and for various stakeholders and organisations within the Austrian health care sector. It is a distributed information system that provides electronic access to patient-related health-data and documents for the patients and participating health care service providers (GesundheitsDiensteAnbieter, short GDA), which are hospitals, care homes, pharmacies, dentists, medical practitioners, social security services, other corporate and public organisations.

The goals of ELGA are (a) a transparent, complete and detailed documentation of patient treatments, (b) the cross-organisational flow of patient health data and improvement of GDA-collaboration, (c) the improvement of patient safety (access to all findings, medications, etc.), and (d) an improvement of the quality of medical documentation (use of standards).

ELGA is a national effort driven by the Austrian Ministry of Health, all nine provinces and the social insurance carriers. The participating GDAs have been tasked to connect their IT-systems into the ELGA-infrastructure and provide patients health care data in standardized formats:

- Discharge summaries (physician, nursery) of public hospitals
- Nursery transfer note (care situation report)
- Laboratory-analyzed findings
- Radiology findings
- Prescribed medication

Additionally, demographics and social security information of patients can be requested by authorized parties. The integration of further information like pathology reports, dental registries, additional imaging data is planned.

4   Stakeholders

First, we address the different stakeholders involved with the sharing of medical data for research purposes, their expectations, their reservations, their requirements, and their limitations.

4.1   Donors

Donors of data will primarily be individuals who donate biological material to biobanks. As such they have been informed about the purpose of donations to medical research and agreed to the provided informed consent. Apart from the ease of use and the assumed desire to support research and science to advance medicine and mankind, a data donor's expectations will mainly be driven by the need for confidence and trust. In order to build this trust the following demands must be met by the other stakeholders, their processes, their infrastructure, as well as by laws and regulations.

- Donated data must be treated with the same care as donated biomaterial.
- The biobank guarantees that donor data and data identity will be secured and protected, that data access is strictly regulated and only temporarily granted to legitimate stakeholders.
- The donor is and stays the data owner, thus he has to agree to data donation and usage by signing an informed consent (opt-in only).
- The donor can withdraw the consent and restrict or extend access and usage limitations at any time, and the requested changes will be effective immediately.
- The donor must have a transparent view on the usage of data and may always request information from the biobank about which data was donated, when it was donated, where it is stored, when it was used for which research studies, and for what it can be used in the future.
- The biobank must inform the donor comprehensively about the mission of the biobank, their terms, stipulations, rules of conduct, ethical guidelines and the exact purpose of conducted research.

4.2   Researchers

The researcher is on the other side of the stakeholder spectrum. Accordingly, her expectations regarding donor data are quite different, and mainly driven by the requirement to maximize the quality of her research results and minimize the effort in order to achieve that.

- Before preparing a study proposal it must be possible to find out if the biobank constitution basically supports the research field, whether the biobank has the required samples and data in the required amount, type, and quality, and for how long and under which conditions access to samples and data is granted.
- To prepare a research study proposal, it must be possible to specify what the research is about (hypothesis), which results are intended to achieve, which samples are required, which data are exactly needed from which (type of) donors.
- For and during research it must be possible to retrieve required data for further analysis, preferably in a format that is machine processable, and interpretable, preferably semantically annotated.
- The whole process of from searching to finally accessing and using material and data should be efficient, well documented, and adequately supported.

4.3   General Public

Expectations of the general public is foremost to improve health care through the development of new therapies and new drugs to treat diseases and preventive measures to avoid illnesses. In addition, the general public has an interest in an effective and efficient use of funds for research.

4.4   Health Care Providers

On one hand health care providers share the expectations and motivation of the general public to promote scientific research for improving healthcare. On the other hand, providing data for biobanks is an additional burden with administrative and technical expenses. Sometimes also the export of prior intramural information is seen critical. For health care providers with an own research agenda also sharing valuable case data before it is exploited in projects and publications is met with considerable reservations.

4.5   Mediators

Mediators like ELGA, national health record registers, but also insurance companies, etc. also see the provision of data for research as an additional service but sometimes also as an additional justification for the establishment of mediating infrastructures. For public mediators, the support of research could be part of the mission of such infrastructures. However, there is a huge variety in the organisation, scope, and services of such infrastructures throughout Europe.

5   Laws and Regulations

The main body of law regulating the collection of patient data is the European GDPR. Besides this regulation and its adoption in the national laws of the member states of the European Union, there are additional laws which have to be considered: special laws addressing the collection and use of data for scientific research, as for example, the Austrian Forschungsorganisationsgestz (FOG), laws regulating the organization and distribution of health records resp. the workings of a national infrastructure for the management, collection and provision of health records, such as the Austrian ELGA law, respectively, other laws concerning potential data mediators.

5.1   European General Data Protection Regulation

The General Data Protection Regulation (GDPR) [4] of the European Union was a major step in the legislation of data protection and privacy preservation and is the major legal framework guiding any collection of data in the European Union.

Important for our scenarios, as summarized by a BBMRI-ERIC FAQ [14], the GPDR demands the following: there must be an agreement, in the form of an informed consent, between organizations (like biobanks), that process data, and data subjects (patients, donors), whose personal data are processed. Regarding their personal data, these data subjects have a right to information, to access, to rectification, to erasure (aka 'the right to be forgotten'), to restrict processing, to data portability and to object. Access means also that they have a right to receive their personal data in a commonly used machine-readable format. Additionally they have a right to nominate controllers who act and decide on behalf of the subject, and to transfer their personal data from one controller to another or have the data transmitted directly between controllers.

Further information about the implementation is also provided by the Article 29 Working Party (WP29) which issued new guidances on three important aspects of the new General Data Protection Regulation:

- the new "Right to Data Portability", an obligation on companies and public authorities to build tools that allow users to download their data or transfer it directly to a competitor [13].
- the new obligation for organizations to appoint a "Data Protection Officer", a quasi-independent role within companies that will be tasked with internal supervision and advice regarding GDPR compliance [12].
- the new "One Stop Shop" mechanism, helping companies identify which "lead" data protection authority will be their main point of contact for multi-country regulatory procedures [11].

5.2   Laws Governing Health Data Mediators

The exchange of health care data (health records) between health care providers is typically governed by national laws. We discuss these laws here with the example of the Austrian national infrastructure for the exchange of health records,

ELGA. The ELGA-law [5] and several other regulations and decrees [6] strictly regulate data and privacy protection, which can be summarized as follows:

- Requirements for the protection and security of sensible health data
- Regulation about which data is to be provided by whom
- Regulation about the quality and structure of provided data
- Access regulations and limitations for participating parties
- Obligations for executive care like storage and handling of data
- Explicit voluntariness of participation - realized with opt-out possibilities for patients
- Imposing sanctions and penalties on breaking laws and neglecting regulations
- Time-plan for the step-wise implementation in Austria

ELGA supports the legal concept of *patient representatives* and in order to gain access to patient data these representatives have to identify themselves personally at the ELGA-ombudsman. ELGA also realizes "Artikel 19" of the Patient Charta (Vereinbarung zur Sicherstellung der Patientenrechte) [9] which states that patients have a right to disclosure, regarding medical documentation about diagnostic, therapeutical, and other health care related measures taken.

With the implementation of the GDPR in national law, Austria amended the law governing the organisation of research (Forschungsorganisationsgesetz FOG [1]) which allows the use of slightly pseudonymized data to be used for scientific research without explicit consent of the data owner under some strict procedures. This applies in particular also to data collected with the ELGA system, such that for these data currently there is no donation procedure as described in [31] necessary. However, there is not yet any jurisdiction addressing this law, there is hardly any ruling of an ethics committee, and the requirements for international cooperation and exchange are not yet sufficiently clear. Therefore, cautionary management of biobanks will treat the collection and provision of data with the same scrutiny as the collection and provision of biological material and include data donations explicitly in informed consents.

6   Interoperability Requirements

A system that allows partners to interoperate by exchanging data in order to gain information requires an architecture that is capable of transferring, processing, validating, transforming, querying, and interpreting data. To do this usually three levels of interoperability are required [2]:

1. Technical interoperability, which means that both parties must agree on a stack of communication and encoding technologies.
2. Organizational interoperability, which means that both parties must follow the same rules and protocols when exchanging documents.
3. Semantic interoperability, which means that both parties must have the same understanding of terms, concepts, and values used in documents.

We discuss here the infrastructure needed for the exchange of health records with the example of our case study on the Austrian ELGA system.

6.1   ELGA Infrastructure

ELGA and ELGA-partners realized all these levels of interoperability. They implemented the national data-exchange architecture and document exchange interfaces based on technical profiles provided by organizations dedicated to create international standards and specifications for interoperability in the domain, like Health Level 7 (HL7), Integrating the Healthcare Enterprise (IHE), the Advancing Open Standards for the Information Society (OASIS), or the World Wide Web Consortium (W3C). Summarized, the ELGA infrastructure works as follows:

- The sources for ELGA's patient health care data are the systems operated by health care providers, which are registered ELGA-partners, in particular their internal databases, health applications, or hospital information systems.
- Each ELGA-partner is tasked to provide the technical infrastructure in order to connect their local systems with the national ELGA infrastructure. Each partner must fulfill all ELGA-terms concerning storage, archiving, security, privacy, access restrictions, and so on, according to the standards and profiles demanded by ELGA laws and regulations.
- Each ELGA-partner must implement data interfaces (adaptors) that transform their proprietary health care data, stored in their local systems, into ELGA-conforming documents. An ELGA-partner must offer at least one adaptor for each document type to be supported (e.g., discharge note, laboratory report, prescription).
- During treatment, therapy, and other related activities the acting health care service provider (which must be an ELGA-partner) requests access to the medical history (health care data in the form of ELGA documents) of the patient concerned, which can then be granted via the ELGA-infrastructure for a limited time period.
- Health care data produced by an ELGA partner will be transformed into ELGA documents and sent to ELGA, extending and completing the patients' national health care records.

6.2   ELGA Documents

Documents in ELGA are based on the document standard *Clinical Document Architecture (CDA)* provided by HL7 [7]. It is an XML-based document markup standard to specify the structure and semantics of "clinical documents" for the purpose of exchange between healthcare providers and patients. In contrast to proprietary data formats and scanned documents CDA-based documents improve (human and machine) readability, usability, and accessibility. A CDA document can contain any type of clinical content, e.g. discharge summaries, reports, or a laboratory report.

The advantage of ELGA documents is based on the usage of standardized schemas and interfaces to retrieve and process well defined, structured, semantically annotated, and versioned XML-based data, which can be automatically

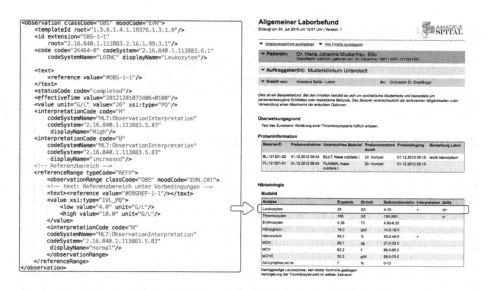

Fig. 2. Semantically annotated XML-representation of the leucocyte count in a CDA Laboratory Report document. Source: [3]

extracted, queried, interpreted, transformed, aggregated, and combined. A standardized structure makes documents machine-readable and the semantic annotations make them machine-interpretable between partners.

Document sections and elements are annotated with semantic information, like LOINC-encodings [8], which allows machines to understand the purpose of the element ("Ok, it should describe a diagnosis"). Furthermore, in ELGA all crucial elements are already prepared to be standard-encoded, which is usually done by demanding values according to specified data types (e.g., a date must be in the format YYYY-MM-DD) or standardized value sets (e.g. "C50", the ICD-10 code for "Malignant neoplasm of breast"). Figure 2 shows a small part (the leucocyte count) of the XML-based encoding of a laboratory report. The XML-fragment contains annotated numbers and codes referencing standardized code-systems, like the above mentioned LOINC to describe document elements and their expected content, as well as predefined lists of values, like HL7:ObservationInterpretation, which specifies rough qualitative interpretations of medical observations (e.g., "normal", "abnormal", "resistent", "indeterminate", and so on).

Summarized, by using the XML-structure and annotation-concepts described by HL7 CDA the following advantages are gained:

- these documents have a unified and standardized document structure which can be automatically parsed and evaluated.
- these documents are machine-readable which enables automatic extraction, processing, and aggregation of information (e.g. summaries of diagnoses, time-series representation of laboratory parameters, and so on).

- these documents contain semantic annotations which enable automatic interpretation of meaning.

Such a structured representation with annotations allows machines to read, parse, and interpret (extract the semantics) from a CDA document without human intervention, which is a cornerstone for the automation of advanced analysis tasks.

7   Incentivizing Data Donation by Building Trust

Even if human research and clinical practice find a way to integrate personal health data, uptake will remain limited, unless people are incentivized to participate [21]. Above all, the main motivations to donate data are: (i) to support research intended to lead to public good, (2) for self-benefit, as well as (3) for the concern for others. Around 60% of people are willing to donate their data for uses that will benefit the public. But the other 40% of people would not give away their data even if it was used for public benefit. For many people, the decision to donate their data depends on for what purpose the data will be used, as well as on assurances on how securely it will be stored. Given there have been so many reports of loss or misuse of personal data it is hardly surprising some are reluctant to give theirs away [35]. *Trust is key* [34].

Sharing personal sensible, especially health-related, data requires a lot information and trust between the data donor and an institution. Trust can only arise if biobanks are regulated by accepted and published laws and bylaws, offer informed consents, secure their data, guarantee the protection of privacy, and additionally adhere to a code of ethics that, among many other things, exactly describes how the institution intends to deal with donated material and data. Several of these requirements are already dictated by ELGA-related laws and regulations, still some more trust-building measures have to be considered when building a data donation platform.

7.1   Security and Privacy

As outlined in Sect. 5 laws and regulations require very strict security obligations to be met by service and data providers. Security mechanisms must ensure that communication is encrypted, data is stored in secured areas where only authorized parties have access. For this purpose, standard security mechanisms for databases and information systems must be applied.

Additionally, data in biobanks must be at least as secure as all health-related data collections as, for example, in hospital information systems, or in the databases of health insurance companies. Security in biobanks can be higher, as typically fewer individuals have access to sensitive data than in hospitals and there is no need to provide access possibilities for emergency situations. However, a main purpose of biobanks is for researchers to access and to use biomaterials and linked data for research. The challenge is how researchers can access data in biobank information systems without compromising the privacy and anonymity of the donors.

7.2   Access Control and Monitoring

Donors and the biobank must be able to control who is allowed to access which type of data, in which context, under which circumstances, and for how long this access is granted. In portals where multiple users with different roles have access this is usually accomplished by personalized role-based access control features, like an account (password, login) which is tied to a person and specific roles (like data owner, donor, researcher, committee member). In these systems access to data can be restricted to certain configurable roles (and the owner). Access can also be temporally limited or allowed for certain document types, and so on. Furthermore, this type of access is the prerequisite for user-specific logging of access and manipulation operations on data, which can be presented to other users in the form of a protocol [29,40].

7.3   Information

According to [14] the obligation to inform data subjects (donors) about the usage and handling of their data is quite pronounced. It demands, among many other things, that donors and the public must be informed about the nature of the data to be collected, for which purposes and by which recipients it will be used, the rules of access, storage and use of data, and how security, privacy, anonymity, and provenance is guaranteed.

7.4   Ethical Principles

The World Medical Association's Helsinki "Declaration of Tapei on ethical considerations in Health Databases and Biobank" lays down ethical principles for medical research involving human subjects, including the importance of protecting the dignity, autonomy, privacy and confidentiality of research subjects, and obtaining informed consent for using identifiable human biological material and data [10].

7.5   Informed Consents

As the donor is the owner of his biomaterial and data in biobanks every activity related to these resources must be backed by an informed consent, which must be approved by an ethical committee and signed by the donor. According to the GPDR the informed consent can also be provided electronically, which means that in this form it also requires electronic signatures. In [27] the following types of informed consents are described:

- General/blanket/open consent: donors can actively consent once for the current study and all future research involving the general use of their samples and information.
- Broad consent: donors can actively consent once for the current study and future research limited to field like cancer, diabetes, and so on.

- Delegated trustee: donors can transfer consents to a trustee (controller) who is at arms-distance length from the biobank and consents on behalf of donors.
- Third-party oversight: donors can actively consent to a general, broad or other model, but an ethics board must approve the study before the commencement of research using stored samples and information. This approach is emerging as a common component of biobanking governance schemes.
- Tiered: donors can actively consent once for the current study and choose one or more broad fields of research or other options, i.e., whether they would be willing to have their samples and information used in research that results in commercialization.
- Re-consent: donors are informed and are required to consent to the current study involving the use of their samples and information.
- Specified informed consent: allows the use of biological specimens and related data only in immediate research; forbids any future study that is not foreseen at the time of the original consent.

Regarding data donation there is one very important scenario not covered by above listed consent types: data donation after death. In most countries it is much more difficult to use data from deceased people than it is to use data from living individuals, as a deceased person cannot be asked to provide an informed consent. To avoid wasting medical data, all citizens should be encouraged to sign up to a data donor register and perhaps carry an associated data donor card. Those registered as data donors will know that their decision will definitely contribute to future research, no matter how they die [33].

8   Electronic Informed Consent with Disclosure Filters

[26] states that in an era when information is shared digitally at the global level, mechanisms of informed consent remain static, paper-based and organised around national boundaries and legal frameworks. Accordingly, they propose a personalised digital communication interface that connects researchers and participants, placing participants at the heart of decision making.

However, informed consents are often rather general regarding the visibility and usage of data linked to samples and donors. They do usually not specify which part of the available personal information is visible to whom, for how long, and for which purpose. Nevertheless, this is one of the most important requirements for donors to donate their personal information (for example in Facebook every user has the possibility to configure and control the visibility of personal information for different user groups for different information categories). This is even more important when dealing with very detailed, fine grained, highly structured HL7-based documents.

To specify the visibility or invisibility of personal data for different stakeholders we propose the application of disclosure filters. Disclosure filters are usually used in data exchange scenarios to control which information is allowed to be transferred between partners [16]. The prerequisites for the specification of personalized disclosure filters are the HL7-based models that describe the structure and semantics of data in health care documents.

Accordingly, we propose to combine dynamic informed consents with disclosure filters to enable donors to maintain their privacy rights harmonized with the necessity of researchers to search for useful material and data. Such a combined interface would perfectly suit the requirement stated in [26] to "facilitate a two-way communication to stimulate a more engaged, informed and scientifically literate participant population where individuals can tailor and manage their own consent preferences".

8.1   Example

A user decides to donate a set of health-related documents and he signs a specified informed consent, allowing the data to be used for cancer research only. Additionally, he wants to exclude certain document types (e.g., exclude medical prescriptions), and specify which information in a specific document type may be used (e.g., only diagnoses codes and laboratory report results) and which parts are prohibited (e.g. personal data, free text entries).

8.2   Electronic Informed Consent (eIC)

To check these restrictions automatically, our system requires an electronic informed consent (eIC) with a data specification that can be specified and electronically signed by the donor. A disclosure filter can then be derived from this specification to be applied in the following three cases: (1) When the donor donates (imports) data everything will be filtered out as specified by the user, before it is stored in a data repository. (2) When a researcher searches for specific data the search results would be filtered according to the filter's specifications. (3) When a researcher requests the data transfer for his analysis, he will only receive the content which he is permitted to see.

8.3   Disclosure Filter Specification

The eIC must be specified by capturing the type of the consent (broad, specified, re-consent, ...) and all other information required by a regular informed consent electronically [27]. Similar, a disclosure filter specifies restrictions on available data specified in several dimensions. [18] lists some filter attributes for transmitting donor data for research studies:

- the field of research (all, cancer, metabolic diseases, etc.),
- type of research (basic research, drug development, etc.),
- type of research lab (university, company, etc.),
- location of the research (country, federation),
- permitted data (case history, lifestyle data, lab data, family data, etc.),
- qualifications of the research organization or researcher,
- or accreditation of a project by some organization or ombudsman.

As structure and semantics of documents are defined by the HL7 CDA standard established in ELGA, a disclosure filter, can even be more specific on the information to be handed over to the biobank or a researcher. This is crucial, as some elements within documents may hold very personal and sensible information, not to be revealed:

- Document type restrictions: disclose certain document types (e.g. disclose discharge notes and laboratory reports, but no prescriptions)
- Document structure restrictions: disclose specific data elements in specific document types or in all document types (e.g. disclose diagnoses and time of diagnoses, but not the attending medical personal)
- Temporal restrictions: disclose all documents or only documents generated in a defined time range (e.g. the last 5 years)
- Temporal access restrictions: unlimited access to documents (forever) or limited access to documents (e.g., only during a study)

Specification Example: A donor restricts donation of his documents with the following specification: exclude all addresses, social security number and status, exclude any free text field, exclude documents of type laboratory report, and exclude any document regarding the venereal disease diagnosis last year. Furthermore, the donor might want to restrict the access on his documents: grant access for cancer studies only, block access for documents before 2010, and block access for genetic research studies. Additionally, the biobank might want to filter out all information about attending doctors and organizations involved (probably in order to avoid potential problems regarding the violation of personal rights), which could be added as default to every disclosure filter.

Particular attention for the development of electronic informed consents has to be given to the evolution of data, schemas and ontologies [19,20], e.g. the succession of different ontologies for diagnosis codes and with the heterogeneity of data stemming from different sources.

9 Discussion and Conclusions

This document presents an elaborated vision how individuals can be empowered to share their health care data with biobanks for medical research. The new General Data Protection Regulation of the EU is a strong enabler for the sovereignty of individuals over their data with the possibility to donate or share data. We analyzed the different stakeholders' roles and expectations and elicited the legal, ethical organizational and technical requirements and constraints in an exploratory study. Many of these requirements and constraints have been collected with best effort, but they still require extended scientific studies for validation and amendments. In our case study [31] we also developed in a design exploration a set of scenarios for the development of information systems studying how data donation can be implemented in technical systems and organisational processes. The case study [31] underlying this paper was performed in

2017, before the new Austrian Forschungsorganisationsgesetz was enacted, which brought new regulations for accessing ELGA data for medical research without explicit consent of donors. Notwithstanding the new possibilities, the core scenarios of this case study remain valid if an explicit consent of the data owners is required or desired. And of course the scenarios and conclusions are relevant for all data sources not covered by the Austrian FOG.

It is our ambition that this document triggers discussions on how to make existing data available for medical research while strictly respecting patients' rights. Further evaluation of the requirements and deeper analysis of possible designs are necessary, but we hope that this explorative study is a step towards improvement of the data basis for medical research and thus for better understanding of diseases and the development of therapies.

Acknowledgments. The authors thank Anna Durnova, Heimo Müller, Karine Sargsyan, Cornelia Stumptner, Melanie Goisauf, Johannes Starkbaum, Iris Eisenberger, Elisabeth Hödl, Margot Ham-Rubisch, and Helga Willinger who provided us with insights into the legal, ethical and organizational context and requirements, were willing to discuss our rough ideas, and provided very valuable feedback on draft versions of this report.

References

1. Datenschutz-Anpassungsgesetz 2018 - Wissenschaft und Forschung - WFDSAG 2018. BGBl. I Nr. 31/2018
2. European commission: ehealth stakeholder group report perspectives and recommendations on interoperability (2014). http://ec.europa.eu/newsroom/dae/document.cfm?doc_id=5168. Accessed Mar 2019
3. elga.gv.at: ELGA - die elektronische Gesundheitsakte (official governmental website) (2016). https://www.elga.gv.at/index.html. Accessed Mar 2019
4. eur-lex.europa.eu: regulation (EU) 2016/679 of the European parliament and of the council of 27 April 2016 on the protection of natural persons with regard to the processing of personal data and on the free movement of such data, and repealing directive 95/46/ec (general data protection regulation) (2016). http://eur-lex.europa.eu. Accessed Oct 2016
5. Gesamte Rechtsvorschrift für Gesundheitstelematikgesetz 2012, Fassung vom 23.01.2017 (2016). https://www.ris.bka.gv.at. Accessed Oct 2016
6. Gesetzliche Grundlagen von ELGA (2016). https://www.elga.gv.at. Accessed Oct 2016
7. Hl7 international: clinical document architecture, CDA release 2 (2016). https://www.hl7.org. Accessed Oct 2016
8. loinc.org: logical observation identifiers names and codes (2016). https://loinc.org. Accessed Oct 2016
9. Parlament.gv.at: Vereinbarung gem. Art. 15a B-VG zur Sicherstellung der Patientenrechte (Patientencharta) (1268) (2016). https://www.parlament.gv.at/PAKT/VHG/XXII/I/L_01268/index.shtml. Accessed Oct 2016
10. WMA declaration of Taipei on ethical considerations regarding health databases and biobanks. Adopted by the 53rd WMA general assembly, Washington, DC, USA, October 2002 and revised by the 67th WMA general assembly, Taipei, Taiwan, October 2016. http://www.wma.net/en/30publications/10policies/d1

11. Article 29 data protection working party: guidelines for identifying a controller or processor's lead supervisory authority. 16/en wp 244. Adopted on 13 December 2016 (2017). http://ec.europa.eu/newsroom/dae/document.cfm?doc_id=5168. Accessed Mar 2017

12. Article 29 data protection working party: Guidelines on data protection officers. 16/en wp 243. Adopted on 13 December 2016 (2017). http://ec.europa.eu/information_society/newsroom/image/document/2016-51/wp244_en_40857.pdf. Accessed Mar 2017

13. Article 29 data protection working party: guidelines on the right to data portability. 16/en wp 242. Adopted on 13 December 2016 (2017). http://ec.europa.eu/newsroom/dae/document.cfm?doc_id=5168. Accessed Mar 2017

14. The EU general data protection regulation - answers to frequently asked questions 1.0. prepared by the BBMRI common service ELSI 1 May 2016 (2017). http://ec.europa.eu/information_society/newsroom/image/document/2016-51/wp242_en_40852.pdff. Accessed Jan 2017

15. Asslaber, M., et al.: The genome austria tissue bank (GatiB). Pathology **74**, 251–258 (2007)

16. Dabringer, C., Eder, J.: Retrieving samples from biobanks. In: Khuri, S., Lhotská, L., Pisanti, N. (eds.) ITBAM 2010. LNCS, vol. 6266, pp. 172–185. Springer, Heidelberg (2010). https://doi.org/10.1007/978-3-642-15020-3_16

17. Eder, J., Dabringer, C., Schicho, M., Stark, K.: Information systems for federated biobanks. In: Hameurlain, A., Küng, J., Wagner, R. (eds.) Transactions on Large-Scale Data- and Knowledge-Centered Systems I. LNCS, vol. 5740, pp. 156–190. Springer, Heidelberg (2009). https://doi.org/10.1007/978-3-642-03722-1_7

18. Eder, J., Gottweis, H., Zatloukal, K.: IT solutions for privacy protection in biobanking. Public Health Genomics **15**, 254–262 (2012)

19. Eder, J., Koncilia, C.: Modelling changes in ontologies. In: Meersman, R., Tari, Z., Corsaro, A. (eds.) OTM 2004. LNCS, vol. 3292, pp. 662–673. Springer, Heidelberg (2004). https://doi.org/10.1007/978-3-540-30470-8_77

20. Eder, J., Koncilia, C., Morzy, T.: A model for a temporal data warehouse. In: Proceedings of Open Enterprise Solutions: Systems, Experiences and Organizations (OES-SEO 2001), Venice, pp. 48–54 (2001)

21. Editorial. Incentivizing data donation. Nat. Biotechnol. **33**(9), 885 (2015)

22. Hainaut, P., Vaught, J., Zatloukal, K., Pasterk, M.: Biobanking of Human Biospecimens: Principles and Practice. Springer, Heidelberg (2017). https://doi.org/10.1007/978-3-319-55120-3

23. Henriksen, A.: Using fitness trackers and smartwatches to measure physical activity in research: analysis of consumer wrist-worn wearables. J. Med. Internet Res. **20**(3), e110 (2018)

24. Hofer-Picout, P., et al.: Conception and implementation of an Austrian biobank directory integration framework. Biopreservation Biobank. **15**, 332–340 (2017)

25. Jankel, C., Speedie, S.: Detecting drug interactions: a review of the literature. DICP Ann. Pharmacother. **24**(10), 982–9 (1990)

26. Kaye, J., et al.: Dynamic consent: a patient interface for twenty-first century research networks. Eur. J. Hum. Genet. **23**(2), 141–146 (2015). PMC. Web. 3 May 2017

27. Klingström, T., Bongcam-Rudloff, E., Reichel, J.: A primer for managing international collaboration and legal compliance in biobank based genomics. Technical report, PeerJ Preprints (2016)

28. Kuhlmann, J., Mück, W.: Clinical-pharmacological strategies to assess drug inter-action potential during drug development. Drug Saf. Int. J. Med. Toxicol. Drug Exp. **24**, 715–725 (2001)
29. Lazouski, A., Martinelli, F., Mori, P.: Usage control in computer security: a survey. Comput. Sci. Rev. **4**(2), 81–99 (2010)
30. Malone, D., et al.: Assessment of potential drug-drug interactions with a prescrip-tion claims database. Am. J. Health Syst. Pharm. AJHP **62**, 1983–1991 (2005). Official journal of the American Society of Health-System Pharmacists
31. Pichler, H., Eder, J.: Supporting donors to donate data for medical research. bbmri.at work package 2 - ELGA report part 2, version 5. Technical report, Alpen-Adria University Klagenfurt, Department of Informatics Systems (2017)
32. Scripture, C., Figg, W.: Drug interactions in cancer therapy. Nat. Rev. Cancer **6**(7), 546–58 (2006)
33. Shaw, D.M., Gross, J.V., Erren, T.C.: Data donation after death. EMBO Rep. **17**(1), 14–17 (2016)
34. Skatova, A., Goulding, J.: Donate your data. How your digital footprint can be used for the public good (2015). http://theconversation.com/donate-your-data-how-your-digital-footprint-can-be-used-for-the-public-good-35525. Accessed April 2017
35. Skatova, A., Ng, E., Goulding, J.: Data donation: sharing personal data for public good? In: Digital Economy All Hands Meeting 2014 (2014)
36. Staffa, J.A., Chang, J., Green, L.: Cerivastatin and reports of fatal rhabdomyolysis. N. Engl. J. Med. **346**(7), 539–540 (2002). PMID: 11844864
37. Tatonetti, N.P., et al.: Detecting drug interactions from adverse-event reports: interaction between paroxetine and pravastatin increases blood glucose levels. Clin. Pharmacol. Ther. **90**(1), 133–142 (2011)
38. Wichmann, H.-E., et al.: Comprehensive catalog of European biobanks. Nat. Biotechnol. **29**(9), 795–797 (2011)
39. Zhan, C., et al.: Suboptimal prescribing in elderly outpatients: potentially harmful drug-drug and drug-disease combinations. J. Am. Geriatr. Soc. **53**, 262–267 (2005)
40. Zhang, X., Parisi-Presicce, F., Sandhu, R., Park, J.: Formal model and policy specification of usage control. ACM Trans. Inf. Syst. Secur. **8**(4), 351–387 (2005)

Survey of XAI in Digital Pathology

Milda Pocevičiūtė[1,2(✉)], Gabriel Eilertsen[1,2], and Claes Lundström[1,2,3]

[1] Department of Science and Technology, Linköping University, Linköping, Sweden
{milda.poceviciute,gabriel.eilertsen,claes.lundstrom}@liu.se
[2] Center for Medical Image Science and Visualization, Linköping University,
Linköping, Sweden
[3] Sectra AB, Linköping, Sweden

Abstract. Artificial intelligence (AI) has shown great promise for diagnostic imaging assessments. However, the application of AI to support medical diagnostics in clinical routine comes with many challenges. The algorithms should have high prediction accuracy but also be transparent, understandable and reliable. Thus, explainable artificial intelligence (XAI) is highly relevant for this domain. We present a survey on XAI within digital pathology, a medical imaging sub-discipline with particular characteristics and needs. The review includes several contributions. Firstly, we give a thorough overview of current XAI techniques of potential relevance for deep learning methods in pathology imaging, and categorise them from three different aspects. In doing so, we incorporate uncertainty estimation methods as an integral part of the XAI landscape. We also connect the technical methods to the specific prerequisites in digital pathology and present findings to guide future research efforts. The survey is intended for both technical researchers and medical professionals, one of the objectives being to establish a common ground for cross-disciplinary discussions.

Keywords: XAI · Digital pathology · AI · Medical imaging

1 Introduction and Motivation

1.1 Background

Artificial intelligence (AI) applications are showing great promise for assisting diagnostic tasks in medical imaging. Nevertheless, it is difficult to translate the technology from academic experiments to clinical use. A central challenge for AI in medicine is that mistakes can have serious consequences. This means that human experts must be able to gauge the trustworthiness of machine predictions, and put it into the context of other diagnostic information. This is the purpose of explainable artificial intelligence (XAI) techniques. XAI research embraces the insight that AI solutions should not only have high accuracy performance, but also be transparent, understandable and reliable from the end user's point of view.

This work was supported by the Swedish e-Science Research Center.

A. Holzinger et al. (Eds.): AI & ML for Digital Pathology, LNAI 12090, pp. 56–88, 2020.
https://doi.org/10.1007/978-3-030-50402-1_4

This survey investigates XAI in the domain of digital pathology. The adoption of digital microscopy, whole-slide imaging (WSI), at clinical pathology departments is progressing at a fast pace in many parts of the world. A key motivation for this investment is the potential to use AI assistance for image analysis tasks. XAI has been described as an essential component to make AI successful in imaging diagnostics [63], and we argue this is particularly pertinent for digital pathology. For example, assume that a pathologist is faced with an AI result marking a WSI region as "malignant tumour", whereas the pathologist deemed it as probably benign. It is easy to see how the pathologist would need further information on the rationale of the machine prediction in order to accept or reject the result that was in conflict with his/her own initial assessment.

There are several motivations to specifically target XAI for digital pathology, as we do in this survey. XAI has so far been dominated by the explainability tailored for AI developers, whereas the needs of pathologists and other medical professionals are distinctly different, as will be described below. Pathology is also quite different from other medical imaging. Gigapixel images are the norm, which are visually scrutinised on many scales. The characteristics of the large histology "landscapes" are very different both from photos such as in ImageNet and from radiological images. We believe that describing the XAI prerequisites in pathology will be valuable for informing much needed future research efforts in this domain.

This survey is a niched drill-down complementing previous more general reviews. There are broad XAI overviews [1, 24, 36, 42, 74], and more specialised reviews such as for Convolutional Neural Network (CNN) methods [122]. A few efforts discuss the potential of XAI for medicine in general [44, 114].

There are several specific contributions in our survey. We have elicited a classification of XAI techniques from three separate aspects: *explanation target*, *result representation*, and *technical approach*. We have identified previous XAI efforts with relevance for digital pathology, most of them not applied to this domain yet, and categorise them into the defined classes. Estimation and visualisation of uncertainty are sometimes treated as a topic separate from explainability. We echo previous researchers arguing against such a separation [4, 44, 109] and incorporate uncertainty methods as an inherent part of the XAI overview in this review. Finally, based on an analysis of the survey outcome, we provide some key findings that could guide future research efforts to solve XAI challenges in digital pathology. We believe that this paper is suitable for both technical researchers and medical domain professionals. For example, the categorisation is made with both target groups in mind, where *result representation* and *explanation target* are of interest to the medical experts, whereas the *technical approach* is separated into an isolated group. Thus, we believe that the survey can assist in understanding across the disciplines by providing a joint structure as a base for discussions.

Our survey places the focus on image recognition tasks as most AI algorithms in digital pathology work with image data. Therefore, all methods described in this survey are applicable for CNN models as, currently, this is the state-of-the-art in digital pathology. We use the terms AI tools, AI solutions and AI algorithms interchangeably.

1.2   AI in Pathology

The workload for pathologists is predicted to increase continuously due to the ageing population, shortage of physicians, increased cancer screening programmes and increased complexity of diagnostic tests [96]. One way of addressing this problem is to introduce digital pathology; that is, new workflows and tools based on the digitisation of microscopy images [113]. The possibility to add assistive AI tools is a major component of the foreseen improvements. As a foundation for our discussion on XAI, we will in this section first provide a brief overview of some important types of AI use cases for the clinical routine setting of digital pathology. For more exhaustive overviews of applied AI research in this area, we refer to previous review efforts [11,42,96], and for an introduction to the diagnostic work of a pathologist, we refer to [88].

A common diagnostic task in pathology is to detect the existence of cancer. Thus, AI development efforts are often directed towards assisting the tumour detection process. One improvement aspect is to make the search more efficient. Since the lesions may be just a handful of cells in a sea of normal tissue, it can be very time-consuming to locate them. For some scenarios the search can stop when a first lesion is found, meaning that normal/benign cases are the most time-consuming as the search then covers the entire sample. Metastasis detection in breast cancer lymph nodes is a common AI research application [26,64]. The other task aspect is to determine whether a finding actually is malignant or not, and often this includes performing a subtype classification of the cancer in question. Illustrative Cresearch efforts in this subarea include a tool for detection and subtype classification of gliomas and non-small-cell lung carcinomas [45], classification of gastric carcinoma [97], and malignancy prediction in breast cancer cytology [35].

Detection tools could also help to reorganise the worklist of a pathologist so that the cases with a high risk of malignant tumours would be prioritised. Apart from tumours, potential detection tasks for AI include needle-in-a-haystack searches for tuberculosis or helicobacter pylori bacteria [71].

In the diagnostic work-up of oncology cases, the pathologist typically provides further granularity in the analysis in the form of grading and staging assessments. These assessments often suffer from poor inter-observer reproducibility as well as high time consumption, making AI assistance attractive. In breast cancer, quantification of cell proliferation is part of the grading. Detecting and counting mitotic cells is a common target for AI methods [9,18,115]. AI solutions are commonly employed also for other cell quantification in breast cancer diagnostics, regarding positive nuclei in sections stained through immunohistochemistry (IHC) [5,41,48,76,117]. Quantified IHC analysis is relevant to predict response for many targeted treatments, with active research efforts in AI method development. Important examples include detection of positive cell membranes in the PD-L1 [56] and HER2 [92] stains.

The Gleason score is used to stage prostate cancer by assessing the extent of different architectural patterns of a tumour. This analysis has been in focus for applied AI research [6, 75] and recent larger studies show results on par with human experts [14, 106].

Another cell identification task is to count lymphocytes, which for example is important for predicting treatment response for immunotherapy on cancer patients. Deep learning methods have shown the potential to provide support for this diagnostic task as well [19, 34, 108].

A pathologist's assessment can be underpinned by other more generic quantification where AI could contribute to higher efficiency. This is relevant for area measures such as tumour/stroma ratio or tumour necrosis rate, and potentially for automation of distance measurements such as tumour thickness in skin cancer and the margin from the tumour to the resection border.

Apart from the tasks described above, neural networks have the potential to be used for content-based image retrieval (CBIR) to find previous cases with similar histology patterns as the patient at hand. This can not only assist the daily work of a pathologist but also improve the education of new physicians [58]. Deep learning has been employed for this purpose, both in research [15] and in a commercial application [47].

Overall, deep learning is a flexible approach that can be used to assist pathologists in many different aspects of their work. However, the path from promising AI models to actual clinical usage is very challenging. We argue that a key part of meeting that challenge is to develop effective and tailored XAI methods. Next, we will drill down into the specific needs of XAI in this domain.

1.3   Needs of XAI in Digital Pathology

XAI serves different purposes depending on the role of the person receiving the explanation, and depending on the reason for interacting with the AI technology. In digital pathology for clinical use we see three main scenarios, having quite different characteristics (Fig. 1). The arguably most common target for XAI is to assist the AI developer working to create or improve the model, which of course is relevant also in this domain. The second scenario is when the clinical end user, typically the pathologist, employs an AI solution in the diagnostic routine. The third XAI target area, perhaps less considered than the others, is healthcare professionals doing quality assurance (QA) of AI solutions. This role may be taken by pathologists or other medical staff, but we may also see data scientists entering the diagnostic departments to carry out such assignments. QA can correspond to initially assessing how well an algorithm performs at the lab in question, for calibrating or configuring the solution to fit local characteristics, to evaluate if there is a drift in performance over time, and more.

The AI developer perspective on XAI needs is fairly generic, at the conceptual level it is the same in digital pathology as in other application areas. We will give an outline here, while further details can be found in the survey by Hohman et al. [42]. Explainability is a key component to support the developer in improving the performance of the trained model. For example, studying

Fig. 1. Overview of the three main scenarios in digital pathology where XAI methods are relevant.

erroneous predictions is effective for evaluating the next development steps to be taken. Prediction accuracy aside, the developer also benefits from XAI analysing the generalisability of the results; is the training data, including augmentations made, representative for wider use, and is there any bias to consider? As collecting and preparing data could be very laborious, often including human experts spending many hours annotating images, the collection may not have sufficient coverage for the intended application. For instance, if there are many classes to separate, some of them may have too few examples in the data collected.

For the routine diagnostic use of AI solutions, there are many situations where explainability would be beneficial. In fact, we argue that effective XAI is essential for broad successful deployment of computational pathology in the clinical environment.

For a physician using AI assistance, a main task is to spot and correct any errors made by the algorithm. XAI would then provide assistance to critically assess the result. The typical ML model always predicts one of its predetermined outcomes, even if the evidence is lacking for any of the alternatives. An important aspect is therefore to convey the uncertainty of the prediction made. This is particularly useful when there is not a black-or-white assessment to be made, but a conclusion from a complex set of contributing factors.

The physician would likely also benefit from a deeper understanding of the source of the AI tool's limitations in the context it is used. For models trained by supervised learning, the representativeness of the training data in relation to the local data characteristics is a key factor, i.e. its ability to generalise. Image differences due to e.g. staining variations is a well-known challenge in computational pathology [105, 111], creating a domain gap between the training data and the data used for inference. There may also be discrepancies in the definition of the diagnostic task trained for and the local diagnostic protocol. Such problems makes it important to highlight when the diagnosis provided by an AI application cannot be trusted due to a lack in its ability to generalise to the current situation.

Achieving the above transparency is useful for making correct conclusions for individual cases, but also to allow the medical professionals to gain trust in the solution in general. Such trust is necessary in order to arrive at an effective division of labour between man and machine. Powerful XAI can, however, induce too high levels of trust, counteracting the objective of critical assessment [49]. Therefore, XAI methods should be carefully designed to provoke sound reflection, rather than just creating blind trust.

An additional benefit of explainable AI predictions is for teaching. Whereas it today is very difficult to verbalise the complex assessments a senior pathologist does [44], XAI visualisations may be able to better convey such knowledge. Furthermore, there is a direct connection to medical research, as XAI may help uncover previously unknown disease characteristics.

In digital pathology, AI researchers face the challenge of dealing with very large data sets, typically gigapixel images. Diagnostic pathology assessments almost always include considering small-scale and large-scale features in tandem, and computational pathology needs to do the same. This is a particular challenge for XAI as well. An AI prediction will likely need to be explained both at local cellular level and at a higher tissue structure level.

The QA scenario shares many of the XAI needs of the diagnostic assessments described above. Identifying errors, assessing uncertainty, and understanding limitations are in focus here as well. The difference is that the focus shifts from individual cases to analyses across larger case sets representing the entire operations at the lab. This poses additional requirements for XAI solutions, to support systematic, in-depth investigations akin to the diligent validation procedures for other lab equipment.

The aspects discussed above clearly show that there is a great diversity of situations where pathology diagnostics require transparency and interpretability. In summary, there is strong rationale for XAI advances tailored for digital pathology.

2   Glossary

XAI: explainable artificial intelligence, a field of study on how to increase transparency and intepretabily of artificial intelligence algorithms such that the results could be understood by a human expert.

Standard Neural Network (NN): the most common type of neural network used in research as well as in practical applications. They are based on frequentist probability theory which states that each parameter of a model has a true fixed value. It is hard and often impossible to find the exact true values, hence the backpropogation algorithm provides a means of approximating them [37]. In the context of the uncertainty estimation, the parameters of a NN are not random variables, hence, probabilies cannot be associated with them and other frequentist techniques have to be used [119].

Bayesian Neural Network (BNN): a type of neural network that is based on Bayesian theory and requires more complex procedures of training and inference. According to the Bayesian approach, a probability is a degree of the belief that a certain event will occur and can be modelled by Bayes' theorem. Bayes' theorem states that the conditional probability of an event depends on the data as well as prior information/belief. The model parameters are viewed as random variables, and Bayesian inference is used to estimate the probability distribution over them. This distribution reflects the strength of the belief regarding what parameter values that are possible, and it is used during forward pass through a BNN to sample some likely parameters and produce a range of possible outcomes [119].

3   State-of-the-Art

In this section, we provide an overview of the current methods that aim to help in developing transparent and interpretable AI solutions. We focus on methods that are specifically developed for, or can be easily applied to, visual detection tasks. There are many ways in which the methods can be grouped. In this work, we provide three alternative taxonomies, namely *Explanation target*, *Result representation* and *Technical approach*. Each taxonomy is described in detail in the corresponding subsection below, followed by examples of representative XAI methods that can be assigned to it. Table 1 in Appendix A contains all reviewed XAI methods, classified according to the three alternative ways of categorisation.

The explanation target gives a general understanding of what can be explained in visual detection tasks and for which group of professionals – AI developers, QA specialists or pathologists – this explanation is most relevant. Result representation illustrates how the explainability may be presented in an AI solution while the Technical approach provides an insight into what techniques and mathematical theories are used in order to achieve the explainability. Many of the existing XAI techniques focus on explaining classification tasks, or at least illustrate their work with examples of classification algorithms. Some methods encompass other computer vision tasks, such as detection, localisation and segmentation. Furthermore, it is important to note that some methods can be or have already been adapted for different tasks which could make them fall under several different categories. We decided to base our categorisation on how the method is described in the original paper.

Figure 2 summarises the reviewed papers based on our three dimensions of categorisation, and Fig. 3 shows the development over time. In Fig. 2, the matrix plot in the top gives an overview of what technical approaches are most commonly used for which explanation targets. In contrast, the plot in the bottom gives an overview of what result presentation types are most commonly used for which explanation targets. We can see that irreducible uncertainty so far has been only presented as an auxiliary measure even though there are quite a few different technical approaches for determining it. In contrast, the explanation of inner workings can be presented in many different ways, but the activation optimisation approach is the most commonly used to achieve the results. Figure 2 not only summarises previous work in XAI but also highlights which combinations of the categories that have not yet been explored.

It is important to note that this section is aimed at providing a general understanding of existing methods, hence the text does not focus on the pathology specific aspects. However, the result representation part is mainly illustrated by

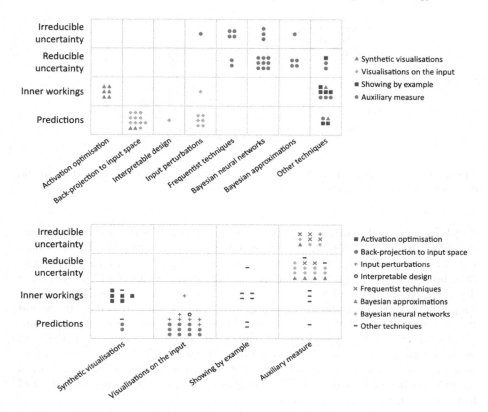

Fig. 2. Summary of the reviewed papers based on the three ways of categorisation. Explanation targets are given on the y-axis. The top plot has Technical approach as x-axis with markers indicating different *Result representations*. Conversely, the bottom plot shows Result representations on the x-axis with the markers indicating the Technical approach. Papers containing two method components representing different categories have been registered twice.

XAI methods applied to histopathological data. Furthermore, a discussion on how the different methods can be used for fulfilling the need for reliable and transparent AI tools of digital pathology is provided in Sect. 5.

3.1 Explanation Target

Explainability could have several objectives in the context of AI assisting visual analysis. Figure 4 illustrates the four targets that an XAI method may help to understand better. In this section we describe in more detail each of the explainability types and illustrate with some examples from the reviewed papers.

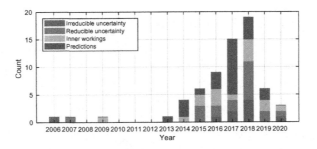

Fig. 3. Time histogram of the methods in Fig. 2. Grouping is made according to the different explanation targets.

Explaining Predictions. Explaining predictions refers to methods that are developed to understand why a certain image led to a corresponding NN output. The expectation is often that the reasoning of an NN would match the logic that human experts use when solving the problem. For example, if an NN is detecting the presence of a tumour, we would like to see that the NN is basing its prediction on the areas of the image that contain tumour cells. This would reassure pathologist that the prediction is trustworthy. Some well-known examples in this category include saliency maps [100], Excitation Backprop [121] and explanations generated using meaningful perturbations [30]. Such explanations could be useful for the AI developers to debug their created algorithms, could aid QA specialists in guaranteeing an appropriate behaviour of an NN, and could foster trust in the community of the end-users.

Explaining Inner Workings. Methods in the category of inner workings explanation aim to increase the understanding of how an algorithm works. There are a few ways that researchers have attempted to achieve this. For example, activation maximisation techniques show the patterns to which neurons react most [28,79,118]. Other methods analyse image representations encoded by the model in order to understand what information is retained and what is lost. This can be done by recreating the original images from the representations saved at different layers of a CNN [23,67]. Finally, some techniques examine what interpretable concepts, such as textures and patterns, that are detected for a specific class of interest. This enables explanation of behavioural properties of deep neural networks [54,62]. This explanation type is most relevant to the AI developers as it can give new insights into what an NN is doing and how its performance could be boosted.

Understanding Reducible Uncertainty. Reducible uncertainty, also known as epistemic uncertainty, refers to when the training of the model has been imperfect, insufficiently covering the phenomenon of the interest. Having high such uncertainty means that the parameters of an NN are not tuned properly to make an informed prediction for some inputs [22], i.e., data points being outliers

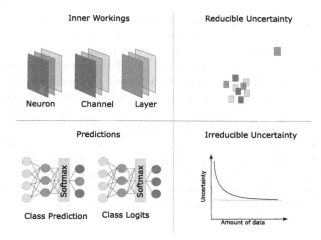

Fig. 4. Illustration of the different explanation targets. In order to understand inner workings, we can explore neurons, channels, layers and the relations between them. Explaining the predictions only focus on a specific class output and what logic the model is using to arrive at them. Understanding reducible uncertainty enables us to detect outliers in the data and warn when an NN is making an uninformed prediction, while the irreducible uncertainty shows how well our model approximates the variability in the phenomenon of interest.

in relation to the training data. This results in the model being incapable of providing informed predictions about outliers as the prior knowledge gathered during training is insufficient. If we would expand the training data and ensure it contains all outliers, this uncertainty could be reduced to zero. Even without more data, an improved training scheme could also reduce the epistemic uncertainty. Explanations targeting this uncertainty type enable us to understand the limitations of our model via training data and how we can improve it to increase prediction accuracy.

There are two main ways of estimating the epistemic uncertainty. It can be modelled on the NN's weights directly [12,40,91]. Other methods use the exploration of the data sets used for training and validating an NN to find out which points that are outliers and tune the uncertainty estimates to match this information [38,84,85].

Understanding Irreducible Uncertainty. The irreducible uncertainty arises due to the intrinsic randomness of a phenomenon of interest and the fact that our model is an approximation of it. It is also known as an aleatoric uncertainty [22]. This uncertainty cannot be reduced by increasing the size of the training data set. For an intuitive understanding, consider that even if we train a model to detect a tumour in WSIs on all of the relevant images existing in the world, our model is still an approximation of the complex phenomenon (tumour in human tissue). Hence, the upcoming new images from new patients may inherit some variability that our model is unable to classify correctly due to the missing variables/parameters that are necessary for capturing it.

So what does such uncertainty explain to us? It reminds the users that they should never trust an AI prediction completely as the nature of the world contains intrinsic variations that none of the models can perfectly capture. Furthermore, aleatoric uncertainty also gives an insight into whether developers chose an appropriate architecture of the model for a particular problem. If the developers observe low epistemic uncertainty but high aleatoric uncertainty, this indicates that the model is too simple to approximate the properties of the phenomenon of the interest well [53]. In an ideal situation, the chosen model would only contain low aleatoric uncertainty and the prediction variability would be as low as possible. Some examples of methods for estimating the aleatoric uncertainty include [7,13,33].

3.2   Result Representation

The categorisation of result representations assesses what type of results the user should expect to receive from applying an explainability technique. This allows users and developers to quickly pick a subgroup of methods that would provide the desired explanation output. We have distinguished four main groups of how the results are presented: *synthetic visualisations, visualisations on an input image, showing by example* and *auxiliary measures*. If we are working on helping a pathologist with a tumour detection task or want to boost the pathologist's confidence in an AI solution, we may be most interested in the techniques that provide visualisations on the original input images or show how an NN works by an example. However, if we are debugging or validating the overall classification strategy of an NN, the methods that generate synthetic visualisations or auxiliary measures may be preferred.

Synthetic Visualisations. Synthetic visualisations is a broad group of methods that all generate a synthetic image as an outcome. The group can be further divided based on what sort of image is generated.

The first subgroup generates surrealistic images from scratch that can be interpreted as illustrations of what some part of the NN reacts to. These methods are also known as activation maximisation: they attempt at finding, through optimisation, the input images that maximally activate a chosen neuron, channel or layer. Some examples of the methods can be found in [17,28,79,81,118]. The visualisations give an insight into what patterns the neurons are looking for. For example, this knowledge may aid the analysis of a domain shift problem [105]. Figure 5 shows an example of patterns that maximally activate some filters of a Mini-GoogLeNet that is trained to classify tumours in WSI patches [105]. The different rows use different strategies for formulating the training data but are all based on the same original dataset. The results show how very different representations are learned by the convolutional layers depending on how the

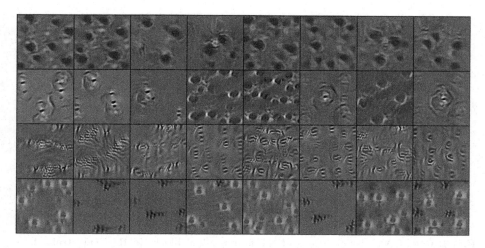

Fig. 5. Activation maximisation of GoogLeNet filters (per channel) trained on histopaphology data. Each row corresponds to filters from the same model, but trained on different formulations of the same original dataset, from top to bottom: unmodified original data, colour and intensity augmentations, stain normalisation, and Cycle-GAN transformation for domain-adaptation between different medical centres. Reproduced with the authors' permission from [105].

data is pre-processed, e.g. how colour augmentation makes the representation less sensitive to absolute colour values in the input (second row).

Another subgroup of methods focuses on using the feature representations in an NN to generate images that resemble parts of the original input. The aim is not to retrieve the original image but to conclude which patterns could be most responsible for the NN's prediction (or a neuron's activation). A well-known method of this category is deconvolutional networks [120]. Other examples that aim to explain the target NN include PatternNet [55] and Guided Backprop [103]. The main drawback these methods have is that they produce visualisations that are not class-specific. This means that the techniques give an insight into which patterns are important in general, but cannot be used to understand why an NN predicted the specific class [80].

Finally, some methods have focused on reconstructing the original images from the feature representations in an NN. They are also known as model inversion methods. This type of visualisation illustrates what information an NN is keeping about the image which, in turn, helps to understand better how an NN works. For example, comparing the reconstructed images to the original input, Dosovitskiy and Brox [23] found that the colour seems to be a crucial feature for the prediction they studied. Similar visualisations can be found in [67,68].

Visualisations on an Input Image. The methods in this group produce three types of visualisations: heatmaps, important patches and receptive fields.

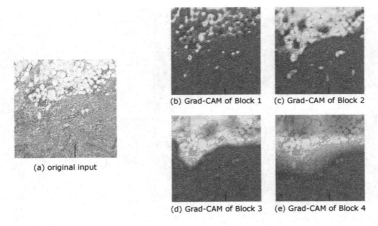

(a) original input

(b) Grad-CAM of Block 1   (c) Grad-CAM of Block 2

(d) Grad-CAM of Block 3   (e) Grad-CAM of Block 4

Fig. 6. Grad-CAM visualisations of the four residual blocks in ResNet18 trained to detect tumours in skin WSIs. In the example, the model's prediction of the absence of a tumour is incorrect: tumour cells are present in the bottom of the patch (image (a)). Observing Grad-CAM visualisations (images (b)–(e)), where high prediction importance is shown in red, we can conclude that throughout the blocks the NN is incorrectly using the presence of fat tissue to indicate absence of tumour; an indication of potential bias in the trained model. (Color figure online)

A heatmap is a graphical representation of 2D scalar data where the values are encoded by colour. With such representation, this first type of visualisation shows how much each pixel contributes to the prediction. This information is visually conveyed by overlaying the colour gradient on the original input image. Well-known techniques that produce heatmaps are Excitation Backprop [121], Grad-CAM [95] and Layer-wise relevance propagation [8]. The second type of visualisation is produced by keeping the important patches (pixel regions) of the original input and cropping out the remaining. These techniques reveal which objects or regions in the input that are contributing to the prediction. However, they do not provide the knowledge of importance distribution over the pixels [90, 124]. The third type of visualisation marks the receptive field, the areas on the original input image that indicate what regions that activate most a target unit [123, 124]. This gives an insight into how neurons in NNs and filters in CNNs work.

Visualisations on an input image methods, such as Grad-CAM, can be used to increase the transparency as well as uncover some potential biases that the model has. Figure 6 shows an example of such a case. We trained a ResNet18 neural network to predict if a patch from a WSI of skin contains a tumour. ResNet18 contains four residual blocks, units consisting of several layers. It is connected with the previous block with a skip connection [39]. We used the

Grad-CAM technique to visualise each of the four blocks. The resulting heatmaps show which pixels that are most important for the prediction. This provides an overview of how the attention of an NN is changing through the layer blocks when the image is classified. The model predicted that there is no tumour, but the patch does contain tumour cells in the lower part of the image. The Grad-CAM method uncovers a potential bias: the model uses fat tissue as an indication of the absence of the tumour cells, which could be caused by an over-representation of fat tissue in patches without a tumour in the training data set.

All methods described so far aim to provide a deeper understanding of an NN trained to do classification. However, AI is not only used for classification tasks. Wu and Song [116] has proposed how to improve the interpretability of a CNN trained for object detection. They create an architecture of an NN based on R-CNN that provides not only the classification score but also the bounding box on the region of interest (the target object). Furthermore, XAI visualisation on the input image can increase the interpretability of the segmentation task. Kwon et al. [59] have used a technique for estimating uncertainty first described by Kendall and Gal [50] and created heatmaps of uncertain regions of the segmentation. A large area of uncertain regions can warn a user that the NN is making a poorly informed guess.

Showing by Example. The methods in this group are diverse but share the foundation that their explanations are based on presenting and discussing examples, either from the original data or from auxiliary data. This is a small group of methods so far, but it has great potential as some research claims that this type of explainability may be the most intuitive for a human user [70].

The first subgroup of methods uses examples from the original data set in order to understand an NN better. Lapuschkin et al. [61] provide a visualisation of clustering input images that an NN determined to be from the same class. The clustered images reveal potential rationale for how an NN assigns samples to a certain class. For example, such exploration may reveal that an image is classified as containing a horse if there is a white fence, if there is a person in a certain position or if there is a clearly visible horse head. Similar results are achieved in work by Kevin et al. [51] where authors grouped WSIs of neuropathological tissue that an NN perceived to be similar. Moreover, at each layer of an NN, we can compare the representations of the input image to the representations of all other images in the data set and see what labels have the k most similar other images [85]. This may help to detect out-of-distribution images. Alsallakh et al. [3] explore a confusion matrix produced by an algorithm in order to determine which classes that are causing most trouble and the possible reason for the confusion.

Other methods show examples that do not come from the original data set. Seah et al. [94] proposed an idea that if we generate the most similar image to the original one but that would be classified to a different class by an NN, we could compare these images and understand which parts or differences are used by the NN to predict the correct class. Figure 7 illustrates such a method

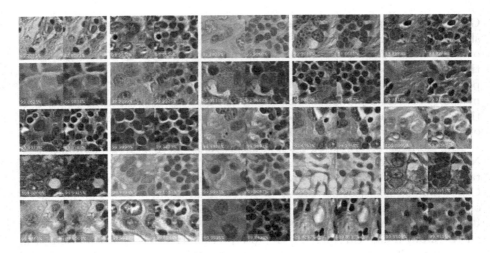

Fig. 7. Cycle-GANs transform a WSI patch with tumour to a synthetic healthy patch. Such counterfactual examples could boost pathologists' confidence that a tumour prediction is correct. The illustration consists of 25 pairs of patches: to the left are original patches with tumour and to the right are their respective transformation that illustrates how the patch could look if it were healthy. The percentage shows how confident the target NN is that the left patch contains tumour and the right patch is healthy, respectively.

used on a tumour classifier. We trained a Cycle-GAN [126] to transform patches that contain tumour cells to healthy ones. The score in the left corner of each image shows the prediction score for each patch by the NN under scrutiny; the high confidence of the NN proves that the transformation was successful. Such counterfactual illustrations could capture and convey complex explanations of diagnostic predictions.

Furthermore, some researchers explore if human-comprehensible concepts, such as striped patterns, gender, or a tie, are influencing an NN [10,54]. These methods require a separate data set that contains the images with the concepts of interest. They can show which images of a certain concept that are most relevant to a chosen class that an NN is predicting. Also, they can reveal which particular images in the original data set that are influenced by the concept most. For example, they can show images with the striped patterns (from the concepts data set) that are most related to a Chief Enterprise Officer (CEO) class in an NN and which images labelled CEO (from the original data set) are mostly influenced by the stripe patterns. This knowledge could potentially alleviate biased predictions in an AI solution.

Auxiliary Measures. This subsection provides an overview of various measures that have been developed for understanding an NN better. They do not necessarily have anything in common apart from the main aim to make an NN more transparent. However, all of them explore an important way of representing the results: providing an informative score or measure.

Uncertainty measures give insight into how much we can trust the outcome of an AI solution. These measures can be used i) to construct prediction intervals that show how much the prediction could vary [87], ii) to create heatmaps as discussed in Sect. 3.2 above, iii) to create plots illustrating uncertainty [7], or iv) to be presented as a score to the user [33].

Other scores provide a measure of importance that helps to understand how an NN makes the prediction. For example, Koh and Liang [57] assigns an importance score for each training image by exploring how the predictions of the target NN would change if the particular image would be removed from the training data.

3.3   Technical Approach

This subsection gives an insight into how the explainability methods work technically. Thus, the categorisation is probably more relevant for readers with a technical background. Knowing what strategies that have been commonly applied in acquiring the visualisations or the scores may provide a good starting point for identifying what technical approaches that have not yet been explored. It is important to note that we do not aim to describe the technical details of each method thoroughly, instead, we provide a general overview of what kind of techniques researchers have used so far.

Activation Optimisation. All methods in this subsection use an optimisation algorithm on the activations of the target NN in order to create their visualisations. There are two distinct ways of how optimisation in the context of neural network understandability may be used. Some techniques aim to explore the inner workings of an NN by finding the patterns that maximise the activation of a chosen neuron or a combination of neurons. The main idea can be illustrated by the following optimisation problem:

$$x^* = \arg \max_x h_{i,j}(\theta, x) + regulariser, \tag{1}$$

where $h_{i,j}$ is the activation of the target neuron with indices i, j, that has been computed from the input sample x.

θ is the set of parameters used for computing the activation and x^* is the estimated sample that maximises the output the neuron at i, j. This objective is usually achieved using gradient descent, and most proposed activation maximisation methods mainly differ in what regulariser they propose to use [17, 28, 79, 81, 118].

Optimisation techniques are also used for inverting NNs. Mahendran and Vedaldi [68] proposed a method to reconstruct the original image from the activations of a chosen layer of an NN. Given that a neural network is some composite function $\Phi_0 = \Phi(x_0)$ with input image x_0, they acknowledge that finding an inverse of Φ_0 is difficult; neural networks are composed of many non-invertable functions. Hence, this method aims to find an image whose representation best matches the target input image by reducing the loss between $\Phi(x)$ of some input x and the target Φ_0. There are a few other efforts where model inversion tools also are proposed to achieve a better understanding of an NN [23,67].

Back-Projection to Input Space. Back-projection methods reflect a prediction score of an NN or activation of a target neuron back to the input space. They generate the patterns that triggered the neuron or create sensitivity maps over the input pixels. We describe this category by highlighting two representative approaches, deconvolution and saliency map.

Deconvolution is a technique that inverts the direction of the information flow in an NN [120]. In a higher layer a target neuron is chosen and the activations of all the other neurons in that layer are set to 0. Then, the activation of the target neuron is passed back through the layers to the input space. In order to invert the max pooling layers which are normally non-invertable, Zeiler and Fergus [120] propose to compute so-called switches during the forward pass: they record which positions that contained the maximum value within each pooling region. The resulting signal in the input layer is used to construct an image which shows what patterns that triggered the activation of the target neuron. Guided Backprop [103] is another method also built on this approach.

Saliency map is a technique that uses Taylor expansion in order to back-project a prediction score to the input space. The technique is based on the idea that the prediction of a neural network can be approximated by a linear function:

$$S_c(x) = w^T x + b, \tag{2}$$

where S_c is the class score, w and b are the weight vector and bias of the model, respectively, and x is the input image. Then the first-order Taylor expansion is used to determine the approximation for a weight vector w^T. The approximated w^T reflects how much each pixel in the input contributed to the final score [100]. There are a few other XAI methods that achieve back-projection to input space by using Taylor expansions [8,73] or other linear approximations that distribute the target score among the input pixels [95,125].

Input Perturbations. Explainability can be achieved by inducing variations of the input. Methods in this category use perturbations on the input images in order to determine the important pixels for a prediction, or to estimate the uncertainty. It is important to note that the methods under this category may or may not analyse each perturbation separately. An example of such an algorithm is Local Interpretable Model-agnostic Explanations (LIME) [90]. The target input image is split into k superpixels. A Ridge regression is then trained on k perturbed images (each time only one superpixel is non-black) to predict the black-box classifier's prediction score of that particular input. The parameters of the Ridge regression are used to determine which superpixel is the most important for the correct prediction.

Another method is using Shapley values for the explanation of a classifier [65]. Normally, these are computed by rerunning the classifier as many times as we have features (pixels in our case) and excluding one feature at a time. This provides an insight to which features that are important for the classification. However, such a procedure becomes very expensive with deep learning, hence the authors have offered several approximations for computing Shapley values for image classification. Similar use of perturbations or approximations of perturbations can be found in other XAI methods [7, 20, 30, 127].

Interpretable Network Design. Another approach to explainability is to modify the architecture of an NN in order to arrive at models that produce more interpretable feature maps. This means that visualising them may give an insight into what objects a unit of an NN is detecting when making a classification decision.

Interpretable CNNs [123] is a method modifying the CNN filters; a special loss function is introduced that enforces the filters to capture human-interpretable objects better. The idea is that visualising the receptive field of such filters could reveal behaviour of NN units, such as using cat head depictions to label the image as a cat. Another example is Interpretable R-CNN [116]. Here, an architecture of an NN based on Faster R-CNN is created that provides not only the classification score but also the bounding box on the region of interest (the target object). This is achieved by introducing a new layer in the model called terminal-node sensitive feature maps that is based on graph theory.

Frequentist Techniques. The methods in the group of frequentist techniques are built for standard neural networks. Therefore, applying such techniques usually does not require heavy modifications to the algorithm or the training pipeline. The methods are based on frequentist statistical theory and there are three main techniques commonly used: ensembles, bootstrapping and quantile regression.

Ensemble methods use multiple learning algorithms to obtain a better predictive performance compared to the learning algorithms alone. Recently it has been proposed to generate the prediction intervals via ensembles of NNs [60, 87], i.e. utilising the variation between different models as a measure of uncertainty.

Bootstrapping is a technique that uses random sampling with replacement in order to approximate the population distribution with the sample distribution. This provides means to estimate statistical measures such as standard error, bias, variance, and confidence intervals [25]. Osband et al. [82] developed an efficient and scalable method that enables generation of bootstrap samples from a deep neural network to estimate the uncertainty.

Finally, quantiles in statistics are dividing the range of the probability distribution or the sample distribution into continuous intervals that have equal probabilities [119]. Quantile regression, methods for estimating quantiles, can be used to build confidence intervals around the target variable (for example, the prediction of the NN) which enables estimation of the uncertainty. Tagasovska and Lopez-Paz [109] have proposed to implement an additional output layer called

Simultaneous Quantile Regression for any deep learning algorithm. Simultaneous Quantile Regression would be trained on a special loss function that learns the conditional quantiles of a target variable.

It is also worth mentioning that while some of the methods described in this section are developed for regression problems, it is also possible to adapt them for classification tasks.

Bayesian Neural Networks. Bayesian Neural Networks (BNNs) are designed to incorporate uncertainty about the networks' parameters, weights and biases. Unfortunately, BNNs are computationally more complex than conventional NNs, require a different training pipeline, and may not scale well to big data sets nor deep architectures that are required for state-of-the-art performance [86]. While it is out of scope for this survey to rigorously describe the research on BNNs, we next provide a brief overview of some key approaches.

Many researchers have worked on producing approximations of the intractable posterior distributions of BNNs – approximations that can be used in practise. This includes, among others, applying Markov chain Monte Carlo methods [77] and variational Bayesian methods [12]. Another challenge in training BNNs is performing the backpropagation, as there is a large number of possible values of the parameters. A few of the efforts have focused on improving the backpropagation algorithm for BNNs by introducing alternative algorithms, namely probabilistic backpropagation [40], Bayes by Backprop [12], and natural-gradient algorithms [52]. Essential work has been done on determining the best way of finding a good prior as it strongly influences the quality of the uncertainty measurement [38]. Finally, some work focused on specifically developing Bayesian convolutional neural networks [32,99], while others developed ways to distribute the estimated uncertainty between epistemic and aleatoric parts in BNNs [21,50,59].

Bayesian Approximations. Bayesian theory can be applied also to standard NNs to estimate uncertainty. In this way, uncertainty awareness can be introduced without having to tackle the shortcomings of BNNs. They use derivations and modifications to a standard NN training in order to incorporate the Bayesian inference.

Pearce et al. [86] showed how to add a Bayesian prior via regularization of the parameters and train an ensemble of standard NNs in order to approximate the posterior distribution. Postels et al. [89] proposed to reduce the computational complexity of ensembles and other resampling-based methods by adding noise to the parameters of an NN during training. Some researchers focused on how to derive Bayesian inference approximations using some common techniques in modern NN training, such as dropout [33] and batch normalisation [112]. Finally, Ritter et al. [91] applied a Laplace approximation to obtain uncertainty estimates after an NN is trained.

Other Techniques. A number of methods base the generation of explanations on techniques that do not fall into any of the previous categories. Some methods use Generative Adversarial Networks (GANs) as part of their XAI solution [78, 94] (similar to Fig. 7). Moreover, uncertainty estimates can be based on conformal prediction; a technique that determines the confidence of a new prediction based on the past experience [84, 85]. The training data set can be explored using influence functions, a classic technique from statistics, which help to detect the points most contributing to a given prediction [57]. Linear binary classifiers and binary segmentation algorithms have also been used to determine to what concepts (defined by a separate data set) a target NN is responding [10, 54]. Finally, techniques for dimensionality reduction, such as t-distributed Stochastic Neighbour Embedding (t-SNE) [66], makes it possible to reduce the dimensionality of feature representations of an NN and highlight which input images the model is perceiving to be similar [51]. It is also possible to extract information on how different NNs relate to each other by considering the weights of a large number of trained models [27].

3.4   XAI Methods in Medical Imaging

In this final subsection of the XAI method overview, we highlight some previous efforts of XAI techniques specifically addressing the medical imaging domain.

Palatnik de Sousa et al. [83] explored an AI algorithm that classifies lymph node metastases by creating heatmaps of the area in the input patch that contributed most to the prediction. The authors found that deep learning algorithms trained for this task have underlying 'reasoning' behind their predictions similar to human logic. Similar findings are reported in a study on classifying Alzheimer's disease [110]. Huang and Chung [46] addressed the need for an informed decision by training a CNN model to predict the presence of cancer for a given WSI. At the test time of this algorithm, XAI methods that explain the predictions by creating visualisations on the input are used to detect the areas of the tissue that are unhealthy. It provides 'evidence' why this WSI should be classified as unhealthy as well as localises the cancerous cells. The authors showed that the detected areas closely correlated with the pathologists labelling. Therefore, it provides a meaningful intuition of why AI categorised the whole slide as containing a tumour.

Incorporating uncertainty measures in AI solutions for digital pathology could help to increase transparency as well. Kwon et al. [59] has shown that the highly uncertain regions in ischemic stroke lesion segmentation often correlate with the pixels that are incorrectly labelled by the algorithm. This means that uncertainty measures provides means for a doctor to spot possibly wrong predictions and understand when he or she should be cautious of the AI decision. Fraz et al. [31] fulfilled this idea by incorporating an uncertainty measure in their model, and showed that the quality of microvessel segmentation did indeed improve.

These results are inspiring and demonstrate the potential of XAI techniques in medical imaging. Nevertheless, the current body of work is still quite limited.

There is a need for more in-depth research on applied XAI methods in the domain, and particularly so in digital pathology, as will be further discussed in the next section.

4 Open Problems

There are several open problems arising with XAI application for digital pathology. The stakeholders involved in XAI development and usage should be aware of the potentially misleading explanations as well as the lack of ways to evaluate different XAI methods.

The first problem is caused due to the design of the explanations and their user interactions. To increase human understanding, it is important to formulate causal explanations, that is, why the AI algorithm made that prediction. Holzinger et al. [43] argue that analysing how an AI solution arrived to the prediction may not always result in a satisfactory explanation as a more thorough understanding of how humans interpret and use explanations is needed. This point is also highlighted by Mittelstadt et al. [70], further detailing that explanations may become damaging if they are phrased confusingly or do not match the users' expected format.

Another pitfall is if the explanation designer has a certain agenda. As there may be a strong incentive to promote trust in the AI predictions, explanation design runs the risk of being more persuasive than informative, as demonstrated in the work by Kaur et al. [49]. This could have especially severe consequences in XAI solutions developed for digital pathology, as overconfidence in them could result in patient hazards, as well as in a setback for the needed development of AI assistance to improve diagnostics.

Even though XAI tools could increase the understandability of an AI solution, so far we lack a solid scientific evaluation framework that would allow us to understand when they work well and what limitations they have. This challenge arises due to the fact that usually the 'ground truth' is unknown for most of the outputs by any XAI technique. There are a few works attempting to answer these questions with some studies showing alarming results that the assessed methods do not always live up to the expectations [2,29,80,93,102]. The question marks about the performance and evaluation of XAI methods remain for both the general case and specifically for digital pathology.

It is often stated that AI algorithms are black boxes that need to become transparent. While this is an illustrative metaphor, it is also necessary to carefully consider what type of transparency that is meaningful and effective in different scenarios and for different stakeholders. In summary, there is strong rationale for XAI advances tailored for digital pathology, however the challenge of constructing meaningful explanation and evaluating the performance of a chosen XAI method still remains.

5   Future Outlook

Our analysis of the overview presented in the previous sections has led to several key findings that can be informative for future research in XAI for digital pathology. A first insight is that the comprehensive list of identified explainability scenarios points to the fact that there are many techniques to consider when developing XAI solutions in the domain. XAI is also an important concept that needs to be incorporated for decision support – due to the potentially high costs of errors in healthcare, pathologists are concerned about using black-box algorithms in their daily practices and call for an increased transparency [72]. Moreover, there is a substantial heterogeneity both in terms of the desired benefits that AI tools should bring, and the types of prediction tasks to be performed. Thus, it appears clear that even within this niche a multi-faceted XAI toolbox will be needed.

In order for the XAI researcher to navigate the digital pathology landscape, it is valuable to consider the three usage scenarios: development, QA, and diagnostic work. For example, for the model developer, all of the explanation types would be relevant, whereas the inner workings of the neural network ought to be of little relevance for QA or diagnostics. Understanding training data quality is probably unnecessary for diagnostic work but may be quite important for the QA specialist to assess limitations of the model at the specific lab.

Similar mappings can be done with respect to result representation. A likely difference between usage scenarios here is that synthetic visualisations would only be valuable to the model developer. There may, however, be exceptions. Mittelstadt et al. [70] argue that counterfactual and contrastive explanations are suitable for intuitive human understanding. The synthesised counterfactual image proposed by Seah et al. [94] is an interesting direction, combining the synthesis and showing by example explanations. It is our expectation that combinations of XAI techniques will be needed in order to be sufficiently effective in most digital pathology applications.

Finally, this survey sheds some light on the role of uncertainty in relation to XAI. Whereas uncertainty estimation sometimes is seen as a separate topic, the survey indicates that uncertainty is an integral part of the XAI scope when seen from an end-user perspective. Our review lists some useful existing methods for performing and evaluating uncertainty estimation. There is, however, ample room for further research efforts, not the least directed towards imaging diagnostics applications. Moreover, we argue that AI solutions for clinical routine need to have some level of uncertainty awareness. While this is not part of bread-and-butter AI development today, we hope that incorporating uncertainty soon will be the standard, which in turn will have a direct positive impact for broad XAI deployment.

A   Reviewed Methods

Table 1. List of methods and their categorisations, ordered by the year of publishing.

Method	Explains	Result representation	Technical approach
Quantile Regression Forests [69]	Irreducible uncertainty	Auxiliary measures	Frequentist techniques
Conformal Prediction [84]	Reducible uncertainty	Auxiliary measures	Other techniques
Activation maximisation [28]	Inner workings	Synthetic visualisations	Activation optimisation
Saliency maps [100]	Predictions	Visualisations on the input	Back-projection to input space
DeconvNet [120]	Predictions	Synthetic visualisations	Back-projection to input space
Guided Backprop [103]	Predictions of NN	Synthetic visualisations	Back-projection to input space
Object detectors in Deep Scene [124]	Prediction; Inner workings	Visualisations on the input	Input perturbations
Layer-wise relevance propagation [8]	Predictions	Visualisations on the input	Back-projection to input space
Probabilistic backpropagation [40]	Reducible uncertainty	Auxiliary measures	Bayesian neural networks
Inverting Deep Image Representations [67]	Inner workings	Synthetic visualisations	Activation optimisation
BCNN with Bernoulli approximations [32]	Reducible uncertainty	Auxiliary measures	Bayesian neural networks
Deep visualization [118]	Inner workings	Synthetic visualisations	Activation optimisation
Bayes by Backprop [12]	Reducible uncertainty	Auxiliary measures	Bayesian neural networks
Bootstrapped DQN [82]	Reducible uncertainty	Auxiliary measures	Frequentist techniques
Multifaceted Feature Visualization [79]	Inner workings	Synthetic visualisations	Activation optimisation
Inverting feature representations [23]	Inner workings	Synthetic visualisations	Activation optimisation
Class activation mapping (CAM) [125]	Prediction	Visualisations on the input	Back-projection to input space
Dropout as Bayesian approximation [33]	Reducible uncertainty	Auxiliary measures	Bayesian approximations
Disco nets [13]	Irreducible uncertainty	Auxiliary measures	Bayesian approximations
Deep generator networks [78]	Inner workings	Synthetic visualisations	GANs methods
Distinct class saliency maps [98]	Prediction	Visualisations on the input	Back-projection to input space
LIME [90]	Prediction	Visualisations on the input	Input perturbations
Uncertainty with deep ensembles [60]	Reducible uncertainty; Irreducible uncertainty of NN	Auxiliary measures	Frequentist techniques
Deep Taylor decomposition [73]	Predictions	Visualisations on the input	Back-projection to input space
SHAP [65]	Predictions	Visualisations on the input	Input perturbations
PatternNet and PatternAttribution [55]	Predictions	Visualisations on the input	Back-projection to input space

(continued)

Table 1. (*continued*)

Method	Explains	Result representation	Technical approach
Integrated Gradients [107]	Predictions	Visualisations on the input	Back-projection to input space
Network Dissection [10]	Inner workings	Showing by example	Other techniques
Grad-CAM [95]	Predictions	Visualisations on the input	Back-projection to input space
Uncertainties in Bayesian deep learning [50]	Reducible uncertainty; Irreducible uncertainty	Auxiliary measures	Bayesian neural networks
Meaningful Perturbation [30]	Predictions	Visualisations on the input	Input perturbations
SmoothGrad [101]	Predictions	Visualisations on the input	Back-projection to input space
Real Time Image Saliency [20]	Predictions	Visualisations on the input	Input perturbations
Prediction Difference Analysis [127]	Predictions	Visualisations on the input	Input perturbations
Influence Functions [57]	Predictions	Auxiliary measures	Other techniques
Interpretable CNNs [123]	Predictions	Visualisations on the input	Interpretable design
Generative Visual Rationales [94]	Predictions	Synthetic visualisations	GANs methods
Weight-perturbation in ADAM [52]	Reducible uncertainty	Auxiliary measures	Bayesian neural networks
Uncertainty in Bayesian Deep Learning [21]	Reducible uncertainty; Irreducible uncertainty	Auxiliary measures	Bayesian neural networks
Monotone composite quantile regression NN [16]	Irreducible uncertainty	Auxiliary measures	Frequentist techniques
Deep k-Nearest Neighbors [85]	Predictions; Reducible uncertainty	Showing by example; Auxiliary measures	Other techniques
Laplace approximation for estimating uncertainty [91]	Reducible uncertainty	Auxiliary measures	Bayesian approximations
TCAV [54]	Inner workings	Showing by example	Other techniques
Bayesian uncertainty in batch normalized NN [112]	Reducible uncertainty	Auxiliary measures	Bayesian approximations
Excitation Backprop [121]	Predictions	Visualisations on the input	Back-projection to input space
Prediction Intervals for Deep Learning [87]	Irreducible uncertainty	Auxiliary measures	Frequentist techniques
Bayesian Ensembling [86]	Reducible uncertainty	Auxiliary measures	Bayesian approximations
Blocks [81]	Inner workings	Synthetic visualisations	Activation optimisation
Class Hierarchy in CNNs [3]	Inner workings	Showing by example	Other techniques
Data augmentation for uncertainty estimation [7]	Irreducible uncertainty	Auxiliary measures	Input perturbations
Visualization and Anomaly detection using t-SNE [51]	Inner workings; Reducible uncertainty	Showing by example	Other techniques
Uncertainty via noise contrastive priors [38]	Reducible uncertainty	Auxiliary measure	Bayesian neural networks
FullGrad [104]	Prediction	Visualisations on the input	Back-projection to input space
SpRAy [61]	Inner workings	Showing by example	Other techniques

(*continued*)

Table 1. (*continued*)

Method	Explains	Result representation	Technical approach
Influence-directed explanations [62]	Predictions; Inner workings	Showing by example	Other techniques
Bayesian CNN with variational inference [99]	Reducible uncertainty	Auxiliary measures	Bayesian neural networks
Uncertainty quantification in Bayesian NN [59]	Reducible uncertainty; Irreducible uncertainty	Auxiliary measures	Bayesian neural networks
Dissecting the weight space of NN [27]	Inner workings	Auxiliary measures	Other techniques

References

1. Adadi, A., Berrada, M.: Peeking inside the black-box: a survey on explainable artificial intelligence (XAI). IEEE Access **6**, 52138–52160 (2018)
2. Adebayo, J., Gilmer, J., Muelly, M., Goodfellow, I., Hardt, M., Kim, B.: Sanity checks for saliency maps. In: Proceedings of the 32nd International Conference on Neural Information Processing Systems, NIPS 2018, pp. 9525–9536. Curran Associates Inc., Red Hook (2018). https://doi.org/10.5555/3327546.3327621
3. Alsallakh, B., Jourabloo, A., Ye, M., Liu, X., Ren, L.: Do convolutional neural networks learn class hierarchy? IEEE Trans. Visual Comput. Graphics **24**(1), 152–165 (2018). https://doi.org/10.1109/TVCG.2017.2744683
4. Alvarez-Melis, D., Jaakkola, T.: A causal framework for explaining the predictions of black-box sequence-to-sequence models. In: Proceedings of the 2017 Conference on Empirical Methods in Natural Language Processing, pp. 412–421. Association for Computational Linguistics, Copenhagen, September 2017. https://doi.org/10.18653/v1/D17-1042
5. Alzubaidi, L., Resan, R., Abdul Hussain, H.: A robust deep learning approachto detect nuclei in histopathological images. Int. J. Innov. Res. Comput. Commun. Eng. **5**, 7–12 (2017)
6. Arvaniti, E., et al.: Automated Gleason grading of prostate cancer tissue microarrays via deep learning. Sci. Rep. **8**(1) (2018). https://doi.org/10.1038/s41598-018-30535-1
7. Ayhan, M.S., Berens, P.: Test-time data augmentation for estimation of heteroscedastic aleatoric uncertainty in deep neural networks. In: Medical Imaging with Deep Learning (Midl 2018), pp. 1–9 (2018)
8. Bach, S., Binder, A., Montavon, G., Klauschen, F., Müller, K.R., Samek, W.: On pixel-wise explanations for non-linear classifier decisions by layer-wise relevance propagation. PLoS ONE **10**(7) (2015). https://doi.org/10.1371/journal.pone.0130140
9. Balkenhol, M., et al.: Deep learning assisted mitotic counting for breast cancer. Lab. Invest. **99** (2019). https://doi.org/10.1038/s41374-019-0275-0
10. Bau, D., Zhou, B., Khosla, A., Oliva, A., Torralba, A.: Network dissection: quantifying interpretability of deep visual representations. In: Proceedings - 30th IEEE Conference on Computer Vision and Pattern Recognition, CVPR 2017, January 2017, pp. 3319–3327. Institute of Electrical and Electronics Engineers Inc., November 2017. https://doi.org/10.1109/CVPR.2017.354

11. Bera, K., Schalper, K.A., Rimm, D.L., Velcheti, V., Madabhushi, A.: Artificial intelligence in digital pathology – new tools for diagnosis and precision oncology. Nat. Rev. Clin. Oncol. **16**(11), 703–715 (2019). https://doi.org/10.1038/s41571-019-0252-y

12. Blundell, C., Cornebise, J., Kavukcuoglu, K., Wierstra, D.: Weight uncertainty in neural networks. In: 32nd International Conference on Machine Learning, ICML 2015, vol. 2, pp. 1613–1622, May 2015

13. Bouchacourt, D., Pawan Kumar, M., Nowozin, S.: DISCO nets: DISsimilarity COefficient Networks. In: Advances in Neural Information Processing Systems, pp. 352–360 (2016)

14. Bulten, W., et al.: Automated deep-learning system for Gleason grading of prostate cancer using biopsies: a diagnostic study. Lancet Oncol. **21**, 233–241 (2020)

15. Cai, C.J., et al.: Human-centered tools for coping with imperfect algorithms during medical decision-making. In: Proceedings of the 2019 CHI Conference on Human Factors in Computing Systems, CHI 2019, Association for Computing Machinery, New York (2019). https://doi.org/10.1145/3290605.3300234

16. Cannon, A.J.: Non-crossing nonlinear regression quantiles by monotone composite quantile regression neural network, with application to rainfall extremes. Stoch. Environ. Res. Risk Assess. **32**(11), 3207–3225 (2018). https://doi.org/10.1007/s00477-018-1573-6

17. Carter, S., Armstrong, Z., Schubert, L., Johnson, I., Olah, C.: Activation atlas. Distill **4**(3) (2019). https://doi.org/10.23915/distill.00015

18. Chen, H., Dou, Q., Wang, X., Qin, J., Heng, P.A.: Mitosis detection in breast cancer histology images via deep cascaded networks. In: Proceedings of the Thirtieth AAAI Conference on Artificial Intelligence, AAAI 2016, pp. 1160–1166. AAAI Press (2016)

19. Chen, J., Srinivas, C.: Automatic lymphocyte detection in H&E images with deep neural networks. CoRR abs/1612.03217 (2016)

20. Dabkowski, P., Gal, Y.: Real time image saliency for black box classifiers. In: Advances in Neural Information Processing Systems, December 2017, pp. 6968–6977 (2017)

21. Depeweg, S., Hernandez-Lobato, J.M., Doshi-Velez, F., Udluft, S.: Decomposition of uncertainty in Bayesian deep learning for efficient and risk-sensitive learning. In: 35th International Conference on Machine Learning, ICML 2018, vol. 3, pp. 1920–1934 (2018)

22. Der Kiureghian, A., Ditlevsen, O.: Aleatory or epistemic? Does it matter? Struct. Saf. **31**, 105–112 (2008). https://doi.org/10.1016/j.strusafe.2008.06.020

23. Dosovitskiy, A., Brox, T.: Inverting visual representations with convolutional networks. In: Proceedings of the IEEE Computer Society Conference on Computer Vision and Pattern Recognition, December 2017, pp. 4829–4837 (2016). https://doi.org/10.1109/CVPR.2016.522

24. Došilović, F.K., Brčć, M., Hlupić, N.: Explainable artificial intelligence: a survey. In: 2018 41st International Convention on Information and Communication Technology, Electronics and Microelectronics (MIPRO), pp. 0210–0215, May 2018. https://doi.org/10.23919/MIPRO.2018.8400040

25. Efron, B., Tibshirani, R.: An Introduction to the Bootstrap. Monographs on Statistics and Applied Probability, vol. 57. Chapman & Hall, London (1994)

26. Ehteshami Bejnordi, B., et al.: The CAMELYON16 consortium: diagnostic assessment of deep learning algorithms for detection of lymph node metastases in women with breast cancer. JAMA **318**(22), 2199–2210 (2017). https://doi.org/10.1001/jama.2017.14585

27. Eilertsen, G., Jönsson, D., Ropinski, T., Unger, J., Ynnerman, A.: Classifying the classifier: dissecting the weight space of neural networks (2020). arXiv preprint, arXiv: 2002.05688

28. Erhan, D., Bengio, Y., Courville, A., Vincent, P.: Visualizing higher-layer features of a deep network. Technical report, Univeristé de Montréal, January 2009

29. Fang, K., Shen, C., Kifer, D.: Evaluating aleatoric and epistemic uncertainties of time series deep learning models for soil moisture predictions (2019). arXiv preprint, arXiv:1906.04595

30. Fong, R.C., Vedaldi, A.: Interpretable explanations of black boxes by meaningful perturbation. In: Proceedings of the IEEE International Conference on Computer Vision, October 2017, pp. 3449–3457 (2017). https://doi.org/10.1109/ICCV.2017.371

31. Fraz, M.M., Shaban, M., Graham, S., Khurram, S.A., Rajpoot, N.M.: Uncertainty driven pooling network for microvessel segmentation in routine histology images. In: Stoyanov, D., et al. (eds.) OMIA/COMPAY -2018. LNCS, vol. 11039, pp. 156–164. Springer, Cham (2018). https://doi.org/10.1007/978-3-030-00949-6_19

32. Gal, Y., Ghahramani, Z.: Bayesian convolutional neural networks with Bernoulli approximate variational inference (2015). arXiv preprint, arXiv:1506.02158

33. Gal, Y., Ghahramani, Z.: Dropout as a Bayesian approximation: representing model uncertainty in deep learning. In: 33rd International Conference on Machine Learning, ICML 2016, vol. 3, pp. 1651–1660 (2016)

34. Garcia, E., Hermoza, R., Castanon, C.B., Cano, L., Castillo, M., Castanñeda, C.: Automatic lymphocyte detection on gastric cancer IHC images using deep learning. In: 2017 IEEE 30th International Symposium on Computer-Based Medical Systems (CBMS), pp. 200–204, June 2017. https://doi.org/10.1109/CBMS.2017.94

35. Garud, H., et al.: High-magnification multi-views based classification of breast fine needle aspiration cytology cell samples using fusion of decisions from deep convolutional networks. In: IEEE Computer Society Conference on Computer Vision and Pattern Recognition Workshops, July 2017, pp. 828–833 (2017). https://doi.org/10.1109/CVPRW.2017.115

36. Goebel, R., et al.: Explainable AI: the new 42? In: Holzinger, A., Kieseberg, P., Tjoa, A.M., Weippl, E. (eds.) CD-MAKE 2018. LNCS, vol. 11015, pp. 295–303. Springer, Cham (2018). https://doi.org/10.1007/978-3-319-99740-7_21

37. Goodfellow, I., Bengio, Y., Courville, A.: Deep Learning. MIT Press, Cambridge (2016). http://www.deeplearningbook.org

38. Hafner, D., Tran, D., Lillicrap, T., Irpan, A., Davidson, J.: Reliable uncertainty estimates in deep neural networks using noise contrastive priors. In: ICLR, pp. 1–14 (2019). https://doi.org/10.1163/156856192X00700

39. He, K., Zhang, X., Ren, S., Sun, J.: Deep residual learning for image recognition. In: 2016 IEEE Conference on Computer Vision and Pattern Recognition (CVPR), pp. 770–778, June 2016. https://doi.org/10.1109/CVPR.2016.90

40. Hernández-Lobato, J.M., Adams, R.P.: Probabilistic backpropagation for scalable learning of Bayesian neural networks. In: 32nd International Conference on Machine Learning, ICML 2015, vol. 3, pp. 1861–1869 (2015)

41. Höfener, H., Homeyer, A., Weiss, N., Molin, J., Lundström, C.F., Hahn, H.K.: Deep learning nuclei detection: a simple approach can deliver state-of-the-art results. Comput. Med. Imaging Graph. **70**, 43–52 (2018). https://doi.org/10. 1016/j.compmedimag.2018.08.010

42. Hohman, F., Kahng, M., Pienta, R., Chau, D.H.: Visual analytics in deep learning: an interrogative survey for the next frontiers. IEEE Trans. Visual Comput. Graphics **25**(8), 2674–2693 (2019). https://doi.org/10.1109/TVCG.2018.2843369

43. Holzinger, A., Carrington, A., Müller, H.: Measuring the quality of explanations: the System Causability Scale (SCS). comparing human and machine explanations. In: Kersting, K. (ed.) Special Issue on Interactive Machine Learning, vol. 34. KI - Künstliche Intelligenz (German Journal of Artificial intelligence) (2020)

44. Holzinger, A., Langs, G., Denk, H., Zatloukal, K., Müller, H.: Causability and explainabilty of artificial intelligence in medicine. Wiley Interdisc. Rev. Data Min. Knowl. Discov. e1312 (2019). https://doi.org/10.1002/widm.1312

45. Hou, L., Samaras, D., Kurc, T.M., Gao, Y., Davis, J.E., Saltz, J.H.: Patch-based convolutional neural network for whole slide tissue image classification. In: 2016 IEEE Conference on Computer Vision and Pattern Recognition (CVPR), pp. 2424–2433 (2016). https://doi.org/10.1109/cvpr.2016.266

46. Huang, Y., Chung, A.C.S.: Evidence localization for pathology images using weakly supervised learning. In: Shen, D., et al. (eds.) MICCAI 2019. LNCS, vol. 11764, pp. 613–621. Springer, Cham (2019). https://doi.org/10.1007/978-3-030-32239-7_68

47. HTI Inc.: Image search engine for pathology (2020). http://www.hurondigitalpathology.com/image-search/. Accessed 17 Jan 2020

48. Jung, H., Lodhi, B., Kang, J.: An automatic nuclei segmentation method based on deep convolutional neural networks for histopathology images. BMC Biomed. Eng. **1**(1), 24 (2019). https://doi.org/10.1186/s42490-019-0026-8

49. Kaur, H., Nori, H., Jenkins, S., Caruana, R., Wallach, H., Wortman Vaughan, J.: Interpreting interpretability: understanding data scientists' use of interpretability tools for machine learning. In: 2020 CHI Conference on Human Factors in Computing Systems, CHI 2020 (2020)

50. Kendall, A., Gal, Y.: What uncertainties do we need in Bayesian deep learning for computer vision? In: Advances in Neural Information Processing Systems, December 2017, pp. 5575–5585 (2017)

51. Kevin, F., et al.: Visualizing histopathologic deep learning classification and anomaly detection using nonlinear feature space dimensionality reduction. BMC Bioinformatics **19**, 173 (2018). https://doi.org/10.1186/s12859-018-2184-4

52. Khan, M.E., Nielsen, D., Tangkaratt, V., Lin, W., Gal, Y., Srivastava, A.: Fast and scalable Bayesian deep learning by weight-perturbation in Adam. In: 35th International Conference on Machine Learning, ICML 2018. vol. 6, pp. 4088–4113 (2018)

53. Khan, M.E.E., Immer, A., Abedi, E., Korzepa, M.: Approximate inference turns deep networks into gaussian processes. In: Wallach, H., Larochelle, H., Beygelzimer, A., d' Alché-Buc, F., Fox, E., Garnett, R. (eds.) Advances in Neural Information Processing Systems, vol. 32, pp. 3088–3098. Curran Associates, Inc. (2019)

54. Kim, B., et al.: Interpretability beyond feature attribution: quantitative testing with concept activation vectors (TCAV). In: 35th International Conference on Machine Learning, ICML 2018, vol. 6, pp. 4186–4195 (2018)

55. Kindermans, P.J., et al.: Learning how to explain neural networks: PatternNet and PatternAttribution. In: 6th International Conference on Learning Representations, ICLR 2018 - Conference Track Proceedings (2018)

56. Koelzer, V., et al.: Digital image analysis improves precision of programmed death ligand 1 (PD-L1) scoring in cutaneous melanoma. Histopathology **73** (2018). https://doi.org/10.1111/his.13528

57. Koh, P.W., Liang, P.: Understanding black-box predictions via influence functions. In: Proceedings of the 34th International Conference on Machine Learning, ICML 2017, vol. 70. p. 1885–1894. JMLR.org (2017). https://doi.org/10.5555/3305381.3305576

58. Komura, D., Ishikawa, S.: Machine learning methods for histopathological image analysis. Comput. Struct. Biotechnol. J. **16** (2017). https://doi.org/10.1016/j.csbj.2018.01.001

59. Kwon, Y., Won, J.H., Kim, B.J., Paik, M.C.: Uncertainty quantification using Bayesian neural networks in classification: application to biomedical image segmentation. Comput. Stat. Data Anal. **142**, 106816 (2020). https://doi.org/10.1016/j.csda.2019.106816

60. Lakshminarayanan, B., Pritzel, A., Blundell, C.: Simple and scalable predictive uncertainty estimation using deep ensembles. In: Advances in Neural Information Processing Systems, December 2017, pp. 6403–6414 (2017)

61. Lapuschkin, S., Wäldchen, S., Binder, A., Montavon, G., Samek, W., Müller, K.R.: Unmasking Clever Hans predictors and assessing what machines really learn. Nat. Commun. **10**(1) (2019). https://doi.org/10.1038/s41467-019-08987-4

62. Leino, K., Sen, S., Datta, A., Fredrikson, M., Li, L.: Influence-directed explanations for deep convolutional networks. In: Proceedings - International Test Conference, October 2018 (2019). https://doi.org/10.1109/TEST.2018.8624792

63. Litjens, G.J.S., et al.: A survey on deep learning in medical image analysis. Med. Image Anal. **42**, 60–88 (2017)

64. Liu, Y., et al.: Detecting cancer metastases on gigapixel pathology images. CoRR abs/1703.02442 (2017)

65. Lundberg, S.M., Lee, S.I.: A unified approach to interpreting model predictions. In: Guyon, I., et al. (eds.) Advances in Neural Information Processing Systems, vol. 30, pp. 4765–4774. Curran Associates, Inc. (2017)

66. Maaten, L.V.D., Hinton, G.: Visualizing data using t-SNE. J. Mach. Learn. Res. **9**, 2579–2605 (2008)

67. Mahendran, A., Vedaldi, A.: Understanding deep image representations by inverting them. Technical report (2015). https://doi.org/10.1109/CVPR.2015.7299155

68. Mahendran, A., Vedaldi, A.: Visualizing deep convolutional neural networks using natural pre-images. Int. J. Comput. Vis. **120**(3), 233–255 (2016). https://doi.org/10.1007/s11263-016-0911-8

69. Meinshausen, N.: Quantile regression forests. J. Mach. Learn. Res. **7**, 983–999 (2006)

70. Mittelstadt, B., Russell, C., Wachter, S.: Explaining explanations in AI. In: Proceedings of the Conference on Fairness, Accountability, and Transparency, FAT* 2019, pp. 279–288 (2019). Association for Computing Machinery, New York (2019). https://doi.org/10.1145/3287560.3287574

71. Molin, J., Bodén, A., Treanor, D., Fjeld, M., Lundström, C.: Scale stain: multi-resolution feature enhancement in pathology visualization (2016). arXiv preprint, arXiv:1610.04141

72. Molin, J., Woundefinedniak, P.W., Lundström, C., Treanor, D., Fjeld, M.: Understanding design for automated image analysis in digital pathology. In: Proceedings of the 9th Nordic Conference on Human-Computer Interaction, NordiCHI 2016, Association for Computing Machinery, New York (2016). https://doi.org/10.1145/2971485.2971561

73. Montavon, G., Lapuschkin, S., Binder, A., Samek, W., Müller, K.R.: Explaining nonlinear classification decisions with deep Taylor decomposition. Pattern Recogn. **65**, 211–222 (2017). https://doi.org/10.1016/j.patcog.2016.11.008

74. Mueller, S.T., Hoffman, R.R., Clancey, W., Emrey, A., Klein, G.: Explanation in human-AI systems: a literature meta-review, synopsis of key ideas and publications, and bibliography for explainable AI (2019). arXiv preprint, arXiv:1902.01876

75. Nagpal, K., et al.: Development and validation of a deep learning algorithm for improving Gleason scoring of prostate cancer. NPJ Digit. Med. **2**(1) (2019). https://doi.org/10.1038/s41746-019-0112-2

76. Narayanan, P.L., Raza, S.E.A., Dodson, A., Gusterson, B., Dowsett, M., Yuan, Y.: DeepSDCS: dissecting cancer proliferation heterogeneity in Ki67 digital whole slide images (2018). arXiv preprint, arXiv: 1806.10850

77. Neal, R.M.: Bayesian learning for neural networks. Ph.D. thesis, CAN (1995). aAINN02676

78. Nguyen, A., Dosovitskiy, A., Yosinski, J., Brox, T., Clune, J.: Synthesizing the preferred inputs for neurons in neural networks via deep generator networks. In: Proceedings of the 30th International Conference on Neural Information Processing Systems, NIPS 2016, pp. 3395–3403. Curran Associates Inc., Red Hook (2016)

79. Nguyen, A., Yosinski, J., Clune, J.: Multifaceted feature visualization: uncovering the different types of features learned by each neuron in deep neural networks (2016). arXiv preprint, arXiv: 1602.03616

80. Nie, W., Zhang, Y., Patel, A.: A theoretical explanation for perplexing behaviors of backpropagation-based visualizations. In: ICML (2018)

81. Olah, C., et al.: The building blocks of interpretability. Distill **3**(3) (2018). https://doi.org/10.23915/distill.00010

82. Osband, I., Blundell, C., Pritzel, A., Van Roy, B.: Deep exploration via bootstrapped DQN. In: Advances in Neural Information Processing Systems, pp. 4033–4041 (2016)

83. Palatnik de Sousa, I., Maria Bernardes Rebuzzi Vellasco, M., Costa da Silva, E.: Local interpretable model-agnostic explanations for classification of lymph node metastases. Sensors **19**(13), 2969 (2019). https://doi.org/10.3390/s19132969

84. Papadopoulos, H., Vovk, V., Gammerman, A.: Conformal prediction with neural networks. In: Proceedings - International Conference on Tools with Artificial Intelligence, ICTAI, vol. 2, pp. 388–395 (2007). https://doi.org/10.1109/ICTAI.2007.47

85. Papernot, N., McDaniel, P.: Deep k-nearest neighbors: towards confident, interpretable and robust deep learning (2018). arXiv preprint, arXiv: 1803.04765

86. Pearce, T., Leibfried, F., Brintrup, A., Zaki, M., Neely, A.: Uncertainty in neural networks: approximately Bayesian ensembling (2018). arXiv preprint, arXiv: 1810.05546

87. Pearce, T., Zaki, M., Brintrup, A., Neely, A.: High-quality prediction intervals for deep learning: a distribution-free, ensembled approach. In: 35th International Conference on Machine Learning, ICML 2018, vol. 9, pp. 6473–6482 (2018)

88. Pohn, B., Kargl, M., Reihs, R., Holzinger, A., Zatloukal, K., Muller, H.: Towards a deeper understanding of how a pathologist makes a diagnosis: Visualization of the diagnostic process in histopathology. In: 2019 IEEE Symposium on Computers and Communications (ISCC), 2019 IEEE Symposium on Computers and Communications (ISCC), pp. 1081–1086 (2019)

89. Postels, J., Ferroni, F., Coskun, H., Navab, N., Tombari, F.: Sampling-free epistemic uncertainty estimation using approximated variance propagation (2019). arXiv preprint, arXiv: 1908.00598

90. Ribeiro, M.T., Singh, S., Guestrin, C.: "Why should I trust you?" Explaining the predictions of any classifier. In: Proceedings of the ACM SIGKDD International Conference on Knowledge Discovery and Data Mining, 13–17 August, pp. 1135–1144 (2016). https://doi.org/10.1145/2939672.2939778

91. Ritter, H., Botev, A., Barber, D.: A scalable Laplace approximation for neural networks. In: ICLR, pp. 1–15 (2018). https://doi.org/10.5121/ijfcst.2014.4504

92. Saha, M., Chakraborty, C.: Her2Net: a deep framework for semantic segmentation and classification of cell membranes and nuclei in breast cancer evaluation. IEEE Trans. Image Process. **27**(5), 2189–2200 (2018). https://doi.org/10.1109/TIP.2018.2795742

93. Samek, W., Binder, A., Montavon, G., Lapuschkin, S., Müller, K.: Evaluating the visualization of what a deep neural network has learned. IEEE Trans. Neural Netw. Learn. Syst. **28**(11), 2660–2673 (2017). https://doi.org/10.1109/TNNLS.2016.2599820

94. Seah, J., Tang, J., Kitchen, A., Seah, J.: Generative visual rationales (2018). arXiv preprint, arXiv: 1804.04539

95. Selvaraju, R.R., Cogswell, M., Das, A., Vedantam, R., Parikh, D., Batra, D.: Grad-CAM: visual explanations from deep networks via gradient-based localization. In: Proceedings of the IEEE International Conference on Computer Vision, October 2017, pp. 618–626 (2017). https://doi.org/10.1109/ICCV.2017.74

96. Serag, A., et al.: Translational AI and deep learning in diagnostic pathology. Front. Med. **6**, 185 (2019). https://doi.org/10.3389/fmed.2019.00185

97. Sharma, H., Zerbe, N., Klempert, I., Hellwich, O., Hufnagl, P.: Deep convolutional neural networks for automatic classification of gastric carcinoma using whole slide images in digital histopathology. Comput. Med. Imaging Graph. **61**, 2–13 (2017). https://doi.org/10.1016/j.compmedimag.2017.06.001. Selected papers from the 13th European Congress on Digital Pathology

98. Shimoda, W., Yanai, K.: Distinct class saliency maps for multiple object images. In: Workshop Track - ICLR 2016, vol. 1 (2016)

99. Shridhar, K., Laumann, F., Liwicki, M.: A comprehensive guide to Bayesian convolutional neural network with variational inference (2019). arXiv preprint, arXiv: 1901.02731

100. Simonyan, K., Vedaldi, A., Zisserman, A.: Deep inside convolutional networks: Visualising image classification models and saliency maps. In: 2nd International Conference on Learning Representations, ICLR 2014 - Workshop Track Proceedings (2014)

101. Smilkov, D., Thorat, N., Kim, B., Viégas, F., Wattenberg, M.: SmoothGrad: removing noise by adding noise (2017). arXiv preprint, arXiv:1706.03825

102. Snoek, J., et al.: Can you trust your model's uncertainty? Evaluating predictive uncertainty under dataset shift. In: Wallach, H., Larochelle, H., Beygelzimer, A., d' Alché-Buc, F., Fox, E., Garnett, R. (eds.) Advances in Neural Information Processing Systems, vol. 32, pp. 13969–13980. Curran Associates, Inc. (2019)

103. Springenberg, J.T., Dosovitskiy, A., Brox, T., Riedmiller, M.: Striving for simplicity: The all convolutional net. In: 3rd International Conference on Learning Representations, ICLR 2015 - Workshop Track Proceedings (2015)

104. Srinivas, S., Fleuret, F.: Full-gradient representation for neural network visualization. In: Wallach, H., Larochelle, H., Beygelzimer, A., d' Alché-Buc, F., Fox, E., Garnett, R. (eds.) Advances in Neural Information Processing Systems, vol. 32, pp. 4126–4135. Curran Associates, Inc. (2019)

105. Stacke, K., Eilertsen, G., Unger, J., Lundström, C.: A closer look at domain shift for deep learning in histopathology (2019). arXiv preprint, arXiv: 1909.11575

106. Ström, P., et al.: Artificial intelligence for diagnosis and grading of prostate cancer in biopsies: a population-based, diagnostic study. Lancet Oncol. **21**, 222–232 (2020)

107. Sundararajan, M., Taly, A., Yan, Q.: Axiomatic attribution for deep networks. In: 34th International Conference on Machine Learning, ICML 2017, vol. 7, pp. 5109–5118 (2017)

108. Swiderska-Chadaj, Z., et al.: Learning to detect lymphocytes in immunohistochemistry with deep learning. Med. Image Anal. **58**, 101547 (2019). https://doi.org/10.1016/j.media.2019.101547

109. Tagasovska, N., Lopez-Paz, D.: Single-model uncertainties for deep learning. In: Wallach, H., Larochelle, H., Beygelzimer, A., d' Alché-Buc, F., Fox, E., Garnett, R. (eds.) Advances in Neural Information Processing Systems, vol. 32, pp. 6414–6425. Curran Associates, Inc. (2019)

110. Tang, Z., et al.: Interpretable classification of Alzheimer's disease pathologies with a convolutional neural network pipeline. Nat. Commun. **10** (2019). https://doi.org/10.1038/s41467-019-10212-1

111. Tellez, D., et al.: Quantifying the effects of data augmentation and stain color normalization in convolutional neural networks for computational pathology. Med. Image Anal. **58**, 101544 (2019)

112. Teye, M., Azizpour, H., Smith, K.: Bayesian uncertainty estimation for batch normalized deep networks. In: 35th International Conference on Machine Learning, ICML 2018, vol. 11, pp. 7824–7833 (2018)

113. Thorstenson, S., Molin, J., Lundström, C.: Implementation of large-scale routine diagnostics using whole slide imaging in Sweden: digital pathology experiences 2006–2013. J. Pathol. Inf. **5** (2014). https://doi.org/10.4103/2153-3539.129452

114. Tjoa, E., Guan, C.: A survey on explainable artificial intelligence (XAI): towards medical XAI (2019). arXiv preprint, arXiv: abs/1907.07374

115. Veta, M., et al.: Predicting breast tumor proliferation from whole-slide images: the TUPAC16 challenge. CoRR abs/1807.08284 (2018)

116. Wu, T., Song, X.: Towards interpretable object detection by unfolding latent structures. In: The IEEE International Conference on Computer Vision (ICCV), October 2019

117. Xue, Y., Ray, N., Hugh, J., Bigras, G.: Cell counting by regression using convolutional neural network. In: Hua, G., Jégou, H. (eds.) ECCV 2016. LNCS, vol. 9913, pp. 274–290. Springer, Cham (2016). https://doi.org/10.1007/978-3-319-46604-0_20

118. Yosinski, J., Clune, J., Nguyen, A., Fuchs, T., Lipson, H.: Understanding neural networks through deep visualization (2015). arXiv preprint, arXiv: 1506.06579

119. Young, G.A., Smith, R.L.: Essentials of Statistical Inference. Cambridge Series in Statistical and Probabilistic Mathematics. Cambridge University Press, Cambridge (2005)

120. Zeiler, M.D., Fergus, R.: Visualizing and understanding convolutional networks. In: Fleet, D., Pajdla, T., Schiele, B., Tuytelaars, T. (eds.) ECCV 2014. LNCS, vol. 8689, pp. 818–833. Springer, Cham (2014). https://doi.org/10.1007/978-3-319-10590-1_53

121. Zhang, J., Bargal, S.A., Lin, Z., Brandt, J., Shen, X., Sclaroff, S.: Top-down neural attention by excitation backprop. Int. J. Comput. Vis. **126**(10), 1084–1102 (2018). https://doi.org/10.1007/s11263-017-1059-x

122. Zhang, Q.S., Zhu, S.C.: Visual interpretability for deep learning: a survey. Front. Inf. Technol. Electron. Eng. **19**(1), 27–39 (2018)

123. Zhang, Q., Wu, Y.N., Zhu, S.C.: Interpretable convolutional neural networks. In: Proceedings of the IEEE Computer Society Conference on Computer Vision and Pattern Recognition, pp. 8827–8836 (2018). https://doi.org/10.1109/CVPR.2018.00920

124. Zhou, B., Khosla, A., Lapedriza, A., Oliva, A., Torralba, A.: Object detectors emerge in deep scene CNNs. In: ICLR 2015 (2014)

125. Zhou, B., Khosla, A., Lapedriza, A., Oliva, A., Torralba, A.: Learning deep features for discriminative localization. In: Proceedings of the IEEE Computer Society Conference on Computer Vision and Pattern Recognition, December 2016, pp. 2921–2929 (2016). https://doi.org/10.1109/CVPR.2016.319

126. Zhu, J.Y., Park, T., Isola, P., Efros, A.A.: Unpaired image-to-image translation using cycle-consistent adversarial networks. In: The IEEE International Conference on Computer Vision (ICCV), October 2017

127. Zintgraf, L.M., Cohen, T.S., Adel, T., Welling, M.: Visualizing deep neural network decisions: prediction difference analysis. In: 5th International Conference on Learning Representations, ICLR 2017 - Conference Track Proceedings (2019)

Sample Quality as Basic Prerequisite for Data Quality: A Quality Management System for Biobanks

Christiane Hartfeldt[1(✉)] ⓘ, Verena Huth[1], Sabrina Schmitt[2] ⓘ,
Bettina Meinung[4], Peter Schirmacher[3], Michael Kiehntopf[4], Cornelia Specht[1],
and Michael Hummel[1] ⓘ

[1] German Biobank Node, Charité - Universitätsmedizin Berlin, Berlin, Germany
`christiane.hartfeldt@charite.de`
[2] BioMaterialBank Heidelberg, Heidelberg University Hospital, Heidelberg, Germany
[3] Institute of Pathology, Heidelberg University Hospital, Heidelberg, Germany
[4] Integrated Biobank Jena, Jena University Hospital, Jena, Germany

Abstract. Artificial intelligence will undoubtedly shape technological developments in the next years – affecting biobanks as well. First concepts already exist for the possible application of AI in biobank processes. Data quality, which depends on sample quality, plays the decisive role here. For this reason, high and also overarching quality standards are important to prepare biobanks for these technological innovations. In addition, the requirements for sample and data quality will be significantly affected by the EU regulation for in vitro diagnostics as its transition period ends in 2022. The demand for human biospecimens will consequently rise.

In order to meet such requirements, the German Biobank Node (GBN) and the German Biobank Alliance (GBA) have established a quality management programme for German biobanks which includes e.g. an extensive quality manual and so-called "friendly" (cross-biobank) audits. The following article describes these developments with regard to their relevance for future biobank workflows using AI methods.

Keywords: Biobank · Quality · Machine learning

1 Introduction and Motivation

Assume it is 2029. The first approval for targeted treatment decisions based on image analysis is in place. Recognition of a distinct histomorphological pattern determines the most effective drug. A new era in precision oncology has begun – requiring considerations regarding the quality of the tissue specimens including their pre-analytical condition. Luckily, grounds for quality assessment and assurance have been laid in 2018/19 facilitating the introduction of morphology based treatment decision systems without any delay. Thanks to the pioneer work of the biobanking community in BBMRI-ERIC [1] and its 21 national nodes, a quality

© Springer Nature Switzerland AG 2020
A. Holzinger et al. (Eds.): AI & ML for Digital Pathology, LNAI 12090, pp. 89–94, 2020.
https://doi.org/10.1007/978-3-030-50402-1_5

system has been established allowing harmonised handling of tissue samples to guarantee comparable and reliable results irrespective of local conditions. The following text describes the components and the establishment of this quality system in Germany in cooperation with BBMRI-ERIC.

2   Glossary

Biobanking: describes biobank processes such as the reception, processing, storage, transport, retrieval, and distribution of biospecimens and associated data for biomedical research.

German Biobank Node and German Biobank Alliance: Led by the German Biobank Node (GBN), the German Biobank Alliance (GBA) is a network consisting of 18 biobank sites and two IT centres in Germany [2]. The alliance partners establish quality standards for biospecimens and related data from different biobanks nationally and internationally available for biomedical research. GBN is the umbrella organisation for university biobanks in Germany. Since 2017 the biobanks of GBA and GBN are funded by the Federal Ministry of Education and Research (BMBF). GBN serves in addition as the German national node for BBMRI-ERIC.

BBMRI-ERIC: is a pan-European infrastructure of national biobank networks [1]. The abbreviation BBMRI-ERIC stands for "Biobanking and Biomolecular Resources Research Infrastructure – European Research Infrastructure Consortium". BBMRI-ERIC's aim is to facilitate access to high-quality biospecimens and associated data as research resources.

Sample Locator: is a web-based search tool enabling scientists to perform cross-biobank searches for biosamples and related data meeting relevant criteria. Currently, GBA biobanks are connected and the IT infrastructure is prepared to include further national or European biobanks. It was developed by GBN in cooperation with the German Cancer Research Center in Heidelberg (DKFZ).

3   State-of-the-Art

Artificial intelligence will shape technological developments in the next years – affecting biobanks as well. First concepts already exist for the possible application of AI in biobank processes. Data quality, which depends on sample quality, plays the decisive role here.

For this reason, high and also overarching quality standards are important to prepare biobanks for these technological innovations. In addition, the requirements for sample and data quality will be significantly affected by the EU regulation for in vitro diagnostics as its transition period ends in 2022. The demand for human biospecimens will consequently rise.

The German Biobank Node (GBN) [2] and the German Biobank Alliance (GBA) have established a quality management programme for German biobanks which includes e.g. an extensive quality manual and so-called friendly (cross-biobank) audits.

3.1   The Quality Management Concept of GBN

The main objective of the activities by GBN and GBA in the field of quality management is the implementation and maintenance of a uniform quality management system (QMS) at all GBA sites. This is accomplished by means of a QM manual of generic biobank documents, an uniform QM software for the management of documents and processes, a cross-GBA audit system, ring trials for the review of sample-processing steps and constant review of the satisfaction of biobank users with the offered services.

3.2   QM Manual

The GBN QM manual consists of generic biobank-specific standard operating procedures. It is based on several standards e.g. ISO 9001, ISO 15189, ISO 20387 and also contains documents for the management level. The manual has been published open access [3].

3.3   Software Solution

The central QM software solution for all GBA biobanks provides a digital interface for various quality applications and reduces the documentation effort by continuous improvement of processes.

3.4   Friendly Audits

Regular audits are an indispensable prerequisite to continuous review and improvement of biobank processes. All applied standards require audits to ensure compliance and improve the quality of biospecimens and related data. The QM core team of GBA developed an audit programme to perform cross-biobank audits based on applied standards and the audit specific standard ISO 20387. During a "friendly audit", auditors from other GBA biobanks audit each participating biobank once a year. As a result, auditors gain a new perspective and deeper understanding of the standards' requirements. For the biobanks, the audit programme supports preparation for external competence evaluation (certification, accredation) – which by 2020 all participating biobanks are likely to have passed. Other national networks such as the German Centers for Health Research (DZG) and the German National Cohort (GNC) have joined the programme in order to harmonise auditing activities on the national level.

3.5   Ring Trials

Interlaboratory comparisons are highly desirable to harmonise and improve pre-analytical processes, and to identify factors which may have an impact on sample quality [4]. To provide a consistently high quality of individual samples, a ring trial concept for different bioresources with the focus on continuous improvement of processes has been established within GBA. During ring trials, reference samples are processed, nucleic acids are isolated and analysed according to the standard operating procedures at the different biobanks. Improvements in handling were discussed in a cross-project exchange with the GBA working group for education of the technical biobank staff. Furthermore, in a pilot ring trial across GBA biobanks, metabolic quality indicators are being validated to become part of the standard quality control procedure for samples before they are stored. The indication whether samples have been tested accordingly will in future be included in GBA Sample Locator [5] as a quality criteria.

3.6   Satisfaction Survey for Biobank Users

To support biobanks in meeting their users' needs, GBN designed an online questionnaire. The results of this survey enable biobanks to adapt internal processes to the needs of their customers to ensure sustainability. The survey is conducted once a year. There are two options to perform the survey: (i) Using the online tool provided by GBN or (ii) applying a biobank own survey tool, which rely, however, covers the same questions and, potenially, some further questions regarding the respective biobank. Irrespective of the option used, GBN performs a comprehensive evaluation with the data of all biobanks. An indication whether this survey is being conducted by a biobank will also be included in the Sample Locator.

4   Challenges and Opportunities

The belief that the main purpose of biobanks is the collection and storage of biosamples is outdated. Modern biobanks should do as much as possible to ensure that their collected and stored samples are also used for biomedical research. If it comes to the use of samples and data from various biobanks harmonisation of (heterogeneous) data sets and samples quality is an additional aspect [6]. Here, biobank networks such as the GBA are indispensable to ensure harmonised standards in order to achieve reliable and comparable sample and data quality and to enhance the visibility of their sample collections.

In addition, it is essential that biosamples are not only linked to medical information but also to research data to enhance their value and to avoid repetition of data generation [7]. Therefore, data and material transfer agreements should be in place to allow the return of research data based on harmonised metadata according to the FAIR principles [8]. This would ensure a much more sustainable use of sample and research data.

5   Outlook

The GBN quality concept for biobanks is a real added value for the biobanking community in Germany. An awareness for quality is built and biobank staff received targeted training. More biobanks will become GBA partners and contribute their experiences and knowledge as well as benefit from the developed products and the exchange within the community.

Establishing harmonised processes on a national and, ultimately, European level is the aim pursued in cooperation with BBMRI-ERIC. This is especially relevant regarding the EU regulation for in vitro diagnostics, which came into force in 2017 – the transition period will end in 2022. The demand for well-characterised human samples will consequently rise and IVD device manufacturers might lay down additional requirements regarding sample quality.

Sample quality is as well a basic requisite for data quality: the collection, evaluation and use of data will become the most important field of competence for biobanks – in some parts of the world that might already be the case. High-resolution digitalisation of tissue sections for virtual microscopy is becoming accessible for an increasing number of biobanks. Machine learning of many histological patterns linked to the medical data generate algorithms enabling pattern recognition for prognostic and potentially therapeutic purposes [9]. In less than ten years from now, huge data pools and algorithms for pattern recognition will be available in pathology which – in combination with molecular alterations – will allow the precise identification of most effective drugs for most successful therapies.

Key for success are official standards which ensure compatibility and interoperability. In addition, samples and data sharing without unnecessary restrictions is mandatory. This might – at least to some extent – need cultural change. Large infrastructures such as BBMRI-ERIC and its national nodes play a central role in this respect. Back to the future: The year 2029. Obstacles such as quality variations, missing data and insufficient interoperability have been overcome. Biobanks play a major role as sources of high quality biospecimens and comprehensive data of all kind. To accomplish this, biobanks have been embedded in well-developed research infrastructures: the future has already started!

References

1. BBMRI-ERIC - Biobanking and BioMolecular Resources Research Infrastructure - European Research Infrastructure Consortium. www.bbmri-eric.eu
2. German Biobank Node (GBN): bbmri.de
3. Schmitt, S., et al.: German Biobank Node: Manual for Quality Management in Biobanking - English Version. https://doi.org/10.5281/zenodo.3697691
4. Herpel, E., Schmitt, S., Kiehntopf, M.: Quality of biomaterials in liquid- and tissue-biobanking. Bundesgesundheitsblatt, Gesundheitsforschung, Gesundheitsschutz **59**(3), 325–335 (2015). https://doi.org/10.1007/s00103-015-2294-3
5. Cooperation between German Biobank Node, German Cancer Research Center in Heidelberg, Biobanking and Biomolecular Resources Research Infrastructure - European Research Infrastructure Consortium. https://samplelocator.bbmri.de/
6. Huppertz, B., Holzinger, A.: Biobanks – a source of large biological data sets: open problems and future challenges. In: Holzinger, A., Jurisica, I. (eds.) Interactive Knowledge Discovery and Data Mining in Biomedical Informatics. LNCS,

vol. 8401, pp. 317–330. Springer, Heidelberg (2014). https://doi.org/10.1007/978-3-662-43968-5_18

7. Müller, H., et al.: State-of-the-art and future challenges in the integration of biobank catalogues. In: Holzinger, A., Röcker, C., Ziefle, M. (eds.) Smart Health. LNCS, vol. 8700, pp. 261–273. Springer, Cham (2015). https://doi.org/10.1007/978-3-319-16226-3_11

8. Wilkinson, M.D.: The FAIR guiding principles for scientific data management and stewardship. Sci. Data **3**, 160018 (2016). https://doi.org/10.1038/sdata.2016.18

9. Courdray, N., et al.: Classification and mutation prediction from non-small cell lung cancer histopathology images using deep learning. Nat. Med. **24**(10), 1559–1567 (2018). https://doi.org/10.1038/s41591-018-0177-5

Black Box Nature of Deep Learning for Digital Pathology: Beyond Quantitative to Qualitative Algorithmic Performances

Yoichi Hayashi[✉]

Department of Computer Science, Meiji University, Kawasaki 214-8571, Japan
hayashiy@meiji.ac.jp

Abstract. Artificial intelligence (AI), particularly deep learning (DL), which involves automated feature extraction using deep neural networks, is expected to be used increasingly often by clinicians in the near future. AI can analyze medical images and patient data at a level not possible by a single physician; however, the resulting parameters are difficult to interpret. This so-called "black box" problem causes opaqueness in DL. The aim of the present study is to help realize the transparency of black box machine learning for digital pathology (DP). To achieve this aim, we review the "black box" problem and the limitations of DL for DP, and attempt to reveal a paradigm shift in DP in which diagnostic accuracy is surpassed to achieve explainability. DL in medical fields such as DP still has considerable limitations. To interpret and apply DL effectively in DP, sufficient expertise in computer science is required. Moreover, although rules can be extracted using the Re-RX family, the classification accuracy is slightly lower than that using whole images trained by a convolutional neural network; thus, to establish accountability, one of the most important issues in DP is to explain the classification results clearly. Although more interpretable algorithms seem likely to be more readily accepted by medical professionals, it remains necessary to determine whether this could lead to increased clinical effectiveness. For the acceptance of AI by pathologists and physicians in DP, not only quantitative, but also qualitative algorithmic performance, such as rule extraction, should be improved.

Keywords: Black box · Interpretability · Explainable AI · Digital pathology · Transparency

1 Introduction

Artificial intelligence (AI) is a branch of computer science that deals with intelligence exhibited by computers. The earliest work related to medical AI dates back to the early 1970s [1]. Almost every type of clinician, ranging from certificated medical specialists to paramedics, is expected to be using AI technology, particularly deep learning (DL), at some point in the near future [2]. DL has been the backbone of computer science in terms of exceeding human ability. It largely involves automated feature extraction

© Springer Nature Switzerland AG 2020
A. Holzinger et al. (Eds.): AI & ML for Digital Pathology, LNAI 12090, pp. 95–101, 2020.
https://doi.org/10.1007/978-3-030-50402-1_6

using deep neural networks (DNNs) that can help discriminate medical images such as pathological slides, skin lesions, and retinal fundus photographs.

While the roots of AI date back over 60 years, it was not until 2012 that deep belief networks [3] were widely accepted as a viable form of AI.

The basic DNN architecture, convolutional neural networks (CNNs) [4], have an input layer, an output layer, and a number of hidden layers, each responding to different image features (e.g., shapes, edges). A key differentiating feature of DL [2] compared with other types of AI is its autodidactic quality; neural networks (NNs) are not designed by humans [5].

AI can analyze a large number of images and patient data at a level not possible by a single physician. However, given a set of parameters, DNNs learn on their own to produce an output. Known inputs and algorithms of AI programs start the process, but the resulting parameters are difficult to interpret [5].

These difficulties (the so-called "black box" problem) cause opaqueness in DL, which has been the subject of many recent studies [6–9]. The aim of this paper is to help realize the transparency of "black box" machine learning for digital pathology (DP). To achieve this aim, we undertake a renewed attack on the "black box" problem and the limitations of DL for DP and attempt to reveal a paradigm shift in DP in which we surpass diagnostic accuracy to achieve explainability.

2   Rule Extraction and the "Black Box" Problem

Rule extraction is not a new concept, being originally conceived for a shallow NN by Gallant [10] for the medical domain. For about the past 30 years, extensive efforts have been made by many researchers to resolve the "black box" problem of trained NNs using rule extraction technology [11–15].

Rule extraction [12] is a powerful and increasingly popular method of data mining that provides explanations and interpretable capabilities for models generated by shallow NNs. Extracted rules need to be simple and interpretable by humans, and must be able to discover highly accurate knowledge in the medical domain. Rule extraction technology has also been recognized as a technique that attempts to find a compromise between the two requirements of accuracy and interpretability by building a simple rule set that mimics how a well-performing complex model (a "black box") makes decisions for users [15].

Recently, as a promising means to address the "black box" problem, a rule extraction technology well balanced between accuracy and interpretability was proposed for shallow NNs [14, 16]. In addition, Uehara et al. [17] reported an actual medical application in hepatology using rule extraction. Hayashi et al. [18] reported a rule extraction approach to explore the upper limit of hemoglobin during anemia treatment in patients with predialysis chronic kidney disease. Hayashi [19] also proposed a method to detect lower albuminuria levels and the early development of diabetic kidney disease using an AI-based rule extraction approach.

3 Renewed Attack of the "Black Box" Problem for Deep Neural Network Architectures

The interpretability of predictive models is important. In fact, the "black box" nature of DL in medicine, especially in pathology and radiology, has been severely criticized. Therefore, the "new black box" problem caused by highly complex DNN models generated by DL must be addressed. To resolve this "new black box" problem, transparency and interpretability are needed in DNNs. However, at present, various "black box" problems remain [20]. Much has been written about the "black box" of algorithms, and substantial controversy around this topic remains. Especially in the case of DNNs, understanding the determination of output will not be possible.

In contrast to conventional image analysis, in DL, the manner in which image features are abstracted is difficult for humans to understand. Consequently, with the aim of making features more interpretable by humans, efforts have been made, using a variety of techniques, to convert DL algorithms into a "glass box" by clarifying the inputs and their relation to measured outputs [21].

4 Limitations and Criticisms of Deep Learning in Digital Pathology

Based on recent trends, DL is the preferred approach for computer vision. Specifically, deep networks pre-trained with natural images, which are relatively easy to set up, enable high performance while reducing the need for domain knowledge substantially. Although the raw-level features underlying the good performance of such methods are of interest, their scientific novelty is limited, usually constrained to hyperparameter settings or network ensembles. In addition, the "black box" nature of DL approaches hinders their application in the medical field, where specialists (e.g., computer scientists) need to understand the reasoning behind the decisions. Aresta et al. [22] suggested that the challenges facing medical imaging could be solved by incentivizing participants to propose novel solutions. For example, it would be of interest to ask participants to produce an automatic explanation of a method's decision. This would require the development of new ground truths and metrics that allow appropriate reasoning for such decisions, thereby making DL suitable for use in clinical practice [22].

4.1 The "Black Box" Nature of Deep Learning in Digital Pathology

In contrast to computer vision tasks, DL in DP and ophthalmology still has considerable limitations in terms of its interpretability and transparency, as expertise in computer science is needed to interpret and apply DL to medical images effectively in the clinical setting. This is because of the "black box" nature of DL, where results are generated with high accuracy but no specific medical-based reasons. Hence, the results from DL can be difficult to interpret clinically, which can limit their use in medical decision-making [23].

Although some researchers have emphasized the importance of improvements in model performance over interpretability, we feel that improvements in the transparency of DL would promote the widespread adoption of such methods for medical imaging in clinical practice [20]. On the other hand, Hayashi [23] noted the importance of transparency for DL in radiological imaging, which provided clue to solving the "black box" problem in DP.

4.2 Detection of Metastatic Breast Cancer in Sentinel Lymph Node Biopsies

DL in the clinical setting (LYmph Node Assistant: LYNA) has achieved an area under the receiver operating characteristic curve of 99.6% for the detection of metastatic breast cancer in sentinel lymph node biopsies [24], but not without limitations. Although a previous study attempted to unpack the "black box" mechanisms underlying LYNA's predictions by computing the degree to which they were affected by each pixel, LYNA is still unable to compare the current field of view with similar cells in less ambiguous regions of the same slide or case, which can be done by a pathologist [24].

The application of CNNs [25], especially for sentinel lymph nodes, also has several limitations; however, this is of limited importance for their clinical application. If CNNs can detect micro- and macro-metastases with high accuracy, then isolated tumor cells can be detected by immunohistochemistry without the need for a pathologist to examine hematoxylin and eosin-stained slides.

What remains a challenge for machine learning is not the ability to identify cancers or metastases in images, a task that a trained pathologist can perform rapidly, but rather, the ability to prognosticate and predict therapy response to treatment for tumors and to complement or work in combination with genomics and transcriptomics for patient stratification [26].

4.3 Detection and Classification of Cancer in Whole Slide Breast Histopathology Images

The generalizability of algorithms for binary cancer compared with no cancer classification remains unclear for more clinically significant multi-class scenarios in which intermediate categories have different risk factors and treatment strategies. Gecer et al. [27] reported the use of a system that classifies whole slide images (WSIs) of breast biopsies into five diagnostic categories. In that system, a saliency detector utilizing a pipeline of four full CNNs trained using samples from pathologists' screenings performs multiscale localization of diagnostically relevant regions of interest in WSIs. Next, a CNN trained from consensus-derived reference samples classifies image patches as showing proliferative or non-proliferative changes in typical ductal hyperplasia, ductal carcinoma in situ, and invasive carcinoma. Finally, saliency and classification maps are fused for pixel-wise labelling and slide-level categorization. However, although this five-category classification formulation is a novel technique, the diagnostic process remains a "black box". Therefore, a rule extraction approach for clinical applications would be useful for pathologists.

4.4 Limitation of Heat Map Visualization of DL Predictions

In a patient with a high-grade tumor, heat map visualization of the AI prediction corresponded to the areas of early microvascular proliferation—a hallmark of malignant progression—identified by a pathologist, thereby providing unique interpretability to the analysis. Such visual attention maps and post hoc analyses of DL methods have also been criticized [28], as they exclude all information about how relevant data are being used. Knowing where a network is looking within the image does not tell the user what it is doing with that part of the image. In fact, saliency maps could be essentially the same for multiple classes.

5 Beyond Diagnostic Accuracy to Explainability for Digital Pathology

At present, various "black box" problems remain for DNNs. By contrast, as machine learning-based predictions become increasingly ubiquitous and affect numerous aspects of our daily lives, the focus of current research has moved beyond model performance (e.g., accuracy) to other factors, such as interpretability and transparency [14].

Recently, Campanella et al. [29] developed a novel framework that leverages multiple instance learning to train DNNs. However, decision trees (DTs) converted from DNNs are very large and complex, and therefore not suitable for rule extraction [20]. However, using rule extraction technologies proposed by the present author [14, 16–19, 30, 31], the characteristics of DTs, based on explicit features, can be well-balanced in terms of both accuracy and interpretability. The rule extraction technologies proposed by the present author can easily explain medical diagnostic results in the form of interpretable and concise rules [17–20].

6 Conclusions

In current medicine practice, physicians are the ones who ultimately need to take responsibility for the output of any type of DL. Despite its limitations, AI is expected to be an integral part of the future of medicine and medical imaging. However, it should also be noted that the interpretability of DL systems may hold different meanings for health care professionals than for experts in machine learning. Although more interpretable algorithms seem likely to be more readily accepted by medical professionals such as pathologists, it remains necessary to determine in applied clinical research whether this is the case and whether it could lead to tangible benefits for patients in terms of clinical effectiveness in the future.

As clinicians and patients remain somewhat concerned about the "black box" nature of AI and DL, the large-scale adoption of AI in the health care setting has yet to take place. For its acceptance by pathologists and physicians in areas such as DP, not only quantitative, but also qualitative algorithmic performance such as rule extraction should be improved. To promote the clinical acceptance of DL systems, it will be important to unravel the "black box" nature of DL using rule extraction technology in future research.

These findings suggest that trust in DL algorithms and synergy effects between pathologists and computer scientists that exceed the performance of either AI or pathologists alone can be achieved by providing qualitative data about the histopathologic features used in a particular instance to the reviewing pathologist.

Acknowledgments. This work was supported in part by the Japan Society for the Promotion of Science through a Grant-in-Aid for Scientific Research (C) (18K11481).

References

1. Kapoor, R., Walters, S.P., Al-Aswad, L.A.: The current state of artificial intelligence in ophthalmology. Surv. Ophthalmol. **64**(2), 233–240 (2019)
2. LeCun, Y., Bengio, Y., Hinton, G.: Deep learning. Nature **521**(7553), 436–444 (2015)
3. Hinton, G.E., Salakhutdinov, R.R.: Reducing the dimensionality of data with neural networks. Science **313**, 504–507 (2006)
4. LeCun, Y., et al.: Handwritten Digit Recognition With a Back-Propagation Network. In: Touretzky, D.S. (ed.) Advances in neural information processing systems, vol. 2, pp. 396–404. MIT Press, Cambridge (1989)
5. Topol, E.J.: High-performance medicine: the convergence of human and artificial intelligence. Nat. Med. **25**, 44–56 (2019)
6. Rahim, S.S., Palade, V., Almakky, I., Holzinger, A.: Detection of diabetic retinopathy and maculopathy in eye fundus images using deep learning and image augmentation. In: Holzinger, A., Kieseberg, P., Tjoa, A.M., Weippl, E. (eds.) CD-MAKE 2019. LNCS, vol. 11713, pp. 114–127. Springer, Cham (2019). https://doi.org/10.1007/978-3-030-29726-8_8
7. Holzinger, A., Kickmeier-Rust, M., Müller, H.: KANDINSKY patterns as IQ-test for machine learning. In: Holzinger, A., Kieseberg, P., Tjoa, A.M., Weippl, E. (eds.) CD-MAKE 2019. LNCS, vol. 11713, pp. 1–14. Springer, Cham (2019). https://doi.org/10.1007/978-3-030-297 26-8_1
8. Holzinger, A., et al.: Interactive machine learning: experimental evidence for the human in the algorithmic loop. Appl. Intell. **49**(7), 2401–2414 (2019). https://doi.org/10.1007/s10489-018-1361-5
9. Holzinger, A., Langs, G., Denk, H., Zatloukal, K., Mueller, H.: Causability and explainability of artificial intelligence in medicine. Wiley Interdisc. Rev. Data Min. Knowl. Discov. **9**(4) (2019), https://doi.org/10.1002/widm.1312
10. Gallant, S.I.: Connectionist expert systems. Commun. ACM **31**, 152–169 (1988)
11. Hayashi, Y.: A neural expert system with automated extraction of fuzzy *if–then* rules and its application to medical diagnosis. In: Lippmann, R.P., Moody, J.E., Touretzky, D.S. (eds.) Advances in Neural Information Processing Systems, vol. 3, pp. 578–584. Morgan Kaufmann, Los Altos (1991)
12. Andrews, R., Diederich, J., Tickele, A.: Survey and critiques of techniques for extracting rules from trained artificial neural networks. Knowl. Based Syst. **8**, 373–389 (1995)
13. Setiono, R., Baesens, B., Mues, C.: Recursive neural network rule extraction for data with mixed attributes. IEEE Trans. Neural Networks **19**(2008), 299–307 (2008)
14. Hayashi, Y., Yukita, S.: Rule extraction using recursive-rule extraction algorithm with J48graft with sampling selection techniques for the diagnosis of type 2 diabetes mellitus in the Pima Indian Dataset. Inf. Med. Unlocked **2**, 92–104 (2016)
15. Fortuny, E.J.D., Martens, D.: Active learning-based pedagogical rule extraction. IEEE Trans. Neural Networks Learn. Syst. **26**, 2664–2677 (2015)
16. Hayashi, Y., Oisi, T.: High accuracy-priority rule extraction for reconciling accuracy an interpretability in credit scoring. New Gener. Comput. **36**(4), 393–418 (2018). https://doi.org/10.1007/s00354-018-0043-5
17. Uehara, D., et al.: The non-invasive prediction steatohepatitis in Japanese patients with morbid obesity by artificial intelligence using rule extraction technology. World J. Hepatol. **10**(12), 934–943 (2018). https://doi.org/10.4254/wjh.v10.i12.934

18. Hayashi, Y., Nakajima, K., Nakajima, K.: A rule extraction approach to explore the upper limit of hemoglobin during anemia treatment in patients with predialysis chronic kidney disease. Inf. Med. Unlocked **17**, 100262 (2019)

19. Hayashi, Y.: Detection of lower albuminuria levels and early development of diabetic kidney disease using an artificial intelligence-based rule extraction approach. Diagnostics **9**, 133 (2019). https://doi.org/10.3390/diagnostics9040133

20. Hayashi, Y.: The right direction needed to develop white-box deep learning in radiology, pathology, and ophthalmology: a short review. Front. Robot. AI **2019**(6), 24 (2019)

21. Abels, E., Pantanowitz, L., Aeffner, F., et al.: Computational pathology definitions, best practices, and recommendations for regulatory guidance: a white paper from the Digital Pathology Association. J Pathol. **249**, 286–294 (2019)

22. Aresta, G., et al.: BACH: grand challenge on breast cancer histology images. Med. Image Anal. **56**, 122–139 (2019)

23. Hayashi, Y.: Toward the transparency of deep learning in radiological imaging: beyond quantitative to qualitative artificial intelligence. J Med. Artif. Intell. **2**, 19 (2019). https://doi.org/10.21037/jmai.2019.09.06

24. Golden, J.A.: Deep learning algorithms for detection of lymph node metastases from breast cancer helping artificial intelligence be seen. JAMA **318**(22), 2184–2186 (2017). https://doi.org/10.1001/jama.2017.14580

25. Litjens, G., et al.: Deep learning as a tool for increased accuracy and efficiency of histopathological diagnosis. Sci. Rep. **6**, 26286 (2016). https://doi.org/10.1038/srep26286

26. Liu, Y., et al.: Artificial intelligence-based breast cancer nodal metastasis detection insights: into the black box for pathologists. Arch. Pathol. Lab. Med. (2018). https://doi.org/10.5858/arpa.2018-0147-OA

27. Gecer, B., et al.: Detection and classification of cancer in whole slide breast histopathology images using deep convolutional networks. Pattern Recogn. **84**, 345–356 (2018)

28. Rudin, C.: Stop explaining black box machine learning models for high stakes decisions and use interpretable models instead. Nat. Mach. Intell. **1**, 206–215 (2019)

29. Campanella, G., et al.: Clinical-grade computational pathology using weakly supervised deep learning on whole slide images. Nat. Med. **25**, 1301–1309 (2019)

30. Hayashi, Y.: Use of a deep belief network for small high-level abstraction data sets using artificial intelligence with rule extraction. Neural Comput. **30**(12), 3309–3332 (2018)

31. Hayashi, Y.: Synergy effects between the grafting and the subdivision in the Re-RX with J48graft for the diagnosis of thyroid disease. Knowl. Based Syst. **131**, 170–182 (2017)

Towards a Better Understanding of the Workflows: Modeling Pathology Processes in View of Future AI Integration

Michaela Kargl[1]([⊠]), Peter Regitnig[2], Heimo Müller[1,2], and Andreas Holzinger[1]

[1] Institute for Medical Informatics, Statistics and Documentation, Medical University Graz, Auenbruggerplatz 2/V, 8036 Graz, Austria
`kargl-schrammel@student.tugraz.at`
[2] Diagnostic and Research Institute of Pathology, Medical University Graz, Neue Stiftingtalstraße 6, 8036 Graz, Austria

Abstract. A profound understanding of the pathology processes is an essential precondition for successful introduction of changes and innovations, such as for example AI and Machine Learning, into pathology. Process modeling helps to build up such a profound understanding of the pathology processes among all relevant stakeholders. This paper describes the state of the art in modeling pathology processes and shows on an example how to create a reusable multipurpose process model for the diagnostic pathology process.

Keywords: Process modeling · Pathology process · Reusable model

1 Introduction and Motivation

Pathology departments are regarded to be rather complex systems, as procedures and workflows in pathology are quite complex and interconnected [18,41]. Many interacting organisational entities as well as people with different professional backgrounds are involved in the diagnostic pathology process [10,18], which is, besides education and research, the main business process in pathology departments [40].

As known from Systems Theory and Systems Engineering, introducing a change to an element in a complex system of interrelated entities can cause (unintended) effects in other parts of the system. Therefore, when introducing changes to an element within a complex system, it is not sufficient to look only at the respective element or part of the system. Moreover, it is essential to apply a system-view and take into account the interrelations and interdependence between the system's elements [9].

This holds true also for the complex system of a pathology department: for successful introduction of innovations, such as for example AI and Machine Learning, into pathology, it is essential to apply a system-view and take into

© Springer Nature Switzerland AG 2020
A. Holzinger et al. (Eds.): AI & ML for Digital Pathology, LNAI 12090, pp. 102–117, 2020.
https://doi.org/10.1007/978-3-030-50402-1_7

account the interrelations and dependencies of the various elements in the pathology system. However, for that, a good understanding of the pathology system is needed. A clear description of the pathology processes in a way that is comprehensible to people with different professional backgrounds, such as medical, office, management and technical staff, is therefore inevitable for any endeavour to introduce optimisation or innovation actions in a pathology department [40].

2   Glossary

Business Process. A business process is a sequence of related tasks (done by people or machines) within an organisation, which produces a specific product or service.

Business Process Modeling is the activity of describing a business process within an organisation in a structured way, so that it can be understood, improved, simulated or automated.

BPMN. Business Process Model and Notation™ (BPMN™) is a graphical modeling language for business processes developed by the Object Management Group (OMG).

Pathology Process. In this paper the term pathology process is used for any business process occurring within a pathology department.

Diagnostic Pathology Process. The diagnostic pathology process describes the business process for developing a pathology diagnosis, from the reception of a case (specimens) at the pathology department to the submission of the respective final pathology report.

Requisite Model. A requisite model is a process model that includes just the right amount of detail that is necessary to solve a specific problem.

Multipurpose Model. A multipurpose model is a generic process model that can be used to develop requisite models of (parts of) that process for different purposes.

3   State-of-the-Art

Process modeling is the state-of-the-art concept for describing technical as well as organisational processes in a standardised, clear, unambiguous and structured way.

3.1   Stakeholder Involvement in Process Modeling

Process modeling is a highly interactive and participatory endeavour, as both knowledge and expertise in modeling as well as the domain knowledge and experience of people familiar with the daily working routines and practical framework conditions of the respective process are needed. In the highly interdisciplinary medical domain the group of relevant practical experts that must be involved in the development of a process model comprises of representatives of the medical, laboratory, technical and administrative staff of all involved departments and units.

Different approaches and methods for the involvement of the practical experts can be applied. The process model could be developed in a fully participatory workshop setting together with all relevant stakeholders [34]. However, in the medical domain this approach is rarely applied in practice, as it is in most cases not feasible to bring together all relevant experts for a series of workshops that last several hours.

Therefore, in practice usually an iterative approach for the development of process models is applied: In a first step, the modeling experts obtain insights of the respective practical processes through interviews and focus-groups with the domain experts or through a contextual inquiry [10,14], a method originally developed for contextual design [3,11]. In a contextual inquiry the modeling expert watches the people working on their tasks, routines and procedures directly on-site at their workplace. A contextual inquiry is especially beneficial for understanding complex processes, as for example in pathology departments, since it helps to reveal important aspects that cannot be obtained through interviews. In a contextual inquiry the modeling expert can directly observe the specific constraints and practical framework conditions at the workplaces, and learn about workarounds applied in practice. Furthermore, in a contextual inquiry the modeling expert may observe also small aspects of routine work that people often do unconsciously and would therefore not tell in an interview setting apart from the workplace context [3].

In the next step, the modeling experts use the information obtained from interviews, focus-groups and contextual inquiry to create a first process model. This first model is further elaborated and refined by seeking the domain experts' feedback regularly throughout the iterative modeling process.

3.2   Process Modeling Language

There are two main types of process modeling languages: modeling languages based on rule specifications and graphical modeling languages [19]. Rule-based modeling languages require a good understanding of the syntax of logical expressions, while graph-based languages are more intuitive, even for people with little technical background [19]. Therefore, for business process modeling the graphical modeling language BPMN^{TM} (Business Process Model & Notation^{TM}) is widely used. Moreover, the modeling language BPMN, developed by the Object

Management Group (OMG) has become a de-facto industry standard for modeling processes [25]. In 2013 BPMN 2.0.1 has been published by the International Organization for Standardization (ISO) as standard ISO/IEC 19510:2013 [15].

BPMN is a graphical modeling language designed for creating flowchart-like, easy to understand process maps. In addition, since BPMN version 2.0, which was released in 2011, BPMN includes a native XML serialization [24]. Thus, a BPMN process model is not only a standardised graphical depiction of a process, which is easily comprehensible by humans, but it is also machine-readable and can be used as basis for process simulation and process automation.

There are many software tools available that support the creation of BPMN business process models. Currently, more than 85 tools are listed on the OMG's BPMN website [26]. Among these tools are commercial software tools, free software tools, and community-driven open source software tools. However, not all of these tools create valid BPMN 2.0 XML serialisations. Therefore, it is recommended to use a tool that is tested by the BPMN Model Interchange Working Group (BPMN MIWG) [27], since those tools can not only draw BPMN diagrams but also export/import BPMN 2.0 compliant XML serialisations, so that the created BPMN models are not only graphical depictions of the modeled process, but can subsequently also be used for simulation and process automation or optimisation tasks.

BPMN 2.0 includes several categories of graphical elements to build diagrams: *Flow Objects* (events, activities, gateways) represent actions that happen in the process, *Connecting Objects* (Sequence Flows, Message Flows, Associations) connect objects with each other, *Swimlanes* (Pools, Lanes) are used to group elements, *Data* (Data Object, Data Stores, Collections, Messages) provide renderings for Data Input and Data Output, and *Artifacts* (Group, Text Annotation) provide additional information that does not affect the sequence or message flows of the process [6,24]. Figure 1 shows some of the basic graphical elements of BPMN version 2.0.

BPMN is often used for modeling processes in the medical domain, since BPMN process graphs are easily understandable by people with different professional and educational backgrounds, such as medical, administrative, technical and laboratory staff [7,38]. Thus, in the highly interdisciplinary field of medicine and healthcare, BPMN facilitates the involvement of all relevant stakeholders into the development of process models. Already in 2008, Rojo et al. [37] have shown that BPMN is suitable for modeling pathology processes.

However, although BPMN is in principle suitable for modeling processes in the medical domain, in many cases the standard features and elements included in basic BPMN are not sufficient for modeling details in complex medical/healthcare processes. Fortunately, the BPMN 2.0 specification provides a defined mechanism for extension of BPMN. In recent years, various extensions for BPMN have been elaborated. Examples for extensions related to processes in the medical/healthcare domain include: BPMN extension for annotation of hospital protocols [36], BPMN extension to support discrete-event simulation for healthcare applications including an explicit representation of queues, attributes

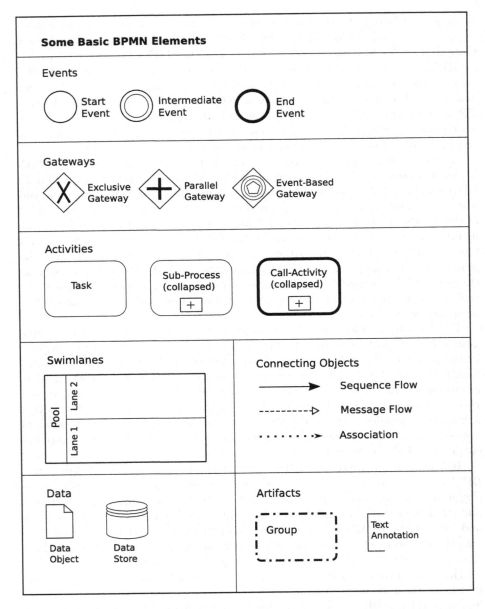

Fig. 1. Some basic graphical elements from the standard version of BPMN 2.0.

and data-driven decision points [28], BPMN extension for batch processing [35], BPMN extension for modeling clinical pathways [4], BPMN security extension for healthcare processes [39], and time-aware BPMN [33].

3.3   Provenance Management

Biobanks collect, preserve, and provide access to samples, e.g. from pathology in
a transparent and quality controlled manner in compliance with ethical, legal,
and regulatory requirements for research, They require access to sufficient numbers of samples and data that properly cover the broad spectrum of disease
sub-entities relevant for targeted therapies [23]. To address this demand, samples and data from different biobanks in different countries must be suitable
for integrated analyses. This is only possible if samples and data meet common
quality criteria. Therefore, international standards (e.g. CEN Technical Specifications or ISO Standards) were implemented for sample pre-analytics, covering
all steps from sample collection from the patient to isolation of bio molecules
[22], and (open-source) software for cataloging and provenance management was
developed, e.g. for rare diseases [8] and for biobanks in low and medium income
countries [2,17].

Provenance information can be seen as the actual documentation of a process
describing the whole workflow from collection, generation, processing and analysis of the biological material to data analysis and statistics. Important parts
of the pre-analytical workflow, as the gross evaluation, sample preparation and
documentation are part of the pathology workflow and generate important information to be stored in biobank information systems. ISO TC 276/WG 5 just
started efforts to standardize the documentation of the whole workflow from
collection, generation, processing and analysis of the biological material to data
analysis and statistics based on existing provenance standards as OPM1 or W3C
PROV2. The main driver behind this is the increasing adoption of data-intensive
technologies, such as next-generation sequencing, high-throughput mass spec-
trometry as used for proteomics or metabolomics, high-throughput microscopy
in digital pathology, and their impact on data collection strategies [21].

3.4   Multipurpose Process Models

In a pathology department, business process models may be used for a range
of very different purposes, such as process analysis for improving the current
workflow, integration of new components or new methods into the workflow,
quality management, communication among different units of the department,
communication with external (non-domain) experts, as well as education and
training [40].

Unfortunately, in process modeling there is no one-fits-all approach: it is not
possible to create a generic model that is suitable for all these different purposes.
However, as BPMN supports to model a process with different levels of detail,
multipurpose models can be developed, which are reusable and can be adapted
to different use cases and situations in a pathology department. Adaptation of
such reusable models to a specific use case is done by modeling relevant parts
of the process in more detail, adding tasks where necessary and sticking to
a more coarse modeling level, wherever this is sufficient, in order to keep the
complexity of the model at a minimum. The main goal is to come up with a

requisite model, this is a model whose form and content are sufficient to solve a particular problem. Such a requisite model is constructed through an interactive process between those, who define the purpose of the model (i.e. the problem to be solved), the domain specialists, and the modeling specialists [29, 30].

Example: Creation of a Multipurpose Process Model for a Diagnostic Pathology Process. In the following paragraphs of this chapter, the creation of reusable BPMN process models of the diagnostic pathology process at an Austrian hospital is described as an example. In this hospital, six organisational units are involved in the diagnostic pathology process, namely the sample-reception unit, the macro-pathology unit, the histology laboratory, the immunohistochemistry laboratory, histopathologists, and the secretary. In BPMN process diagrams these actors are modeled with so-called lanes, and all activities assigned to a specific actor are placed in the respective lane. As a preparatory step for modeling the process, a contextual inquiry was conducted in all organisational units along the whole process in order to gain insights to the diagnostic pathology process: all activities along the process were observed on-site and complementary questions for clarification were addressed to the involved people directly at their workplace.

For the business process modeling work described in this example, the software tool CAMUNDA Modeler [5] was used. This tool was chosen, because it supports BPMN 2.0, can be used for free, and is open source software written in Java, which makes it possible to develop and add BPMN 2.0 extensions, if needed.

First Step: Creation of a High-Level Model of the Process. In a first step, a high-level model of the diagnostic pathology process was developed. This model should be as simple as possible, and depict only high-ranking tasks without going into details. Figure 2 shows the high-level BPMN model of the diagnostic pathology process, with one lane for each of the actors, which are the six organisational units mentioned above. In the following paragraphs, this high-level model is called "level-1 model". From Fig. 3, which provides a closer look at a section of the "level-1 model" diagram, it can be seen that this high-level model is rather coarse-grained: The process is shown as a sequence of comprehensive higher-order tasks, such as for example "receive specimen", "gross specimen", "process tissue" etc. No further details of these activities are modeled in the "level-1" process diagram.

However, in addition to the sequence flows among the high-level tasks, also the associations with the pathology laboratory-information-system (which is called "PAS" in this hospital) are depicted in the "level-1 model", as these connections of the process with the pathology laboratory-information-system mark quite important points in the diagnostic pathology process, which will be helpful for model verification at a later stage of the process modeling procedure.

At the end of this first modeling step, the "level-1 model" was validated in a feedback-round with the people working within that diagnostic pathology process in practice.

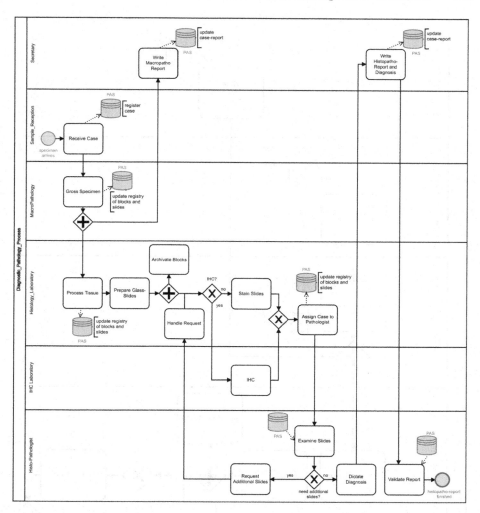

Fig. 2. In a first step, a high-level model ("level-1 model") of the diagnostic pathology process is developed.

Second Step: Modeling Complex Tasks as Separate Processes. In the second step, the higher-order tasks included in the "level-1 model" were further detailed and modeled as separate processes. In the following these models are called "level-2 models". When developing "level-2 models", it must be kept in mind that also these models should be as simple as possible. Any complex tasks in these processes should be depicted as a single task in the "level-2 model", and subsequently modeled as a separate process in a "level-3 model".

As an example, this procedure is explained for the task "Receive Case", which is the first task in the "level-1 model" shown in Fig. 2 and Fig. 3.

110   M. Kargl et al.

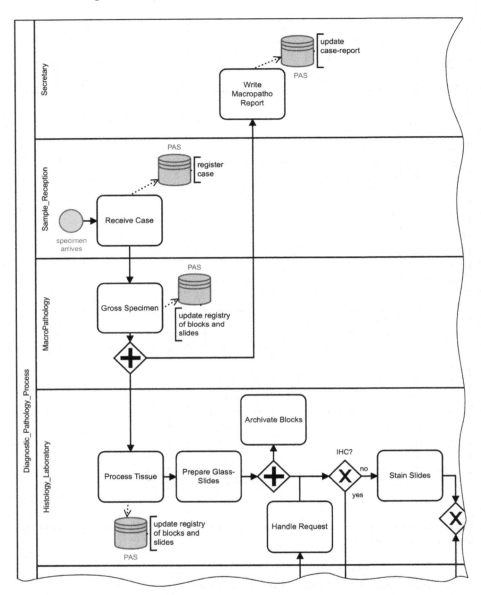

Fig. 3. In the "level-1 model" the process is broken down into high-ranking, comprehensive tasks, which are not modeled in detail.

As can be seen in Fig. 4, in the "level-2 model" for this task, the respective process "Receive Case" is broken down into two tasks: the task "Handle Case Reception" and the subsequent task of transporting the specimen to the macro-pathology unit. However, this transport task is quite special: rather than transporting each specimen individually to the macro-pathology unit, the staff waits until there is a tray full of specimens ready for transport - the specimens are transported in batches. This is an example for a special concept that is not integrated in the basic BPMN 2.0 specification. Therefore, to model this task, an extension for BPMN 2.0 must be developed. Fortunately, research revealed that such an extension of BPMN 2.0 for batch activities had been developed and published at the University of Potsdam recently [35]. That extension was used for modeling the task "Batch Transport to MacroPatho" shown in Fig. 4. Since the values assigned to the properties of the batch task in the BPMN model constitute important information for the model validation, but are encoded to the model only in machine readable format, a text annotation describing these values was added to the process diagram to make these properties visible for humans and facilitate model validation by the staff working on these tasks in practice.

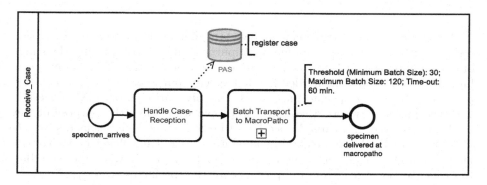

Fig. 4. The "level-2 model" of the high-level task "Receive Case".

Next, a "level-3 model" for the task "Handle Case Reception" was elaborated to model that task in more detail. As can be seen in Fig. 5 the respective process model "Handle Case Reception" is already quite fine-grained and shows for example also the distribution of the tasks between the secretary and the Biomedical Analyst (BMA) working in that unit. In further modeling levels, each of the tasks included in this process can be modeled in more detail and broken down into smaller tasks, as needed.

This procedure of further refining the modeling details level-by-level is repeated until a sufficient grade of model detail is reached, whereby each modeling level should be validated with the staff working at these activities in practice.

Third Step: Composing Requisite Process Models. The result of the modeling work in the previous steps, is a set of related process models in various levels, whereby a task "XY" in a "level-n model" is further refined by a process "XY" in the "level-(n+1) model". This set of related process models in various levels constitutes a re-usable, multipurpose model for the diagnostic pathology process.

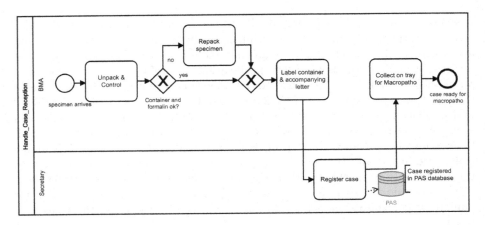

Fig. 5. The "level-3 model" of the task "Handle Case Reception".

For any purpose, a tailor-made model of the diagnostic pathology process can be derived based on this re-usable, multipurpose model. By utilising the chain of refined process models for the respective tasks, each section of the process can be modeled as detailed as needed for that specific purpose. Creating a requisite process model for a specific purpose is a highly participatory task: together with the problem owners, these are the people who define the purpose of the modeling endeavour, a careful selection of black box modeling elements, which will not be modeled in more detail, and white box modeling elements, which will be elaborated in detail, must be made to avoid complexity where possible but to explicitly model features of importance for the specific use case [1].

Technically, the refinement of the model for a specific task is done by transforming the respective Task element in the BPMN model into a Call Activity element linked to the respective refined process model of that task. This is shown for the example of the task "Receive Case" in Fig. 6.

4   Open Problems

As shown in this paper, in principle BPMN is suitable for modeling pathology processes. However, some features of pathology processes, such as for example batch processing, cannot be modeled with the elements included in basic BPMN 2.0. To overcome this problem, extensions for BPMN can be created. Since 2011, when BPMN 2.0 was released, numerous extensions for BPMN have been developed and published, whereby many of those BPMN extensions could also be relevant for process modeling in the medical domain.

However, two issues with BPMN extensions can be denoted: First, it is difficult to get an overview of available BPMN extensions, since there is no central repository or platform for BPMN extensions. This problem has already been described in a Bachelor thesis at the University of Stuttgart in 2016, and at that

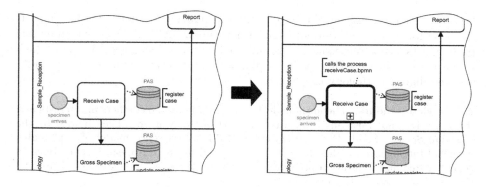

Fig. 6. For refining the BPMN model of the task "Receive Case", the *Task* element (shown in the left section) is transformed into a *Call Activity* element (shown in the right section), which is linked to the respective process model constituting a more detailed modeling-level of the task.

time, almost 40 BPMN extensions could be found in scientific publications [16]. The number of existing BPMN extensions has certainly increased since. Thus, although many of the existing BPMN extensions are open source and could probably be quite useful for pathology process modeling, it is rather difficult to find these existing solutions, and the probability is high to end up 're-inventing the wheel'. The other issue is, that process models relying on non-standard solutions, such as self-developed BPMN extensions, require also special solutions when it comes to process simulation or automation. For these models it is not possible to use existing simulation software out of the box.

5   Future Outlook

Based on the current developed model it should be possible to improve the diagnostic pathology workflow process towards a lean system. In a first pilot phase we could already describe peaks within a working day and follow the further processing of specimens until sign-out. The goal of every pathology laboratory is to report results to clinicians and patients as fast as possible. Therefore, pathology-lab workflows were developed over many decades and with experience, however, neither in a statistical nor mechanistic model. Workflow optimization with such a model will help to develop a nearly continuous workflow without accumulation of specimens at certain processing steps. Implementing whole slide scanning of tissue slides and implementing AI algorithms for morphological evaluation or quantification of tissue sections will introduce further work steps within an already complex and interacting system. Thus, a model will also be necessary, at least it will be of advantage, to see how changing one or multiple elements in that complex system of interrelated work-processes can cause (un-)intended effects in other parts of the system. For future AI supported workflows in digital pathology we need a clear understanding of how pathologists make diagnoses

[31], and also a good insight into possible visualization methods [32]. This is essential for design and development of new human-AI interfaces, which enable pathologists to ask questions [12,13] interactively via dialog systems [20], which would help to increase the quality of diagnoses and is the ultimate goal of an AI assisted digital pathology pipeline.

Acknowledgements. The authors declare that there are no conflicts of interests and the work does not raise any ethical issues. Part of this work has been funded by the Austrian Science Fund (FWF), Project: P-32554 "A reference model of explainable Artificial Intelligence for the Medical Domain", and by the European Union's Horizon 2020 research and innovation programme under grant agreements No 824087 "EOSC-Life" and No 826078 "Feature Cloud".

References

1. Bedford, T.: Requisite reliability modelling in complex engineered systems. In: 11th International Conference on Mathematical Methods in Reliability MMR 2019, Hong Kong (2019)
2. Bendou, B., et al.: Baobab laboratory information management system: development of an open-source laboratory information management system for biobanking. Biopreserv. Biobank. **15**(2), 116–120 (2017)
3. Beyer, H., Holtzblatt, K.: Contextual Design: Defining Customer-Centered Systems. Morgan Kaufmann Publishers Inc., San Francisco (1997)
4. Braun, R., Schlieter, H., Burwitz, M., Esswein, W.: BPMN4CP revised - extending BPMN for multi-perspective modeling of clinical pathways. In: 2016 49th Hawaii International Conference on System Sciences (HICSS), pp. 3249–3258. IEEE (2016). https://doi.org/10.1109/HICSS.2016.407
5. Camunda Services GmbH, Berlin: Camunda Modeler - The developer-friendly desktop app for editing BPMN process diagrams and DMN Decision Tables (2018). https://camunda.com/de/products/modeler/. Accessed 24 Nov 2019
6. Chinosi, M., Trombetta, A.: BPMN: an introduction to the standard. Comput. Stand. Inter. **34**, 124–134 (2012). https://doi.org/10.1016/j.csi.2011.06.002
7. De Ramon Fernandez, A., Ruiz Fernandez, D., Sabuco Garcia, Y.: Business process management for optimizing clinical processes: a systematic literature review. Health Inform. J. (2019). https://doi.org/10.1177/1460458219877092. Accessed 24 Nov 2019. OnlineFirst
8. Gainotti, S., et al.: The RD-connect registry & biobank finder: a tool for sharing aggregated data and metadata among rare disease researchers. Eur. J. Hum. Genet. **26**(5), 631–643 (2018)
9. Haberfellner, R., de Weck, O., Fricke, E., Vössner, S.: Systems Engineering - Grundlagen und Anwendung. Orell Füssli, Zürich, 13. aktualisierte auflage 2015 edn. (2015)
10. Ho, J., Aridor, O., Parwani, A.V.: Use of contextual inquiry to understand anatomic pathology workflow: implications for digital pathology adoption. J. Pathol. Inform. **3**(35) (2012). https://doi.org/10.4103/2153-3539.101794
11. Holtzblatt, K., Beyer, H.: Contextual design: evolved. In: Carroll, J.M. (ed.) Synthesis Lectures on Human-Centered Informatics. Morgan & Claypool, San Rafael (2014). https://doi.org/10.2200/S00597ED1V01Y201409HCI024. Accessed 13 Nov 2019

12. Holzinger, A., Carrington, A., Müller, H.: Measuring the quality of explanations: the system causability scale (SCS). KI - Künstliche Intelligenz, 1–6 (2020). https://doi.org/10.1007/s13218-020-00636-z

13. Holzinger, A., Langs, G., Denk, H., Zatloukal, K., Müller, H.: Causability and explainability of artificial intelligence in medicine. Wiley Interdisc. Rev. Data Min. Knowl. Discov. 9(4) (2019). https://doi.org/10.1002/widm.1312

14. Holzinger, A., et al.: Machine learning and knowledge extraction in digital pathology needs an integrative approach. In: Holzinger, A., Goebel, R., Ferri, M., Palade, V. (eds.) Towards Integrative Machine Learning and Knowledge Extraction. LNCS (LNAI), vol. 10344, pp. 13–50. Springer, Cham (2017). https://doi.org/10.1007/978-3-319-69775-8_2

15. International Organisation for Standardization ISO: ISO/IEC 19510:2013 Information technology - Object Management Group Business Process Model (2013). https://www.iso.org/standard/62652.html. Accessed 13 Nov 2019

16. Karner, P.: Analyse verschiedener BPMN Extensions. OPUS Online Publikationen der Universität Stuttgart (2016). http://dx.doi.org/10.18419/opus-9866. Accessed 16 Nov 2019

17. Klingstrom, T., et al.: Supporting the development of biobanks in low and medium income countries. In: 2016 IST-Africa Week Conference. IEEE, May 2016. http://dx.doi.org/10.1109/istafrica.2016.7530672, https://doi.org/10.1109/istafrica.2016.7530672

18. Lester, S.C.: Manual of Surgical Pathology, 3rd edn. Elsevier Inc., Saunders, Philadelphia (2010). https://doi.org/10.1016/C2009-0-38878-9

19. Lu, R., Sadiq, S.: A survey of comparative business process modeling approaches. In: Abramowicz, W. (ed.) BIS 2007. LNCS, vol. 4439, pp. 82–94. Springer, Heidelberg (2007). https://doi.org/10.1007/978-3-540-72035-5_7

20. Merdivan, E., Singh, D., Hanke, S., Holzinger, A.: Dialogue systems for intelligent human computer interactions. Electron. Notes Theor. Comput. Sci. **343**, 57–71 (2019). https://doi.org/10.1016/j.entcs.2019.04.010

21. Müller, H., Dagher, G., Loibner, M., Stumptner, C., Kungl, P., Zatloukal, K.: Biobanks for life sciences and personalized medicine: importance of standardization, biosafety, biosecurity, and data management. Curr. Opin. Biotechnol. **65**, 45–51 (2020)

22. Müller, H., et al.: From the evaluation of existing solutions to an all-inclusive package for biobanks. Health Technol. **7**(1), 89–95 (2017). https://doi.org/10.1007/s12553-016-0175-x

23. Müller, H., et al.: State-of-the-art and future challenges in the integration of biobank catalogues. In: Holzinger, A., Röcker, C., Ziefle, M. (eds.) Smart Health. LNCS, vol. 8700, pp. 261–273. Springer, Cham (2015). https://doi.org/10.1007/978-3-319-16226-3_11

24. Object Management Group OMG: About the Business Process Model and Notation Specification Version 2.0.2 (2014). https://www.omg.org/spec/BPMN/. Accessed 13 Nov 2019

25. Object Management Group OMG: Business Process Model & Notation (BPMN) (2019). https://www.omg.org/bpmn/. Accessed 13 Nov 2019

26. Object Management Group OMG: Object Management Group - Business Process Model and Notation (2019). http://www.bpmn.org/. Accessed 24 Nov 2019

27. Object Management Group (OMG) Model Interchange Working Group: BPMN Tools tested for Model Interchange (2019). https://bpmn-miwg.github.io/bpmn-miwg-tools/. Accessed 24 Nov 2019

28. Onggo, B.S., Proudlove, N., D'Ambrogio, A., Calabrese, A., Bisogno, S., Ghiron, N.L.: A BPMN extension to support discrete-event simulation for healthcare applications: an explicit representation of queues, attributes and data-driven decision points. J. Oper. Res. Soc. **69**, 788–802 (2017). https://doi.org/10.1057/s41274-017-0267-7

29. Phillips, L.D.: A theory of requisite decision models. Acta Psychol. **56**, 29–48 (1984). https://doi.org/10.1016/0001-6918(84)90005-2

30. Phillips, L.D.: Requisite decision modelling for technological projects. In: Vlek, C., Cvetkovich, G. (eds.) Social Decision Methodology for Technological Projects. Theory and Decision Library. Series A: Philosophy and Methodology of the Social Sciences, vol. 9, pp. 95–110. Kluwer Academic Publishers, Dordrecht (1989). https://doi.org/10.1007/978-94-009-2425-3-6

31. Pohn, B., Kargl, M., Reihs, R., Holzinger, A., Zatloukal, K., Müller, H.: Towards a deeper understanding of how a pathologist makes a diagnosis: visualization of the diagnostic process in histopathology. In: IEEE Symposium on Computers and Communications (ISCC 2019). IEEE (2019). http://dx.doi.org/10.1109/ISCC47284.2019.8969598

32. Pohn, B., Mayer, M.C., Reihs, R., Holzinger, A., Zatloukal, K., Müller, H.: Visualization of histopathological decision making using a roadbook metaphor. In: 23rd International Conference Information Visualisation (IV). IEEE (2019). http://dx.doi.org/10.1109/IV.2019.00073

33. Posenato, R., Zerbato, F., Combi, C.: Managing decision tasks and events in time-aware business process models. In: Weske, M., Montali, M., Weber, I., vom Brocke, J. (eds.) BPM 2018. LNCS, vol. 11080, pp. 102–118. Springer, Cham (2018). https://doi.org/10.1007/978-3-319-98648-7_7

34. Proudlove, N.C., Bisogno, S., Onggo, B., Calabrese, A., Levialdi Ghiron, N.: Towards fully-facilitated discrete event simulation modeling: addressing the model coding stage. Eur. J. Oper. Res. **263**, 583–595 (2017). https://doi.org/10.1016/j.ejor.2017.06.002

35. Pufahl, L.: Modeling and executing batch activities in business processes. Ph.D. thesis, Digital-Engineering-Fakultät of Hasso-Plattner-Institute and University Potsdam (2017)

36. Ramos-Merino, M., Álvarez-Sabucedo, L.M., Santos-Gago, J.M., Sanz-Valero, J.: A BPMN based notation for the representation of workflows in hospital protocols. J. Med. Syst. **42**(10), 181:1–181:10 (2018). https://doi.org/10.1007/s10916-018-1034-2

37. Rojo, M.G., et al.: Implementation of the Business Process Modeling Notation (BPMN) in the modeling of anatomic pathology processes. In: New trends in digital pathology: Proceedings of the 9th European Congress on Telepathology and 3rd International Congress on Virtual Microscopy, vol. 3, Supplement 1, S22. BioMed Central (2008). http://dx.doi.org/10.1186/1746-1596-3-S1-S22

38. Ruiz, F., et al.: Business process modeling in healthcare. In: Garcia-Rojo, M., Blobel, B., Laurinavicius, A. (eds.) Perspectives on Digital Pathology - Results of the COST Action IC0604 EURO-TELEPATH, pp. 75–87. IOS Press, Amsterdam (2012). https://doi.org/10.3233/978-1-61499-086-4-88

39. Sang, K.S., Zhou, B.: BPMN security extensions for healthcare process. In: 2015 IEEE International Conference on Computer and Information Technology; Ubiquitous Computing and Communications; Dependable, Autonomic and Secure Computing; Pervasive Intelligence and Computing Proceedings, pp. 2340–2345. IEEE (2015). http://dx.doi.org/10.1109/HICSS.2016.407

40. Schrader, T., Blobel, B., Garcia-Rojo, M., Daniel, C., Slodkowska, J.: State of the art in pathology business process analysis, modeling, design and optimization. In: Garcia-Rojo, M., Blobel, B., Laurinavicius, A. (eds.) Perspectives on Digital Pathology - Results of the COST Action IC0604 EURO-TELEPATH, pp. 88–102. IOS Press, Amsterdam (2012). https://doi.org/10.3233/978-1-61499-086-4-88

41. Slaoui, M., Fiette, L.: Histopathology procedures: from tissue sampling to histopathological evaluation. In: Gautier, J.C. (ed.) Drug Safety Evaluation. Methods in Molecular Biology (Methods and Protocols), vol. 691, pp. 69–82. Humana Press, New York (2011). https://doi.org/10.1007/978-1-60761-849-2_4

OBDEX – Open Block Data Exchange System

Björn Lindequist[1,2(✉)], Norman Zerbe[2,3], and Peter Hufnagl[1,2,3]

[1] Center for Biomedical Image and Information Processing (CBMI), HTW University for Applied Sciences Berlin, Berlin, Germany
[2] Institute for Pathology, Charité Universitätsmedizin Berlin, Berlin, Germany
{bjoern.lindequist,peter.hufnagl}@charite.de
[3] ZeBanC - Central Biomaterial Bank Charité, Berlin, Germany

Abstract. Biobanks have become central structures for the provision of data. Raw data such as whole slide images (WSI) are stored in separate systems (PACS) or in biobank information systems. If segmentation or comparable information is to be exchanged in the context of the compilation of cases for the application of AI systems, the limits of proprietary systems are quickly reached. In order to provide these valuable (meta-) data for the description of biological tissue samples, WSI and analysis results, common standards for data exchange are required. Such standards are not currently available. Ongoing standardization developments, in particular the establishment of DICOM for digital pathology in the field of virtual microscopy, will help to provide some of the missing standards. DICOM alone, however, cannot close the gap due to some of the peculiarities of WSIs and corresponding analysis results. We propose a flexible, modular and expandable storage system - OBDEX (Open Block Data Exchange System), which allows the exchange of meta- and analysis data about tissue blocks, glass slides, WSI and analysis results. OBDEX is based on the FAIR data principles and uses only freely available protocols, standards and software libraries. This facilitates data exchange between institutions and working groups. It supports them in identifying suitable cases and samples for virtual studies and in exchanging relevant metadata. At the same time, OBDEX will offer the possibility to store deep learning models for exchange. A publication of source code, interface descriptions and documentation under a free software license is planned.

Keywords: Biobanking · Virtual microscopy · Digital pathology · FAIR data · DICOM · Annotation exchange for AI

The work presented here was funded by the Federal Ministry of Education and Research (BMBF) as part of the "BB-IT-Boost" research project.

A. Holzinger et al. (Eds.): AI & ML for Digital Pathology, LNAI 12090, pp. 118–135, 2020.
https://doi.org/10.1007/978-3-030-50402-1_8

1   Introduction and Motivation

In recent years application of artificial intelligence – especially deep learning – has made tremendous progress. In the developed world, almost everyone to some extent uses devices or services that use AI, such as photo apps on smartphones or shopping sites with product suggestions from previous purchases. The same technology is also used in many areas of ongoing medical research [1–5]. The possibilities are manifold and range from relatively simple tasks such as automated text indexing to more complex problems such as predicting the probability of the presence of tumors in MRI images.

Large training data sets are required for the successful training of neuronal networks. In many cases the creation of training data is only possible by a few experts. However, the compilation of larger data sets is also difficult for reasons such as data protection, data privacy or other legal reasons. If the data are collected in the current clinical context and continue to be used for the treatment of patients, the problems become even greater.

It is precisely at this interface that biobanks are increasingly prepared to make data available on a larger scale in pseudonymized or anonymized form. In the past, biobanks were mainly used for the storage of samples of different origins, but recently more and more sample-related data have come to the fore.

In this process the scope of biobanks has changed from being merely a diagnostic archive to a modern, research supporting core facility [6]. The use of whole slide images (WSI), which are managed in parallel to histological sections and blocks, offers several advantages [7]. For example, the suitability of cases for use in a study can be assessed directly on the monitor. It is not necessary to search for blocks or histological sections. Users of a biobank can search for cases independently and do not need the assistance of biobank staff if they have the right to view such cases for selection purposes. Using image analysis and pattern recognition techniques, the application examples can be extended from quality control at incoming material through quantification of biomarkers to virtual studies. Only the data from one or more biobanks are used and the analyses are performed on these data. For example, the correlation between two biomarkers and their significance for the assessment of the malignancy of a tumor could be achieved by a virtual combination of the corresponding data.

Therefore, the integration of virtual microscopy into biobank information systems has begun recently [8]. However, this integration is still limited. On the one hand, WSIs can be assigned to the respective physical slides and may be used for (remote) case selection, quality control or even viewing. On the other hand, analysis results based on image data can be stored as additional sample data using the data structures of the biobank systems, usually as key-value pairs, e.g. Ki-67 positivity. From the analysis of virtual slides, however, very high-quality data can be obtained, for example segmented cell nuclei, histoarchitectural structures (e.g. glands) or complex tissue models. An example for such high value analysis results is shown in Fig. 1. The image represents a heatmap overlay for Ki-67 positivity based on the cell nuclei classification for an entire WSI.

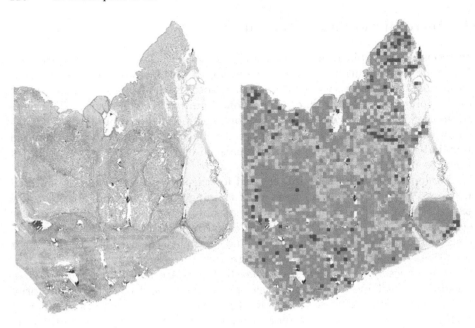

Fig. 1. Heatmap of Ki-67 positivity for breast cancer (red – high Ki-67 score, green – low Ki-67 score). (Color figure online)

A biobank could increase the value of WSIs by offering such additional data to their users or even to the scientific community. In the context of machine learning (especially deep learning) where huge sets of data are needed, biobanks would be able to provide highly valuable data for training and validation of new models.

An important question at this point is whether a biobank system should actively occupy the role of data storage for the image analysis results from WSIs, or whether it should interface with systems that are more suitable for such a task. In the first case, the development of common formats and standards, due to different and incompatible solutions of the individual providers of biobank information systems, is significantly more difficult. Such fragmentation impedes the exchange of data and complicates the collaboration of different institutions and research groups. In the second case, an obvious solution would be the DICOM standard (Digital Imaging and Communications in Medicine), already well established in many clinical disciplines especially in radiology. Unlike other types of medical image data, e.g. CT or MRI, the DICOM standard in digital pathology, especially for virtual slides and supplemental data, is not yet widely used. Decisive steps - the involvement of major industrial companies, manufacturers of slide scanners and distributors of PACS (picture archiving and communication system), or the waiver of royalties for patents - have significantly advanced the DICOM standard in terms of virtual microscopy in recent years [9–13].

The use of DICOM would offer a valid bridge between clinical infrastructure, biobank information system and researchers. Nevertheless, there are open questions and problems that still need to be addressed, e.g. the integration of DICOM into biobank systems, the adaptation of existing PACS to fully support WSIs or the filing of analysis results in DICOM in accordance with the standard. The last point is the subject of this paper.

2 Glossary and Key Terms

Biobank. A (core/key) facility that is responsible for storing bio samples at hospitals or research institutes, but also as an external service provider for smaller institutions. In recent years biobanks have become more important in research by providing samples and corresponding data (meta-data, data concerning the quality of samples, analytical data) to compile large collectives for e.g. clinical studies

Digital Pathology (DP). Digital pathology includes the acquisition, management, sharing and interpretation of pathology information - including slides and data - in a digital environment. Digital slides are created when glass slides are captured with a scanning device, to provide a high-resolution image that can be viewed on a computer screen or mobile device [Royal College of Pathologist].

Whole Slide Image (WSI, digital slide). A WSI is a digitized image of a tissue sample on a glass slide. They are digitized at a very high resolution (up to 100.000 dpi), have large dimensions (up to 1 Mio. pixel width and/or height) and are large in terms of storage space (up to several GBytes). The use of WSIs enables processing of image data of entire tissue samples and is in the focus of DP solutions.

Virtual Microscopy. An important component of workflows in digital pathology. Virtual Microscopy refers to the work with WSIs. This includes viewing, annotating POIs/ROIs, digital image processing and the ability to collaborate directly with colleagues around the world. In the context of AI-based applications, Virtual Microscopy plays an important role in the creation of learning, validation and test sample collections.

DICOM. Digital Imaging and Communications in Medicine (DICOM) is the standard for the communication and management of medical imaging information and related data [14]. DICOM was first presented in the 1980s (at that time under a different name) to enable the exchange of radiological images (mainly CT and MRI). After the first release more and more imaging modalities were incorporated (e.g. Ultrasound, endoscopy, microscopy). The main advantage of DICOM is that compatible devices and applications can communicate and exchange data without restriction.

Picture Archiving and Communication System (PACS). PACS is a medical imaging technology to provide storage and access to images needed in medical facilities. The storage and transfer format used in PACS is DICOM.

FAIR. FAIR data is a concept that describes data that meet certain conditions to facilitate the exchange of data and promote global cooperation [15]. The conditions for FAIR data are (a) findability (b) accessibility (c) interoperability and (d) reusability. In recent years, more and more researchers and institutions have endorsed the idea of FAIR data.

Representational state transfer (REST). REST is a software architecture used to create web services. Web services that are conform to the REST architecture provide uniform and stateless operations to access and manipulate resources.

Nginx. A free and open-source web server. Nginx supports many state-of-the-art web technologies and protocols, for example WSGI.

Web Server Gateway Interface (WSGI). WSGI is a calling convention to forward web requests to Python services, applications or frameworks. WSGI is used to establish a connection between web servers (e.g. Nginx) and components written in Python (e.g. a Flask web service).

FLASK. A lightweight micro web framework written in Python. Flask incorporates the REST architecture and is WSGI compliant. The main advantage of Flask is the ease of use, low system requirements, fast development and extensibility.

Relational Database Management System (RDBMS). A database management system based on the relational model to represent data as tuples, grouped into relations. A RDBMS can be queried in a declarative manner.

Object-relational mapping (ORM). ORM is a technique to convert data between incompatible type systems using object-oriented programming languages. A common use case for ORM is to map objects used in program code onto tables in a relational database. All access to or changes in the state of objects are automatically translated into commands understandable by the database.

3   State-Of-The-Art

The possibilities of machine learning in general and recent developments in artificial neural networks (especially convolutional neural networks – CNNs) are applied in more use cases every year. These applications of artificial intelligence (AI) to process huge amounts of data are the basis for many products and services presented in the last few years. For many medical disciplines, including pathology, AI-based applications have been the subject of extensive research in recent years. In the following section we will present and discuss some of the up-to-date AI-focused research in digital pathology. This overview is very limited, but gives a general impression of the current development.

3.1   Current Developments of AI in Digital Pathology

In line with the objective of OBDEX, we concentrate on AI-based applications for the processing of histological sections. AI is already successfully used for many technical approaches for the evaluation of histological sections, e.g. image analysis, 3D reconstruction, multi-spectral imaging and augmented reality [16]. It provides both commercial and open source tools to assist pathologists with specific tasks (e.g. quantifying biomarkers or registering consecutive slides). The authors of the cited survey come to the conclusion that the AI will continue to expand its influence in the coming years.

A similar prediction of developments in digital pathology is outlined in [17]. This overview focuses on the integrative approach to combine different data sources, such as histological image data, medical history or omics data, to make predictions to assist pathologists. Such a combination of heterogeneous data into a Machine Aided Pathology (also [17]) would benefit development towards personalized medicine.

Another important aspect when using the assistance of computer generated/analyzed data to make a decision (for diagnosis as well as in research) is the ability to understand and explain why this decision was made. There are researchers who are working on approaches fostering transparency, trust, acceptance and the ability to explain step-by-step the decision-making process of AI-based applications [17,18]. First steps to understand and evaluate the predictions of trained AI models for image data have been taken [19]. These methods were used to evaluate the automated detection of tumor-infiltrating lymphocytes in histological images [4]. Building trust in predictions from AI-based applications is of utmost importance. A pathologist who does not trust the results of a software will not use it.

Trust, understanding and explainability is not only important regarding the acceptance of AI among pathologists but also when legal or regulatory approval is concerned. In [20] a roadmap is set out to help academia, industry and clinicians develop new software tools to the point of approved clinical use.

3.2   Conclusion

Many researchers predict an increasing importance of AI-based applications in digital pathology for the next years. In addition to the ongoing development of new methodologies and the transfer to new use cases other aspects are equally important. Integration data from different sources, building trust among users and satisfying legal and regulatory conditions must not be neglected.

In the scope of this work the standardization of data formats, communication and transfer protocols and interfaces is of particular interest. The impact of AI in digital pathology could be increased further, if (meta-)data of biological samples, analysis results, (labeled) data sets for training, validation and testing and/or partially or fully trained prediction models would be shared within the medical and scientific community. To realize this, common standards are needed as soon as possible to counteract the development of many individual solutions that are not compatible.

4   OBDEX – Open Block Data Exchange System

We propose an extensible and flexible storage system for analysis data of virtual slides to address the issues described above. The scope of this system is to provide access to and to allow the exchange of detailed results based on the analysis of WSIs. On one hand it will be possible to access a complex step-by-step evaluation (e.g. model of histoarchitecture) on already existing results (e.g. classified cell nuclei) and on the other hand to compare the results between different algorithmic solutions on several levels.

The general structure of meta and analytical data for tissue slides (or more generally whole tissue blocks) is more or less hierarchical. The topmost (first) level contains data describing the physical tissue block. The type of material (biopsy, OP material) and the spatial location within the organ are examples for such data. The first level is followed by the second level, with all data concerning the glass slides generated from the tissue samples and their corresponding WSIs. It should be noted here that no primary image data (raw data) is stored in OBDEX, but only data newly generated by analysis (e.g. contours of cell nuclei) or transformation (e.g. registration) is stored. Image data must be stored in other information systems designed for such a task, ideally a fully DICOM conform PACS.

Between the first (tissue block) and second level (individual slides/WSIs) there is an intermediate level to address data that combines information from more than one single slide. An example for such multi-slide data is the registration of consecutive WSI of the same block. Such registration is necessary if WSI with different staining are to be viewed in parallel. Reconstructing 3D models

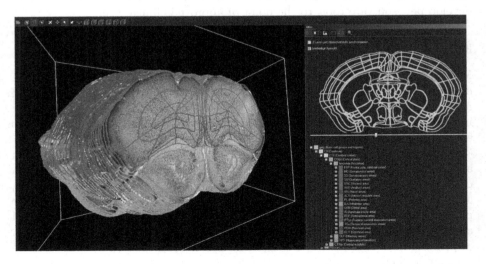

Fig. 2. 3D reconstruction of tissue (example reconstruction of mouse brain) [21].

of complex anatomical structures based on large stacks of consecutive slides is another use case where registration data is needed (see Fig. 2).

On the third level (and all levels following thereafter) analytical results based on individual slides are arranged. The data on these levels can be very diverse and can depend on each other (e.g. a tissue classification depends on a tissue segmentation). Figure 3 illustrates the basic structure of the hierarchical data arrangement and possible dependencies.

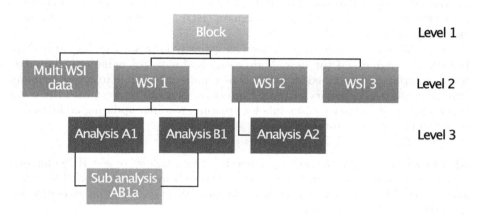

Fig. 3. Hierarchical data structure - example for dependencies between analysis results.

Taking into account the increasing adaptation of DICOM to the requirements of digital pathology, the system we propose can be used in conjunction with an appropriate PACS, perhaps as a DICOM addition in the future. Beside the image data DICOM supports handling of other, even sensible data in a save way. So (meta-)data concerning the slide (e.g. image acquisition parameters, modality data) are stored in the DICOM series. Complex analysis results (e.g. graph-based topological/object representations as discussed in [22]) that cannot be represented on the basis of DICOM are stored in OBDEX. In some cases (e.g. segmentation) a redundant storage in both systems can be desirable to address different use cases more comfortably. A DICOM viewer expects segmentation data according to the DICOM standard. A data scientist performing further data analysis or composing a data set to train artificial neural networks based on segmentations may use different data formats (e.g. XML or CSV files). From their point of view, it is neither necessary nor useful to work directly with the DICOM format. In this case, parallel storage in both systems makes sense, provided that the data is synchronized.

4.1 OBDEX Implementation

The technical infrastructure of hospitals and research facilities can be very versatile. An important feature of a storage system is its flexibility to be used in as many contexts as possible. In order to achieve this necessary flexibility, OBDEX is divided into the two components storage engine and middleware.

Storage Engine. The purpose of the storage engine is to store the analysis data. The actual implementation of the Storage Engine is interchangeable to be as flexible as possible so that it can be adapted to the needs or requirements of a particular infrastructure, provided a common interface is used with the middleware. This offers the possibility to use different database systems (e.g. PostgreSQL, MySQL) or file-based formats (HDF5 - hierarchical data format) as storage engines.

The middleware component is used as gateway between the data stored by the storage engine and the user. Middleware and storage engine are connected by the interface as described in Sect. 2. The middleware is able to access as many storage engines as necessary. A second interface serves to interact with the users by providing all necessary endpoints for creating, reading, updating and deleting data from connected storage engines.

Middleware. From a technical perspective, the middleware is a RESTful web application implemented in Python using the web micro-framework Flask [23] and is served by a Nginx [24] proxy server and uWSGI [25] to be accessible for multiple users simultaneously.

If the middleware is used in combination with database systems as storage engines, the ORM toolkit SQLAlchemy [26] is used to handle all accesses to the databases. Additionally, if a supported relational database management system is used, all database tables can be created automatically as well.

Extensibility. In its base form the user-interface of the middleware can handle standard analysis results, for example annotations, segmentations and classifications, in a predefined JSON format. Both data format and supported analysis result types can be extended. To add a new data format a parser for this format must be provided. A new parser can include only data input or output or both and must implement methods to access (input only), validate and write (output only) the data in the new format. If needed the validation can be done by using an additionally provided XML or JSON schema.

To add a new analysis type the provided data model must be extended. This can be done by using all existing models (e.g. deriving a new model or aggregating existing models) or by defining completely new models. All user provided data formats and analysis results will be loaded and integrated beside the standard format and data models on server start.

System Overview. Based on the components introduced the storage system is a flexible composition of middleware and one or more storage engines. Figure 4 shows an example of the general structure of the storage system.

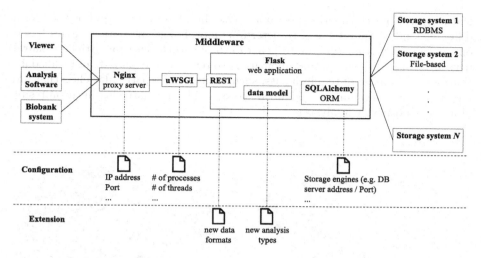

Fig. 4. Structure of OBDEX. The figure shows the internal components of the middleware, connected storage engines as well as the possibilities of configuration and extension.

The FAIR data principles [15] for research data as a basis for international scientific cooperation are a crucial reason for the specific form of the proposed storage system. In accordance with these principles all used protocols, software libraries and data structures are freely available, open source and documented.

4.2   Use Cases

To demonstrate the flexibility and ease of use of the OBDEX system, we will consider the following two use cases: (1) use of intermediate results, (2) composition of ground truth data for AI-based analysis.

Ki-67 Positivity, Original Data Access Versus Heatmap Exchange. A tile-based Ki-67 positivity analysis should be performed for a WSI to generate a heatmap overlay (as shown above). The planned analysis is composed of four steps for each image tile of the WSI: cell nuclei segmentation, nuclei feature calculation, nuclei classification and Ki-67 positivity score calculation (as described in [27]). It would be sufficient to store only the final results for each tile (the positivity score) to generate the heatmap. But in terms of reusability and data exchange the storage of all intermediate results would be much better. The OBDEX system can provide that possibility.

If intermediate analysis results are stored and arranged in an appropriate structure, researchers can retrieve them at any stage in the analysis process and use them for their own research purposes. In the case of a Ki-67 analysis with the results of all stored process steps, it would be possible to retrieve only the classification of the nuclei (together with the segmentation result and the calculated features) without considering positivity. The obtained results could be used for a different kind of analysis, e.g. to determine morphological characteristics based on nuclei of a certain type or to generate basic truth data for artificial neural networks. In addition, it would allow users to retrieve only subsets of result data that meet a number of requirements, such as nuclei of a particular class that are larger than a minimum area. Figure 5 shows an intermediate classification result of a Ki-67 positivity analysis.

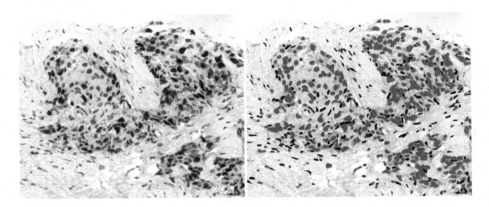

Fig. 5. Determination of Ki-67 index, left: original image; right: nuclei classification results (red: Ki-67 positive tumor, green: Ki-67 negative tumor, black: no tumor). (Color figure online)

Composition of Ground Truth Data for AI Based Analysis. The aim is to train an AI model to recognize certain morphological structures in histological images. In order for a data scientist to be able to fulfill this task, corresponding annotated image data are required as basic truth. If the existing infrastructure consists for example of a biobank information system for samples and clinical data, an image archive (PACS) for WSIs and OBDEX for the storage of analysis results, such a basic truth could be put together. Figure 6 shows the information flow and interaction between the systems involved in such a use case.

4.3   First Reference Implementation

A first implementation of the OBDEX system is used in conjunction with the ePathology platform CoPaW (Collective Pathology Wisdom) [28]. In this project it is possible to exchange cell nuclei segmentations for entire WSIs or a specific field of view including the possibility of live viewing of all segments. The same mechanism is used for the exchange of annotations within an open discussion of cases between groups of pathologists. Figure 7 show a screenshot of the CoPaW platform.

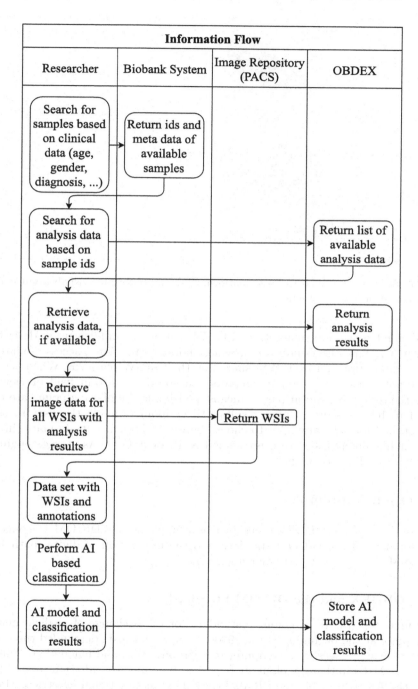

Fig. 6. Composing ground truth data for an AI based analysis by using OBDEX to access analytical data and to store results and AI model.

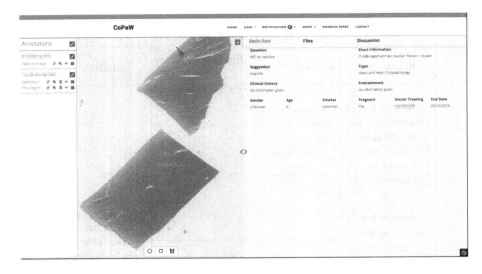

Fig. 7. Screenshot of the CoPaW platform – Example for the visualization of the annotations of different users.

This reference implementation of OBDEX uses the middleware as described in Sect. 4.1. The REST-interface provides endpoints to create, access, update or delete annotations for each WSI shared on the CoPaW platform. When accessing annotations, additional parameters can specify a certain field of view to filter the returned annotations by means of visibility. Similar endpoints are provided to handle segmentation results. All endpoints enable the user to send an optional format parameter to choose between different data formats (in the current implementation state predefined XML or JSON). As storage engine a PostgreSQL database is used.

5   Open Problems

Due to the fact that OBDEX is designed as a supplement to DICOM, the ongoing development of the DICOM standard and the integration of digital pathology and WSIs into it, is of particular importance.

5.1   OBDEX and the DICOM Standard

The first step towards a common standard for the exchange of medical images took place at the beginning of the 1980s, when radiologists demanded the possibility of using images from computer tomography (CT) and magnetic resonance imaging (MRI) in therapy planning (e.g. dose planning for radiation therapy). In 1985 the American College of Radiology (ACR) and National Electrical Manufacturers Association (NEMA) introduced the ACR/NEMA 300 standard. After two major revisions the third version of the standard was released in 1993 and renamed to DICOM. Currently DICOM is used in all imaging systems in radiology and nuclear medicine to store, visualize and exchange image and corresponding supplemental data. DICOM has been extended to most other medical specialties that use images, videos or multidimensional image data, such as sonography, endoscopy or dentistry.

The use of DICOM in digital pathology was somewhat hesitant. A major problem is the huge size of WSIs, so specific parts of the DICOM standard could not be adapted one-to-one. This can be seen, for example, in the use of annotations and segmentations. Of course, these can be managed in DICOM, but not for millions of segmented objects, neither in number nor in speed. We discussed the possibilities of DICOM for digital pathology and WSIs with David Clunie[1] in an email conversation in 2018. His answer concerning the huge number of segments or annotations in a single WSI was:

> Without extending the DICOM standard, the two ways to store WSI annotations that are currently defined for general use are: On a pixel by pixel basis, as a segmentation image, where each pixel is represented as a bit plane ...; there may be multiple segments (e.g. nuclei, membranes), but this approach does not anticipate identifying individual nuclei ... As contours (2D polylines) outlining objects, stored as either DICOM presentation states (not ideal, no semantics) or DICOM structured reports (SR) (each graphic reference may have attached codes and measurements and unique identifiers (UIDs). The biggest problem with the coordinate (SR) representation is that it is not compact (though it compresses pretty well), so while it may be suitable for identifying objects in small numbers of fields (tiles, frames) it probably doesn't scale well to all the nuclei on an entire slide.

His comment on dealing with graph based analysis results (e.g. Delaunay triangulation with different cell types) was:

> However, there is no precedent for encoding the semantics of graph-based methods as you discuss.

Our conclusion from these statements is that DICOM is currently not suitable to cover all of the use cases described in the above sections. Most are more or less feasible (in a cumbersome way), some are not.

One of the main challenges will be to find out where the limits of DICOM as the used standard are and where OBDEX can be used additionally to enable applications beyond the limits of DICOM.

5.2 Integration into Existing Clinical Infrastructures

As discussed in the previous sections OBDEX is focused to handle all relevant data concerning tissue samples. This includes data for the entire block but also

---

[1] David Clunie is a member of the DICOM committee.

for a single slide/WSI. When OBDEX is used as a supplement to other systems (e.g. biobank system or laboratory information management system) collaboration between the systems is needed to link the data for individual samples. It is to be expected, that such links could require an adaptation of other systems or the need to provide a joint search interface to fully integrate all available data of a sample into a single query. Another aspect of integration that needs to be taken into account is the synchronization of data that is stored redundantly in both systems for convenience and ease of use.

Some clinical use cases require that different samples (blocks) of a patient must be considered together, for example a metastatic tumor. In the case of two tumors, for example, the question may arise as to whether one tumor is a metastasis of the other or whether it is an independent tumor. All samples and their associated data are needed to make the final diagnosis. In laboratory information systems, this information is linked on a case-by-case basis. In its current design state OBDEX is not able to link samples from different tissue blocks. If such links are needed, they have to be established in other systems. From a technical perspective OBDEX could be extended to be able to realize such links by itself. However, it would be preferable if links between different blocks could be established by other systems, e.g. biobank systems. In a biobank system, at best all samples of a patient are semantically connected. Adding the functionality to link samples in OBDEX would be comparatively easy. However, bi-directional interfaces to LIS or LIMS would have to be established and data protection aspects would have to be taken into account.

6   Conclusion, Further Developments and Future Outlook

The OBDEX system for meta and analytical data for tissue blocks, glass slides and WSI is flexible, modular and extensible. By using open and extensible interfaces and complying with FAIR data principles, it offers the possibility to facilitate data exchange between institutions and working groups. By linking to biobank, pathology and other medical information systems, relevant data can be provided to support AI applications.

The hierarchical structure of the interconnected measurement results and data opens a channel for the exchange of intermediate results at different levels of a complex algorithm.

In the future, DICOM will be an important standard in both digital pathology and biobanking. Regardless of the specific features of DICOM discussed in this paper, dimensions such as image acquisition, image management, patient planning information, image quality, media storage, security, etc. form the basis for future use of the standard in pathology and biobanking.

The OBDEX system can help to remedy the current lack of common standards until DICOM becomes more widely used, covering applications that DICOM cannot or cannot comfortably handle.

6.1   Further Developments

The further development of OBDEX will concentrate on four essential aspects: Data protection, support of additional data formats, simplification of use and integration with other information systems (Biobank IS, Pathology IS).

In the current implementation the system does not contain any ID data and does not log any data to identify individual users by their IP addresses. Within specific research context or clinical studies it may be necessary to protect data from unauthorized access. Therefore, an authentication and authorization concept is required. A sensible solution is to control access to the data via another platform on which the users are already authenticated. If, for example, analysis data is to be accessed for visualization with a viewer, the user's login information is transferred to the query at OBDEX in order to check whether he has access to the queried data. When implementing such scenarios, the GDPR (General Data Protection Regulation) must of course be taken into account.

To increase the number of input and/or output data formats supported by OBDEX, additional format parser must be provided. The focus is on common formats of widely used analysis tools or platforms. Import and export from or to DICOM should be realized as soon as possible.

Analysis results derived from deep learning applications should be sufficiently complemented by metadata describing important attributes of the model used and the underlying ground truth data. Ideally, the results could be complemented by the model from which the data was generated. Then other users who do not have the ability to create a sufficient model themselves can reuse it for their own analysis. This requires a common standard for the exchange of these models. For example, ONNX (Open Neural Network Exchange) [29] could be used. However, it should be examined whether this can be brought into line with the FAIR principles.

Easy handling is also an important goal. Therefore, the storage system should be as easy to install and operate as possible. A direct way to achieve this would be to use preconfigured docker images that can be customized with only a few configuration files. In a standard installation (default settings for ports of the web server, number of processes and threads of the Flask application) without self-created format or analysis extensions, only the external IP address would have to be configured. In order to use OBDEX with such default settings, only two Docker Container (middleware and storage engine) have to be started. New types of storage engines could also be easily distributed as docker images. Docker would also make it easier to connect several separate middleware instances to shared storage engines and could form the basis of a decantralized research infrastructure. The first steps towards a docker-based distribution have already been taken.

OBDEX and all necessary supplemental documentation will be released under a suitable open source software license in the near future.

Acknowledgements. We thank David Clunie for his feedback on the current state of DICOM for digital pathology and his comments on OBDEX ideas. We also thank Tobias Dumke, Pascal Helbig and Nick Zimmermann (HTW University of Applied Sciences Berlin) for implementing the CoPaW ePathology platform and collaborating on the integration of the OBDEX system. Finally, we would like to thank Erkan Colakoglu for his work on adaptations for distributing OBDEX via Docker.

References

1. Geert, L., et al.: A survey on deep learning in medical image analysis. Med. Image Anal. **42**, 60–88 (2017)
2. Song, Y., et al.: A deep learning based framework for accurate segmentation of cervical cytoplasm and nuclei. In: 36th Annual International Conference of the IEEE Engineering in Medicine and Biology Society, pp. 2903–2906, IEEE (2014)
3. Henning, H., et al.: Deep learning nuclei detection: a simple approach can deliver state-of-the-art results. Comput. Med. Imaging Graph. **70**, 43–52 (2018)
4. Klauschen, F., et al.: Scoring of tumor-infiltrating lymphocytes: from visual estimation to machine learning. Semin. Cancer Biol. **52**(2), 151–157 (2018)
5. Sharma, H., et al.: Deep convolutional neural networks for automatic classification of gastric carcinoma using whole slide images in digital histopathology. Comput. Med. Imaging Graph. **61**, 2–13 (2017)
6. Hufnagl, P., et al.: Virtual microscopy in modern tissue-biobanks - the ZeBanC example. In: 27th European Congress of Pathology, Extended Abstracts, pp. 41–45. Springer (2015)
7. Weinstein, R.S., et al.: Overview of telepathology, virtual microscopy, and whole slide imaging: prospects for the future. Human Pathol. **40**(8), 1057–1069 (2009)
8. Kairos - Biobanking 3.0. https://www.kairos.de/referenzen/konsortium/biobanking-3-0. Accessed 29 Nov 2019
9. Jodogne, S.: The orthanc ecosystem for medical imaging. J. Digit. Imaging **31**(3), 341–352 (2018)
10. Clunie, D., et al.: Digital imaging and communications in medicine whole slide imaging connectathon at digital pathology association pathology visions 2017. J. Pathol. Inform. **9** (2018)
11. Herrmann, M., D. et al.: Implementing the DICOM standard for digital pathology. J. Pathol. Inform. **9** (2018)
12. DICOM Working Group 26. https://www.dicomstandard.org/wgs/wg-26/. Accessed 29 Nov 2019
13. Godinho, T.M., et al.: An efficient architecture to support digital pathology in standard medical imaging repositories. J. Biomed. Informat. **71**, 190–197 (2017)
14. DICOM PS3.1 2019d - Introduction and Overview - 1 Scope and Field of Application. dicom.nema.org/medical/dicom/current/output/chtml/part01/chapter1.html. Accessed 29 Nov 2019
15. Wilkinson, M.D., et al.: The FAIR Guiding Principles for scientific data management and stewardship. Sci. Data **3** (2016)
16. Janardhan, K.S., et al.: Looking forward: cutting-edge technologies and skills for pathologists in the future. Toxicologic pathology (2019). 0192623319873855
17. Holzinger, A., et al.: Machine learning and knowledge extraction in digital pathology needs an integrative approach. In: Holzinger, A., Goebel, R., Ferri, M., Palade, V. (eds.) Towards Integrative Machine Learning and Knowledge Extraction. LNCS (LNAI), vol. 10344, pp. 13–50. Springer, Cham (2017). https://doi.org/10.1007/978-3-319-69775-8_2

18. Pohn, B., et al.: Visualization of histopathological decision making using a road-book metaphor. In: 23rd International Conference Information Visualisation (IV). IEEE (2019)

19. Bach, S., et al.: On pixel-wise explanations for non-linear classifier decisions by layer-wise relevance propagation. PLoS ONE **10**, 7 (2015)

20. Colling, R., et al.: Artificial intelligence in digital pathology: a roadmap to routine use in clinical practice. J. Pathol. **249**(2), 143–150 (2019)

21. Norman, Z., et al.: Creation and exploration of augmented whole slide images with application to mouse stroke models. In: Modern Pathology, vol. 31 Supplement 2, p. 602 (2018)

22. Sharma, H., et al.: A comparative study of cell nuclei attributed relational graphs for knowledge description and categorization in histopathological gastric cancer whole slide images. In: 2017 IEEE 30th International Symposium on Computer-Based Medical Systems (CBMS), pp. 61–66. IEEE (2017)

23. Flask (A Python Microframework). http://flask.pocoo.org/. Accessed 29 Nov 2019

24. NGINX. https://www.nginx.com/. Accessed 29 Nov 2019

25. The uWSGI project. https://uwsgi-docs.readthedocs.io/en/latest/. Accessed 29 Nov 2019

26. SQLAlchemy - The Database Toolkit for Python. https://www.sqlalchemy.org/. Accessed 29 Nov 2019

27. Klauschen, F., et al.: Standardized Ki67 diagnostics using automated scoring–clinical validation in the GeparTrio breast cancer study. Clin. Cancer Res. **21**(16), 3651–3657 (2015)

28. CoPaW - Collective Pathology Wisdom, A Platform for Collaborative Whole Slide Image based Case Discussions and Second Opinion. http://digitalpathology.charite.de/CoPaW. Accessed 29 Nov 2019

29. ONNX: Open Neural Network Exchange Format. https://onnx.ai/. Accessed 29 Nov 2019

Image Processing and Machine Learning Techniques for Diabetic Retinopathy Detection: A Review

Sarni Suhaila Rahim[1,2], Vasile Palade[1], and Andreas Holzinger[3(✉)]

[1] Faculty of Engineering, Environment and Computing, Coventry University, Priory Street,
Coventry CV1 5FB, UK
sarni@utem.edu.my, {ad0490,ab5839}@coventry.ac.uk
[2] Faculty of Information and Communication Technology, Universiti Teknikal Malaysia
Melaka, Hang Tuah Jaya, 76100 Durian Tunggal, Melaka, Malaysia
[3] Institute for Medical Informatics, Statistics and Documentation, Medical University Graz,
Graz, Austria
andreas.holzinger@medunigraz.at

Abstract. An effective automatic diagnosis and grading of diabetic retinopathy would be very useful in the management of the diabetic retinopathy within the national health system. The detection of the presence of diabetic retinopathy features in the eyes is a challenging problem. Therefore, highly efficient and accurate image processing and machine learning techniques must be used in order to produce an effective automatic diagnosis of diabetic retinopathy. This chapter presents an up-to-date review on diabetic retinopathy detection systems that implement a variety of image processing techniques, including fuzzy image processing, along various machine learning techniques used for feature extraction and classification. Some background on diabetic retinopathy, with a focus on the diabetic retinopathy features and the diabetic retinopathy screening process, is included for better understanding. The chapter also highlights the available public databases, containing eye fundus images, which can be currently used in the diabetic retinopathy research. As the development of an automatic diabetic retinopathy screening system is a very challenging task, some of these challenges together with a discussion pertaining the automatic diabetic retinopathy screening are also presented in this chapter.

Keywords: Diabetic retinopathy · Eye screening · Fundus images · Image processing · Machine learning

1 Introduction

Diabetic Retinopathy (DR) is a disorder of the retinal vasculature. It develops to some degree in nearly all patients with long-standing diabetes mellitus and can result in blindness. It is one of the diabetes mellitus complications that damages blood vessels inside the retina.

© Springer Nature Switzerland AG 2020
A. Holzinger et al. (Eds.): AI & ML for Digital Pathology, LNAI 12090, pp. 136–154, 2020.
https://doi.org/10.1007/978-3-030-50402-1_9

The International Diabetes Federation reported the estimation of diabetes prevalence for 2017 as well as the projection for 2045, in age groups from 20 to 79 years, worldwide and per region (North America and Caribbean, Middle East and North Africa, Europe, South and Central America, Africa, South East Asia and Western Pacific). The report estimated a 48% increase from 2017 to 2045, i.e., from 425 million people worldwide in 2017 to 629 million by 2045 [1]. In addition, the report reveals that the number of people with diabetes aged 65–79 years is 98 million (in 2017), which will increase to 191 million by 2045, while for the diabetic people aged 20–64 years, the prevalence increases from 327 billion (2017) to 438 million (2045). According to Mathers and Loncar [2], in the year of 2014, the number of diabetic people worldwide was 422 million. Therefore, it shows that the prevalence of diabetes in the world is increasing rapidly.

An article published by the World Health Organization (WHO) [3], indicated that the number of visual impaired people worldwide was estimated to be 285 million of all ages, where 39 million people are blind and 246 million are having low vision problem. The report stated that the main cause of global visual impairment is the retinal diseases. Moreover, the report stated that the total number of visual impairments and blindness because of diabetic retinopathy, glaucoma and age-related macular degeneration is comparable to corneal opacities and trachoma. Education, support services and rehabilitation related to the eye care system developments are required to overcome those eye diseases, as suggested in the report. In a more recent report of the World Health Organization in 2018 [4], it is revealed that diabetes is a major cause of blindness as well as kidney failure, stroke, heart attack and lower limb amputation [4]. In addition, it is claimed in [4] that approximately 1.3 billion people currently live with some sort of vision impairment worldwide. Furthermore, people aged 50 years or over form the majority with vision impairment, and 80% of all vision impairment is considered avoidable [4]. One of the leading causes of vision impairment is diabetic retinopathy, besides cataract, glaucoma, uncorrected refractive errors, age-related corneal opacity, macular degeneration and trachoma [4]. Therefore, it can be concluded that one of the most important visual impairment and blindness causes is diabetic retinopathy. Hence, before this eye problem worsens, it should be properly addressed.

There is another survey on the diabetic retinopathy global prevalence according to region as well as ethnicity, conducted by Sivaprasad et al. [5]. This survey claims that the African, Latin American and South Asian populations suffer from diabetic retinopathy and macular edema higher than people of European origin. Hence, it is claimed that one of the factors that contributes to the incidence rates of diabetic retinopathy is the ethnicity, besides other factors, such as the severity of hyperglycemia and length of exposure, hypertension and hyperlipidemia. Moreover, obesity, sedentary lifestyles, diet changes, urbanization are the factors that will increase the healthcare demands for many ethnicities, and especially in Asia.

Regular screening of diabetic retinopathy is essential for both early detection and early treatment. In order to perform an effective classification of the retinal images, an accurate retinal screening is required. An effective clinical screening system would greatly contribute to and support the diabetic retinopathy detection and management. It is envisaged that such clinical screening systems will contain automatic detection techniques that will assist clinicians to diagnose the diabetic retinopathy at an early stage.

The chapter presents a complete review on diabetic retinopathy screening, comprising the diabetic retinopathy incidence, the screening process of diabetic retinopathy, the public databases available for diabetic retinopathy research, various image processing as well as features extraction and machine learning classifiers used in the automatic detection of diabetic retinopathy, and also some challenges of diabetic retinopathy screening and detection.

The chapter is organised as follows. Section 2 presents the background of diabetic retinopathy, comprises of the incidence of the diabetic retinopathy and the features of each of the diabetic retinopathy stages. Section 3 describes in details the diabetic retinopathy screening process. Meanwhile, Sect. 4 presents the available public databases used in diabetic retinopathy research. The image processing techniques that are employed for the detection of diabetic retinopathy, comprises of the traditional image processing as well as fuzzy image pre-processing, are presented in Sect. 5. The features extracted for diabetic retinopathy detection are presented in Sect. 6. Machine learning classifiers including the deep learning approach used for the diabetic retinopathy classification are described in Sect. 7. Finally, Sect. 8 presents some conclusions and discussions on diabetic retinopathy screening and automatic diabetic retinopathy detection systems.

2 Diabetic Retinopathy

Diabetic retinopathy is a complex disease and with diverse clinical findings. There are several stages, or classifications, of the diabetic retinopathy. According to Learned and Pieramici [6], the major forms of diabetic retinopathy are: the proliferative diabetic retinopathy (PDR), the non-proliferative diabetic retinopathy (NPDR) and the diabetic macula edema (DME).

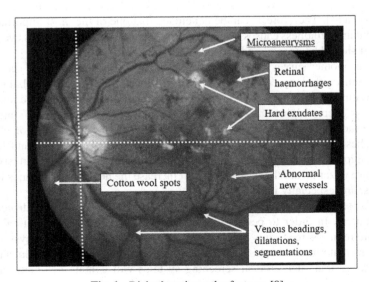

Fig. 1. Diabetic retinopathy features [8]

The initial reported signs of the diabetic retinopathy are the enlargement of the veins found in the retina. Some blockings in the small capillaries may result in small vascular wall swellings, named microaneurysms. This early stage is termed as the minimal non-proliferative diabetic retinopathy, and, at this particular stage, the sight may not affected. Due to the vascular blocking and leakage, small haemorrhages as well as other changes of blood vessels in the eye fundus appear. Consequently, from minimal to mild stage, the retinopathy progresses causing hard exudates, retinal haemorrhages and nerve layer infarct appearance. Moreover, due to intra-retinal microvascular irregularities and venous beading, moderate non-proliferative diabetic retinopathy may occur. Severe non-proliferative diabetic retinopathy is characterized usually by the presence of more microaneurysms, haemorrhages, abnormalities of intra-retinal microvascular system and also venous beading in moderate non-proliferative diabetic retinopathy [7]. The following diabetic retinopathy severe stage, called proliferative diabetic retinopathy, happens when new vessels are detected (called neovascularisation). This stage is considered as being of high risk, which can cause blindness. A visualisation of these features of diabetic retinopathy is presented in Fig. 1. A comparison between the normal retina and a retina with diabetic retinopathy signs is shown in Fig. 2, where the normal retina, which is free of any diabetic retinopathy features, is shown in Fig. 2 (a). The retina with several diabetic retinopathy features, for example microaneurysms, exudates, haemorrhages, cotton wool spots and maculopathy is shown in Fig. 2 (b).

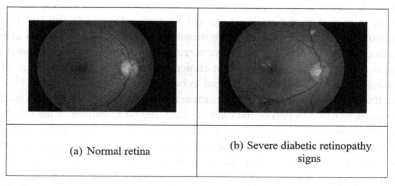

(a) Normal retina	(b) Severe diabetic retinopathy signs

Fig. 2. Visualisation of normal retina and retina with signs of diabetic retinopathy

3 Diabetic Retinopathy Screening

Regular diabetic population testing, which aims to identify people showing features that could be early symptoms, or indicators related to a certain condition is called screening [9]. The detection whether or not the people require referral for further treatment, in order to prevent blindness, is the main purpose of diabetic retinopathy screening [9]. The diabetic eye disease, which does not affect sight until reaches an advanced stage, is one major problem in ophthalmology [9]. Treatment, such as laser treatment, can save sight, but only if this is applied during the initial phases of the disease. This shows the importance of having regular screening, which would detect the diabetic patients at an early phase of diabetic retinopathy. Moreover, by regular screening, any signs of retinopathy could be identified earlier, which could assist in the detection of blood pressure or blood glucose management changes, in order to slow the progression rate.

There are several available screening methods that can be used in the screening of diabetic retinopathy, including eye fundus photography, direct ophthalmoscopy, the binocular indirect ophthalmoscopy and the slit-lamp bio-microscopy with contact lens. However, different screening modalities will come up with different the sensitivity and specificity scores. In the current practice, usually, all registered patients with diabetes will first perform a visual acuity (VA) test. Next, eye fundus photography is done using an eye fundus camera, and a further assessment to the visual acuity test will then take place. The captured eye fundus images will be graded by a trained paramedic into the diabetic retinopathy classes, depending on the abnormalities found in the eye fundus images. Based on the identified retinopathy stage, the management of the patient condition will be decided upon, comprising a schedule of follow-ups or a referral to an ophthalmologist for further diagnosis.

The American Academy of Ophthalmology (AAO) and the American Diabetes Association (ADA) established the recommendations for retinopathy screening [10]. Factors, such as inadequate resources to complete the screening task, and inadequate diabetic eye screening program, and poor patient awareness or available information are among the challenges of the screening of diabetic retinopathy.

Retinal digital imaging is usually implemented as a tool of screening, including in the UK as indicated by the National Retinal Screening Project Group [9]. However, implementing efficient and cost-effective measures is a challenge that needs to be considered in establishing and deploying eye screening systems nationally. Retinal digital imaging is considered as one of the best choices of screening from this point of view. Five retinal screening principles that need to be followed are underlined in [9], which include: the availability of an efficient screening system, regular screening assurance, eye screening practice as part of the diabetes care, the participation of the ophthalmologist's in the screening system planning and operation, and, finally, the quality control of the screening process. There are four main requirements in the systematic screening programmes developed for the diabetic retinopathy, as recommended by Scanlon et al. [11], i.e., effective treatment, opportunistic and systematic screening, quality assurance and coverage screening.

4   Publicly Available Datasets

Several public data sets containing eye fundus images are available for download to researchers working on diabetic retinopathy detection. The most popular ones are: the Standard Diabetic Retinopathy Database Calibration Level 0 (DIARETDB0), the Standard Diabetic Retinopathy Database Calibration Level 1 (DIARETDB1), Digital Retinal Images for Vessel Extraction (DRIVE), Methods to Evaluate Segmentation and Indexing techniques in the field of Retinal Ophthalmology (MESSIDOR), STructured Analysis of the REtina (STARE), the Retinopathy Online Challenge (ROC), the Retinal Vessel Image set for Estimation of Widths (REVIEW), the Diabetic Retinopathy Detection Kaggle dataset, and the Indian Diabetic Retinopathy Image Dataset (IDRiD).

The Standard Diabetic Retinopathy Database Calibration Level 0, or DIARETDB0 [12], is one of first databases made available, offering diabetic retinopathy as well as normal eye fundus images. The data set contains a total of 130 eye fundus images, out of which 20 are identified as normal (no DR), and the other 110 images contain some signs of diabetic retinopathy, such as microaneurysms, soft exudates, hard exudates, haemorrhages and neovascularisation.

The images were captured using a 50° field-of-view digital fundus camera, sized 1500 × 1152 pixels and stored in the PNG format [12]. The research group on Machine Vision and Pattern Recognition from the Lappeenranta University of Technology, Finland, which made this dataset available, later developed another data set, called the Standard Diabetic Retinopathy Database Calibration Level 1 (DIARETDB1) [13]. This data set offers a total of 89 eye fundus images in colour, where 84 images show mild stages of non-proliferative diabetic retinopathy signs (i.e., microaneurysms) in addition to five normal (no DR signs) images [13]. The DIARETDB0 and DIARETDB1 datasets provide a small number of eye fundus images. Therefore, they are unsuitable to build an effective automatic systems due to the limited data.

The MESSIDOR database is another data set made available mainly to evaluate segmentation and indexing techniques in the field of retinal ophthalmology, and offered by the French Ministry of Research and Defence in order to assist research on diabetic retinopathy diagnosis [14]. A total of 1,200 colour eye fundus images were captured using a colour video 3CCD camera on a Topcon TRC NW6 non-mydriatic device with a 45° field-of-view. The images consist of three different sizes: 1440 × 960 pixels, 2240 × 1488 pixels and 2304 × 1536 pixels, and all with 8 bits colour representation [14]. In addition to the original dataset, Messidor-2 is an alternative publicly available dataset, which have been used by researchers for diabetic retinopathy detection benchmarking, and which consists of 1,748 colour eye fundus images.

The Digital Retinal Images for Vessel Extraction (DRIVE) is another retinal image database, which provides colour eye fundus images and allow automatic segmentation of blood vessels [15]. The dataset comprises of 40 images, where 33 of them do not show any diabetic retinopathy signs and the remaining 7 images show signs of mild diabetic retinopathy. The eye fundus images, sized at 768 × 584 pixels, were captured using a non-mydriatic camera model Canon CR5 3CCD, with a 45° field-of-view and 8 bits colour representation [15].

A project from the University of California, San Diego, led by Dr. Michael Goldbaum [16] and funded by the U.S. National Institute of Health, proposed another database with retinal colour images, called STructured Analysis of the REtina (STARE). The dataset consists a total of 400 images, provided with a list of diagnosis codes as well as a diagnosis for each image. There are 80 images used for optic nerve detection [16], while 40 of these images involves blood vessel segmentation work [17].

The DRIVE and STARE datasets are two very good datasets that can be used for retinal vessel segmentations, however both databases do not contain measurements of width. Therefore, in order to fill this gap, the REtinal Vessel Image set for Estimation of Widths (REVIEW) [18] database was made available. This dataset consists of 193 vessel segments from 16 images together with a variety of pathologies and types of vessels. An accurate measurements of width and four subgroups of images, categorised in four classes, i.e., high resolution, vascular disease, central light reflex and kick-points, are presented in this database. The retinal vessel segmentation techniques from REVIEW database used to produce vessel profiles has been described by Al-Diri et al. [18].

An online competition, called the Retinopathy Online Challenge (ROC), presented numerous methods for the detection of microaneurysms [19]. The published dataset consists of 50 images for training with available reference standard, together with another 50 images for testing, where the reference standard was withheld by the organisers. There are three different sizes of images, i.e., 768 × 576 pixels, 1058 × 1061 pixels and 1389 × 1383 pixels. The outcome of this competition shows that the detection of microaneurysms is a big challenging for automatic approaches as well as human experts.

One recent and large public dataset for diabetic retinopathy detection is the Diabetic Retinopathy Detection Kaggle dataset, provided by EyePACS [20]. It is a large high-resolution retina image dataset containing 88,702 images using different types of cameras, where for every subject, both left and right fields are provided. The diabetic retinopathy presence in each image has been rated according to the following scale: no diabetic retinopathy, mild, moderate, severe and proliferative diabetic retinopathy stages. This dataset is especially useful when using deep learning methods, which require a large amount of labelled data.

In addition to the public data sets presented above, Rahim et al. [21] developed a new data set, containing normal and Diabetic Retinopathy (DR) eye fundus images, collected from the Eye Clinic of the Department of Ophthalmology, Melaka Hospital, Malaysia. This dataset collected from 300 patient's folders comprises of 600 colour eye fundus images. There are minimum two images for each patient, where one was captured on the right side and the other on the left side, with two different angles, i.e., the optic disc in centre or the macula in centre. The original images, which were captured using a KOWA VX-10 digital fundus camera are stored in a JPEG format sized 3872 × 2592 pixels, providing high quality and detailed images. Three medical experts from the Department of Ophthalmology, Melaka Hospital, Malaysia, were involved in classifying the eye fundus images into ten retinopathy classes, i.e., No Diabetic Retinopathy, Mild DR without maculopathy, Mild DR with maculopathy, Moderate DR without maculopathy, Moderate DR with maculopathy, Severe DR without maculopathy, Severe DR with maculopathy, Proliferative DR without maculopathy, Proliferative DR with maculopathy and Advanced Diabetic Eye Disease (ADED). Each image in the dataset was labelled by the 3 experts, and a majority voting was performed in order to obtain a more confident classification. One significant feature of this dataset is that it represents the South Asian population, unlike other publicly available datasets, which mainly involved Caucasian individuals.

In addition to the dataset presented by Rahim et al. [21], which is representative for the Malaysian population, there is another ethnic related database, called the Indian Diabetic Retinopathy Image Dataset (IDRiD) [22]. This is the first database representing an Indian population. The data set consists of 516 fundus images with 4288 × 2848 pixels resolution, in JPG file format. A Kowa VX-10 alpha digital fundus camera with 50° field-of-view, located at the Eye Clinic in Nanded, Maharashta, India, was used to capture the eye fundus images, and all of the images taken are centered near to the macula. The dataset provides typical lesions of diabetic retinopathy expert annotation. In addition, the information on the diabetic retinopathy severity level and the diabetic macula edema for each image is provided.

It can be concluded that along developing automatic diabetic retinopathy screening detection systems, researchers also developed and made available eye fundus image datasets to promote image processing research and the retinal-imaging research area, particularly for diabetic retinopathy screening purposes. Moreover, the developed datasets are not only useful for diabetic retinopathy screening, but also for screening of other retinal diseases, like glaucoma, cataracts and hypertensive retinopathy.

5 Diabetic Retinopathy Image Processing

Image processing techniques are increasingly used as a way of diagnosing diseases, including diseases of the eye. Tools such as computer-aided imaging are effectively used in the diagnosis of the diabetic retinopathy signs. It is vital to save patients from major eye damage and detect the disease earlier, which would offer the best way of protecting patients' valuable vision. An automatic grading system for diabetic retinopathy would allow a faster and more efficient diagnosis.

The screening and detection of diabetic retinopathy is currently a popular area of research. The first type of diabetic retinopathy screening development concerns a general detection of retinopathy, i.e., whether or not the diabetic retinopathy is present [23–35]. In order to detect more specific features of the retinopathy, such as exudates, microaneurysms, haemorrhages and others, several image processing methods and techniques were implemented in [36–61]. In addition, other researchers proposed the detection of maculopathy in order to assist the diabetic retinopathy management [62–66]. The detection of yellow lesions near the macula called maculopathy, is important as it will eventually cause the vision loss if the affected macula is not treated in time. For the detection of maculopathy, various techniques and methods were proposed and reported in the literature [62–66] to produce a reliable system. It can be concluded that in producing an efficient and reliable diabetic retinopathy system, various image pre-processing techniques, feature extraction methods and machine learning classification techniques were used and novel methods developed.

5.1 Traditional Image Pre-processing

The process of improving or enhancing the features of an image for the following processing tasks is termed as image pre-processing. Sonka et al. [67] classified the image pre-processing methods into four categories, which are local pre-processing, pixel brightness transformations, geometric transformations and image restoration. However, other authors classify the image pre-processing methods into image restoration and image enhancement only.

The greyscale conversion, extraction of green channel, image filtering, contrast enhancement, morphological operations, segmentation and thresholding are among the pre-processing techniques used in the present diabetic retinopathy screening system. Two main processes, which are optic disc localisation and blood vessel removal are widely used as an additional task within the scope of diabetic retinopathy detection, before the subsequent tasks are performed. In addition, for the detection of the maculopathy, the localisation of the fovea and of the macula are important. Some pre-processing techniques are also required for the detection of such retinal structures.

The change of the colour retinal image into a greyscale colour format is a popular pre-processing technique used, as greyscale format is typically an enhanced format for image processing. Besides the greyscale conversion, the extraction of the green and red channels from the colour eye fundus image, which comprises of the three primary colours (i.e., red, green and blue channels), is performed. In most of the diabetic retinopathy screening research that has been developed so far, the green channel is extracted for locating the lesions caused by diabetic retinopathy, for example microaneurysms, haemorrhages as well as the blood vessels. The green channel contains more structural information, while the red channel is somewhat saturated. Therefore, the green channel extraction is sensible to be used for the morphological and segmentation operations, as many image processing tools work better for greyscale only.

Another pre-processing technique implemented for diabetic retinopathy detection is contrast enhancement. This technique works by changing the pixel intensities, and this produces a better image than the original one [68]. Contrast Limited Adaptive Histogram Equalisation (CLAHE), Histogram Equalisation (HE), Histogram Stretching and Brightness Preserving Histogram modification techniques are the several contrast enhancement techniques available. It is more challenging to use colour fundus images than the other types of fundus photography examination, which are the red-free and angiography. Hence, in order to improve the contrast of the eye fundus images for better visualisation as well as better detection, such appropriate techniques need to be implemented.

For the purpose of improving the image quality or restoring the digital image, which tends to contain a variety of noise types, image filtering is performed. Equipment associated factors, like dirty computer screen or lens, may result in poor photo quality. In addition, poor quality fundus photographs are generated due to the surroundings distractions, for example a too bright room. Therefore, the process of filtering is required to solve this problem and enable the image for further effective processing and grading tasks. Popular edge detection filtering techniques suggested for the blood vessels' detection and segmentation in colour retinal images are Sobel, Prewitt, Kirsch. In addition, the median filter, the Gaussian filter and the Frangi filter can also be implemented.

Morphological operations could be also used for the purpose of improving the structure of an object, image pre-processing, object segmentation from the background, as well as for the objects' quantitative description [67]. In the development of a diabetic retinopathy system, for the blood vessel extraction, the morphology operators comprising erosion and dilation operations are usually implemented. A closing operation for retinal blood vessel segmentation is proposed by Joshi and Karule [69], employing disk shaped structuring element is implemented. Nonetheless, the diabetic maculopathy detection in retinal images is also investigated through the use of morphological operations. For example, Vimala and Kajamohideen [63] proposed the transforms of top-hat and bottom-hat as the morphological operations for the detection of macula.

In more recent literature, Lam et al. [28] proposed the diabetic retinopathy detection by implementing the Otsu's method in order to isolate the coloured image of the retina, followed by normalisation and finally contrast adjustment, performed using the contrast limited adaptive histogram equalisation. Sreng et al. [70] implemented pre-processing steps such as the green channel, median filter and gamma correction when building their automated diabetic retinopathy screening system.

In addition to the pre-processing techniques listed above, other techniques, such as shade correction and thresholding were usually used in previous diabetic retinopathy detection research [23, 38, 43, 46, 47, 51, 64, 65].

5.2 Fuzzy Image Preprocessing

In the development of image processing systems, fuzzy approaches were widely implemented and reported in the literature, mostly for non-medical images, but also for medical image processing in a smaller number of cases. The fuzzy image pre-processing methods that can be usually employed are fuzzy contrast enhancement, fuzzy filtering, fuzzy edge detection and fuzzy image segmentation.

Rahim et al. [71] proposed a microaneurysms detection by using fuzzy image processing. As it is more challenging to use the colour retinal images compared to the other modes of fundus photography examination, therefore contrast enhancement should be implemented as a way to obtain better visualisation and more precise detection. The system reported in [71] consists of two variants, where a combination of image pre-processing techniques and circular Hough transform for the localisation and detection of the microaneurysms is proposed in the first subsystem, while the second variant proposed the microaneurysms detection using fuzzy image pre-processing, by employing the Fuzzy Histogram Equalisation method. Both systems are compared in order to investigate the ability of the implemented fuzzy image processing techniques. From the obtained results, it was concluded that improved contrast for eye fundus images is generated with the implementation of fuzzy pre-processing techniques, and it can greatly help in the detection of microaneurysms. The Brightness Preserving Dynamic Fuzzy Histogram Equalisation (BPDFHE), a modified equalisation of brightness preserving technique developed by Sheet et al. [68], was implemented in [71]. The fuzzy domain allows the representation and processing of images to manage the grey level values inexactness in a better way, in order to improve the overall performance. The performance of this technique has been compared with the other two contrast improvement techniques, i.e., HE and CLAHE, and, as a result, the image brightness is conserved in the BPDFHE much better than when using the other two proposed techniques. Good performance of the BPDFHE method, particularly in medical images, for instance pathology images, is described by Garud et al. in [72].

Due to the encouraging results in the implementation of the fuzzy histogram equalisation technique for the microaneurysms detection, the microaneurysms detection system was improved in the next develop variants in [75]. The implementation of fuzzy edge detection and fuzzy filtering, in addition to the fuzzy histogram equalisation, for the automatic detection of microaneurysms was proposed in [73]. The Noise Adaptive Fuzzy Switching Median (NAFSM) filter, an extension to the Fuzzy Switching Median (FSM) filter, developed by Toh et al. was proposed in [74]. This technique worked well by integrating fuzzy reasoning in correcting the detected noisy pixel, in removing salt-and-pepper noise, and also conserving image details and textures. There are two modules in this techniques: firstly, the salt-and-pepper noise detection module, and, secondly, the fuzzy noise cancellation module. The analysis shows that better contrast enhancement is provided by the employment of the fuzzy pre-processing techniques as well as other enhancements, such as image brightness and better segmentation of fundus images. The fuzzy image pre-processing techniques are capable of generating better image quality and, eventually, obtain enhanced performance. In addition to the fuzzy filtering, the fuzzy edge detection is implemented as well. The two uniform regions' boundary, called edge, can be identified by comparing the neighbouring pixels intensity. However, small differences of intensity between two neighbouring pixels do not always represent an edge, since uniform regions are not crisply defined, and it might represent a shading effect. Therefore, the problems can be solved by defining the degree of pixel intensity with the use of membership functions, if it belongs to an edge or to a uniform region. As a result, better detection of edges and better output image are provided as the output of the using the fuzzy membership functions for the edge detection.

Due to the reported capabilities of fuzzy image processing, as outlined above, Rahim et al. [75] investigated the implementation of a combination of several fuzzy image processing techniques for the diabetic retinopathy detection as well as for the maculopathy detection in retinal images. The system consists of a combination of techniques with several fuzzy approaches in the image pre-processing part, which combine fuzzy filtering, fuzzy histogram equalisation, and followed by fuzzy edge detection. The combination of different fuzzy image processing techniques further enhanced the performance of the diabetic retinopathy and maculopathy when retinal structures segmentation was used in [21]. This research presented a novel combined diabetic retinopathy and maculopathy detection in eye fundus images using fuzzy image pre-processing. The results showed that a reliable diabetic retinopathy screening system can be created by employing fuzzy image pre-processing techniques alongside the extraction of retinal structures.

A variety of other fuzzy techniques can be applied and explored for image processing. In order to produce a more effective screening system, other fuzzy image processing, dealing with local pre-processing, image restoration, geometric transformations and pixel brightness transformations can be implemented. Furthermore, the extraction of the retinal structures can be implemented in the screening of the diabetic retinopathy, where the Fuzzy Circular Hough Transform can be used as an alternative technique for the detection of the optic disc, for example.

6   Diabetic Retinopathy Feature Extraction

Feature extraction takes place after performing the pre-processing techniques, in order to obtain several features from images that can be further used in the classification stage.

Basic features include area, mean and standard deviation of on/white pixels, as used for the diabetic retinopathy detection systems proposed in [24, 76]. There are many other feature values that can used in the development of a DR detection system, where the features used are appropriate for the characteristics of the particular diabetic retinopathy signs that are looked for. For example, since a microaneurysm has specific characteristics, such as red colour and circular shape, therefore appropriate features such as the object perimeter, the area of the pixels, the major and minor axis length, its circularity and its aspect ratio should be extracted to ensure reliable feature extraction and classification.

Generally, the features can be categorised into colour features, shape features, intensity features, and also Fourier descriptor features. In addition to these major types of feature values, there are features based on the texture analysis, such as contrast, entropy, homogeneity, correlation, energy, which are extracted from the grey level co-occurrence matrix and can be also used to detect the severity of the diabetic retinopathy.

The feature values for the detection of microaneurysms proposed in [38–40, 42, 48, 50, 52, 53], consists of area, eccentricity, perimeter, compactness, aspect ratio, mean and standard deviation, circularity, total number of microaneurysms, entropy, correlation, energy, contrast and homogeneity values. Meanwhile, the feature values for the detection of exudates, such as the number of exudates patches, exudates area, exudates perimeter and statistical features are presented in [23, 25, 38, 40, 47, 48, 50, 53, 62]. Besides the shape features, the intensity features, such as intensity value of pixel and standard deviation, hue of pixel, average intensity of the pixel's cluster, are also reported for the exudates detection [38]. Mookiah et al. [23] employed texture features, which are local binary patterns, laws texture energy, as well as the entropy for the exudates signs.

Meanwhile, Akram et al. [38] proposed features for the neovascularisation detection by using feature values such as energy, area, mean and standard deviation of gradient, mean intensity, intensity variation, blood vessel density, vessels segments, vascular segment width and vascular direction variation. For the detection of retinal structures, (such as blood vessels), feature values such as the area of blood vessels, mean and standard deviation of on pixels, the energy are proposed in [23, 25, 40, 42, 47, 50, 53].

Recently, Sreng et al. [70] proposed 208 features extracted from eight features extractors, i.e., colour features, intensity features, morphological features, first order statistical features, Gray Level Run Length Matrix (GLRLM) features, Gray-Level Co-occurrence Matrix (GLCM) features, Tamura's texture features and local binary pattern features, for their automated diabetic retinopathy screening system.

7 Machine Learning Classifiers for Diabetic Retinopathy Detection

In the classification phase, different machine learning classifiers can be trained using the features extracted after the image pre-processing step, in order to classify the images into their respective classes. Another approach is to employ deep learning, where feature extraction is practically embedded in the classification stage.

7.1 Deep Learning

Deep learning is a popular and upcoming area of machine learning, where a model automatically extracts the necessary features from the input data. Deep learning requires large amounts of labeled data and considerable computing power.

Deep learning has been previously used in medical research, including the diabetic retinopathy screening. Automated diabetic retinopathy detection systems in eye fundus images using deep learning have been proposed in [28–35]. In addition, research works using deep learning and focusing on the diabetic retinopathy signs detection, such as microaneurysms, exudates and haemorrhages, were reported in [54–61]. These research papers proposed different neural network architectures and different datasets, reporting various results and performances. Several image pre-processing techniques were used by researchers in order to first enhance the quality of the image and, eventually, increase the deep learning system classification accuracy. Among the pre-processing techniques employed are resizing, normalisation, denoising, scaling, centering, cropping, green channel extraction and contrast enhancement.

Deep convolutional neural networks are the most popular deep learning approach implemented in diabetic retinopathy classification. Pratt et al. [34] proposed a convolutional neural network (CNN) method with image pre-processing techniques, i.e., resizing and normalisation, in order to diagnose into five classes of diabetic retinopathy. Meanwhile, Rakhlin [31] implemented the diabetic retinopathy detection using a deep CNN, using two datasets i.e., the Kaggle and Messidor-2 datasets. In order to make the retinal images uniform, the images have been normalised, scaled, centered and cropped. Rajanna et al. [33] evaluated the efficiency of the proposed neural network based classifiers with a combination of pre-processing techniques, such as resizing, green channel extraction and histogram equalisation. In addition, Ghosh et al. [35] proposed a CNN approach to classify into two classes, and then five classes, of diabetic retinopathy by using the Kaggle public dataset. Xu et al. [30] explored the use of deep CNNs for the diabetic retinopathy automatic classification using colour fundus images, and obtained 94.5% accuracy. An implementation of deep learning system for diabetic retinopathy automated detection in retinal fundus photographs have also been proposed by Gulshan et al. [32] and Voets et al. [29].

In addition, pretrained networks, such as GoogleNet, AlexNet, ResNet and others, were implemented to classify the eye fundus images into the respective categories. Lam et al. [28] demonstrated the implementation of a CNN on colour fundus images for the diabetic retinopathy detection. The results show that contrast limited adaptive histogram equalisation for the image pre-processing and ensuring fidelity of datasets by expert verification of class labels increase the recognition of subtle features. The accuracies of transfer learning on pre-trained GoogleNet and Alexnet models from ImageNet are 74.5%, 68.8% and 57.2%, respectively, on 2-ary, 3-ary and 4-ary classification models [28].

It can be concluded that various approaches and different deep learning architectures were proposed for DR detection. In order to produce a good performance, a large and diverse range of data is required by deep learning algorithms. It is then possible to get a convolutional neural network to segment the features of diabetic retinopathy on a wide range of eye fundus images with reasonable accuracy. However, it is challenging to implement deep learning classifiers when only a small amount of data is available. Lam et al. [55] developed an automated method of localising diabetic retinopathy lesions with limited amount of data. The method was validated on 148 retinal images with microaneurysms and 47 showing exudates signs. The research work presented a combination of image patches manually cropped that comprise lesions and sliding windows. The 1,324 image patches from the Kaggle dataset, containing either microaneurysms, hemorrhages, exudates, neovascularisation or normal-appearing structures, were used to train the CNN to predict the five classes' presence. The probability maps across the entire image was generated by using a sliding window approach. The proposed method achieved 0.94 and 0.95 for a pixel-wise classification of the area under the curve of the receiver operating characteristic, and 0.86 and 0.64 for a lesion-wise area under the precision recall curve, for microaneurysms and exudates, respectively.

7.2 Other Machine Learning Classifiers

Various other machine learning classifiers, namely the K-nearest neighbour, decision trees, Naïve-Bayes, support vector machines, were also used in diabetic retinopathy classification to train and classify fundus images into the respective categories or classes.

One of the most popular techniques used for classification is Support Vector Machines (SVM). SVMs have been widely used in medical image processing and analysis as well as for other pattern classification problems. A computer-based system for diabetic retinopathy for identifying normal, non-proliferative diabetic retinopathy (NPDR) and proliferative diabetic retinopathy (PDR) classes was developed and proposed by Priya and Aruna [24]. Colour retinal images were used, where the features were extracted from the original image using image processing techniques and later fed to a support vector machine classifier for classification. As a result, it shows that the classifier provides an enhanced accuracy, with 99.45% for sensitivity and 100% for specificity. Other SVM classifiers were proposed and reported in the literature [36, 37, 42, 43, 46–48, 50] to produce a dependable diabetic retinopathy grading system.

Classification is one of the neural networks main applications. Neural network based classifiers have been reported and used in [23, 43, 45, 47, 53, 65]. A development of a computing system for diabetic retinopathy, identifying normal, NPDR and PDR classes, by using two types of classifiers, i.e., a Probabilistic Neural Network (PNN) and a Support Vector Machine (SVM), was developed by Priya and Aruna [25]. The classifiers were defined in detail and their performances compared. From the results obtained, it was shown that the SVM model is more effective compared to the PNN. Priya and Aruna [47] investigated a comparison of three classification models; namely a Bayesian classifier, a SVM and a PNN in the developed system. The results show that the SVM classier outperforms all other models and again this proves that the SVM is a more effective classifier for diabetic retinopathy detection and diabetic retinopathy categories classification. The detection and classification of diabetic retinopathy by using a Radial Basis Function Neural Network (RBFNN) classifier has also been reported in [26]. However, the experimental results showed a low accuracy of the proposed system (76.25%) and it was recommended to find more relevant features and combine them with other classification methods to improve its accuracy.

Another popular approach for implementing classifiers is decision trees. This machine learning technique has been used in previous diabetic retinopathy classification detection research in [23, 66]. An alternative machine learning classifier used for diabetic retinopathy grading purposes is the Naïve Bayes classifier, which was reported in [58, 66].

8 Conclusions and Discussions

The screening and detection of diabetic retinopathy is a popular research area and many researchers focused on the development of automatic machine learning based systems in this application. Some researchers concentrated on contributing a truthful technique or method for identifying certain diabetic retinopathy features, through exploring the eye fundus images. There are still lacunae, and rooms for improvement, although there has been enormous progress in this research area in the last decade. The different techniques proposed in the reviewed research works will mostly benefit the realm of image processing in a number of areas or ways that include the provision of accurate methods for effectively detecting features, in particular diabetic retinopathy features.

Despite the existence of a wide range of available image processing techniques, the need for effective and specialised image processing techniques in this case is very important. In addition, good performance of employed classification methods is significant, as it can help increase the likelihood of accurate grading of diabetic retinopathy.

Diabetic retinopathy screening is considered to be a complicated process, as there is a need to identify and detect a wide range of signs in order to produce a complete screening system. The detection of the diabetic retinopathy signs is challenging, as each particular sign comes up with different characteristics. It can be concluded that the screening of diabetic retinopathy is not an easy task, because before any practical diagnose can be made, there are many criteria that need to be thoroughly examined.

As the diabetic retinopathy disease itself is complex and the automatic detection of diabetic retinopathy is challenging, efficient computational methods are required to decrease the manual detection burden as well as increase the performance of current automatic methods. This can be addressed by employing effective image processing techniques and adequate machine learning techniques, which are capable to converge faster to the desired solution and obtain better accuracy. In the future it will be important to take into consideration explainability and causability [77, 78].

Acknowledgements. This study is a part of postdoctoral research currently being carried out at the Faculty of Engineering, Environment and Computing, Coventry University, United Kingdom. The deepest gratitude and thanks go to the Universiti Teknikal Malaysia Melaka (UTeM) for sponsoring this postdoctoral research.

References

1. International Diabetes Federation: IDF Diabetes Atlas, 8th edn. IDF, Belgium (2017)
2. Mathers, C.D., Loncar, D.: Projections of global mortality and burden of disease from 2002 to 2030. PLos Med. **3**(11), e442 (2006)
3. World Health Organization: Global data on visual impairments 2010. WHO, Geneva (2012)
4. World Health Organization. http://www.who.int/en/news-room/fact-sheets/detail/blindness-and-visual-impairment. Accessed 20 Mar 2019
5. Sivaprasad, S., Gupta, B., Crossby-Nwaobi, R., Evans, J.: Prevalence of diabetic retinopathy in various ethnic groups: a worldwide perspective. Surv. Ophthalmol. **57**(4), 347–370 (2012)
6. Learned, D., Pieramici, D.: Epidemiology and natural history of diabetic retinopathy. In: Baumal, C.R. (ed.) Current Management of Diabetic Retinopathy. Elsevier, St. Louis (2018)
7. Health Technology Assessment Unit, Medical Development Division, Ministry of Health Malaysia: Report screening for diabetic retinopathy. Ministry of Health Malaysia, Kuala Lumpur (2002)

8. Ministry of Health Diabetic Retinopathy Screening Team: Handbook guide to diabetic retinopathy screening -Module 5-2012. Ministry of Health Malaysia, Putrajaya (2012)
9. Taylor, R., Batey, D.: Handbook of Retinal Screening in Diabetes: Diagnosis and Management. Wiley, Chichester (2012)
10. American Academy of Ophthalmology Retina Panel: Preferred practice pattern guidelines. Diabetic retinopathy. American Academy of Ophthalmology, San Francisco (2008)
11. Scanlon, P.H., Wilkinson, C.P., Aldington, S.J., Matthews, D.R.: A Practical Manual of Diabetic Retinopathy Management. Wiley-Blackwell, Chicester (2009)
12. Kauppi, T., et al.: DIARETDB0: Evaluation Database and Methodology for Diabetic Retinopathy Algorithms. Lappeenranta University of Technology, Finland (2006)
13. Kauppi, T., et al.: DIARETDB1 Diabetic Retinopathy Database and Evaluation Protocol. Lappeenranta University of Technology, Finland (2007)
14. Messidor. http://www.adcis.net/en/third-party/messidor/. Accessed 28 Jan 2019
15. Staal, J.J., Abramoff, M.D., Niemeijer, M., Viergever, M.A., Ginneken-van, B.: Ridge based vessel segmentation in color images of the retina. IEEE Trans. Med. Imaging **23**, 501–509 (2004)
16. Hoover, A., Goldbaum, M.: Locating the optic nerve in a retinal image using the fuzzy convergence of the blood vessels. IEEE Trans. Med. Imaging **22**(8), 951–958 (2003)
17. Hoover, A., Kouznetsova, V., Goldbaum, M.: Locating blood vessels in retinal images by piece-wise threshold probing of a matched filter response. IEEE Trans. Med. Imaging **19**(3), 203–210 (2000)
18. Al-Diri, B., Hunter, A., Steel, D., Habib, M., Hudaib, T., Berry, S.: REVIEW-A reference data set for retinal vessel profiles. In: Proceedings of the 30th Annual International Conference of the IEEE Engineering in Medicine and Biology Society, pp. 2262–2265. IEEE, USA (2008)
19. Niemeijer, M., et al.: Retinopathy online challenge: automatic detection of microaneurysms in digital color fundus photographs. IEEE Trans. Med. Imaging **29**(1), 185–195 (2010)
20. Diabetic Retinopathy Detection. https://www.kaggle.com/c/diabetic-retinopathy-detection. Accessed 28 Jan 2019
21. Rahim, S.S., Palade, V., Shuttleworth, J., Jayne, C.: Automatic screening and classification of diabetic retinopathy and maculopathy using fuzzy image processing. Brain Inform. **3**(4), 249–267 (2016). https://doi.org/10.1007/s40708-016-0045-3
22. Indian Diabetic Retinopathy Image Dataset. https://idrid.grand-challenge.org/Home/. Accessed 28 Jan 2019
23. Mookiah, M.R.K., et al.: Evolutionary algorithm based classifier parameter tuning for automatic diabetic retinopathy grading: a hybrid feature extraction approach. Knowl.-Based Syst. **39**, 9–22 (2013)
24. Priya, R., Aruna, P.: Review of automated diagnosis of diabetic retinopathy using the support vector machine. Int. J. Appl. Eng. Res. **1**(4), 844–863 (2011)
25. Priya, R., Aruna, P.: SVM and neural network based diagnosis of diabetic retinopathy. Int. J. Comput. Appl. **41**(1), 6–12 (2012)
26. Priya, R., Aruna, P., Suriya, R.: Image analysis technique for detecting diabetic retinopathy. Int. J. Comput. Appl. **1**, 34–38 (2013)
27. Shome, S.K., Vadali, S.R.K.: Enhancement of diabetic retinopathy imagery using contrast limited adaptive histogram equalization. Int. J. Comput. Sci. Inf. Technol. **2**(6), 2694–2699 (2011)
28. Lam, C., Yi, D., Guo, M., Lindsey, T.: Automated detection of diabetic retinopathy using deep learning. In: AMIA Joint Summits on Translational Science Proceedings. AMIA Joint Summits on Translational Science 2017, pp. 147–155 (2018)
29. Voets, M., Mollersen, K., Bongo, L.A.: Replication study: development and validation of a deep learning algorithm for detection of diabetic retinopathy in retinal fundus photographs. https://arxiv.org/pdf/1803.04337.pdf (2018)

30. Xu, K., Feng, D., Mi, H.: Deep convolutional neural network-based early automated detection of diabetic retinopathy using fundus image. Molecules **22**(12), 1–7 (2017)
31. Rakhlin, A.: Diabetic retinopathy detection through integration of deep learning classification framework (2017). https://www.biorxiv.org/content/biorxiv/early/2018/06/19/225508.full.pdf
32. Gulshan, V., Peng, L., Coram, M., et al.: Development and validation of a deep learning algorithm for detection of diabetic retinopathy in retinal fundus photographs. JAMA **316**(22), 2402–2410 (2016). https://doi.org/10.1001/jama.2016.17216
33. Rajanna, A.R., Aryafar, K., Ramchandran, R., Sisson, C., Shokoufandeh, A., Ptucha, R.: Neural networks with manifold learning for diabetic retinopathy detection. In: Proceedings of IEEE Western NY Image and Signal Processing Workshop. https://arxiv.org/pdf/1612.03961.pdf (2016)
34. Pratt, H., Coenen, F., Broadbent, D.M., Harding, S.P., Zheng, Y.: Convolutional neural networks for diabetic retinopathy. Procedia Comput. Sci. **90**, 200–205 (2016)
35. Ghosh, R., Ghosh, K., Maitra, S.: Automatic detection and classification of diabetic retinopathy stages using CNN. In: 4th International Conference on Signal Processing and Integrated Networks (SPIN), pp. 550–554. IEEE, USA (2017)
36. Adal, K.M., Ali, S., Sidibe, D., Karnowski, T., Chaum, E., Meriaudeau, F.: Automated detection of microaneurysms using robust blob descriptors. In: SPIE Medical Imaging-Computer Aided Diagnosis, vol. 8670, no. 22 (2013)
37. Adal, K.M., Sidibe, D., Ali, S., Chaum, E., Karnowski, T.P., Meriaudeau, F.: Automated detection of microaneurysms using scale-adapted blob analysis and semi-supervised learning. Comput. Methods Programs Biomed. **114**, 1–10 (2014)
38. Akram, M.U., Khalid, S., Tariq, A., Khan, S.A., Azam, F.: Detection and classification of retinal lesions for grading of diabetic retinopathy. Comput. Biol. Med. **45**, 161–171 (2014)
39. Akram, M.U., Khalid, S., Khan, S.A.: Identification and classification of microaneurysms for early detection of diabetic retinopathy. Pattern Recogn. **46**, 107–116 (2012)
40. Alipour, S.H.M., Rabbani, H., Akhlaghi, M.R.: Diabetic retinopathy grading by digital curvelet transform. Comput. Math. Med. **2012**, 1–11 (2012)
41. Antal, B., Hajdu, A.: Improving microaneurysm detection in color fundus images by using context-aware approaches. Comput. Med. Imaging Graph. **37**, 403–408 (2013)
42. Aravind, C., Ponnibala, M., Vijayachitra, S.: Automatic detection of microaneurysms and classification of diabetic retinopathy images using SVM technique. In: IJCA Proceedings on International Conference on Innovations in Intelligent Instrumentation, Optimization and Electrical Sciences ICIIIOES, no. 11, pp. 18–22 (2013)
43. Hatanaka, Y., Inoue, T., Okumura, S., Muramatsu, C., Fujita, H.: Automated microaneurysm detection method based on double-ring filter and feature analysis in retinal fundus images. In: Soda, P. (eds.) Proceedings of the 25th International Symposium on Computer-Based Medical Systems, CBMS, pp. 1–4. IEEE, USA (2012)
44. Kose, C., Sevik, U., Ikibas, C., Erdol, H.: Simple methods for segmentation and measurement of diabetic retinopathy lesions in retinal fundus images. Comput. Methods Programs in Biomed. **107**, 274–293 (2012)
45. Lichode, R.V., Kulkarni, P.S.: Automatic diagnosis of diabetic retinopathy by hybrid multi-layer feed forward neural network. Int. J. Sci. Eng. Technol. Res. (IJSETR) **2**(9), 1727–1733 (2013)
46. Prakash, J., Sumanthi, K.: Detection and classification of microaneurysms for diabetic retinopathy. Int. J. Eng. Res. Appl. **4**, 31–36 (2013)
47. Priya, R., Aruna, P.: Diagnosis of diabetic retinopathy using machine learning techniques. J. Soft Comput. **3**(4), 563–575 (2013)

48. Punnolil, A.: A novel approach for diagnosis and severity grading of diabetic maculopa-thy. In: Proceedings of the 2013 International Conference on Advances in Computing, Communications and Informatics, pp. 1230–1235. IEEE, New York (2013)

49. Saleh, M.D., Eswaran, C.: An automated decision-support system for non-proliferative dia-betic retinopathy disease based on Mas and HAs detection. Comput. Methods Programs Biomed. **108**, 186–196 (2012)

50. Selvathi, D., Prakash, N.B., Balagopal, N.: Automated detection of diabetic retinopathy for early diagnosis using feature extraction and support vector machine. Int. J. Emerg. Technol. Adv. Eng. **2**(11), 762–767 (2012)

51. Sopharak, A., Uyyanonvara, B., Barman, S.: Automated microaneurysm detection algorithms applied to diabetic retinopathy retinal images. Maejo Int. J. Sci. Technol. **7**(2), 294–314 (2013)

52. Sujithkumar, S.B., Vipula, S.: Automatic detection of diabetic retinopathy in non-dilated RGB retinal fundus images. Int. J. Comput. Appl. **47**(19), 26–32 (2012)

53. Sundhar, C., Archana, D.: Automatic screening of fundus images for detection of diabetic retinopathy. Int. J. Commun. Comput. Technol. **2**(1), 100–105 (2014)

54. Chudzik, P., Majumdar, S., Caliva, F., Al-Diri, B., Hunter, A.: Microaneurysm detection using deep learning and interleaved freezing. In: Proceedings SPIE 10574, Medical Imaging 2018: Image Processing 1057411, pp. 1–9 (2018)

55. Lam, C., Yu, C., Huang, L., Rubin, D.: Retinal lesion detection with deep learning using image patches. Invest. Ophthalmol. Vis. Sci. **59**(1), 590–596 (2018)

56. Hatanaka, Y., Ogohara, K., Sunayama, W., Miyashita, M., Muramatsu, C., Fujita, H.: Auto-matic microaneurysms detection on retinal images using deep convolution neural network. In: International Workshop on Advanced Image Technology (IWAIT), pp. 1–2 (2018)

57. Dai, L., Fang, R., Li, H., Hou, X., Sheng, B., Wu, Q., Jia, W.: Clinical report guided retinal microaneurysm detection with multi-sieving deep learning. IEEE Trans. Med. Imaging **37**(5), 1149–1161 (2018)

58. Harangi, B., Toth, J., Hajdu, A.: Fusion of deep convolutional neural networks for microa-neurysm detection in color fundus images. In: 2018 40th Annual International Conference of the IEEE Engineering in Medicine and Biology Society (EMBC), pp. 3705–3708 (2018)

59. Shan, J., Li, L.: A deep learning method for microaneurysm detection in fundus images. In: 2016 IEEE First International Conference on Connected Health: Applications, Systems and Engineering Technologies (CHASE), pp. 357–358 (2016)

60. Haloi, M.: Improved microaneurysm detection using deep neural network. https://arxiv.org/pdf/1505.04424.pdf (2016)

61. Tan, J.H., et al.: Automated segmentation of exudates, haemorrhages, microaneurysms using single convolutional neural network. Inf. Sci. **420**, 66–76 (2017)

62. Tariq, A., Akram, M.U., Shaukat, A., Khan, S.A.: Automated detection and grading of diabetic maculopathy in digital retinal images. J. Digit. Imaging **26**(4), 803–812 (2013)

63. Vimala, A.G.S.G., Kajamohideen, S.: Detection of diabetic maculopathy in human retinal images using morphological operations. Online J. Biol. Sci. **14**, 175–180 (2014)

64. Siddalingaswamy, P.C., Prabhu, K.G.: Automatic grading of diabetic maculopathy severity levels. In: Mahadevappa, M. et al. (eds.) Proceedings of the 2010 International Conference on Systems in Medicine and Biology, pp. 331–334. Excel India Publishers, New Delhi (2010)

65. Hunter, A., Lowell, J. A., Steel, D., Ryder, B., Basu, A.: Automated diagnosis of referable maculopathy in diabetic retinopathy screening. In: Proceedings of 2011 Annual Interna-tional Conference of the IEEE Engineering in Medicine and Biology Society, EMBC 2011, pp. 3375–3378. IEEE, USA (2011)

66. Chowriappa, P., Dua, S., Rajendra, A.U., Muthu, R.K.M.: Ensemble selection for feature-based classification of diabetic maculopathy images. Comput. Biol. Med. **43**(12), 2156–2162 (2013)

67. Sonka, M., Hlavac, V., Boyle, R.: Image Processing, Analysis, and Machine Vision. Cengage Learning, United States of America (2008)

68. Sheet, D., Garud, H., Suveer, A., Mahadevappa, M., Chatterjee, J.: Brightness preserving dynamic fuzzy histogram equalization. IEEE Trans. Consum. Electron. **56**(4), 2475–2480 (2010)

69. Joshi, S., Karule, P.T.: Retinal blood vessel segmentation. Int. J. Eng. Innov. Technol. **1**(3), 175–178 (2012)

70. Sreng, S., Maneerat, N., Hamamoto, K., Panjaphongse, R.: Automated diabetic retinopathy screening system using hybrid simulated annealing and ensemble bagging classifier. Appl. Sci. **8**(7), 1198 (2018)

71. Rahim, S.S., Jayne, C., Palade, V., Shuttleworth, J.: Automatic detection of microaneurysms in colour fundus images for diabetic retinopathy screening. J. Neural Comput. Appl. **521**, 1–16 (2015)

72. Garud, H., et al.: Brightness preserving contrast enhancement in digital pathology. In: Siddavatan, R., Ghrera, S.P. (eds.) Proceedings of the 2011 International Conference on Image Information Processing (ICIIP 2011), pp. 1–5. IEEE, USA (2011)

73. Rahim, S.S., Palade, V., Shuttleworth, J., Jayne, C., Omar, R.N.R.: Automatic detection of microaneurysms for diabetic retinopathy screening using fuzzy image processing. In: Iliadis, L., Jayne, C. (eds.) EANN 2015. CCIS, vol. 517, pp. 69–79. Springer, Cham (2015). https://doi.org/10.1007/978-3-319-23983-5_7

74. Toh, K.K.V., Mat Isa, N.A.: Noise adaptive fuzzy switching median filter for salt-and-pepper noise reduction. IEEE Signal Process. Lett. **17**(3), 281–284 (2010)

75. Rahim, S.S., Palade, V., Jayne, C., Holzinger, A., Shuttleworth, J.: Detection of diabetic retinopathy and maculopathy in eye fundus images using fuzzy image processing. In: Guo, Y., Friston, K., Aldo, F., Hill, S., Peng, H. (eds.) BIH 2015. LNCS (LNAI), vol. 9250, pp. 379–388. Springer, Cham (2015). https://doi.org/10.1007/978-3-319-23344-4_37

76. Rahim, S.S., Palade, V., Shuttleworth, J., Jayne, C.: Automatic screening and classification of diabetic retinopathy fundus images. In: Mladenov, V., Jayne, C., Iliadis, L. (eds.) EANN 2014. CCIS, vol. 459, pp. 113–122. Springer, Cham (2014). https://doi.org/10.1007/978-3-319-11071-4_11

77. Holzinger, A., Langs, G., Denk, H., Zatloukal, K., Mueller, H.: Causability and Explainability of Artificial Intelligence in Medicine. Wiley Interdiscip. Rev. Data Mining Knowl. Discov. **9**(4) (2019)

78. Holzinger, A., Carrington, A., Müller, H.: Measuring the Quality of Explanations: The System Causability Scale (SCS). Comparing Human and Machine Explanations. KI - Künstliche Intelligenz (German Journal of Artificial intelligence), Special Issue on Interactive Machine Learning, Edited by Kristian Kersting, TU Darmstadt, vol. 34, no. 2, pp. 193–198 (2020)

Higher Education Teaching Material on Machine Learning in the Domain of Digital Pathology

Klaus Strohmenger[1,2]([✉]) [iD], Christian Herta[1,2] [iD], Oliver Fischer[1,2] [iD], Jonas Annuscheit[1,2] [iD], and Peter Hufnagl[1,2,3]

[1] HTW Berlin - University of Applied Sciences,
Wilhelminenhofstr. 75a, 12459 Berlin, Germany
{klaus.strohmenger,christian.herta,oliver.fischer,
jonas.annuscheit,peter.hufnagl}@htw-berlin.de
[2] CBMI - Centre for Biomedical Image and Information Processing,
Ostendstraße 25 1a, 12459 Berlin, Germany
[3] Charité Universitätsmedizin Berlin - Institute for Pathology,
Charitépl. 1, 10117 Berlin, Germany
peter.hufnagl@charite.de
https://cbmi.htw-berlin.de/

Abstract. Machine learning (ML) and especially deep learning (DL) are doubtless one of the key technologies of the last couple of years and future decades. Learning its theoretical concepts alone is a big challenge as it requires a strong background in mathematics and computer science. Once students and researchers have built up on the core concepts and recent algorithms using toy data sets and want to move forward tackling real-world application scenarios, they are confronted with additional problems, specific to the application domain. Digital pathology is one of those domains that has many of these additional issues, such as: New file formats, large images, and the amount of medical expertise needed to capture the underlying problem is relatively large. In our project deepteaching.org we provide teaching materials to introduce computer science students to the use of ML for digital pathology. As example, we present the application of pathologic N-stage (pN-stage) classification by dividing it into sub-tasks and propose - step by step - how different machine and deep learning, as well as computer vision techniques, can be combined to contribute to the main objective.

Keywords: Higher education · Machine learning · Digital pathology · Cancer detection

1 Introduction and Motivation

The year 2012 marks the beginning of a new chapter in ML and computer vision. It was the first time a convolutional neural network (CNN) won the ImageNet

Supported by the German Ministry of Education and Research (BMBF), project number 01IS17056.

A. Holzinger et al. (Eds.): AI & ML for Digital Pathology, LNAI 12090, pp. 155–174, 2020.
https://doi.org/10.1007/978-3-030-50402-1_10

Large Scale Visual Recognition Challenge (ILSVRC), reducing the top-5 error from approximately 26% to 15% [15]. Since then CNNs attained a lot of interest, accelerating research of neural networks (NNs) and DL in general. 2014 almost human accuracy (5.1%) was achieved with GoogLeNet (6.7%) [28] and surpassed in 2015 with an ensemble of deep residual nets (3.6%) [22].

In the meantime ML, and especially DL have made its way from benchmarks data sets into practical real-world applications. This includes various speech assistants, e.g. Google Now, Amazon's Alexa or Apple's Siri [26], driver-assistance systems, various neural machine translation systems for translation of written text or even Microsoft's Skype Translator for real-time voice translation [10]. The trend suggests, that ML will most likely keep capturing more and more areas of life. This means also, that the need for ML experts will also keep increasing. Therefore, in 2018 the German government decided to establish 100 new professorships for artificial intelligence (AI) to meet the upcoming need in industry and research [6].

When we focus on medicine and image recognition tasks, we also notice some great recent advances: In 2017, a CNN achieved performance comparable to dermatologists in classifying skin cancer [20], even more, human expert level has also been reached in detecting tumorous tissue on whole-slide-images (WSIs) of Hematoxylin and Eosin (H&E) stained slides [24]. Yet, until we reach a state in which an augmented pathology software or even a fully autonomous digital pathologist is ready for productive usage, a lot of barriers still have to be taken [23]. This includes hardware limitations, but also more reliable and explainable algorithms, for which again, more ML experts are needed.

ML is a tough topic and proper education is not an easy task to accomplish. Students of computer science oriented degrees often have a hard time understanding the mathematics needed to understand basic concepts like loss functions, gradient descent, backpropagation or convolution operations, whereas students of more mathematical oriented degrees have difficulties with computer science tasks, like file formats, data pre- and post-processing, hardware limitations or usage of programming languages and frameworks in general. And even when students manage to overcome their deficiencies in the mentioned topics, they still miss one important skill to truly be able to contribute to ML applications for real-world problems. That is domain knowledge of the application and also problems and limitations of computer science, specific to the scope conditions of that domain. Figure 1 depicts this constellation in general. The center term data science in the diagram is described by the author as the combination of mathematics, statistics, and hacking skills - which gets you ML - and additionally on top substantive expertise to ask the right questions about the scenario and to form valuable hypotheses, that can be validated with the former mentioned ML skills [7].

For pN-stage classification e.g., this expertise knowledge includes: Why examine especially the local lymph nodes in case of breast cancer. What are pN-stages. How are micro- and macrometastases defined. How to read the slide scanners

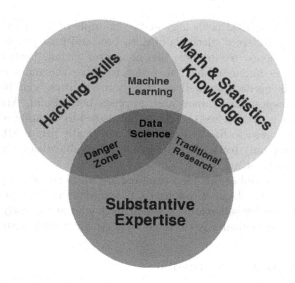

Fig. 1. Often cited Venn Diagram from Drew Conway (CC-BY-NC 3.0) showing the skills needed by a data scientist. Mathematics, statistics, and hacking skills, gets you ML. Substantive expertise knowledge, in addition, is required to formulate the right questions [7].

file formats. Why you can not read a complete WSI into random-access memory (RAM) at once and how to solve this.

Another problem is, that during the study of ML, problems are often viewed in isolation and explained using toy data sets. The aim is to understand and practice algorithms of ML. While facing real-world scenarios, it can be very hard to recognize which problems might be solvable with currently available and approved methods of AI and how. In most cases, a task cannot be considered as a whole, but must be divided into sub-tasks beforehand. Each sub-task requires different methods and techniques. In the context of pN-stage classification this is already given by the fact, that the pN-stage of a patient cannot be determined at once. The pN-stage is determined by the class of multiple WSIs from that patient, each showing tissue of one lymph node local to the primary tumor. A WSI can neither be classified at once, simply because of the RAM limitations of common desktop computers. Reading in and uncompressing one WSI, with a file size of four gigabytes, into a three dimensional array (width, height, colors) of eight-bit unsigned integer values (uint8) can easily exceed 50 GB or more [23]. Therefore, the problem must be divided into sub-problems. Afterwards, the intermediate results of the sub-problems must be combined hierarchically to get the result for the pN-stage.

To help students and upcoming researchers to overcome the gap from artificial toy examples to practical applications of ML, we developed the deep-teaching.org platform. Besides courses teaching the fundamentals of ML theory, including the mathematics, we offer well prepared and presented real-world application scenarios, one being digital pathology at the example of pN-stage classification. In these scenarios, different methods of data pre- and post-processing, ML and other computer science techniques, like computer vision, have to be used to solve the sub-tasks and combined in order to solve the main objective. The different methods needed, as well as their mathematics, can be learned and practiced in corresponding courses and exercises beforehand. Another purpose of these scenarios is also to keep students motivated in learning as they can see exactly what they need to finally implement practically useful ML applications. In contrast, solving only toy exercises without a tangible vision quickly becomes tiresome and demotivating.

All teaching-material of the deep-teaching.org platform is freely available. Its aimed audience are teachers of ML and DL, students and everyone who wants to learn these topics by self-study or researchers who are already familiar with them but want to specifically get started with AI for digital pathology.

2   Glossary and Key Terms

Artificial intelligence (AI) is intelligence, demonstrated by a machine, in contrast to natural intelligence. It is a superset including the subsets ML and DL. A simple rule based decision-making program, defined beforehand by a human expert already classifies as AI.

Application Program Interface (API) (application programming interface). A set of functions, classes, and other constructs enabling access to the features of a library, framework or any other service.

A *convolutional neural network (CNN)* is a special form of NN, utilizing convolutional operations to achieve translation equivariance of groups of features. Typically used for two-dimensional data like images, but can also be used on other dimensional data, where locality of features matters, e.g. speech or text for one-dimensional data.

Deep learning (DL) is a subset of ML and - in contrast to it - is able to extract features on its own, ideally to completely making manual feature extraction superfluous. Typically realized as some form of NN.

Data Science: Interdisciplinary field incorporating computer science, mathematics, statistics, and domain knowledge to make valuable use of structured or unstructured data.

Hematoxylin and Eosin (H&E) is a widely used combination of histological stains. Stains the cell nuclei blue and extracellular matrix and cytoplasm pink.

A *Heatmap* is a small resolution, greyscale image of a WSI, depicting the confidence for tumorous tissue of the classifier.

Isolated tumor cells (ITCs). Strictly not a metastasis. A region of tumorous tissue up to 200 cells and/or smaller than 0.2 mm [4].

Macro metastases. A region of tumorous tissue with a size of at least 2.0 mm [4].

Micro metastases. A region of tumorous tissue of more than 200 cells or size between 0.2 and 2.0 mm [4].

Machine learning (ML) is a subset of AI and superset of DL. In contrast to rule-based AI, with the rules defined beforehand, ML methods can derive their own rules from labeled training data.

Neural network (NN) is a short form for artificial neural network, a ML algorithm based on non-linear transformations of input features, loss function, gradient descent and backpropagation. It shares some similarities with a biological neural network, like hierarchically ordered neurons to process and forward information. A neuron might get activated if the summed up incoming signal of preceding neurons is strong enough.

The *pN-stage* is part of the tumor nodes metastasis (TNM) system focusing on the pathologic N-stage [1].

Random-access memory (RAM) is a volatile form of system memory. Its benefits are, that read and write access is almost the same everywhere independently of the physical location inside the memory and a several hundred times faster access than for information stored on magnetic hard discs.

A *tile* is a small region of a WSI with a fixed size, e.g. 256×256 pixels. It can be of any magnification level.

Tumor nodes metastasis (TNM) System: "A system to describe the amount and spread of cancer in a patient's body, using TNM. T describes the size of the tumor and any spread of cancer into nearby tissue; N describes spread of cancer to nearby lymph nodes; and M describes metastasis (spread of cancer to other parts of the body). This system was created and is updated by the American Joint Committee on Cancer (AJCC) and the International Union Against Cancer (UICC). The TNM staging system is used to describe most types of cancer. Also called AJCC staging system" [3].

Whole-slide-image. "A digitized histopathology glass slide that has been created on a slide scanner. The digitized glass slide represents a high-resolution replica of the original glass that can then be manipulated through software to mimic microscope review and diagnosis. Also referred to as a virtual slide" [5].

3   Teaching Concept

In this section, we will briefly describe the concept of the deep-teaching.org platform as a whole and the pN-stage classification application scenario in detail.

3.1   The Deep Teaching Platform

To understand the descriptions of the pN-stage classification application scenario it is necessary to also describe the deep-teaching.org platform, as the underlying teaching concepts are roughly the same and interconnections between courses and application scenarios exist. For example, there is an exercise on decision trees and random forests using a toy data set in the course *Introduction to Machine Learning* and a decision tree is the proposed solution to classify WSIs based on extracted features of heatmaps which were generated with the help of a CNN.

Teaching Material. The teaching material is realized in the form of Jupyter Notebooks, which can be viewed and edited in the Jupyter Notebook[1] environment. The idea behind Jupyter Notebook is to store an experiment as a whole in a single file. This includes a description of the experiment, the code to load and preprocess the data, code to visualize the data, code to execute the experiment and finally code to post-process and analyze the results. A notebook file consists of an arbitrary amount of code and markdown cells, which can be added, edited and executed anytime. The markdown cells support markdown syntax as well as pure HTML syntax and are therefore capable of capturing text, tables, and images. These cells are suitable to, e.g. store the experiment description, the conclusion, intermediate interpretation or explanation of code cells. Code cells house blocks of code and can be executed individually. So when the code of a cell to process data or to learn a ML model did not work as expected, one does not have to rerun the whole experiment. Instead, changes can be made to the corresponding cells, which then can be rerun individually. These features are not only ideally suited to present experiments but also to present teaching material, including theoretical concepts, exercise descriptions, exercises with optionally boilerplate code (e.g. to load the data set) and code to check the results for correctness.

Courses and Application Scenarios. The Jupyter Notebooks are organized in courses and application scenarios. Notebooks of courses mainly focus on a single ML algorithm or technique, as small as possible, and understanding and practicing its underlying math. Although many of these algorithms are implemented and optimized for performance in modern ML libraries and frameworks like scikit-learn[2], TensorFlow[3] or PyTorch[4], it is very much advisable to also understand them. Else, when working with these frameworks, development of ML applications is likely to become an untargeted try and error process with a questionable result. Currently available course are: *Introduction to Machine Learning, Introduction to Neural Networks, Convolutional Neural Networks, Bayesian Learning, Sequence Learning, Differentiable Programming.*

Application scenarios do not focus on a single algorithm or technique, but on a main objective, like pN-stage classification for the scenario called *Medical Image Classification.* As the main objective can not be approached at once, several sub-tasks have to be solved beforehand. Other than most course notebooks, the exercises of application scenarios often are not closed in itself and working on certain exercises relies on the results of preceding ones. Also, it is advised to have worked through certain courses before approaching an application scenario. For the scenario *Medical Image Classification*, the recommended courses are *Introduction to Machine Learning, Introduction to Neural Networks* and

---

[1] https://jupyter.org/.
[2] https://scikit-learn.org/stable/.
[3] https://www.tensorflow.org/.
[4] https://pytorch.org/.

Convolutional Neural Networks. Other available scenarios are *Robotic Autonomous Driving* and *Natural Language Processing.*

Website and Repository. All teaching material is stored in a git repository to allow collaborative development including all benefits of a version control system. The solutions to exercises are maintained in a separate repository, which is in contrast to the former, not publicly available. The code for the website also resides in an additional repository. When new material is uploaded, changes to existing material or changes of the code for the website are made, a so-called hookup, configured in the repositories, informs the server hosting the deep-teaching.org website, which then downloads the recent version. This way the website is at all times automatically up to date.

The website, therefore, includes all courses, application scenarios and a non-editable preview of the exercises. To interactively work on them, the website further gives instructions on how to install all needed software, the most important being a recent python version, the Jupyter Notebook environment, and python libraries and frameworks like NumPy[5], matplotlib[6], scikit-learn, TensorFlow and PyTorch.

3.2   Medical Image Classification

The main purpose of the presented application scenario is to introduce students into the field of ML for digital pathology, but also to show how to approach real-world problems in general including their side problems. The presented task of pN-stage classification is based on the Camelyon16 and Camelyon17 challenges and its data sets. That means, after completing all exercises, a student will have built a complete data processing and ML pipeline as it is needed to participate in the challenges. For teaching purpose, the proposed solutions are not too complex, therefore the pipeline will not yield optimal results when compared to the top performing submission of the Camelyon17 challenge. Though, after each exercise, tips and links to literature are given on how to improve the results. The intention of this approach is to equip the students with a working pipeline as fast and easy as possible. After that, further improvements are up to him/her.

3.3   Summary Page

At the summary page[7], students first find a brief introduction into the problem, that is, determining the pN-stage of a patient based on the analysis of given WSIs. The summary page also includes explanations about breast cancer in general, the role of pathology, the TNM system, the pN-stages, WSIs, ITCs, micro- and macrometastases, the data set, and soft- and hardware requirements.

Next follows a short description of the sub tasks which have to be worked through one after another, organized in four bigger groups:

---

[5] https://NumPy.org/.

[6] https://matplotlib.org/.

[7] https://www.deep-teaching.org/courses/medical-image-classification.

1. WSI Preprocessing (see Sect. 3.6):
   - Introduction into the handling of WSI data.
   - Dividing WSIs into smaller tiles.
   - Creating a fast accessible data set of tiles for training a CNN.
2. Tile Classification (see Sect. 3.7):
   - Training a CNN to predict whether a tile contains metastases or not.
   - Predicting/Assigning a score between 0.0 and 1.0 to each tile of the WSIs in the test set.
   - Combining all prediction results of a WSI to form a heatmap.
3. WSI classificationn (see Sect. 3.8):
   - Manually extract features of the heatmaps, e.g. area of the biggest region of high confidence (score).
   - Training a decision tree with extracted features.
   - Predicting each slide if it contains no metastases, ITCs, micro- or macro-metastases.
4. pN-stage classificationn (see Sect. 3.9):
   - Assigning the pN-stage to each patient based on the predicted labels (normal, ITC, micro, macro)
   - Calculating the weighted kappa score for the pN-stage predictions.

Most of these steps or similar ones were also followed by the majority of teams that participated in the Camelyon17 challenge [16]. Each sub-task is briefly described on the summary page and corresponding exercises are linked. The exercises contain additional information on the sub-task, but less with the big picture in mind and more related to the sub-task itself. Besides these exercises specific to the application scenario, more generic exercises on the ML algorithm or technique used are linked as well.

3.4 Camelyon Data Set

The data set is divided into two sub data sets, the Camelyon16 and the Camelyon17 data set. They are named after their competitions, see [2] for more details. Participating at the later one did not require participating at the first one officially but technically, as efficiently solving the Camelyon17 challenge requires the results of its precursor.

The Camelyon16 data set consists of 270 WSIs in the training set and 130 in the test set. The WSIs of the training set are only labeled with positive (contains metastases) or negative (no metastases). Also, XML files are included for positive slides, containing coordinates for polygons to describe the metastatic regions. The XML files for the test set were not publicly available until the end of the Camelyon16 challenge in November 2016. Together with the XML files, the labels *normal, ITC, micro* and *macro* were released.

The Camelyon17 training set, as well as the test set, contains 100 patients each. Each patient consists of five WSIs. The labels are *normal, ITC, micro* and *macro*. In contrast to the Camelyon16 data set, XML files describing the tumorous regions are only provided for 50 WSIs of the training set. Labels of the test set are still not publicly available, so it is still possible to submit results (Table 1).

Table 1. Summary of the data set. *Labels* column shows the number of examples for each label. *Annotations* shows the number of WSIs for which XML files, containing information about the tumorous tissue locations.

Data set	Labels	Annotations
Camelyon16 train	160 normal, 110 tumor	110
Camelyon16 test	80 none, 28 micro, 22 macro	50
Camelyon17 train	313 none, 35 ITC, 64 micro, 88 macro	50
Camelyon17 test	500 unknown	–

Since the data sets only contain WSIs of H&E stained slides and only five slides per patient, it is not possible to distinguish between all 18 pN-stages of breast cancer. For example, to distinguish between pN2- and pN3-stages, 10 or more WSIs per patient would be required. To distinguish between pN0 and pN0(i-), the absence of ITCs must be confirmed by immunohistochemistry stained slides [14]. Therefore the labels are limited to the five pN-stages, shown in Table 2.

Table 2. The five pN-stages which can be determined by examining five WSIs of H&E stained slides.

pN-stage	Description
pN0	Only normal tissue
pN0(i+)	At most ITCs found
pN1mi	At most micrometastases found
pN1	Metastases found in 1–3 nodes. At least one being a macrometastasis
pN2	Metastases found in 4–9 nodes. At least one being a macrometastasis

3.5   Requirements

To work on the exercises, we provide instructions on how to prepare, though at the moment we only provide instructions for the operating system Ubuntu 18.04. Windows, OSX and other Linux distributions should also work but are not tested by us. The suggested installation on Ubuntu is via conda[8]. After having conda installed the following commands can be used to create a virtual environment, to install openslide[9], Jupyter, NumPy and other python packages:

---

[8] https://docs.conda.io/.
[9] https://openslide.org/.

```
conda install scipy=1.3.1
conda install tensorflow-gpu=1.14
conda install -c bioconda openslide=3.4.1
conda install -c conda-forge libiconv=1.15
conda install -c bioconda openslide-python==1.1.1
pip install openslide-python==1.1.1
pip install progress==1.5
pip install scikit-image==0.16.2
```

To work through the application scenario from the beginning to the end, at least 3.5 TB of disk space are required to store the Camelyon16 and Camelyon17 data sets and a preprocessed Camelyon16 data set. Further, a GPU with at least 8 GB of RAM is recommended, e.g. the Nvidia Geforce 1070 GTX or better. As a lot of students cannot afford such hardware, we provide downloadable heatmaps for all WSIs of the Camelyon16 and Camelyon17 data set. Using these, the exercises of the first two groups (WSI pre-processing, Tile classification) can be skipped and students can start with the exercises of the third group (WSI classification). Nevertheless, we strongly suggest to still read through the whole summary page and also the Jupyter Notebooks of the first two groups to get the big picture of the data processing pipeline.

3.6 WSI Preprocessing

Transitioning from ML tutorials using common image benchmark or toy data sets, the first hurdle is the file format of WSIs. Having completed a beginners ML tutorial for images, chances are very high, either the MNIST[10] or cifar10[11] data set has been used. These data sets are typically stored in an easy to read format. For example, the cifar10 data set is downloadable as Python cPickled[12] object. Unpickeling it yields a dictionary including the elements *labels* and *data. labels* is just a list object storing the class labels and data is a multidimensional NumPy array of uint8 values. Both are ready to use with a ML library of choice. In the meantime, some libraries, like TensorFlow even have incorporated functions to load such toy data sets in their API[13], so one does not even have to download external files anymore.

Most WSIs come in JPEG2000 or TIFF format. TIFF formats themselve further differ depending on the slide scanners vendor. These files can neither be read by any default image viewer that comes pre-installed on Windows, OSX or Linux distributions and they can nor be read by any popular image processing library for programming languages. Besides proprietary vendor software, there is only a small number of open source software to read these formats. One of them is openslide. Its functionality is not officially supported by the slide scanner vendors, but readable formats include Aperio (.svs, .tif), Hamamatsu (.vms, .vmu,

---

[10] http://yann.lecun.com/exdb/mnist/.
[11] https://www.cs.toronto.edu/~kriz/cifar.html.
[12] https://docs.python.org/2/library/pickle.html.
[13] https://www.TensorFlow.org/datasets/.

.ndpi), Leica (.scn), MIRAX (.mrxs), Philips (.tiff), Sakura (.svslide), Trestle (.tif), Ventana (.bif, .tif) and Generic tiled TIFF (.tif) [12]. To use openslide, first about 10 other dependencies, some in very specific versions, have to be installed. Then source files can be downloaded from openslide.org and the program can be build. Luckily openslide was added to the package manager conda, which takes care of all of this. We also provide instructions for manual installation, but conda is suggested. Further, the python package *openslide-python* is required as an interface to openslide within a python program.

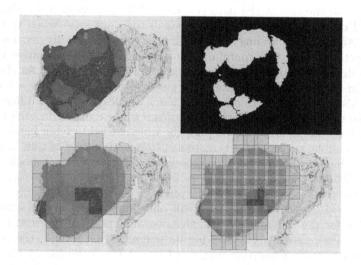

Fig. 2. Camelyon16 WSI *tumor_110*, visualized in the first notebook *data-handling-usage-guide*. The top left shows a thumbnail of the whole WSI. The top right is a binary mask, created from the corresponding XML file with coordinates of the tumorous regions. The bottom left shows which tiles whould be extracted on magnification level 6 (from 0 to 9), with a tile size of 128 × 128 pixels and no overlapping of the tiles. The bottom right shows the same but with 32 pixels overlap.

The first notebook *data-handling-usage-guide* comes with a small library, written by us, to easily access WSIs programmatically. It can be used as-is, or serve as an example on how to use the openslide interface in combination with the XML files for positive slides to find regions with tumorous tissue. It is mostly intended to give students a feeling of how to process WSIs. WSIs typically have a size of approximately 200.000 × 100.000 pixels. A practical approach to find out which regions contain tumorous tissue is to slice the whole WSI into smaller tiles. We will refer to this process as *tiling*. After that, we can train a CNN to predict whether a tile contains metastases (positive) or not (negative). Combining predictions of all tiles of a WSI will give us a heatmap. Figure 2 shows a WSI of the Camelyon16 data set labeled containing tumorous tissue. Executing the example code snippets of the first notebook we can, for example, get a thumbnail of the WSI (top left), a tumor mask, created with the information from the XML file (top right) and tiles of the regions containing tumorous tissue with varying overlapping parameter (bottom). So from the figure we can already see, on which things the notebook gives food for thought concerning the tiling process: Which size shall the tiles have? Which magnification level to chose? Shall they overlap or not, if so how much? For positive slides, what minimum percentage of the pixels must be tumorous so we label them as positive for our training set? For negative slides, how much percentage of the pixels must contain tissue (in contrast to slide background) so we use them as negative training tiles?

Because of the size of the data set, we will have to read in batches of tiles from hard drive (opposed to RAM for small toy data sets) when training the classifier. Additionally, finding suitable tiles is a computationally demanding task as we have to filter out tiles containing mostly background for negative WSIs and tiles containing not enough tumorous tissue for positive WSIs. As slides from different institutions or even different staining processes can vary a lot, e.g. in color, we also would prefer to compose a batch of tiles of as many different WSIs as possible to get a good representation of the whole data set in each batch. To fulfill these requirements while keeping the time needed to fetch batches of tiles as low as possible, we propose to create a custom training set of tiles beforehand.

This is done in the notebook *create-custom-dataset*. The notebook gives two options: *Option A* uses the highest possible magnification level (level 0) and resulting tiles will be of size 312×312 pixels, whereas *option B* only uses magnification level 2 and resulting tiles will only have a size of 256×256 pixels. The reason for the different sizes is, that we want positive slides to contain at least 60% tumorous tissue. If working on magnification level 3, the number of tiles containing 60% tumorous tissue will be a lot less the bigger the tile size. Although we will later train a CNN with tiles of 256×256, having bigger tiles allows us to use data augmentation by random cropping. From a single 312×312 tile we can get $(312-256)^2 = 3.136$ different 256×256 tiles, efficiently increasing the data set size. Concerning the tiling of negative WSIs, we want our data set to contain only tiles with at least 20% tissue. Similar parameters have been used by successful teams of the Camelyon challenge [8,18]. Both options will extract up to 1.000 tiles from each WSI. The time needed to create the data set will be about 10 times higher choosing *option A* (about 60 h). So if the user only wants to get familiar with the data processing pipeline and cares less about the results, there is an alternative consuming less time.

To store the tiles we use the HDF5 format, which is widely used for storing data sets. While the proprietary WSI formats of different scanner vendors vary in performance for random access, HDF5 has a stable and good performance for it, which will be beneficial when composing batches of tiles [21,29]. We also cannot do anything about the compression level of the WSI and therefore their reading performance, but we can adjust the compression level of the HDF5 file.

3.7   Tile Classification

Before we continue with the training of a CNN, we mention the necessity for color normalization. Slides from different institutions and even slides created within the same institution but in a different staining process can vary greatly in color. Figure 3 shows excerpts from two different WSIs of the Camelyon data set. Next, a generic exercise notebook on data augmentation for images, from the course *Convolutional Neural Networks* is linked. In it, the techniques rotation, mirroring, cropping and the application of Gaussian noise can be explored and practiced.

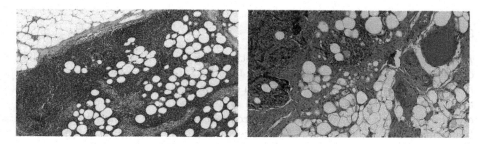

Fig. 3. Excerpts from two different WSIs of the Camelyon data set with strongly differing H&E staining. Left *Radboud University Medical Center, Nijmegen, Netherlands*, right *University of medical Center Utrecht, Netherlands*.

The notebook *exercise-train-cnn-TensorFlow* comes pre-equipped with a generator class featuring data augmentation by mirroring, rotations of multiples of 90° and cropping. TensorFlow suggests the use of a generator class. It allows parallel preloading of batches by multiple workers, while the NN still trains on the current batch. Color normalization, by subtracting the mean of each color channel and dividing by the standard deviation, is partly implemented and has to be completed. At the end of the notebook, hints for further improvement are given, which are adding Gaussian noise for more data augmentation and links to papers studying color normalization techniques specific to digital pathology [25,27]. As CNN architecture we suggest a InceptionResNetV2, a variant of the ResNet101, also used in [18] and [8]. The TensorFlow API allows loading a InceptionResNetV2 with weights pre-trained on the ImageNet data set. This way some training time can be saved as the first convolutional layers tend to develop similar filters for any data set [30].

The next step then is to use the trained CNN to predict all tiles of the Camelyon17 training set and the Camelyon16 test set. For each tile we will receive a score between 0.0 (no metastases) and 1.0. In order to generate a heatmap, the score must not yet be thresholded as this would result in a loss of information. Instead, we build a matrix, saving the score of each tile at the corresponding position. The most important thing to consider here is the overlap (or stride) in the tiling process. If no overlapping of the tiles was used, chances are high that a lot of tumorous regions will be miss classified as an originally big area of tumorous tissue might be split onto multiple tiles, where it only fills a minor percentage of the tile. Also, the higher the overlap, the higher the resolution of the resulting heatmap. The opposite of no overlap is the maximum overlap by only striding 1 pixel, which would result in heatmaps with the same resolution than their WSIs minus once the tile size in height and width. This would not only leave us with problems on how to further store and process the results but also require an unbearable amount of time for classification. A good compromise is an overlap of half the tile size, which is 128 pixels in height and width. The resulting heatmaps will therefore have $\frac{1}{128}$ of the original WSIs size.

3.8   WSI Classification

At this point, students can proceed with the heatmaps created by themselves or with the provided heatmaps. Figure 4 shows three examples of the provided heatmaps. They have been created with similar parameters. Notable differences are the color normalization process, in which specific lookup tables had been created for every WSI and the CNN architecture, which consisted of the combination of two inception v4 CNNs, one working on the highest magnification level and one on the second highest. For more details see [17].

The objective now is to predict whether a WSI, resp. its heatmap, contains no tumorous tissue, only ITCs, micro- or macrometastases. In contrast to the task of tile classification, where we had millions of tiles available for training, we now only have heatmaps of 500 WSIs of the Camelyon17 training set and 130 of the Camelyon16 test set. In addition, classes are very imbalanced, e.g. there only exist 35 WSIs with the label ITCs. It has been shown that this is not enough data to automate the process of feature extraction by using another CNN [17]. Almost all participating teams of the Camelyon challenge manually implemented handcrafted features extractors. The corresponding notebook in the application scenario is *exercise-extract-features*.

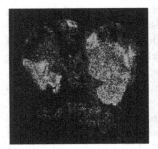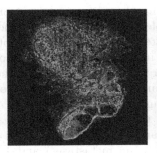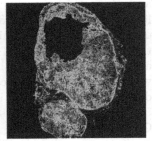

Fig. 4. Three samples of the provided heatmaps, generated with the implementation described in [17]. Original heatmaps are greyscale and have been colorized for visualization purpose, red indicating high confidence for tumorous tissue. (Color figure online)

The six proposed features to extract from each heatmap are shown in Fig. 5. Two of them can be directly extratced, which are *highest value on the heatmap (red)* and *average value (out of values greater than 0.0) (green)*. Before extracting the other four features, a threshold has to be applied to clearly distinguish between tissue likely to be tumorous or not. First, we propose a value of 0.5 as this would be the logical threshold one would choose to classify the tiles. Though it is not said, that this is the best value. Higher values will result in less noise, but they have also a higher chance that an in fact connected tumorous region might become split up into two or even more unconnected regions. Tuning of the threshold value is one of the suggested things for improvement at the end of this exercise. Following the approach of other successful teams [13,19], one could even extract the features multiple times with different thresholds and use them all together. If choosing a low threshold, some teams use morphological closing (dilation followed by erosion) to connect nearby regions after thresholding [13,17]. A more advanced technique than this could include clustering algorithms, e.g. DBSCAN [9]. It could also be worth trying to not only extract the morphological features of the biggest connected area but also of the second and third biggest connected region after thresholding [9,17].

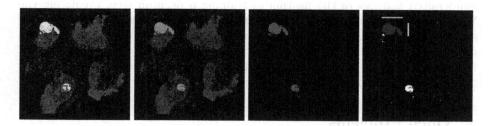

Fig. 5. We propose to extract six features: Highest value on the heatmap (red), average value (out of values greater than 0.0) (green), number of pixels after thresholding (magenta), major side length of the bounding box of the biggest area of connected pixels after thresholding (orange), minor side length of the biggest area after thresholding (yellow), number of pixels of the biggest area after thresholding (blue). (Color figure online)

When all heatmaps have been processed and the extracted features are stored in CSV files, a classifier, e.g. a decision tree can be trained and evaluated. As the size of the labeled data set (630 WSIs) is very small and training and evaluating a decision tree is only a matter of seconds, we suggest 10 fold cross-validation. The benefit of a simple decision tree is that it can easily be visualized and the students can see which features contribute the most. Afterwards, trying and evaluating other classifiers available in pythons scikit-learn library is easy and straight forward. Besides this notebook (*exercise-classify-heatmaps*) on the application scenario, generic notebooks on decision trees and entropy are linked on the summary page.

As a sidenote: The heatmaps, at first only being intermediate results to the final goal of pN-stage classification, are further reusable in the context of explainable AI. Although the reasons for the classification result of individual tiles (positive, negative) remain unknown without further modifications of the CNN, the predicted class of a WSI (e.g. micro or macro metastasis) can be validated by inspecting its regions highlighted (or not highlighted) on the heatmap.

3.9 pN-Stage Classification

So far, the classifier was only evaluated with accuracy and F_1 scores of the individual WSIs regardless of the patient they belong to. Now the pN-stages of the patients have to be determined. This is a simple rule base process, shown by Table 2. The quality of the final classification can then be calculated with a script provided by the Camelyon17 challenge, which calculates the weighted kappa score. The calculation of the kappa score as well as other evaluation metrics, e.g. accuracy and F_1 score, can be looked up and practiced in a generic notebook, which is linked on the summary page as well.

Students now have implemented a working data processing pipeline from reading pure WSIs, tiling of the WSIs, training a CNN to predict tiles, extracting handcrafted features of the heatmaps, training a decision tree, predicting the WSIs classes and finally determining a patient's pN-stage. Results on the training set, obtained via cross-validation, can be compared with the official results on the Camelyon17 website[14]. It has to be noted, that results on the Camelyon17 test set are likely to have a 5–10% lower kappa score, depending how much the classifier was fine-tuned on the available labeled data.

4   Open Problems

Scientific papers have to be as detailed as necessary and as formal as possible. This is not always the case for teaching material. Especially when it is also intended to be used for self-study. It is a balancing act between presenting as much information as possible, preserving formalism and at the same time avoiding to overwhelm students. Presenting too much complex information or writing exhaustive texts might lead to demotivation or skipping the read at all. Therefore, theoretical parts, as well as the exercise, will certainly have to be reworked after receiving more feedback. At this point, we also want to inform the reader, that we welcome any feedback on the teaching material via the issue tracker of the git repository[15]. Also, the ratio between predefined code in the exercises, to guide the direction, and code to be completed by the students might have to be adjusted.

While creating the teaching material of the application scenario, TensorFlow's latest version was 1.14. In the meantime a new major version 2.0 was

---

[14] https://camelyon17.grand-challenge.org/evaluation/results/.
[15] https://gitlab.com/groups/deep.TEACHING/-/issues.

released. The code from either version is not compatible with the other. To build and train a NN in TensorFlow version 1.x, a computational graph had to be defined, as well as a cost function and an optimizer. Once everything was set up, a statement to execute the computation was needed. Version 2.0 is designed around eager execution. That means, operations are evaluated as soon as they are executed and no complete graph has to be defined beforehand. The main reason for this change is probably that it feels more natural to the imperative programming style of python and debugging might also be easier. Additionally, many deprecated API calls and 'tf.contrib' have been removed [11]. So far the teaching material is not adapted to the newer version of TensorFlow. There are several ways of approaching the situation. The least effort would be required to just keep the instructions of the application scenarios requirements section as they are, which are to install TensorFlow 1.15, the latest 1.x version. The downside is that students would learn an outdated API, which is not effective concerning time spent on learning. This alone could still be justifiable because working on and extending applications based on much older libraries and frameworks (legacy code) is a big part of the daily work of many software developers and has to be practiced as well. The much bigger downside is, that exercises based on an outdated API will certainly attract fewer students for self-study. The second solution would be to use wrapper functions for 1.x code, provided by TensorFlow 2.0, which are promised to work throughout version 2.x [11]. However, this would entail the same problems and the code will most likely become more complex on top. The third solution would be to rewrite the teaching material in native TensorFlow 2.0 code. This would solve the problems mentioned, but most likely also require the most effort. Also, the same dilemma might arise again with the next new major version and the trend is towards even faster lifecycles of libraries and frameworks. Another solution would be to rewrite the teaching material to be completely independent of any DL framework. However, this would not allow us to provide the students with sample code, e.g. to guide the exercises. Although these kinds of problems are certainly not specific to our situation and apply to all kinds of rapidly evolving fields, computer science and especially DL has shown that it changes extremely fast. Unluckily there does not seem to be a general solution and arguments have to be weight differently in each case.

5 Future Challenges

We planned to keep the application scenario as easy as possible while still equipping the students with a working data processing pipeline covering the entire process from reading WSIs to tiling, tile prediction, heatmap creation, feature extraction, WSI prediction, and finally pN-stage classification. Completing only the least required in each of the exercises, the results are not competitive with the top performing submissions of the Camelyon challenge. Therefore, we added hints and references to recent papers at the end of each exercise to leave improvements up to the student. The most important improvements include:

Advanced color normalization techniques, specifically for histopathological images to improve the generalization abilities of the CNN [25,27]. Utilization of the CNN architecture to incorporate the benefits of Scannet [24]. While the approach with a standard InceptionResNetV2 uses one tile as input, e.g. 256×256, and outputs a single score for it, Scannet works with much bigger tiles, e.g. 2.868×2.868 pixels and outputs a map of 86×86 scores. The time needed to process a whole WSI in the prediction process is hundreds of times faster. Still the results for detection of micro- and macrometastases are competitive and even surpass human performance [24]. It is a method worth studying (and teaching) as it provides the speed needed for a lot of applications, e.g. real-time augmentation in virtual microscopy. For post-processing of the heatmaps, most promising approaches seem to be a combination of applying multiple thresholds, e.g. 0.1, 0.2, ..., 0.9, and using a clustering algorithm, e.g. DBSCAN [9], to group nearby regions before extracting morphological features.

We have made the experience, that just references to recent papers are not enough to encourage students to incorporate improvements on their own and that most papers seem to be too overwhelming. Therefore we plan to develop a follow-up application scenario to also cover these topics.

References

1. Background section of the hompage of the Camelyon17 challenge. https:// camelyon17.grand-challenge.org/background/. Accessed 18 Nov 2019
2. Data section of the hompage of the Camelyon17 challenge. https://camelyon17. grand-challenge.org/evaluation/. Accessed 18 Nov 2019
3. Definition of TNM System, Website of the National Cancer Institute. https:// www.cancer.gov/publications/dictionaries/cancer-terms/def/tnm-staging-system. Accessed 18 Nov 2019
4. Evaluation section of the hompage of the Camelyon17 challenge. https:// camelyon17.grand-challenge.org/evaluation/. Accessed 18 Nov 2019
5. Glossary on the hompage of the Digital Pathology Association. https:// digitalpathologyassociation.org/glossary-of-terms_1. Accessed 18 Nov 2019
6. Hegemann, L.: Wenn Politik auf künstliche Intelligenz trifft. In: Zeit Online (2018). https://www.zeit.de/digital/internet/2018-11/digitalisierung-ki-strategie-investitionen-bundesregierung. Accessed 18 Nov 2019
7. Hompage of Drew Conway. http://drewconway.com/zia/2013/3/26/the-data-science-venn-diagram. Accessed 04 Nov 2019
8. Lee, B., Paeng, K.: Breast Cancer Stage Classification in Histopathology Images. In: Submission results Camelyon17 challange. https://camelyon17.grand-challenge. org/evaluation/results/. Accessed 18 Nov 2019
9. Lee, S., Oh, S., Choi, K., Kim, S.: Automatic classification on patient-level breast cancer metastases. In: Submission results Camelyon17 challange. https:// camelyon17.grand-challenge.org/evaluation/results/. Accessed 18 Nov 2019
10. Lewis, W.: Skype translator: Breaking down language and hearing barriers. In: Translating and the Computer (TC37), London, pp. 125–149 (2015)
11. Migration guide of the Tensorflow hompage. https://www.tensorflow.org/guide/ migrate/. Accessed 19 Nov 2019

12. Openslide homepage. https://openslide.org/. Accessed 18 Nov 2019
13. Pinchaud, N., Hedlund, M.: Camelyon17 grand challenge. In: Submission results Camelyon17 challange. https://camelyon17.grand-challenge.org/evaluation/results/. Accessed 18 Nov 2019
14. Quick reference on cancer staging - Hompage of the American Joint Committee on Cancer. https://cancerstaging.org/references-tools/quickreferences/Documents/BreastMedium.pdf. Accessed 18 Nov 2019
15. Results of the ImageNet Large Scale Visual Recognition Challenge (ILSVRC) 2012. http://image-net.org/challenges/LSVRC/2012/results.html. Accessed 01 Nov 2019
16. Results section of the hompage of the Camelyon17 challenge. https://camelyon17.grand-challenge.org/evaluation/results/. Accessed 18 Nov 2019
17. Strohmenger, K., Annuscheit, J., Klempert, I., Voigt, B., Herta, C., Hufnagl, P.: Convolutional neural networks and random forests for detection and classification of metastasis in histological slides. In: Submission results Camelyon17 challange. https://camelyon17.grand-challenge.org/evaluation/results/. Accessed 18 Nov 2019
18. Unkown Author (alias Ozymandias): AI breast cancer detection. In: Submission results Camelyon17 challange. https://camelyon17.grand-challenge.org/evaluation/results/. Accessed 18 Nov 2019
19. Zhao, Z., Lin, H., Heng, P.: Breat Cancer pN-Stage classification for whole slide images. In: Submission results Camelyon17 challange. https://camelyon17.grand-challenge.org/evaluation/results/. Accessed 18 Nov 2019
20. Esteva, A., et al.: Dermatologist-level classification of skin cancer with deep neural networks. Nature **542**(7639), 115–118 (2017). https://doi.org/10.1038/nature21056
21. Folk, M., Heber, G., Koziol, Q., Pourmal, E., Robinson, D.: An overview of the HDF5 technology suite and its applications. In: Proceedings of the EDBT/ICDT 2011 Workshop on Array Databases, AD 2011, pp. 36–47. ACM, New York (2011). https://doi.org/10.1145/1966895.1966900, http://doi.acm.org/10.1145/1966895.1966900
22. He, K., Zhang, X., Ren, S., Sun, J.: Deep residual learning for image recognition. In: 2016 IEEE Conference on Computer Vision and Pattern Recognition (CVPR), pp. 770–778, June 2016. https://doi.org/10.1109/CVPR.2016.90
23. Holzinger, A., et al.: Towards the augmented pathologist: challenges of explainable-AI in digital pathology (2017)
24. Lin, H., Chen, H., Dou, Q., Wang, L., Qin, J., Heng, P.: Scannet: a fast and dense scanning framework for metastastic breast cancer detection from whole-slide image. In: 2018 IEEE Winter Conference on Applications of Computer Vision (WACV), pp. 539–546, March 2018. https://doi.org/10.1109/WACV.2018.00065
25. Magee, D., et al.: Colour normalisation in digital histopathology images. In: Proceedings Optical Tissue Image analysis in Microscopy, Histopathology and Endoscopy (MICCAI Workshop), January 2009
26. Parvat, A., Chavan, J., Kadam, S., Dev, S., Pathak, V.: A survey of deep-learning frameworks. In: 2017 International Conference on Inventive Systems and Control (ICISC), pp. 1–7, January 2017. https://doi.org/10.1109/ICISC.2017.8068684
27. Roy, S., kumar, J.A., Lal, S., Kini, J.: A study about color normalization methods for histopathology images. Micron **114**, 42–61 (2018). https://doi.org/10.1016/j.micron.2018.07.005. http://www.sciencedirect.com/science/article/pii/S0968432818300982

28. Russakovsky, O., et al.: Imagenet large scale visual recognition challenge. Int. J. Comput. Vision **115**(3), 211–252 (2015). https://doi.org/10.1007/s11263-015-0816-y
29. Satyanarayanan, M., Goode, A., Gilbert, B., Harkes, J., Jukic, D.: OpenSlide: a vendor-neutral software foundation for digital pathology. J. Pathol. Inform. **4**(1), 27 (2013). https://doi.org/10.4103/2153-3539.119005. https://doi.org/10.4103%2F2153-3539.119005
30. Shin, H., et al.: Deep convolutional neural networks for computer-aided detection: CNN architectures, dataset characteristics and transfer learning. IEEE Trans. Med. Imaging **35**(5), 1285–1298 (2016). https://doi.org/10.1109/TMI.2016.2528162

Classification vs Deep Learning in Cancer Degree on Limited Histopathology Datasets

Pedro Furtado[(✉)] [iD]

Universidade de Coimbra, 3000 Coimbra, Portugal
pnf@dei.uc.pt
http://eden.dei.uc.pt/~pnf

Abstract. Today deep learning techniques (DL) are the main focus in classification of disease conditions from histology slides, but this task used to be done by more traditional machine learning pipeline algorithms (MLp). The first can learn autonomously, without any feature engineering. But some questions arise: can we design a fully automated MLp? Can that MLp match DL, at least in some tasks? how should it be designed? Can both be useful and/or complement each other? In this chapter we try to answer those questions. In the process, we design an automated MLp, build DL architectures, apply both to cancer grading, compare accuracy experimentally and discuss the remaining issues. Surprisingly, a carefully designed MLp procedure (acc. 86.5%) compared favorably to deep learning (best acc. 82%) and to humans (acc. 84%) when detecting degree of atypia for breast cancer prognosis on limited-sized publicly available Mytos dataset, with the same DL architectures that achieved accuracies of 97% on a different cancer classification task. Most importantly, we discuss advantages and limitations of alternatives, in particular what features make DL superior and may justify that choice, but also how MLp can be almost fully automated and produce useful structures characterization. Finally, we raise challenges, identifying how MLp and DL should evolve to offer explainability and integrate humans in the loop.

Keywords: Digital pathology · Deep learning · Machine learning · Classification

1 Introduction

1.1 The Problem and Motivation

The definitions and procedures related to cancer prognosis based on histopathology analysis are well described in [6]. If a tumor is suspected to be malignant, a

Supported by U. Coimbra.

© Springer Nature Switzerland AG 2020
A. Holzinger et al. (Eds.): AI & ML for Digital Pathology, LNAI 12090, pp. 175–194, 2020.
https://doi.org/10.1007/978-3-030-50402-1_11

doctor removes all or part of it during a procedure called a biopsy. A pathologist then examines the biopsied tissue to determine whether the tumor is benign or malignant and the tumor's grade, identifying other characteristics of the tumor as well. The tumor grade is the description of a tumor based on how abnormal the tumor cells and the tumor tissue look under a microscope. It is an indicator of how quickly a tumor is likely to grow and spread. Lower grade tumors, with a good prognosis, can be treated less aggressively, and have a better survival rate. Higher grade tumors are treated more aggressively, and their intrinsically worse survival rate may warrant the adverse effects of more aggressive medications. An important aspect of expert analysis of the tissue is to detect variations in tissue and on its structures between different degrees of illness. Automatic grading of histopathology slides offers interesting challenges in terms of classification due to the convolved properties of the tissues and structures in histopathology slides. Deep learning (DL) using convolution neural networks (CNN) is state-of-the-art in this task, due to high accuracy and autonomous learning capabilities. Figure 1 shows an example from our own experiments classifying degree of atypia using DL on Mytos Atypia dataset [40], where the left image was correctly classified as grade 2 with 99.5% confidence, and the right image was correctly classified as grade 3 with 87.4% probability. DL has displaced techniques based on machine learning pipelines (MLp) that require custom-made code to segment, identify, extract and represent features of specific structures. The need to hand-code parts is usually identified as the main problem of MLp approaches, but in fact the crucial advantage of deep-learning approaches is end-to-end autonomous backpropagation learning, where a large number of iterations of gradient descent on error backpropagation allows the networks to adjust their weights until they have learnt how to estimate the required quantities as best as possible.

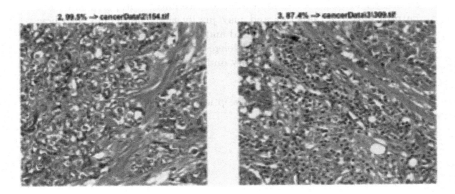

Fig. 1. Inception-V3 example classifications.

Given the lack of backpropagation learning and dependence on coding and operations choices in MLp, it is easy to design it in a very sub-optimal way, lacking the ability to extract and pick the best features for classification. This raises two main questions: can we design a code-free fully automated MLp, or close to such, that is potentially competitive with DL, at least in some tasks? Can both be useful and/or complement each other? We also investigate future challenges in the context of classification of disease conditions from histology slides and in other medical imaging classification tasks. Those challenges include how the techniques should evolve to enhance their clinical/medical usefulness, how to provide explainability and how to integrate humans in the loop.

1.2 Contributions

In order to answer the questions posed we build state-of-the-art DL classifiers to be applied in the classification of histology slides, and we develop an automated MLp approach that is as optimized as we can possibly devise to maximize accuracy. The design of the MLp approach with its ability to find the appropriate features is an important contribution. Another contribution concerns applying the two experimentally and comparing the results in a specific problem of atypia grading using a publicly available dataset (Mytos Atypia), the same DL architectures also being applied to another well-known cancer detection problem (BreakHis) to confirm their capabilities. We conclude that the well-design MLp approach is competitive and even surpasses DL in the atypia grading problem with limited dataset, achieving (acc. 86.5%), versus deep learning (best acc. 82%) and humans (acc. 84%). Another contribution in this work is to discuss how the two paradigms can be used and/or complement each other. We expect this discussion to help in terms of clarifying the strengths of each paradigm and pointing directions for research. As part of future challenges, we highlight the need to make both DL and MLp more interpretable and explainable [1] and the need to work further in integration of humans in the loop [2]. We also discuss briefly how analysis of features in MLp can in the future be explored to help the objective of explainability. The study of MLp versus DL and the discussions on how to address future challenges based on these two techniques are very relevant in the definition of how future clinical/medical AI systems should be designed.

1.3 Structure

This chapter is structured as follows: Sect. 2 is the glossary, introducing used terms to ensure a common understanding. Section 3, state-of-the-art, describes both related work, the state-of-the-art DL architectures used and the design of the automated MLp approach. Then it discusses materials and methods for the experimental data on grading and classifying cancers, reports and compares results and concludes. Section 4 discusses challenges and open issues. In the light of the experience gained with the designs and experiments, we discuss the advantages and limitations of the two paradigms. Section 5, Future Outlook, proposes how automated MLp approaches and DL approaches may evolve to play together, complement or simply improve their capabilities.

2   Glossary

Artificial Intelligence, AI - a broad concept related to models and algorithms that make computer systems able to perform tasks normally requiring human intelligence.

Machine learning, ML - the term machine learning is defined as algorithms and statistical models designed to perform tasks without explicit instructions, relying on patterns and inference instead.

Machine learning pipeline, MLp - in this chapter we define MLp as a sequential pipeline consisting of the machine learning steps of segmentation, feature extraction, feature selection and classification.

Deep Learning, DL - Deep learning is a class of machine learning algorithms that uses multiple layers to progressively extract higher level features from the raw input. The word deep comes from having many layers and the word learning from the capacity to learn a model from data.

Convolution neural network (CNN) - The convolution neural network is the most frequent type of DL used to classify images into categories. It uses multiple layers with convolutions based on a large number of filters to capture properties automatically from more local fields of view, then it progressively extracts higher level features as it merges the feature maps into smaller, more generalized convolutions.

Segmentation - the process of partitioning a digital image into multiple segments or regions. The goal of segmentation is to delineate and locate structures or objects and boundaries in images.

Semantic segmentation - the task of classifying each and very pixel of an image as a class. The classes are the structures or objects that are to be discovered, such that all pixels belonging to those structures should be classified as such.

Feature extraction, features - given some image or data, feature extraction derives a set of values (features) intended to describe the main characteristics of the original data, to be used in subsequent learning, classification and generalization steps. In the case of image classification, the features are most frequently numeric quantities summarizing some properties of regions, e.g. colour, texture or shape properties.

Feature selection - feature selection means selecting a subset of all features that were extracted from the image. In general, in a classification problem, "good" features are features that contribute significantly to distinguish the class, and redundant features are features that are highly correlated. Feature selection should try to find the best describing features and drop redundancy as much as possible.

Dimensionality reduction - the process of reducing the number of features by obtaining a smaller set of principal variables. Dimensionality reduction can be obtained by either feature selection or feature projection. Feature selection was defined previously, feature projection involves a transformation of the variables into a space of fewer dimensions. An example of feature projection is principal components analysis, where the variables are replaced by a smaller set of principal components that are computed from those variables and "summarize" the most relevant characteristics of those variables.

Classification - the problem of identifying to which of a set of categories an observation belongs, usually training from a set of data observations (or instances) whose category is known.

3 State-of-Art

3.1 Related Work

The field of cancer detection and classification using computerized techniques has gained increasing popularity during the last decade or so, given a large increase of computational power, the enormous advances in machine learning and the proposal and evolution of procedures that are able to analyze medical images automatically and classify or detect a degree of disease from those. Up to around 2013, most image analysis and classification techniques were machine learning pipelines (MLp), following a certain sequence of vaguely defined steps to segment, extract features and further analyze the images. Then Convolution Neural Networks (CNNs) started to gain popularity as highly accurate classifiers, new architectures were developed and beat previous approaches in terms of accuracy [16]. Looking at results from past works, accuracies on the order of 95% or 100% are very common in both MLp and DL paradigms. For instance, in [7] MLp using features describing characteristics of the cell nuclei present in the image result in accuracies of 96% to 97.5% using repeated 10-fold cross-validation. Likewise, state-of-the-art CNN approaches for classes cancer/no cancer on the BreakHis dataset [8] achieved 80 and 90% accuracy and, using patches and a myriad of modifications, others [9,10] report more than 95% accuracy on the same problem. But in [7], there seems to be a considerable amount of manual work to achieve the result. Can we automate all the steps, to make it less disadvantageous when compared with DL? And are there possible advantages in the use of MLp to complement DL? In MLp approaches segmentation and feature extraction that individualizes cells and measures a set of specific properties of those cells is needed. For instance, Loukas et al. [11] explored a technique that pre-selected 65 regions of interest to grade cancer into 3 degrees of malignancy (I-III), the neural network classifier achieving 90% accuracy; [12] achieved 80 to 95% accuracy grading prostate and breast cancers using three scales of low-level pixel values, high-level information based on relationships, and structural constraints; [13] used multi-wavelet grading of prostate pathological images, achieving a precision of 97% discriminating prostate tissue cancer/ no cancer and 81% for different degrees of low and high Gleason. More related works exploring analysis of regions of interest or structures can be reviewed in [14] and [15]. In our own previous work we also explored regions characterization [4] and [5]. More recently Convolution neural networks (CNNs) achieved top accuracies [8–10] and replaced feature extraction by convolution layers applying convolution operations [18]. Given the prior work on MLp and the highly practical and accurate CNN paradigm, a question arises on whether it is possible to design a fully automated MLp that might also be easy to apply and accurate. The closest to our intended MLp design would be CellProfiler in [21–23], since it at least offers some interface for deciding and collecting features, but using it in a complete MLp still requires a lot of manual human intervention to code, test and experiment with alternatives in steps of the pipeline, from segmentation to feature selection and classification. The automated MLp extracts objects, characterizes them and processes the extracted structures to build the classifier model automatically, and is applied automatically to classify new images as well.

Explainability/causability is another very relevant issue related to this kind of systems. In medicine there is growing demand for AI approaches that are trustworthy, transparent, interpretable and explainable for a human expert, and this is especially relevant in the clinical domain [1]. The authors in [1] argue that the best performing statistical approaches today are black-boxes and do not foster understanding, trust and error correction. This implies an urgent need for explainable models, explanation interfaces and causability. The systems should give answers to questions such as "Why did the algorithm do that?", "Can I trust these results?", "How can I correct an error?", so that the medical expert would be able to understand why, learn and correct errors and re-enact on demand. The need to make both DL and MLp more interpretable and explainable should be answered in the future, and post-processing of the features extracted by MLp, DL or mixed approaches can be explored further to improve explainability. We call the attention to this future research challenge, at the same time that we briefly illustrate with a small example how MLp features can be useful for further analysis and explainability. We believe DL and MLp can "collaborate" in this issue using extracted features to explain better what is happening and why.

3.2   Deep Learning Architectures Used

MatlabTM 2018's InceptionV3 [20] and Resnet-101 [19] networks are pre-trained implementations of the state-of-the-art InceptionV3 and Resnet architectures pre-trained on more than a million images from the ImageNet database to classify images into 1000 object categories. Not only each of these represents specific architectural details, as the number of layers increases as we move from InceptionV3 to Resnet. While InceptionV3 is a 48 layers deep network based on the Inception architectural features, Resnet-101 is a 101 layers deep network following the Resnet architecture.

3.3   Design of the Machine Learning Pipeline (MLp)

The building of the typical MLp has steps (1) segment, (2) extract features, (3) characterize the image, (4) reduce features space and (5) build classifier. The first part of MLp is an approach to characterize an image based in three main steps (segment, extract features, characterize the image). In each step it is necessary to take precautions to avoid losing information that is important for accuracy of the approach. In step (1), the image is segmented, and structures are identified from the resulting regions. In the case of histopathology slides, examples of structures include cells of specific types, interstitial tissue, groups of cells, adipocytes and others. The outcome of this step is a set of image regions, I = ri and a mapping from regions to structures. In this step it is important not only to segment the structures well, but also to do it such that each image pixel will be assigned to some structure (semantic segmentation). This is important since tissue modifications related to disease conditions can occur in any type of structure that is present in the images. As an example, the fabric/texture of interstitial tissue is expected to change in a cancer condition, therefore the interstitial tissue should be one of the classes. Also, the classes should be aligned with the output of segmentation. For instance, since cells are frequently over-lapped, class "cell cluster" is created to represent that structure. In step (2) a set of features [Fj] are extracted per region, so that each region ri is mapped into that set of features. While in DL end-to-end error backpropagation tunes feature extraction automatically, the only way to avoid losing important features in MLp is to define all potentially useful features and extract them all. Step (3) builds structure probability distribution functions (sPDF). Given the regions of each type of structure Sl, and for each feature Fj, the sPDFlj is represented as a histogram Hlj where, for each interval of possible values, the probability of occurrence is recorded (FPy). This histogram represents the probability that some structure takes some value in an interval for some specific feature. The second part of MLp concerns reduction of the feature space and building of the classifier. Next we provide more details on the steps.

Segmentation of Histopathology Slides. Segmentation algorithms that could be used have been studied extensively in the past, including traditional unsupervised approaches (e.g. [24–28, 30, 32–35]) or semantic segmentation using in deep learning networks [36] (e.g. fully convolutional network [37], U-net [38] or deeplab [39]). For our purpose, the most relevant issue in the design of the MLp is not segmentation algorithm but a tool that separates the image into meaningful regions, such as what CellProfiler does [21–23]. As in CellProfiler, we created a tool for the user to obtain segmentations and tune segmentation parameters. Figure 2 shows an example output after we configured it to define 12 structures. Note that the different structures can overlap partially. The tool options are threshold intervals, morphological operations, geometric properties and grids (to divide regions that may extend over the whole image), and to individualize regions the tool uses labeling of connected components (bwlabel). Note that Fig. 2 structures include cells, clusters of cells, interstice, adypocits, but also halos or aureoles. A halo is also a structure but one which captures the vicinity of another type of structure.

After the user configures segmentation the MLp becomes autonomous segmenting any image of that type, and since all the remaining MLp steps are completely autonomous, the whole pipeline runs automatically for both training and use.

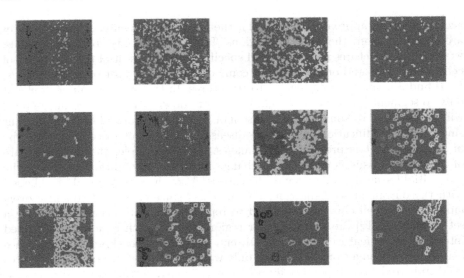

Fig. 2. A segmentation into 12 structures.

Describe Characteristics of Regions. The objective of this step is to characterize discovered regions using visual properties useful for distinguishing disease conditions. Since MLp does not learn which features to extract, it needs to extract all region features that could potentially be relevant for classification. The features that cover all properties that might be useful are counts and densities (D), shapes (S), geometries (G), texture (T) and color (C). Counts and densities (D) are aggregate measures counting the number of occurrences of each type of structure (number of regions of each structure) in images, and the number of occurrences per unit area in each of a number of grid divisions of the image (a nxn grid). A histogram describes the densities encountered. These details can capture for instance an abnormal concentration of small black cells, or any other abnormality in terms of densities of structures. Geometry (G) is a set of aggregate measures taken on each individual region that characterize the extent of the region (the pixels) as an aggregate. Shape (S) characterizes the form of the contours, not as aggregates (captured by geometry), but how the contour curves evolve. Texture (T) captures modifications in the general fabric of a specific structure such as interstitial tissue or cells. The ensemble of all extracted features is denoted as DSGTC features (Density, Shape, Geometry, Texture and Colour). All these features are extracted independently for each region, and since each region is of a specific structure type, structures are characterized by the distributions of those properties for all regions of the structure. The feature extraction process is completely automated, with no human intervention in any phase.

Feature Selection. Feature selection is needed to eliminate useless features, reduce the dimensionality of the dataset and to reveal the contribution of individual features to the outcome. Given ns structures, nf DSGTC features and nbin bins per histogram, the final number of probability features, describing all structures for a specific disease condition, is given by n = ns × nf × nbin. The value n is expected to be very large, since it represents all probability histogram bins for an already large number of features and for each structure. As an example, we had n= 12 structures × 600 features × 10 bins = 12 × 6000 probability features. Only a small fraction of those are relevant to determine the class (e.g. degree of atypia). Either feature projection or feature selection could be applied at this stage. We applied feature selection separately to each structure, reducing from 6000 to 50 most revealing features per structure. Three feature selection methods were used in conjunction: correlation analysis of each feature to the class (Y-correlation), correlation analysis between pairs of features (X1X2 correlation) and sequential feature selection (sequentialfs). Sequentialfs creates candidate feature subsets by sequentially adding each of the features not yet selected. For each candidate feature subset, sequentialfs performs 10-fold cross-validation by repeatedly evaluating classification with different training and test subsets, choosing the candidate feature with best accuracy. The number of features is reduced from 6000 to 100 by correlation analysis prior to calling sequentialfs.

Classification. Any classifier model can be tried in this step. We experimented a set of classifiers that included neural networks, random trees ensemble classifiers and nearest-neighbour. The classifiers were built using 5-fold cross-validation over the dataset, and the accuracy metrics collected over the test folds included precision, recall and F-Score, which were used to compare with DL.

3.4 Experimental Setup

The Mytos Atypia contest has provided a set of selected and annotated slides of breast cancer biopsy. The slides were stained with standard hematoxylin and eosin (H&E) dyes and they have been scanned by two slide scanners: Aperio Scanscope XT and Hamamatsu Nanozoomer 2.0-HT. In each slide, the pathologists selected several frames at X20 magnification located inside tumours. These X20 frames were used for scoring nuclear atypia. A X20 frame scanned using Aperio Scanscope XT is 755.649 × 675.616 μm^2, 1539 × 1376 pixels, one from Hamamatsu Nanozoomer 2.0-HT is 755.996474 × 675.76707 μm^2, 1663 × 1485 pixels. The number of frames is variable from slide to slide. In the training data set there are 284 frames at X20 magnification. Note that the dataset is limited in size, both patching and data augmentation were included as experiments to increase the size and variability in DL training. The frames are RGB bitmap images in TIFF format. The nuclear atypia score is provided as a number 1, 2 or 3. Score 1 denotes a low grade atypia, score 2 a moderate grade atypia, and score 3 a high grade atypia. This score has been given independently by two different senior pathologists. There are some frames for which the pathologists disagree and gave a different score. We account those as incorrect classifications by human experts. In those cases a third senior pathologist would give the final score. Nuclear atypia score is a value, 1, 2 or 3, corresponding to a low, moderate or strong nuclear atpyia respectively. Instead of focusing on segmenting and measuring the nuclei solely, both the DL and MLp approaches developed and tested in this work take the whole tissue images and detect atypical characteristics that dictate the degree of atypia. For experiments, the image datasets were collected and 5-fold cross-validation was applied. In 5-fold cross-validation 5 runs are ran with 80% training, 10% testing and 10% validation data. Patching refers to dividing the images of the dataset into multiple smaller images (e.g. 128 × 128 patches) to be fed to the DL. Those can better individualize structures and may provide a convenient degree of detail about regional structures, while also augmenting the dataset, by dividing an image into many patches. A stride (e.g. start a patch every 10 pixels) can be defined to obtain overlapping patches. Data augmentation is a different technique designed to increase the size and variability of the training dataset based on simple operations such as scaling, rotation, shearing or translation. This can contribute to increase the variability of training images, resulting in more and more diverse training instances.

Experimental Setup Details. We defined the following alternatives for experimentation: HExpert, MLp, CLASS, Iv3, R101, Iv3 augment, R101patch and Iv3patch. Hexpert is the accuracy of medical doctors, measured as the degree of agreement assigning the grades; MLp is the machine learning pipeline described in this work; CLASS is an ML classifier that does not differentiate structures, it simply applies segmentation and extracts a set of features (GLCM, LBP, gray level intensities) from all regions indistinctively, then applies feature reduction and a neural network classifier. CLASS represents a simpler ML pipeline; InceptionV3 (Iv3), Resnet-101 (R101), InceptionV3 with data augmentation (Iv3 augment), and versions of Iv3 and R101 with 128 × 128, 10 pixels stride patching (R101patch, Iv3patch) are DL alternatives built using Matlab 2018 implementations of state-of-the-art CNNs, including InceptionV3 (Iv3) and Resnet-101 (Res). The imageAugmenter used for data augmentation applied Random X Reflection, and both X and Y translation. The DL training options included the following: (stochastic gradient descent with momentum ('sgdm'), miniBatchSize 10, maxEpochs 700, initial learn rate 1e−4, validation frequency 3. In what concerns the MLp setup, after tuning with a few images the segmentation tool divided images into 5 intensity levels based on 3 thresholds (130, 180, 230), followed by a sequential set of operations to obtain the types of structures from those levels. The operations included removal of small noise (removal of very small regions inside larger regions resulting from thresholding), filling of holes and closing to fill and improve contours of small dark and mammarian cells, opening of interstitial tissue regions, individualizing regions by labeling connected regions (bwlabel), dividing white regions based on size, filling and closing those regions, applying circularity to distinguish rounded from non-rounded large white regions, applying a grid to interstice. After these steps comes the step of creating halo structures, which are structures capturing the vicinity of the previously individualized regions for each structure type. Creating the halos involves dilating the regions (imdilate) and then retrieving only the dilation ring. The resulting regions were 'darknCells', 'cells', 'cellsExtraFilled', 'fatSmall', 'fatLargeRound', 'fatLargeNotRound', 'interstice', 'darknCellsHalo', 'cellsHalo', 'fatSmallHalo', 'fatLargeRoundHalo', 'fatLargeNotRoundHalo'. Features of individual regions included area, solidity, major axis, minor axis, eccentricity, convex area, extent and others, contour slopes and variations of slopes (dslope), gray-level co-occurrence matrix (GLCM) [42], local binary patterns (LBP) [41], plus 2D texture histograms (spatial distance x colour intensity distance). Feature selection ran automatically and separately per structure. The first step involved pruning out features with a correlation less than 0.1 with the class. The second step involved removing features that were correlated above 95% with their class-correlation-ranked neighbours, followed by an additional class-correlation based pruning to keep only the top 100 features. Finally, sequential feature selection was used with the classifier F-score as the criteria to choose the subset of 50 best features for each structure. After this step all chosen 50 × 12 features representing all structures were again reduced into 100 final features using the same procedure. The last step of model building involved building of a classifier based on the 100 final features. We experimented neural network (see Matlab2018 patternnet) with a configuration of two hidden layers of 10 neurons each, random trees ensemble classifier (see Matlab2018's TreeBagger Bag of decision trees), with a default number of 10 trees, and k-nn with 3 neighbours. All the classifiers were built using 5-fold cross-validation over the dataset. From our experiments we report accuracy metrics that include precision, recall and F-Score.

Hardware Details. Experiments were ran in a PC running windows, with an intel core i5 at 3.4 GHz, 16 GB RAM and an SSD disk of 1TB. The PC had an NVIDEA GForce GTX 1070 GPU installed (Pascal architecture with 1920 cores, 8 GB GDDR5, 8 Gbps memory speed), and the experiments were all setup and ran in Matlab 2018a.

3.5   Experimental Results

Testing Accuracy of DL with BreakHis. In this experiment we tested Resnet-101 on the (yes/no) problem of detecting cancer on the BreakHis dataset [8], with 128 × 128 image patches. This served as a calibration test, resulting in a validation accuracy of 97%, as shown in the screenshot of Fig. 3 (and a test accuracy of 96.7% as well). This result coincides with results of other authors, giving us confidence that the DL approaches were well configured.

Results of DL with Mytos Atypia. Table 1 shows the results obtained by DL on the Mytos Atypia dataset. It reveals accuracies between 73% and 82.5%, the best approach being Iv3 with data augmentation.

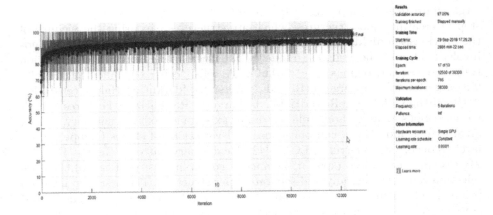

Fig. 3. Calibration run: Resnet on breakHis patches 128 × 128.

Table 1. Comparison of DL results on Mytos Atypia.

Approach	Iv3+augm	Iv3	Iv3+patch	R101+patch	R101
Test accuracy	82.50%	81.20%	79.30%	77.60%	73.00%
C1 = low grade atypia	76.20%	67.10%	77.43%	79.80%	76.20%
C2 = moderate-grade atypia	71.40%	81.30%	73.20%	68.10%	57.20%
C3 = high-grade atypia	100%	95.20%	87.24%	84.90%	85.70%

Results of MLp on Mytos Atypia. Table 2 shows the results we obtained for MLp, including accuracy, precision and recall. The table shows the metrics for all classes and the metrics obtained for each class. Precision was 86.5%, and grade 2 has the lowest precision, probably because the boundary between grades is fuzzy.

Table 2. Accuracy, precision and recall of MLp.

Approach	Acc	Precision	Recall
All	86.5%	86%	87%
Grade 1	93%	94%	90%
Grade 2	79%	71%	91%
Grade 3	90%	99%	80%

Table 3 shows accuracy of MLp using different classifiers and also CLASS. The superiority of MLp is clear compared to CLASS, and all MLp classifiers had good accuracy, with random forests being the best.

Table 3. Accuracy, precision and recall of MLp.

Classifier	MLp	CLASS
knn-3	83.5%	74%
Random forest	86.5%	70%
Neural net	82.8%	73.5%

MLp Runtimes. Figure 4 shows image segmentation times (average 1.8 s) and Fig. 5 shows features extraction time per structure and per image (average 11.3 s). Since regions of 12 structures were extracted, each image took an average of 1.8 + 136 s to be processed. This time is incurred during classifier construction. For classification of new images, it is possible to speedup execution by extracting only the 100 selected features. Feature selection takes a lot more time (average 52.5 min in five runs), due to the sequential feature selection step that calls the classifier on each step. Note however that this step is only necessary during model building.

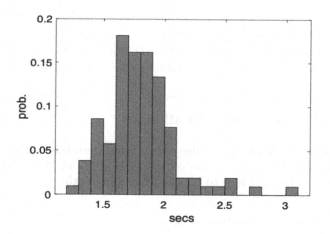

Fig. 4. image segmentation (mean = 1.8 s) and per-structure feature extraction (mean = 11.3 s).

Comparing MLp to DL. Table 4 compares the results of the two best DL approaches to those of MLp on the Mytos Atypia dataset. We also include the accuracy of human experts, measured as the fraction of agreement between the two pathologists labeling the images.

These results show that the state-of-the-art DL approaches did not achieve as high an accuracy as the well-designed MLp classifier. This can also be seen from the partial per-class accuracies, with MLp being superior in classifying low, moderate and high-grade atypia, with the exception of high-grade atypia by Iv3 with data augmentation, but at the expense of the remaining classes.

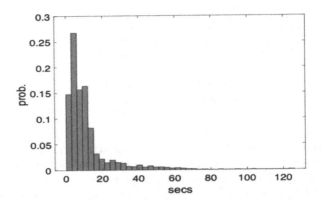

Fig. 5. Image segmentation (mean = 1.8 s) and per-structure feature extraction (mean = 11.3 s).

Table 4. Comparison DL to MLp and others on Mytos Atypia

Approach	MLp	HExpert	Iv3 augm	R101patch
Test accuracy	86.30%	84%	82.5%	77.6%
C1 = low grade atypia	93.10%	76.20%	79.80%	–
C2 = moderate-grade atypia	79.40%	71.40%	68.10%	–
C3 = high-grade atypia	90.20%	100%	84.90%	–

4   Open Problems and Challenges

There are open problems and challenges resulting from this study, both related to the design and use of MLp, the comparative study of MLp and DL, future improvements of DL and how to benefit from using both.

4.1   Degree of Automation of MLp

The MLp is able to run completely automatically over a dataset, but a prior human-based configuration of segmentation parameters to elicit structures was necessary, and the structures that were obtained are an important factor for accuracy. In the future this pre-configuration step can be replaced by deep-learning-based semantic segmentation using groundtruth segmentations. In that case MLp uses DL in one of its steps, and we need to provide the groundtruth segmentations, but the whole MLp procedure becomes totally automated with no need to pre-configure anything. Further work would also be required in improving semantic segmentation based in DL.

4.2   Accuracy Comparison DL to MLp

We created an automated MLp designed to recognize structures, characterize them and then classify disease conditions based on properties of those structures. We had to be careful in every step to avoid losing accuracy, by keeping as much information as possible up to feature selection, and "learning the best features" during feature selection. Our experiments have shown that MLp matched DL accuracy (and even improved it) in a specific experiment, with a limited sized dataset (Mytos Atypia). A large effort is welcome in the future to further compare well-designed MLp to DL in this and other contexts, with different and larger quantities of imaging data, and to evaluate under which circumstances one could be better than the other. Even in this experiment, although MLp achieved better accuracy than DL, it required prior manual configuration and tuning of segmentation parameters and some iterations of the whole pipeline to tune the segmentation to achieve top accuracy. Consequently, we have only shown that MLp can be competitive in some problems, but with some tuning still required.

4.3   Autonomous Learning Ability of DL Versus MLp

The advantage of DL compared with MLp is its capacity to learn end-to-end iteratively, where end-to-end means from the inputs (images) to the output, classification, based in error backpropagation [17]. Its main potential limitation is the difficulty to converge its inner weights to find the best solution. In contrast, MLp learns using a feature selection algorithm that is given a very large number of possible features, and a classifier building algorithm that is finding the most suitable parameters for the classifier. MLp does not learn segmentations iteratively currently, but that step could be replaced by deep learning-based semantic segmentation in the future. Still, MLp also does not backpropagate the classification error from output to input to improve accuracy along epochs of training. In spite of these limitations, MLp was still more accurate than DL in our experiment because it was able to find the most discriminating features among all relevant properties of structures. As a conclusion, DL seems to be the best choice in general, because it can learn more globally and adapt all of its weights automatically by back-propagating the error, to tune what it extracts and from where. Additionally, future work can bring improvements to DL that might make it more accurate still. But a well-designed MLp can still be more accurate, at least in some problems, and as long as it is fully or almost fully automated, it can always be used to provide extra information and characterization capabilities. The two paradigms can be applied simultaneously, and MLp can provide complementary information and characterizations.

4.4   Characterization of Disease Markers

MLp can be used to better characterize disease conditions based on which most relevant features of which structures are modified by disease conditions. We illustrate this by doing a short study using the MLp results. Figure 6 is taken from our results and shows that texture features are important disease markers in interstitial tissue and in clusters of cells (groups of juxtaposed cells). This means detection of variations in the texture of the tissue itself and of agglomerates of cells helps distinguish disease conditions based on those structures. That is consistent with the hypothesis that modifications in tissue fabric, such as hypercellular and more irregular altered tissue architecture, are indicative of higher cancer grades; In contrast to that analysis, in what concerns mammarian cells, shape and geometry features gain a lot of importance. Additionally, the mix for cells clusters also indicates some relevance of shape features, although less prominent. These observations agree with the fact that increased irregularity of cells and contours, some bigger cells and more irregular shapes are indicative of higher grades of cancer. Finally, shape and geometry were also chosen as relevant discriminators in vacuoles and adipocytes, probably signaling the importance of detecting more squeezed structures and more irregularity in their shapes due to altered tissue architecture in higher cancer grades. This study could be enhanced in the future, with more detailed analysis of which features are most revealing and so on.

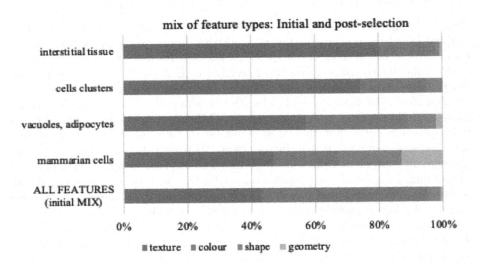

Fig. 6. Feature selection mixes for each structure.

4.5 Towards Explainability/Causability

As reviewed in the related work section, explainability/causability is one of the most relevant issues for adoption of AI models and techniques in medicine clinical practice [1]. The ability to characterize disease markers that we discussed in the previous subsection is one of multiple possible mechanisms that can be integrated to build explainable/causable AI systems. This means that MLp might be used as part of automated procedures to explain classifications and to establish causability, and it can be mixed with DL in practical systems as well. Most importantly, one of the most relevant future challenges in either MLp, DL or a mix of both is how to achieve explainability/causability instead of just having a black box system that is unable to provide very relevant explanatory power to users.

5   Future Outlook

Deep learning has displaced prior approaches and is here to stay. Its superiority is not a guarantee that it achieves better accuracy, but the fact that it learns autonomously, iteratively and end-to-end is a great advantage. We should expect future research to improve DL approaches further and to apply them to most classification and segmentation problems related to medical imaging in general and digital pathology in particular. If we had to choose only one approach between DL and MLp, we would choose DL because of its end-to-end, backpropagation-based learning that tries to optimize accuracy completely autonomously. MLp also searches for the best features and classifier model, but it still lacks end-to-end error backpropagation. The future outlook for MLp seems grimmer than that of DL, but MLp can still have a role together with DL. Since MLp is fully automated after an initial configuration of segmentation step, we can apply both in a specific context and test their accuracy; Instead of deciding between the two, we can have the results of both to gain more evidence. Most importantly, MLp can complement DL by characterizing structures and providing explanatory information. It can tell us which types of features and which features are more discriminative to detect a disease condition, and how those features reveal the disease condition. More generically, a crucial future challenge is to design systems that have explainability/causability capabilities using MLp, DL or both. Another distinctive opportunity to apply MLp together with DL is to segment medical images into structures using DL and then apply the MLp pipeline we designed to identify the properties of structures that change with disease conditions and how they change. It would also be important to fully integrate humans in the loop in the future, as human experts should be able to interact with the AI system in much richer ways [2]. That includes integrating physicians high-level expert knowledge into the process, by acquiring his/her relevance judgments regarding a set of initial results [3]. Either MLp, DL or mixed systems should be designed to integrate the human-in-the-loop, adding interactivity and learning from both sides (humans and algorithms).

References

1. Holzinger, A., Langs, G., Denk, H., Zatloukal, K., Müller, H.: Causability and explainabilty of artificial intelligence in medicine. Wiley Interdisc. Rev. Data Min. Knowl. Discov. **9**, e1312 (2019)

2. Holzinger, A.: Interactive machine learning for health informatics: when do we need the human-in-the-loop? Brain Inf. **3**(2), 119–131 (2016)
3. Akgul, C.B., Rubin, D.L., Napel, S., Beaulieu, C.F., Greenspan, H., Acar, B.: Content-based image retrieval in radiology: current status and future directions. J. Digit. Imaging **24**(2), 208–222 (2011)
4. Furtado, P.: Objects characterization-based approach to enhance detection of degree of malignancy in breast cancer histopathology. In: Medical Imaging 2019: Image Processing, vol. 10949, p. 109491R. International Society for Optics and Photonics (2019)
5. Pereira, J. Barata, R., Furtado, P.: Experiments on automatic classification of tissue malignancy in the field of digital pathology. In: Second International Workshop on Pattern Recognition, vol. 10443, p. 1044312. International Society for Optics and Photonics (2017)
6. NCI Dictionary of Cancer Terms. https://www.cancer.gov/publications/dictionaries/cancer-terms/def/tumor-grade. Accessed 4 Oct 2019
7. Wolberg, W.H., Street, W.N., Heisey, D.M., Mangasarian, O.L.: Computer-derived nuclear features distinguish malignant from benign breast cytology. Hum. Pathol. **26**, 792–796 (1995)
8. Spanhol, F.A., Oliveira, L.S., Petitje, C., et al.: A dataset for breast cancer histopathological image classification. IEEE Trans. Biomed. Eng. **63**(7), 1455–1462 (2016)
9. Wang, D., Khosla, A., Gargeya, R., Irshad, H., Beck, A.H.: Deep learning for identifying metastatic breast cancer. arXiv preprint: arXiv:1606.05718 (2016)
10. Motlagh, N.H., et al.: Breast cancer histopathological image classification: a deep learning approach. In: bioRxiv, 242818 (2018)
11. Loukas, C., Kostopoulos, S., Cavouras, D.: Breast cancer characterization based on image classification of tissue sections visualized under low magnification. In: Computational and Mathematical Methods in Medicine (2013)
12. Naik, S., et al.: Automated gland and nuclei segmentation for grading of prostate and breast cancer histopathology. In: 5th IEEE International Symposium on Biomedical Imaging: From Nano to Macro, ISBI 2008. IEEE (2008)
13. Jafari-Khouzani, K., Soltanian-Zadeh, H.: Multiwavelet grading of pathological images of prostate. IEEE Trans. Biomed. Eng. **50**, 697–704 (2013)
14. Mitko, V., Pluim, J.P.W., van Diest, P.J., Viergever, M.A.: Breast cancer histopathology image analysis: a review. IEEE Trans. Biomed. Eng. **61**(5), 1400–1411 (2014)
15. Aswathy, M.A., Jagannath, M.: Detection of breast cancer on digital histopathology images: present status and future possibilities. Inf. Med. Unlock. **8**, 74–79 (2017)
16. Krizhevsky, A., Sutskever, I., Hinton, G. E. : ImageNet classification with deep convolutional neural networks. In: Advances in Neural Information Processing Systems, pp. 1097–1105 (2012)
17. Rumelhart, D.E., Hinton, G.E., Williams, R.J.: Learning representations by back-propagating errors. Nature. **323**(6088), 533–536 (1986)
18. Alom, Md.Z., et al.: The history began from AlexNet: a comprehensive survey on deep learning approaches. ArXiv Preprint ArXiv:1803.01164 (2018)
19. He, K., Zhang, X., Ren, S., Sun., J.: Deep residual learning for image recognition. In: Proceedings of the IEEE Conference on Computer Vision and Pattern Recognition, pp. 770–778 (2016)

20. Szegedy, C., Vanhoucke, V., Ioffe, S., Shlens, J., Wojna, Z.: Rethinking the Inception Architecture for Computer Vision. In: The IEEE Conference on Computer Vision and Pattern Recognition (CVPR), pp. 2818–2826 (2016)
21. Yu, K.-H., et al.: Predicting non-small cell lung cancer prognosis by fully automated microscopic pathology image features. Nat. Commun. **7**, Article number: 12474 (2016)
22. Carpenter, A.E., et al.: Cell profiler - image analysis software for identifying and quantifying cell phenotypes. Genome Biol. **7**(10), R100 (2006)
23. Kamentsky, L., et al.: Improved structure, function and compatibility for cell profiler: modular high-throughput image analysis software. Bioinformatics **27**, 1179–1180 (2011)
24. Kass, M., Witkin, A., Terzopoulos, D.: Snakes: active contour models. Int. J. Comput. Vis. **1**(4), 321 (1988)
25. Vincent, L., Soille, P.: Watersheds in digital spaces - an efficient algorithm based on immersion simulations. IEEE Trans. Pattern Anal. Mach. Intell. **13**(6), 583–598 (1991)
26. Otsu, N.: A threshold selection method from gray-level histograms. IEEE Trans. Sys. Man. Cyber. **9**(1), 62–66 (1979). https://doi.org/10.1109/TSMC.1979.4310076
27. Liao, P.-S., Chen, T.-S., Chung, P.-C.: A fast algorithm for multilevel thresholding. J. Inf. Sci. Eng. **17**(5), 713–727 (2001)
28. Zhu, N., Wang, G., Yang, G., Dai, W.: A fast 2D otsu thresholding algorithm based on improved histogram. In: Chinese Conference on Pattern Recognition, CCPR 2009, pp. 1–5 (2009)
29. Deing, Y., Manjunath, B.S.: Unsupervised segmentation of color-texture regions in images and videos. Trans. Pattern Anal. Mach. Intell. **23**(8), 800–810 (2001)
30. Hartigan, J.: Clustering Algorithms. Wiley, Hoboken (1975)
31. Achanta, R., et al.: Slic superpixels. In: EPFL Internal Report, No. EPFL-REPORT-149300 (2010)
32. Nock, R., Nielsen, F.: Statistical region merging. IEEE Trans. Pattern Anal. Mach. Intell. **26**(11), 1–7 (2004)
33. Ester, M., et al.: A density-based algorithm for discovering clusters in large spatial databases with noise. In: Proceedings of the Second International Conference on Knowledge Discovery and Data Mining (KDD-96), pp. 226–231. AAAI Press (1996). ISBN 1-57735-004-9
34. Boykov, Y., Veksler, O., Zabih, R.: Fast approximate energy minimization via graph cuts. IEEE Trans. Pattern Anal. Mach. Intell. **23**(11), 1222–1239 (2001)
35. Cheng, Y.: Mean shift, mode seeking, and clustering. IEEE Trans. Pattern Anal. Mach. Intell. **17**(8), 790–799 (1995)
36. Ouaknine, A.: Review of deep learning algorithms for image semantic segmentation. https://medium.com/arthur_ouaknine/review-of-deep-learning-algorithms-for-image-semantic-segmentation-509a600f7b57. Accessed October 2019
37. Long, J., Shelhamer, E., Darrell, T.: Fully convolutional networks for semantic segmentation. In: Proceedings of the IEEE Conference on Computer Vision and Pattern Recognition, pp. 3431–3440 (2015)
38. Ronneberger, O., Fischer, P., Brox, T.: U-net: convolutional networks for biomedical image segmentation. In: Navab, N., Hornegger, J., Wells, W.M., Frangi, A.F. (eds.) MICCAI 2015. LNCS, vol. 9351, pp. 234–241. Springer, Cham (2015). https://doi.org/10.1007/978-3-319-24574-4_28

39. Chen, L.C., Papandreou, G., Kokkinos, I., Murphy, K., Yuille, A.L.: DeepLab: semantic image segmentation with deep convolutional nets, atrous convolution, and fully connected crfs. IEEE Trans. Pattern Anal. Mach. Intell. **40**(4), 834–848 (2017)

40. Mitos-Atypia-14. https://mitos-atypia-14.grand-challenge.org/Dataset/. Accessed October 2019

41. Wang, L., He, D.: Texture classification using texture spectrum. Pattern Recogn. **23**(8), 905–910 (1990)

42. Haralick, R., Shanmugam, K., Dinstein, I.H.: Textural features for image classification. IEEE Trans. Syst. Man Cybern. **SMC–3**(6), 610–621 (1973)

Biobanks and Biobank-Based Artificial Intelligence (AI) Implementation Through an International Lens

Zisis Kozlakidis[(✉)] ⓘ

International Agency for Research on Cancer, World Health Organization, Lyon, France
kozlakidisz@iarc.fr

Abstract. Artificial Intelligence (AI) is gradually changing medical practice. With recent progress in digitized data acquisition, machine learning and computing infrastructure, AI applications are expanding into areas that were previously thought to be the exclusive domain of human experts. One such area is biobanking, which forms a natural extension for AI-driven activities, both because biobanking is a foundational activity for downstream precision medical research, as well as because biobanking can increasingly accommodate high-throughput sample-, image- and data-handling operational models. The increasing AI-driven appetite for higher volumes of data and images often necessitates the cross-border collaboration of biobanks; likely to develop to one of the major forces dictating the international biobanking collaboration in the near future. However there are significant challenges ahead at the same time: firstly key practical issues surrounding the implementation of AI into existing research and clinical workflows, including data standardization, data sharing and interoperability across multiple platforms. Secondly governance concerns such as privacy, transparency of algorithms, data interpretation and how the latter might impact patient safety. Here a high-level summary of these opportunities and challenges will be presented from the perspective of AI driving more and stronger international collaborations in biobanking.

Keywords: Biobank · Biobanking standards · Artificial Intelligence · High-throughput · Implementation drivers

1 Introduction and Motivation

Over the last few decades computer-driven approaches have been central in the development of laboratory research, clinical practice, biobanking and their automation since the associated increase in biospecimen pathway complexity requires intelligent instrumentation and integrated communication between systems and equipment [1]. Biospecimens (such as the commonly collected blood and tissue samples, and urine) contain the information that doctors and researchers use to understand what type of disease a patient has and to determine possible treatment options that should be used for their clinical management. The information in the different biospecimens can now be readily and routinely extracted through new technological approaches, leading to vast amounts of

A. Holzinger et al. (Eds.): AI & ML for Digital Pathology, LNAI 12090, pp. 195–203, 2020.
https://doi.org/10.1007/978-3-030-50402-1_12

digital data being captured and stored in machine-readable forms. This 'datafication' of biospecimens generates different types of imaging and '-omics' data (genomics, transcriptomics, proteomics, metabolomics, epigenomics) reflecting the molecular events ongoing in the disease. This complexity of medically-relevant information must be captured in meaningful and actionable ways. As the impacts of use of digital information to the healthcare system have been emerging, personalised medicine will be directed by computational scientists and data analysts active in the biomedical domains. In doing so, tissue-based science is also becoming an informatics-driven challenge.

However, in order to realize the full benefit of these approaches communication and information exchange needs to be truly integrated, rather than simply connecting single instruments, datasets and surrounding information systems [2]. As such approaches based on Artificial Intelligence (AI) have been utilized in order to impact on the benefits from the ongoing accrual of detailed clinical information.

The current chapter aims to review the efforts made to introduce Artificial Intelligence approaches in the field of biobanking. The available evidence relating to the application of AI-driven approaches to biobanking are reviewed through an international perspective, and not restricted to a particular application or geographical location. For clarification purposes, some key terms are defined in the next section, followed by Sect. 3 discussing the current state-of-the-art approaches. Section 4 will highlight significant challenges that are facing the clinical and academic communities, while providing an outline to future outlooks in Sect. 5.

2 Glossary and Key Terms

Artificial Intelligence is usually defined as the theory and development of computer systems that perform tasks normally requiring human intelligence, such as visual perception, speech recognition and decision-making amongst others [3].

The terms biobank and biobanking, although there is currently no universally accepted definition, commonly refer to a large collection of tissue samples with associated biological and medical data, such as surgical biopsies (fresh frozen or in paraffin sections), blood and serum samples, different cell types, DNA, RNA; all carefully collected for research purposes [4].

3 Introduction and Motivation

3.1 Current Efforts for AI Implementation on Biobanked Data

The notion of implementing computer-based approaches able to handle, analyze and interpret high-throughput clinical tests has been discussed for some decades, though with little conviction. It was strengthened as a call to arms in the wake of the Human Genome Project, [5] with considerable investment to allow for such approaches to emerge. Successful examples of AI-driven implementation in clinical practice include the continuous monitoring and detailed analysis of patients' tympanic temperature allowing for the distinction between patients with infectious versus non-infectious fever [6]. Furthermore, the analysis of basic electronic medical record (EMR) denominators such as admission notes, vital signs and requested diagnostic tests can stratify patients with infections with reasonable accuracy, [7] while AI-driven programs for effectively reducing antibiotic usage have already been introduced [8]. Developments in this field are in their infancy and mature solutions seem to be restricted to particular clinical questions and geographical locations that provide a full infrastructural complement to the public health environment [9] waiting for 'bigger and better' data to become available in the decades to come [10].

There have been international collaborative efforts showcasing an interpretable and actionable use of biobanked data through AI implementation. These include for example the identification of new indicators of heart disease risk present in the pre-existing biobank images of retinas [11], the use of biobanked samples to investigate early stage colorectal cancer detection on genomic data (from whole genome sequencing) [12], and the utilization of Cardiomyopathy related samples and data to improve patient clinical care [13]. These efforts, albeit limited in number, form only the vanguard of a number of international consortia in existence- as such there is still great optimism on the potential impact.

3.2 The Main Drivers of AI Implementation in Biobanking

The discussions on AI implementation in the field of translational medicine, medical research and biobanking are not new, and have been presented previously in some detail [14]. It is clear that translational research, using new techniques and the more holistic approaches in data management, supports the overall feasibility of consolidated biobanking and of high-throughput downstream analyses of both samples and data. A number of high profile translational research initiatives are based on the availability of big infrastructural units (100,000 Genomes Project in the UK; the Precision Medicine Initiative in the USA) that would support the eventual technological transfer of high-throughput analytical approaches from the research into the (consolidated) biobanking facility and subsequently (or in some cases in parallel) to the clinical laboratory. The interaction of consolidated clinical biobanks and their ensuing networks with basic academic health sciences is perhaps inevitable under the umbrella of such large consortia [15]. As a result, the speed at which promising technologies move through the academic pipeline into clinical application(s) can possibly increase, while at the same time maintaining the breadth of creative approaches for biobanking.

Indeed, the expanded use of AI-driven techniques promises to lessen the level of expertise required of bench technologists to rapidly, accurately, and consistently perform repetitive tasks, e.g. identify micro-organisms or process biological samples. In parallel, the rationalisation of public health costs has led to an increased pressure for the cost containment of infrastructural units such as biobanks. In this perspective, a number of biobanks have already undergone a process of consolidation involving a shift towards cross-institutional amalgamation and closer real-time informational linkage with other biobanks in collaborating institutions. Through this consolidation activity, an operational model has started to emerge with centralized 'virtual' units linking information from a network of biobanks [16]. It is expected that AI will ultimately facilitate high-throughput biobanking and will help to bridge the gap in a cost- and time-effective manner between a shortage in qualified personnel; the increasing volume, multi-disciplinary character and complexity of biobanking processing needs; and will provide an easy solution to universally accessible downstream abilities to query databases.

3.3 High-Throughput Biobanking

Collecting clinical specimens for retrospective use and combining these with extensive clinical, diagnostic, geographic and demographic data in biobanks is essential for research purposes, the development of improved diagnostic tools and by contributing to patient care on the basis of retrospective tracing of specific pathogens/conditions. The NIH Human Microbiome Project, which served as a catalyst for human microbiome research, highlights the added value of large consolidated biobanking [17]. The International Agency for Research on Cancer (IARC) biobank, the UK Biobank and the China Kadoorie Biobank are three other major examples. While the latter two reflect large national population cohorts, the IARC Biobank is centered on a certain pathology across a large number of geographical areas [18]. Large consortia and multi-national projects and the sheer number of specimens they process will directly affect biobanks by increasing their operational capacities and flexibility through greater automation and connectivity/integration to healthcare workflows and/or middleware in order to ensure their effectiveness and sustainability [19]. Sharing samples, patients' data, and methods through networks is now more important than ever and often requires interaction with less traditional collaborating specialties such as engineering, law and computer science to foster translational medicine [20].

As a result, biobanks are expected to be repositioned from Mertonian functionalism (for the 'good of society' as a whole) to agency-based frameworks that focus on performance-measured processes [21]. Biobanking will become increasingly embedded in healthcare systems that use longitudinal samples from individuals as part of their personal care, and favoring of translational research, aiming to bring products and therapies quickly to market [22, 23]. This is anticipated by the creation of new standards (ISO 20387:2018 Biotechnology–Biobanking) and alignment with existing best practices, supporting the deeper clinical integration of such infrastructure facilities [24]. Once more, AI-driven solutions are expected to emerge creating the framework and necessary operational environment for the above to take place effectively, both in terms of turnaround times and costs.

4   Open Problems

4.1   The Challenges in AI Implementation

Within biomedical research, centralisation of its core activities into aggregated facilities, such as biobanks, is a well-entrenched practice. Current tissue handling practices seek to aggregate biological samples into sizeable facilities that are linked to databases of annotated clinical and research data, including informed consent and ethical approval documents [25]. However, such larger centralised facilities have not yet realized their potential and struggle with utilization rates [26]. The reasons for this are multifaceted and influenced by the following issues: capacity planning, poor business models, separation of samples from the data, as well as the inability to release samples and associated data to researchers in a timely and interpretable manner [27].

Such centralization attempts suffer from disadvantages typically known to plague centralization models and therefore impact the AI implementation in biobanking. Specifically, biospecimen aggregation creates single points of failure within the system which require excessive protections and constant vigilance to maintain security for both samples and data. A deeper understanding and appreciation of these data aggregation and handling processes would be highly desirable. The need for more deeply developed digital approaches is not negligible since it is clear that "big data" management will be at the core of the quality of future clinical research.

Despite the much anticipated revolution in healthcare, the path from big data to clinical impact for specific research questions remains unclear. Clinically oriented biobanks are important sources of research-ready tissue as well as associated data under best practices, as an added-value proposition to their users. However, they do face a dual harmonization bottleneck of analytical laboratory and of digital techniques (data collection, curation, and storage). Both of these aspects affect directly any AI-driven initiatives and can impact significantly the biobank utilization rates and long-term biobank sustainability [28]. Yet data are critical for the initial training of AI technologies, while a continued supply can ensure ongoing training, validation and improvement of algorithms. The current lack of harmonization directly affects the ability to share data across multiple locations globally.

Furthermore, the needed and anticipated sharing of data raises the question of scalability on ethical, legal and governance aspects of biobanking, as the data would need to be anonymized and/or de-identified in ever increasing volumes, while informed consent processes will need to include the possibility of wide distribution globally. As such, the notions of informed consent and data protection would need to be repositioned on extended foundations to facilitate the AI-driven solutions in biobanking [29, 30]. This is likely to remain a major stumbling block for the international sharing of data in the foreseeable future, as a common global reference framework on 'digital-era ethics' does not exist. Additionally, in developing countries the ability to face these ethical, legal and governance challenges remains incredibly variable. For example in a recent review of 49 sub-Saharan African countries, 29 had some form of national ethics guidance, yet fewer had specific guidance on consent (14), ownership (6), reuse (10), storage (9), and export/import/transfer (13) of human biological samples and data [31].

It should be noted that the interoperability of AI-driven solutions in biobanking, as well as routine clinical laboratory operations, for all sample specimen type workflows remains a real challenge. Variable and often limited types and volumes (cerebrospinal fluid, corneal fluid, etc.) as well as preparation sub-methodology (extraction, sonication, crushing, etc.), and prioritizing test protocols for precious surgical specimens add another layer of complexity for biobanking operations possibly not fully compatible with AI requirements [32]. Indeed the same sample may be subjected to multiple preparation scenarios over different time windows. To this end, the biobanking workflow should accommodate those specimens needing for example simple separation, nucleic acid extraction, direct immuno-chemistry assays, or a combination of each. Clearly, it is not always the size and throughput of the biobank that is the sole defining factor for the introduction of AI-driven technologies. For some biobanks, the number and types of special specimens received are likely to define the value of the processes. Equally important may be the fact that for some of the special specimens, classical technologies have to be maintained. Still, the opportunities in the AI-driven field are considered revolutionary by many [33].

For these reasons, modularity and scalability (e.g. integration of multiple incubation/imaging systems, free standing incubators, integrated workstations) become important design considerations for manufacturers, such that any size biobank would have access to components of the complete system. In addition, incorporation of AI-driven technologies in biobanks within geographic regions where competition for skilled labor is high or acute shortages of qualified personnel occur would likely be advantageous. As such, a balance needs to be reached between AI-driven, lean and consistent universal approaches and sufficiently "open" systems for the often needed "independent" orchestration of specimen workflow by an intelligent middleware. "Openness" remains a clear challenge for manufacturers due to both instrument design aspects and regulatory requirements, among others. Nevertheless this apparent gap demonstrates the clear need for more and better collaboration between private and public sectors in the sphere of biobanking with a global viewpoint [34–36].

The final challenge in AI-driven implementation in biobanking is that of transparency, at multiple levels. In the case of machine learning the accuracy of predictions relies heavily on the accuracy of the data training set inputted into the algorithm. Poor data will yield poor results, thus the transparency of the available data such that others can critically evaluate the training process is paramount to ensuring confidence in the system [37]. However, transparency relates most importantly to model interpretability or the 'Explainable AI' notion - in other words, humans should be able to understand or interpret how a given technology reached a certain decision or prediction [38–40]. This kind of 'transparent' AI contrasts against the 'opaque' or 'black box' approach as it is thought that if the system's reasoning can be explained, then humans can verify whether the reasoning is sound. If the system's reasoning cannot be explained (for example on a particular diagnosis, treatment recommendation, or outcome prediction) such an evaluation would not be practically feasible. However, there are tradeoffs - in certain instances, enforcing transparency and interpretability can potentially result in decreased accuracy or predictive performance of a model [41].

5   Future Outlook

In conclusion, progress is being made in this field. However, the question of the successful application of AI-driven technological support in biobanking is not one of if, but when and where. There are many challenges in the development of the biobank of the future. These range from the expanding need for automation, enhanced data governance and management and their meaningful AI-driven interpretation, care of data privacy and protection, continuous introduction of new and mostly high-throughput and data-intense technologies in routine practice. Providing solutions that generate optimal integrated and affordable services needs to be at the core of all of these activities.

It has to be noted that the true cost of AI-driven technologies still remains to be largely determined. Outcome studies that assess these issues are still needed, especially as the implementation of AI technologies in biobanking is likely to be strongly dependent on the national and/or regional context within which biobanking facilities need to operate. We consider that the speed with which this happens will relate to the "ownership" of the strategy in each case and its implementation. By this we mean that several stakeholders are involved, such as (at a minimum) the institutions, the biobanks, the staff, as well as the algorithm developers. It is currently far from clear how these essential parties will work best together to make this happen, especially in the developing countries.

If tissue-based science is becoming an informatics problem, then biospecimens should be viewed as the first block in the chain of information flow, and the different options for potential data utilization have to become a de facto part of the biobank operational planning. Bold and innovative strategies are needed for biospecimen derived informatics to impact digital health initiatives through AI implementation. Shifting the current aggregative biobanking towards a model that manages biospecimens as an integral part of a digital health information flow will revolutionise how we learn from biospecimen-derived information. The likely future impact in the biobanking field is that successful distributed models are likely to emerge alongside aggregative models, as distributed models rely on the presence of many independent participants that manage processes together through common standards performed in parallel – and such standards now exist for biobanking and data handling.

Lastly, the maintenance of biobanking competency at the highest level needs to be supported by technological innovation, aiding clinician-specialist interactions. This is a key aspect where those with skills need to be properly aligned with skillful decision-making technologies. Biobanking would need to interface with downstream analytical systems and workflow changes will be required to realize these advantages in the timeliness and quality of the results.

References

1. Burnham, C.A., Dunne Jr., W.M., Greub, G., Novak, S.M., Patel, R.: Automation in the clinical microbiology laboratory. Clin. Chem. **59**(12), 1696–1702 (2013)
2. Bourbeau, P.P., Ledeboer, N.A.: Automation in clinical microbiology. J. Clin. Microbiol. **51**(6), 1658–1665 (2013)
3. Beam, A.L., Kohane, I.S.: Translating artificial intelligence into clinical care. JAMA **316**(22), 2368–2369 (2016)
4. Parodi, B.: Biobanks: a definition. In: Mascalzoni, D. (ed.) Ethics, Law and Governance of Biobanking. The International Library of Ethics, Law and Technology, vol. 14, pp. 15–19. Springer, Dordrecht (2015). https://doi.org/10.1007/978-94-017-9573-9_2
5. Roses, A.D.: Pharmacogenetics and the practice of medicine. Nature **405**, 857–865 (2000)
6. Dakappa, P.H., Prasad, K., Rao, S.B., Bolumbu, G., Bhat, G.K., Mahabala, C.: Classification of infectious and noninfectious diseases using artificial neural networks from 24-hour continuous tympanic temperature data of patients with undifferentiated fever. Crit. Rev. Biomed. Eng. **46**(2), 173–183 (2018)
7. Tou, H., Yao, L., Wei, Z., Zhuang, X., Zhang, B.: Automatic infection detection based on electronic medical records. BMC Bioinf. **19**(Suppl 5), 117 (2018)
8. Nault, V., Pepin, J., Beaudoin, M., Perron, J., Moutquin, J.M., Valiquette, L.: Sustained impact of a computer-assisted antimicrobial stewardship intervention on antimicrobial use and length of stay. J. Antimicrob. Chemother. **72**(3), 933–940 (2017)

9. Wong, Z.S.Y., Zhou, J., Zhang, Q.: Artificial intelligence for infectious disease big data analytics. Infect. Dis. Health **24**(1), 44–48 (2019)

10. Van den Wijngaert, S., et al.: Bigger and better? Representativeness of the influenza a surveillance using one consolidated clinical microbiology laboratory data set as compared to the Belgian sentinel network of laboratories. Front. Public Health **7**, 150 (2019)

11. Poplin, R., Varadarajan, A., Blumer, K., Liu, Y., McConnell, M., Corrado, G., et al.: Predicting cardiovascular risk factors from retinal fundus photographs using deep learning. Nat. Biomed. Eng. **2**, 158–164 (2018)

12. Niehous, K., et al.: Early stage colorectal cancer detection using artificial intelligence and whole-genome sequencing of cell-free DNA in a retrospective cohort of 1,040 patients. Am. J. Gastroenterol. **113**, S169 (2018)

13. Sammani, A., Jansen, M., Linschoten, M., et al.: UNRAVEL: big data analytics research data platform to improve care of patients with cardiomyopathies using routine electronic health records and standardised biobanking. Neth Heart J. **27**(9), 426–434 (2019)

14. Holzinger, A., Roecker, C., Ziefle, M.: Smart Health. Springer, Switzerland (2015). https://doi.org/10.1007/978-3-319-16226-3

15. Thompson, R., et al.: RD-connect: an integrated platform connecting databases, registries, biobanks and clinical bioinformatics for rare disease research. J. Gen. Int. Med. **29**, S780–7 (2014)

16. Vande Loock, K., Van der Stock, E., Debucquoy, A., et al.: The Belgian virtual tumorbank: a tool for translational cancer research. Front. Med. **6**, 120 (2019)

17. NIH Human Microbiome Portfolio Analysis Team: A review of 10 years of human microbiome research activities at the US National Institutes of Health, Fiscal Years 2007–2016. Microbiome. **7**(1), 31 (2019)

18. Mendy, M., Caboux, E., Sylla, B.S., Dillner, J., Chinquee, J., Wild, C.: Infrastructure and facilities for human biobanking in low- and middle-income countries: a situation analysis. Pathobiology **81**, 252–260 (2014)

19. Simeon-Dubach, D., Henderson, M.K.: Sustainability in Biobanking. Biopreserv. Biobank. **12**(5), 287–288 (2014)

20. Hulsen, T., et al.: From big data to precision medicine. Front. Med. **6**, 34 (2019)

21. Doucet, M., Yuille, M., Georghiou, L., Dagher, G.: Biobank sustainability: current status and future prospects. J. Bioreposit. Sci. Appl. Med. **5**, 1–7 (2017)

22. Caulfield, T., Burningham, S., Joly, Y., et al.: A review of the key issues associated with the commercialization of biobanks. J. Law Biosci. **1**(1), 94–110 (2014)

23. Kinkorová, J., Topolčan, O.: Biobanks in horizon 2020: sustainability and attractive perspectives. EPMA J. **9**, 345 (2018)

24. Simeon-Dubach, D., Kozlakidis, Z.: New standards and updated best practices will give modern biobanking a boost in professionalism. Biopreserv. Biobank. **16**(1), 1–2 (2018)

25. Gliklich, R.E., Dreyer, N.A.: Registries for evaluating patient outcomes: a user's guide. 3rd edition Editor: Michelle B Leavy. Agency for Healthcare Research and Quality (U.S.), Rockville, MD (2014)

26. Cadigan, R.J., Juengst, E., Davis, A., Henderson, G.: Underutilization of specimens in biobanks: an ethical as well as a practical concern? Genet. Med. **16**(10), 738–740 (2014)

27. Catchpoole, D.R.: Biohoarding: treasures not seen, stories not told. J. Health Serv. Res. Policy **21**(2), 140–142 (2016)

28. Kozlakidis, Z.: Biobanking with big data: a need for developing "big data metrics". Biopreserv. Biobank. **14**(5), 450–451 (2016)

29. Char, D.S., Shah, N.H., Magnus, D.: Implementing machine learning in health care—addressing ethical challenges. N. Engl. J. Med. **378**, 981–983 (2018)

30. Paul, S., Gade, A., Mallipeddi, S.: The state of cloud-based biospecimen and biobank data management tools. Biopreserv. Biobank. **15**(2), 169–172 (2017)

31. Barchi, F., Little, M.T.: National ethics guidance in Sub-Saharan Africa on the collection and use of human biological specimens: a systematic review. BMC Med. Ethics **16**, 64 (2016)
32. Ledeboer, N.A., Dallas, S.D.: The automated clinical microbiology laboratory: fact or fantasy? J. Clin. Microbiol. **52**(9), 3140–3146 (2014)
33. Krittanawong, C., Zhang, H., Wang, Z., Aydar, M., Kitai, T.: Big data, artificial intelligence, and cardiovascular precision medicine. J. Am. Coll. Cardiol. **69**(21), 2657–2664 (2017)
34. Caulfield, T., Borry, P., Gottweis, H.: Industry involvement in publicly funded biobanks. Nat. Rev. Genet. **15**, 220 (2014)
35. Hämäläinen, I., Törnwall, O., Simell, B., Zatloukal, K., Perola, M., van Ommen, G.-J.B.: Role of academic biobanks in public–private partnerships in the european biobanking and biomolecular resources research infrastructure community. Biopreserv. Biobank. **17**(1), 46–51 (2019)
36. Hofman, P., Bréchot, C., Zatloukal, K.: Public-private relationship in biobanking: a still underestimated key component of open innovation. Virchows Arch. **464**(1), 3–9 (2014)
37. Hashimoto, D.A., Rosman, G., Rus, D., Meireles, O.R.: Artificial intelligence in surgery: promises and perils. Ann. Surg. **268**, 70–76 (2018)
38. Garattini, C., Raffle, J., Aisyah, D.N., Sartain, F., Kozlakidis, Z.: Big data analytics, infectious diseases and associated ethical impacts. Philos. Technol. **32**(1), 69–85 (2019)
39. Patrzyk, P.M., Link, D., Marewski, J.N.: Human-like machines: transparency and comprehensibility. Behav. Brain Sci. **40**, e276 (2017)
40. Holzinger, A., Langs, G., Denk, H., Zatloukal, K., Mueller, H.: Causability and explainabilty of artificial intelligence in medicine. WIREs Data Min. Knowl. Discov. **9**, e1312 (2019)
41. Sussillo, D., Barak, O.: Opening the black box: low-dimensional dynamics in high-dimensional recurrent neural networks. Neural Comput. **25**, 626–649 (2013)

HistoMapr™: An Explainable AI (xAI) Platform for Computational Pathology Solutions

Akif Burak Tosun[1], Filippo Pullara[1], Michael J. Becich[1,2],
D. Lansing Taylor[1,3,4], S. Chakra Chennubhotla[1,4], and Jeffrey L. Fine[1,5,6(✉)]

[1] SpIntellx, Inc., Pittsburgh, PA, USA
{burak,chakra,jeff}@spintellx.com
[2] Department of Biomedical Informatics,
University of Pittsburgh School of Medicine, Pittsburgh, PA, USA
[3] Drug Discovery Institute, University of Pittsburgh, Pittsburgh, PA, USA
[4] Department of Computational and Systems Biology,
University of Pittsburgh School of Medicine, Pittsburgh, PA, USA
[5] Department of Pathology, University of Pittsburgh School of Medicine,
Pittsburgh, PA, USA
[6] UPMC Magee-Womens Hospital, Pittsburgh, PA, USA
http://www.spintellx.com

Abstract. Pathologists are adopting whole slide images (WSIs) for diagnostic purposes. While doing so, pathologists should have all the information needed to make best diagnoses rapidly, while supervising computational pathology tools in real-time. Computational pathology has great potential for augmenting pathologists' accuracy and efficiency, but concern exists regarding trust for 'black-box AI' solutions. Explainable AI (xAI) can reveal underlying reasons for its results, to promote safety, reliability, and accountability for critical tasks such as pathology diagnosis. Built on a hierarchy of computational and traditional image analysis algorithms, we present the development of our proprietary xAI software platform, HistoMapr, for pathologists to improve their efficiency and accuracy when viewing WSIs. HistoMapr and xAI represent a powerful and transparent alternative to 'black-box' AI. HistoMapr previews WSIs then presents key diagnostic areas first in an interactive, explainable fashion. Pathologists can access xAI features via a "Why?" button in the interface. Furthermore, two critical early application examples are presented: 1) Intelligent triaging that involves xAI estimation of difficulty for new cases to be forwarded to subspecialists or generalist pathologists; 2) Retrospective quality assurance entails detection of potential discrepancies between finalized results and xAI reviews. Finally, a prototype is presented for atypical ductal hyperplasia, a diagnostic challenge in breast pathology, where xAI descriptions were based on computational pipeline image results.

Keywords: Computational pathology · Artificial Intelligence (AI) · Explainable AI (xAI) · Breast pathology · Digital pathology · Computer assisted diagnosis

© Springer Nature Switzerland AG 2020
A. Holzinger et al. (Eds.): AI & ML for Digital Pathology, LNAI 12090, pp. 204–227, 2020.
https://doi.org/10.1007/978-3-030-50402-1_13

1   Introduction and Motivation

A growing number of pathologists have transitioned to viewing digital images of patient slides on computer monitors with the recent growth of digital pathology whole slide image (WSI) platforms. Following a protracted course, the U.S. Food and Drug Administration has approved two WSI systems as class II medical devices [1,2] and there are several more WSI platform vendors in the digital pathology market [3]. In response to these new market forces and to recent technology advances outside of pathology, a new field of computational pathology is emerging that applies machine learning and image analytics to WSIs [4,5]. This has also led to innovative new concepts such as computer assisted diagnosis for pathologists (pCAD), that propose methods for integration of machine learning techniques into pathology workflows [6–18].

Deep learning in the form of convolutional neural networks has been popular in early computational pathology efforts. While powerful in isolated, lower level applications such as mitosis counting or cancer detection [19–23], deep learning has not yet yielded validated, comprehensive, high level systems [24]. There is also pathologist fear and skepticism about the application of AI to pathology, and there is no consensus about how pathologists should supervise or work with AI-powered computational pathology systems. A crucial new concept is explainable AI (xAI) [25,26], which refers to AI that can justify its results with data. Although xAI term recently used for explaining black-box AI tools, it is actually a broader concept in machine learning, covering all AI algorithms that generate human-understandable statements for its conclusions.

xAI is intended to address bias, transparency, safety, and causality [27]. Bias refers to potentially flawed AI resulting from biased training data, which might appear to work initially but could later fail catastrophically; xAI could prevent such occurrences by providing real-time feedback to its users [28]. Transparency is related as xAI can justify its results to users, providing them with all of the information needed to make good decisions based on its recommendations. In pathology, patient safety is paramount and is the result of a complex interaction between pathologist, other physicians and laboratory personnel, and computer systems including computational pathology applications. Patient safety can be improved by xAI not only by reducing undetected bias or by providing transparency to the pathologist, it is also related to the pathologist being able to monitor xAI's functionality in real-time, on individual patient samples. Finally, causality refers to scientifically understanding the pathological mechanisms underlying xAI systems.

Many deep learning efforts chase engineering statistics (e.g., area under the curve, accuracy, etc.) and some try to provide explanations as a post-processing step (e.g., explaining the black-box AI decisions by showing a group of pixels or a heat map on the image that led the black-box to make the call). All these efforts are far away from human understandable explanations and do not provide new insights into diagnostic pathology. A common discussion point is that xAI sacrifices accuracy for interpretability, but this is not necessarily true especially when the data representation is structured in terms of a dictionary of histological patterns that aid in differential diagnosis [24]. In addition, xAI has the potential to allow researchers understand new disease mechanisms that can lead to meaningful diagnostic or therapeutic advances [29]. These attributes make xAI a critical component of computational pathology.

Pathologists have been conservative about making large practice changes as pathology is considered the gold standard of medical diagnosis. It is likely that xAI can facilitate adoption of computational pathology and it can help drive scientific understanding of pathology underlying cancer and other diseases, which have been elusive. It is important to note that such use of xAI is to support the pathologist in making efficient and more accurate diagnoses, not to replace them. The goal is to allow the pathologist to focus on the most important decisions that only they can make, while having all the necessary information available.

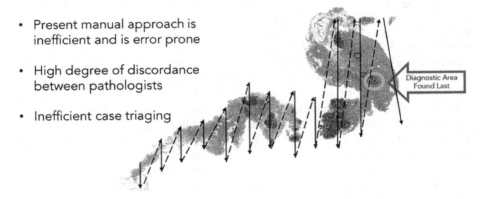

- Present manual approach is inefficient and is error prone

- High degree of discordance between pathologists

- Inefficient case triaging

Diagnostic Area Found Last

Fig. 1. A simplified, usual microscope or manual WSI viewing pattern (dashed and solid black arrows). Pathologists must view the tissue in a systematic fashion to ensure that all tissue was viewed. This leads to an efficiency issue wherein the diagnostic area (yellow circle), is discovered unpredictably and without warning. It could even be missed if small or subtle. The ongoing search for potential diagnostic areas is also slower than the confident review after decisions have been made. Finally, there is no before-hand knowledge of whether an individual pathology case will be difficult, or whether it needs to be expedited. (Color figure online)

There is currently tremendous interest in computational pathology despite any potential concerns, as seen on recent conferences' websites [30,31]. Traditional, manual pathology diagnosis, either with glass microscope slides or with manual WSIs, is inefficient and error-prone (Fig. 1). For example, one group reported low diagnostic concordance between pathologists when diagnosing difficult lesions in breast biopsies such as atypical ductal hyperplasia (52% concordance); this report also noted that different kinds of pathologists (i.e. breast pathologists vs. general pathologists) were subject to different levels of performance [32]. Regarding efficiency, manual WSI viewing may not provide adequate efficiency, versus traditional glass slide microscopy, to justify its implementation for primary diagnosis given the cost and workflow changes of WSI including time delay for slide scanning. This is based on unpublished data but is also borne out by the sluggish adoption of digital pathology for primary diagnosis in recent years despite a regulatory opening in 2017 [33]. According to our simulations of a pCAD model, computational pathology could be 56% more efficient than traditional microscopy for breast core biopsies [34]. Efficiency gains appeared to come from several factors: earlier discovery of diagnostic regions of interest (ROIs); decreased uncertainty with triaging; ability to review less diagnostic ROIs in an expedited fashion after major diagnostic decisions were made.

To address the unmet needs of efficiency and accuracy in pathology diagnosis, and to accelerate the adoption of computational pathology in pathology practice we are developing an xAI software platform called HistoMapr. In this particular chapter, we will be focusing on HistoMapr's example applications on breast pathology, namely HistoMapr-Breast (Fig. 2).

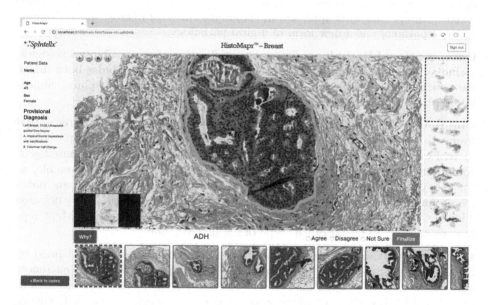

Fig. 2. A prototype of HistoMapr-Breast. The central panel shows the WSI viewing area with a computer-provided ROI outline in green. The panel to the right shows the WSIs, the panel to the left shows patient information and a provisional diagnosis that is based on the interactive work with HistoMapr. The bottom panel shows key elements of HistoMapr, including a "Why?" button for xAI, a HistoMapr diagnostic label of "ADH" (atypical ductal hyperplasia), pathologist buttons to indicate agreement, disagreement, or uncertainty about the HistoMapr label. Under this panel, ROIs are sorted in a way such that highest risk ROIs are shown to the pathologist first on the left. This is a highly-optimized method that enables the pathologist to make the most impactful diagnoses as early as possible during review of a specimen. In this example, ROIs are triaged from most atypical to least atypical. (Color figure online)

2 Glossary

The following terms are defined for common understanding of this chapter;

Pathology Case: This is a patient specimen that is submitted to a laboratory by a physician, such as a breast core biopsy or a collection of specimens such as a mastectomy with separate lymph node biopsies. These specimens, or cases are described and processed into glass microscope slides that may be subsequently imaged as whole slide images (WSIs). Pathologists view microscope slides and/or WSIs to make diagnostic decisions, which are then issued as a results report.

Digital Pathology: This refers to the use of digital imaging in pathology. Initial efforts focused on remote viewing of microscopy with both manual and robotic remote-controlled microscopes, or basic image analysis including biomarker reads. Whole slide images (WSIs) are a more recent area of digital pathology, both for earlier applications (e.g. telepathology or image analysis) and for more recent primary diagnosis applications (i.e. replacement of microscopes). Computational pathology is a new form of digital pathology.

Computational Pathology: This is the application of computing technologies, including machine learning or AI, to pathology data. This includes both image data such as WSIs, and non-image data such as patient demographics, clinical information, or pathologists' observations.

Computer Assisted Diagnosis for Pathologists (pCAD): A conceptual framework that lays out a path forward for applying computational pathology to real-world practice. The intent is to augment pathologists with intelligent computer guidance that allows pathologists to delegate everything possible, so that they can focus on the critical decisions that only pathologists can make. This requires high level integration of pathology case information, highly detailed clinical situation plans, and computational pathology pipelines. HistoMapr represents an early iteration of this type of intelligent guide.

Pointwise Mutual Information (PMI): Two-dimensional maps, defined by the total number of cellular phenotypes, for recording the relative co-occurrences and anti-associations of spatially distributed cellular phenotypes in a tissue sample. A PMI map with strong diagonal entries and weak off-diagonal entries describes a tumor sample that is locally homogeneous but global heterogeneous with respect to the spatial distribution of the cellular phenotypes. PMI maps with strong off-diagonal entries describe a tumor with many localized interactions between different cellular phenotypes, thus signifying a tumor sample exhibiting strong local heterogeneity.

Explainable Artificial Intelligence (xAI): Also known as Transparent AI, or Interpretable Machine Learning, is an artificial intelligence system whose actions can be trusted and easily understood by humans. xAI algorithms are programmed to describe its purpose, rationale and decision-making process in a transparent way that can be understood by lay person. xAI is often confused with explanations provided by post-processing steps of deep learning algorithms. There is a big difference between inherently interpretable machine learning models and explaining black box models as a post-processing step. xAI models that are inherently interpretable provide their own explanations, which are more faithful to what the model actually computes and plays an important role in the FAT ML model (fairness, accountability and transparency in machine learning). The methods presented in this chapter relates to inherently interpretable xAI.

3   State-of-the-Art

3.1   Objective

HistoMapr echoes the natural hierarchies found in the spatial organization of human tissues, as illustrated in a pyramidal diagram (Fig. 3). Lowest level, simple

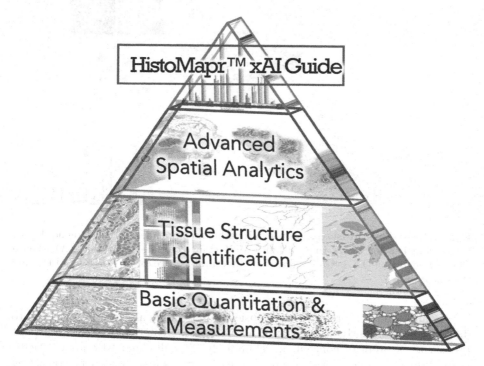

Fig. 3. HistoMapr xAI Guide: Hierarchical integration from cellular quantification to computational guides. Lowest level comprises basic image analyses such as nuclear size/shape, mitosis counting, or color optimization. Next level includes techniques such as PMI mapping to identify potential features in the WSIs such as breast ducts, inflammatory infiltrates, or tumor and their locations within regions of interest (ROIs). The next layer includes analysis of identified ROIs to apply diagnostic labels based on identified spatial relationships of structures and cell populations. These lead to the apex, which are intelligent computer guides that can help pathologists.

image analyses, such as nuclear size/shape or mitosis counts, can be integrated with PMI maps at the second level to identify and classify tissue structures such as ducts in breast tissue. Diagnostic regions of interest (ROIs) are labeled based upon the tissue structures' spatial relationships at the third level with diagnostic information and triaged based on diagnostic significance. In this fashion, the xAI HistoMapr guides emerge at top level; WSIs are re-represented as a *guided review* of triaged ROIs in the context of the pathologist's diagnostic tasks.

This approach is unlike the traditional slide examination pattern as described in Fig. 1 and more efficient since pathologists can view diagnostically relevant ROIs within whole set of WSIs of a patient at once. Furthermore, relationships between distinct cellular populations of the tissue microenvironment (e.g., tumor, stromal and immune cells) can also enable precision medicine approaches to be incorporated into routine diagnostic and prognostic activities.

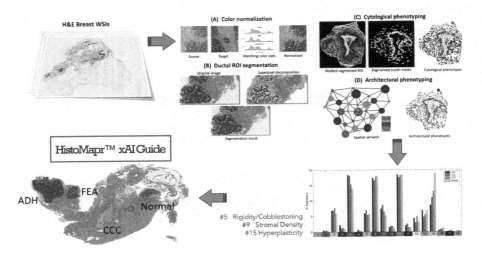

Fig. 4. HistoMapr-Breast computational pathology pipeline. An end-to-end breast lesion classifier for WSIs that includes WSI stain color normalization (A), ductal ROI segmentation (B), cytological and architectural feature extraction (C and D), and classification.

As an example, breast core biopsies can be difficult for pathologists to diagnose concordantly [32,35,36]. Therefore, we created a HistoMapr-Breast prototype as proof of concept, a deliberately difficult diagnostic area. Briefly, HistoMapr-Breast analyzes an entire breast core biopsy specimen, consisting of one or more WSIs, using both basic image analyses and PMI maps to locate regions of interest (ROIs) that contain diagnostic breast tissue structures such as ducts, blood vessels, or stromal infiltrates (Fig. 4) [18,37]. HistoMapr-Breast then analyzes the ROIs to find pre-trained features and quantitate them if present. This analysis is used to label the ROIs with diagnostic terms such as "atypical ductal hyperplasia" or "invasive carcinoma" based on analysis of the feature patterns and strengths. HistoMapr can also indicate its confidence in the label using a "Confidence Score" that incorporates the features and feature quantities. The labeled ROIs are then triaged based upon both the diagnostic labels and the Confidence Scores of those labels. For example, ROIs may be sorted from benign to malignant, or if cancer is not present, then from benign to atypical. Within a diagnostic category, ROIs can be triaged based on the Confidence Score. These steps occur before the pathologist begins viewing the case, possibly overnight or during weekend off hours.

Using a pathologist-centric interactive interface, HistoMapr displays the ROIs in the triage order, so that the pathologist sees the most malignant or most atypical areas first, if present (Fig. 2). Critically, the pathologist is always fully in control and may take manual control of the WSI viewer software at any time if they need to review all or part of the WSIs manually. xAI manifests as a "Why?" button that provides one or more panels of supplementary information (Fig. 5). The pathologist thus has complete situational awareness and is able to make the very best diagnostic decisions. HistoMapr also facilitates the pathologist's work by managing diagnostic information and tracking the pathologist's agreement or disagreement with the provided diagnostic labels; the pathologist may also indicate uncertainty and HistoMapr collects this information for possible additional stain work-up or consultation. When the pathologist is ready to finalize the case, HistoMapr automatically constructs a results report using the pathologist's interpretations of the ROIs review, and also using suggested/standardized terminology. Early study of the prototype HistoMapr-Breast prototype performed well and showed 83% f-measure concordance for atypical ductal hyperplasia (N = 300 WSIs and 2,000 ROIs) [18].

In addition to pathologist diagnostic guides, HistoMapr platform also includes technology for additional applications, such as rapid ground truth data labeling, image-content based distribution of pathology work, and archival of key diagnostic information for longitudinal continuity of care or clinical research. Ground truth data labeling is necessary for machine learning training but has historically been a bottleneck. Poorly implemented labeling tools can also squander scarce pathologist time. HistoMapr effectively addresses this with both automated ROI discovery and with the pathologist-friendly interface. As discussed above, HistoMapr can analyze one or more WSIs and extract ROIs in an unsupervised fashion. Using an efficient and friendly interface, pathologists can rapidly apply diagnostic labels to the ROIs without any need of hand drawing or label typing. In our experience pathologists can label at least 750 ROIs an hour (Fig. 6). The ROI labels can then be used to train HistoMapr; corrected labels derived from diagnostic work can also be used to improve HistoMapr based on real-world pathology diagnoses.

The previously mentioned Confidence Scores can be automatically generated during WSI previewing. Aggregated Confidence Score data can then be used to estimate the difficulty of a case, and also combined with the number of ROIs to estimate the amount of worktime required to view the case. This permits work triage based upon case attributes; difficult cases might be assigned to an expert

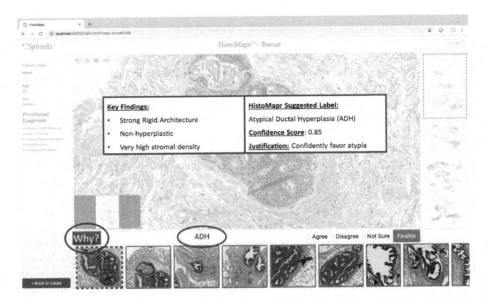

Fig. 5. xAI interface in HistoMapr-Breast. Pathologists can interpret the xAI output by accessing an interface panel or page through clicking a "Why?" button. The output of HistoMapr's xAI shows the green bounded region of interest is classified as "ADH" (circled in red). To the left of this output there is a button named "Why?" (circled in blue) that opens the explanation panel named "Key Findings", where justifications from the ROI in question are shown to the pathologists as the reasons and confidence of HistoMapr-Breast in classifying this region as ADH. (Color figure online)

subspecialist pathologist rather than a generalist pathologist (Fig. 7). Pathology work could also be distributed evenly to a pool of pathologists, thereby improving efficiency of pathologist time utilization. A "Why?" button would show how or why HistoMapr made its triage decision for a case, including Confidence Scores, and potential for ambiguity in the diagnosis. As we go from explaining classification of ROIs to explaining triaging decisions for a case, an updated terminology is needed for pathologists who are viewing a triaged case list and having the option to ask "Why?" to HistoMapr's decisions on triaging. In the xAI interface for case triaging, each triaged case will have an explanatory information field about why the case is triaged this way. These textual justifications can indicate the difficulty of the case (e.g., "difficult case involving atypical findings", "easy case with definite invasive findings") and why it is difficult based on the evidence that HistoMapr quantified. HistoMapr will also indicate its confidence in the triaging decision using a "Confidence Score" that incorporates the features, feature quantities, and confidence on ROI classifications within the case. The cases are triaged based upon both the diagnostic labels and the confidence intervals of those labels. This can be achieved by defining confidence intervals within the ML pipeline with respect to weighted features. This is an early and compelling application for HistoMapr.

The xAI derived statistics of ROIs or of entire cases are a fingerprint of sorts that can also be used for other content-based purposes. The statistics include features present, quantitation of those features, and the previously-mentioned Confidence Scores. These permit matching of an ROI with libraries of known diagnostic images for decision support, for education, for quality assurance activities, or for image content searching and retrieval. Content-based analysis could also facilitate clinical trials by supplementing or automating patient screening and/or central review of the pathology.

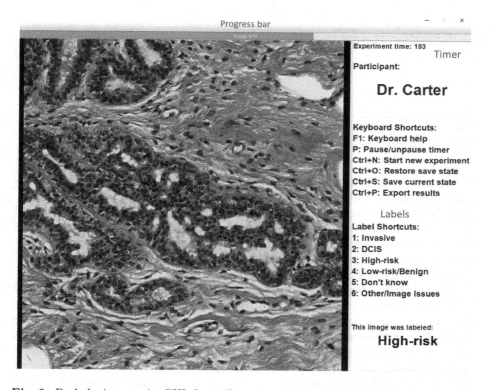

Fig. 6. Pathologist-centric GUI for collecting annotations from automatically segmented ROIs. We employ a GUI in Java environment to be easily used in any operation system, since the software is used in pathologists' workstation or personal computer. The software is a plug-in and play, installed in an encrypted USB drive together with ROI images to be labeled. The GUI design for ground truth annotation is easy to learn and efficient to use. Pathologists do not need to hand-draw or type their inputs, instead they are shown a series if ROIs and asked to hit keyboard buttons from 1 to 6, each corresponding to labels "Invasive", "DCIS", "High-risk Benign", "Low-risk Benign", "Don't know", or "Other". The option "Don't know" is used by pathologists in case they couldn't decide on the label of ROI and "Other/Image issues" is used if there is a problem with the segmented ROI's quality. The pathologists are asked to complete sets of 250 ROIs at a time, with an option of saving to be able continue the process later. We then create a relational database to store, manage and retrieve the ground truth annotations.

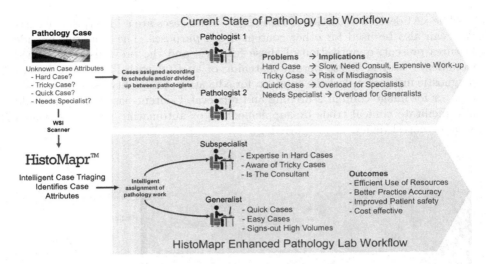

Fig. 7. Intelligent targeted case distribution - getting the right case to the right pathologist rapidly.

As noted above in the xAI discussion of causality; archived HistoMapr information could be used to facilitate subsequent re-visiting of a prior biopsy case. This includes comparison of older biopsies with newer materials or centralized review for clinical trials; pathologists can immediately view the diagnostic ROIs without need to manually search through the WSIs. Previously recorded computational features may also play a role in research where diagnostic entities are re-evaluated for risk or diagnostic criteria.

Finally, HistoMapr can review previously finalized cases for retrospective QA. The xAI features can be used to help identify potential pathology result discrepancies or errors. This important QA activity can reduce risk, improve clinician confidence and help pathologists monitor their diagnostic work in a timely fashion. As with other HistoMapr applications, a "Why?" button would provide details that supported the possibility of a QA issue, such as strong likelihood of malignancy in a biopsy diagnosed as benign, or perhaps a very weak Confidence Score for the diagnosis that was rendered.

HistoMapr is designed for transmitted light applications where tissue samples are stained with Hematoxylin and Eosin (H&E), immunohistochemistry (IHC) labels, and/or other stains (e.g., special stains, chromogenic in situ hybridization, enzyme metallography, etc.).

3.2   Evaluation

Pilot Study 1: In this first study [37], we addressed the classification of breast lesions into benign usual ductal hyperplasia (UDH) versus malignant ductal carcinoma in situ (DCIS), which requires careful examination of diagnostic criteria, including cellular features, tissue architecture, and spatial extent. We developed a prototype HistoMapr algorithm using a publicly available dataset that contained 167 cases (100 DCIS and 67 UDH). In a four-way classification of UDH versus low, moderate or high-grade DCIS, HistoMapr achieved 88% area under the curve (AUC), which represented a 25% improvement (from 70%) over other previously published methods C-path and DCIS CAD system.

Pilot Study 2: In this second study [18], we addressed the challenging problem of classifying high-risk benign breast lesions with data generated by our research group. This study focused on atypical ductal hyperplasia (ADH), which is a known diagnostic dilemma and is also a diagnosis that confers significant cancer risk [32,35]. Flat epithelial atypia, columnar cell change (CCC), and several benign entities were also included in the study, unlike any other studies in literature.

Using our own WSI data (n = 46 cases, 269 WSIs, 1759 ROIs) we constructed a more robust HistoMapr computational pathology pipeline than in the first pilot study above, one that scales to entire WSIs. Briefly, there was a novel color normalization step we previously developed, based on an opponent color space optimized for hematoxylin and eosin (H&E) stained WSIs [38]. Next there was a ductal ROI segmentation which found potentially diagnostic ROIs using our proprietary spatial statistical technology to create pointwise mutual information (PMI) maps. This was followed by cytological then architectural phenotyping; three different phenotyping methods were used, focused on nuclei, on color, or on both, including stromal and lumen superpixels. Using k-means clustering, 18 patterns were found to describe 95% of the input variance. These patterns were later analyzed then described using pathologist-friendly language for the purpose of xAI.

The training step was innovative, using a java-based tool to rapidly and efficiently gather ground truth data using; a pathologist was able to annotate 1009 training ROIs in about one hour (Fig. 6). This is a significant advance; in our experience, ground truth labeling can be a severe bottleneck if an optimal software strategy is not used.

The evaluation step used the same annotation tool and three pathologists were able to very rapidly label a set of 750 ROIs. As noted in the literature, even breast pathologists had some disagreement with one another. Only 4% of the ROIs contained unanimous atypia labels; 12% had at least two pathologist atypia labels; and 21% of ROIs were labeled atypical by one of the three pathologists. The overall Fleiss' kappa score was 0.55, or moderate agreement between pathologists.

For the pipeline, we constructed architectural feature vectors for different scenarios based (e.g., cytologic features, color features, etc.). For both architectural and cytological features, we find that these feature sets outperform the majority classification and perform comparably to the average single expert pathologist classification (F-measure 0.78 versus F-measure 0.83). These results highlight the value of using HistoMapr-Breast to guide the pathologist in diagnosing atypical breast lesions. A key contribution of this study is in demonstrating how to encode morphometric properties of nuclear atypia (cytological) and combine them with the spatial distribution of the nuclei in relationship to stroma and lumen (architectural). Although there are several studies on cancer detection in breast tissue images, our pipeline was the first of its kind in detecting high-risk benign breast lesions from WSIs.

Pilot Study 3: In the third study we studied the efficiency rendered by an AI driven pathology assistant, such as HistoMapr-Breast [34]. We collected time data from pathologists diagnosing breast core biopsies using sound, which permitted us to know how long pathologists spent on each field of view under the microscope. Using models of HistoMapr style workflow we used this data to simulate the time it would take to diagnose those breast core biopsies with an AI driven pathology assistant. Comparing the simulated and actual biopsy review times, we observed that the HistoMapr-Breast driven diagnosis required 56% less time. This is a very significant and novel result that supports the hypothesis that a computer-augmented pathology diagnosis assistant is potentially much more efficient than current manual diagnostic practice.

3.3   Innovative Features of HistoMapr

1. HistoMapr effectively changes pathologists' view of a case from one or more WSIs into a guided series of triaged, diagnostically relevant regions of interest (ROIs). HistoMapr previews entire WSIs to discover relevant structure/features. For breast core biopsies, HistoMapr-Breast finds ducts, vascular structures, and stromal features using patented spatial statistics based on pairwise mutual information (PMI). By analyzing PMI maps, HistoMapr can find ROIs that contain these structures. Once ROIs are identified, HistoMapr then analyzes them for certain features. For example, a prototype version of HistoMapr-Breast used 18 features to classify ROIs as atypical or not atypical. In this analysis, HistoMapr finds which features are present in an ROI, and it quantitates each feature that it finds. The ROI analyses are patterns that can be matched to HistoMapr's library of diagnostic labels. The combination of diagnostic labeling and ROI quantitation is then used to triage the ROIs.
   For breast core biopsies, HistoMapr-Breast triages ROIs in a clinical spectrum from invasive cancer at one end, to low-risk benign at the other. In an interactive work session, the pathologist reviews the entire case, ROI by ROI, in a triaged fashion. This approach is highly efficient because HistoMapr presents the most clinically impactful ROIs to the pathologist first; this guidance enables the pathologist to focus on the hardest decisions first. If necessary, HistoMapr also keeps track of ROIs that may need further workup with additional stains, or ROIs that may require consultation with another pathologist.
2. HistoMapr expedites ground truth data labeling for training the machine learning—pathologists can rapidly view ROIs and provide streamlined diagnosis labels; this unique approach can provide hundreds of labeled ROIs per

hour. In automating ROI discovery, HistoMapr is much more efficient than traditional ground-truth labeling and effectively addresses what was a bottleneck in machine learning. HistoMapr has a pathologist-centric graphical user interface (GUI) for efficient annotation of segmented ROIs, which employs a GUI in Java environment to be easily used in any operation system, since the software will be used in pathologists' workstation or personal computer. The GUI design for ground truth annotation is easy to learn and efficient to us (Fig. 6). Pathologists do not need to hand- draw or type their inputs, instead they are shown a series of ROIs and asked to hit buttons from 1 to 6. HistoMapr has a database to store, manage and retrieve the ground truth annotations. In our initial experiments, pathologists were able to label around 750 ROIs in an hour after getting used to the software.

3. xAI analysis of HistoMapr output yields multiple features (with quantitation of those features) that can be described in pathologist-friendly language, thereby linking impactful features with diagnostic labels that can be used to explain HistoMapr labels in subsequent clinical sessions, providing pathologists with all the information that they need to make the best decisions possible. Using the output of our prototype computational pathology pipeline output, ROIs were reviewed in the context of the 18 features, especially features 5, 9 and 15 which were differentially seen in atypical vs non-atypical ducts (Fig. 8). Feature 5 appeared to correlate with architectural rigidity and cobblestoning of cells; feature 9 appeared to represent stromal density immediately surrounding ducts; and feature 15 seemed to correlate with hyperplasticity of the duct. Review of these ROIs suggested several opportunities for creation of software tools specifically for xAI (e.g., an AI feedback overlay, automatic presentation of Feature examples, etc.) (Fig. 5).

4. xAI visualization in real-time - a software "Why?" button can provide complete transparency by presenting additional information in real-time that explains HistoMapr's labels, fleshes out the relevant differential diagnosis, and acknowledges the strength of HistoMapr's analysis via a Confidence Score. HistoMapr can display the results of its ROI analysis to the pathologist. A HistoMapr-Breast prototype uses a "why?" button to achieve this. As previously mentioned, HistoMapr finds then quantitates features in the ROIs. When the pathologist presses the "Why?" button, they see a visualization of the ROI analysis by HistoMapr, in pathologist-friendly language (e.g., strong rigid architecture, highly monomorphic nuclear patterns, etc.).

   (a) Pathologists can interpret the xAI output by accessing an interface panel or page through clicking a "Why?" or "Explain" button

   (b) Which features were present in the ROI, with quantitation of the features

   (c) A Confidence Score analysis of the features, which transparently provides HistoMapr's estimate of the strength of its labeling and of the difficulty of the ROI

   (d) Examples of similar ROIs from other cases that can serve as a reference guide, for decision support

(e) A cartoon representation of the features in question, with a control (e.g., a slider) that allows the pathologist to view the continuum of that feature from low to high

(f) HistoMapr xAI system presents its differential diagnosis and displays pros and cons of various diagnoses under consideration; if ambiguous HistoMapr can suggest further work-up with stains, or expedited consultation with another pathologist electronically.

5. Confidence score based (content based) triage of patient biopsies; cases above a certain difficulty threshold can be distributed to subspecialty expert pathologists, whereas other cases can be sent to front-line general pathologists. HistoMapr xAI estimate of case difficulty and image volume can also be used to distribute pathology cases to a group of pathologists more evenly for better utilization of professional resources. Even for this application, a "Why?" xAI button means that HistoMapr can justify its case distribution and triage decisions. For pathologist guide applications, it is possible for HistoMapr to provide data that supported its diagnostic label including a measure of the data's strength. This is a powerful communication from HistoMapr to the pathologist, for it permits the pathologist to understand why HistoMapr labeled the ROI as it did and whether HistoMapr considers the ROI to be difficult or ambiguous. This permits the pathologist to have all of the necessary information for making a diagnosis, and it permits the pathologist to fully examine HistoMapr's performance in real time. At a higher level, this assessment can also be harnessed to drive case triage; difficult appearing cases can be routed to subspecialty expert pathologists for review instead of front-line general pathologists (Fig. 7).

6. Using standardized terminology for diagnosis labels, HistoMapr can encourage pathologists to report results in a more uniform fashion, a quality improvement. As the pathologist and HistoMapr work through the case together, HistoMapr uses the pathologist's decisions to construct the pathology report in real-time, using standardized language. This standardizes practice and improves quality of a practice's reports by making them easier to understand due to standardization of practice.

7. A case or its individual ROIs, via xAI, are annotated by HistoMapr. In addition to the diagnostic labels there are the features, feature quantitation, and Confidence Scores. These form a fingerprint that can be used to match ROIs with other cases, with libraries of known diagnoses, or with other pathologists' cases for many purposes:

(a) Decision support - showing the pathologist examples of similar ROIs from other cases, from libraries of known diagnoses, or from didactic materials

(b) Education - comparison of an ROI with known good examples of a diagnosis, and comparison of an ROI to almost-similar ROIs that have different diagnoses (i.e. presenting the differential diagnosis)

(c) Quality assurance (QA) activities - partial automation of second review of pathologists' work by other pathologists (e.g. QA reviews, standard second-opinion situations, etc.). Also, ongoing monitoring of HistoMapr performance as part of a pathology practice's QA framework

(d) Clinical Trials - computer-assisted screening of patient suitability for potential clinical trials, streamlining central review of pathology materials (i.e. ROI presentation without need to review an entire case)

(e) Content-based image searching for the above purposes or for any other reason.

8. Post-finalization quality assurance (QA) - After cases are finalized, or signed out, they can be re-reviewed by HistoMapr for concordance with the pathology diagnosis

(a) Risk reduction by detecting significant discrepancies (e.g., benign versus malignant)

(b) Evidence to regulators of ongoing and effective QA activities

(c) Improve clinician and patient confidence in diagnoses, especially difficult diagnoses such as breast atypias

(d) "Why?" button provides transparency and shows why a case was potentially discrepant.

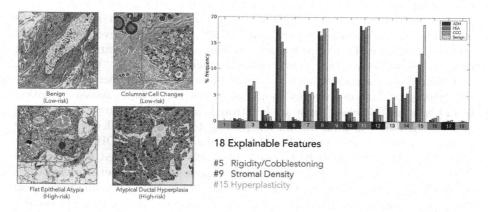

Fig. 8. Micro-spatial discriminant features in breast ROIs. Sample ductal ROIs representing (A) atypical ductal hyperplasia (ADH), (B) flat epithelial atypia (FEA), (C) columnar cell change (CCC), and (D) normal duct. Visualization of architectural patterns discovered in sample ROIs are overlaid on original images. Patterns are derived from a combination of cytological and architectural features and visualized by color coded objects (see x-axis of histogram in center). Note the overexpression of pattern #5 in ADH, #7 in FEA, and #15 in normal ducts. This observation is further supported by the histogram in center, where we measure relative proportions of architectural patterns separately in each one of the categories: ADH, FEA, CCC, and normal. These architectural patterns are further named based on the visual properties they are representing by our expert pathologists.

3.4   Example Session with HistoMapr

HistoMapr previews entire breast core biopsy cases overnight and assigns each case an xAI confidence score. This allows the laboratory to evenly distribute pathology work to multiple pathologists while ensuring that difficult cases are assigned to breast pathologists, while allowing simpler cases to be assigned to general pathologists. For a breast pathologist in this example, HistoMapr has further triaged cases based on factors such as pathologist preferences, laboratory policies such as expediting cases from specific clients, etc. For example, this breast pathologist prefers to look at cases which might need additional stains first so that there is adequate time to get these cases finalized before the end of the day. The pathologist is confident that HistoMapr has triaged the cases properly, and they feel comfortable selecting the first case on the list.

This brings up the HistoMapr-Breast software Fig. 2. After reading provided clinical information in the sidebar, the pathologist now reviews the WSIs. However, instead of manually clicking and dragging through the case the pathologist is whisked through in an intelligently guided path. Just as with traditional manual microscopy, the pathologist views the entire case, but in stark contrast HistoMapr-Breast provides a triaged, highly optimized ROI viewing order that is based upon showing most diagnostic areas to the pathologist first.

The pathologist proceeds to look at the first ROI, which HistoMapr has labeled as "atypical ductal hyperplasia (ADH)". There were several potentially atypical areas, but HistoMapr has selected this area to display first because it is most diagnostic-appearing. The pathologist clicks on the xAI "Why?" button, and HistoMapr graphically outlines its findings including a numerical confidence score that provides transparency about how strong HistoMapr's recommendation is and why; in this case, there are be strongly rigid architecture with bridging and round, monomorphic cell nuclei, leading to a high confidence score. The pathologist feels quite certain that this ROI does represent ADH, and they are able to rapidly agree with HistoMapr. The next four displayed ROIs are also ADH, but they are not classic-appearing and have lower confidence scores. This is OK, because the pathologist has already made the most difficult decision on the easiest-to-recognize ADH area. This means that the pathologist can rapidly review these next ROIs. Finally, the first ROI displayed was actually near the edge of the last WSI of the case; HistoMapr was able to identify and promote this critical ROI to the pathologist's attention thereby optimizing review.

xAI promotion of most-diagnostic ROIs is a critically important feature of pCAD enabled systems such as HistoMapr-Breast. In a manual review, without HistoMapr, the pathologist would have had to wade through almost the entire case before discovering the most-diagnostic area last. Worse, the pathologist would have had to evaluate and spend time with the four less-diagnostic areas first, which is highly inefficient because the pathologist could have rapidly and confidently made the ADH diagnosis on that last area due to it's textbook ("classic") appearance. Worst, if the critical finding is near the edge of an image, it is also possible that the pathologist could miss it entirely, due to an error in manual WSI viewing (a "driving" error in microscopy terms). If not seen, then it cannot be diagnosed. In our simulation study, unguided biopsy review is markedly less efficient (56% less efficient, unpublished data).

There may be other diagnoses in addition to the main one; in this case, the pathologist continues to work through the case with HistoMapr, looking at the entire case. They agree with automatically provided labels for other diagnoses such as columnar cell change and fibrocystic changes. HistoMapr-Breast tracks the pathologist's decisions about the diagnostic labels, and uses these to automatically construct a results report. The pathologist had access to manual WSI viewer controls, but did not need to use them in this case; the pathologist was always in full control of the case if necessary.

After the pathologist has finished the HistoMapr guided case review, they are ready to finalize the case. HistoMapr provides a finalization screen where the pathologist has an opportunity to review their diagnostic decisions, including any that were uncertain, or that were not in agreement with the xAI-generated labels; these ROIs are easily accessed for re-review via thumbnails. A preliminary result report is also provided automatically, a significant time saver because the pathologist did not have to manually take notes, record diagnoses, or even choose which words to use. Significantly, HistoMapr used standardized terminology and language, which is a subtle but concrete quality improvement that facilitates clinical patient management even at other institutions by promoting greater uniformity of pathology results reporting. The pathologist is rapidly able to finalize the result which is then transmitted to the clinical team via electronic health record. For this patient, the radiologist would review the report, notify the patient, and then would recommend a surgical consult. The patient would then see a surgeon, who would understand the current need to perform a larger, surgical biopsy based on the finding of ADH. Use of standardized terminology facilitates patient management by these other physicians, including the surgeon's ability to have an informed discussion with the patient.

4   Open Problems

Currently, almost all AI efforts in pathology applications are based upon Deep Learning methods. However, it is not currently possible to ask a Deep Learning system, "why?" [39]. This is a crucial feature for early computational pathology systems, because it will be necessary for pioneer pathologists to begin building trust even with highly-validated intelligent software guides (Fig. 9) [40,41].

Another importance of using xAI technology comes from possible future regulations on use of AI in decision-making procedures that might affect human rights. A proposed regulation before the European Union prohibits "automatic processing" unless user's rights are safeguarded [42]. Users now have a "right to an explanation" concerning algorithm-created decisions that are based on personal information. Future laws may further restrict AI use in professional practices, which represents a huge challenge to industry [43]. Moreover, business and clinical owners do not aim for full automation of machine learning

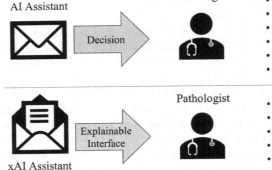

Pathologist

- Why did you do diagnose as DCIS?
- Why not something else?
- When do you correctly diagnose?
- When do you fail?
- When can I trust your decisions?
- How do I correct a misdiagnosis?

Pathologist

- I understand why DCIS
- I understand why not
- I know when you correctly diagnose
- I know when you fail
- I know when to trust your decisions
- I know how to correct your errors

Fig. 9. Machine learning is the core technology but machine learning models are opaque, non-intuitive, and difficult for people to understand. There is an unmet need for explanations in critical software such as computational pathology platforms.

models because they will not blindly trust a model. Because, there is no confidence in how the machine learning model is working and transparency is inadequate [44, 45].

The regulatory constraints that healthcare must operate within, provide an opportunity for explainable AI. The main concern of the regulatory body is that the black boxes should not be granted power to make decisions that deeply affect human lives. If the only solution to this problem is to provide post-hoc explanations of black boxes, unfortunately, the problem of building trust and transparency with the end users is further compounded by continued development of black-boxes that are inherently non-interpretable. Therefore, HistoMapr with an interpretable AI pipeline addresses these concerns.

Pathology is often considered to be the gold standard for patient diagnosis, and therefore pathologists have been conservative in adopting digital pathology [46]. We regard xAI as a critical feature that differentiates HistoMapr from other AI technologies. It is critical to emphasize that the purpose of the xAI in HistoMapr is not to make a diagnosis independent of the pathologist, but to assist the pathologist in being more accurate and efficient.

In the design of HistoMapr xAI system, key concepts of measurement for the evaluation of xAI systems and human-machine performance are considered [47–51]. These key concepts are explanation goodness, explanation satisfaction, curiosity metric, and user performance. Briefly, explanation goodness stands for clarity and precision of the explanation provided by the xAI system. The evaluation for this criterion can be made by simply asking yes/no questions to the user to learn: a) if the explanation helps them to understand how the software works, b) if the explanation is satisfying, sufficiently detailed and complete, c) if the explanation is actionable (i.e. helps user know how to use the tool), d) if the explanation lets the user know how accurate and reliable the software is, and e) if the explanation lets the user know how trustworthy the software is. Equally important measure on explanation goodness is the quality of the explanations (i.e., causability), is a measurement for the evaluation of explanatory interfaces. As HistoMapr provides detailed feature explanations in the explanation interface (e.g., confidence level, effect of features on the decision, detailed explanation of features, lets user to act on the output), we expect explanation goodness metric will be highly scored for HistoMapr.

Explanation satisfaction is to tell the degree to which users feel that they understand the AI system, or the process explained to them. This criterion is common for most xAI systems as it aims to serve the user's goals in understanding the software. In order to satisfy this criterion, the xAI system should be able to address users' questions such as, a) how do I avoid the failure modes? (shows user's desire to mitigate errors), b) what do I do if it gets it wrong? (shows user's desire to avoid mistakes), c) what does it achieve? (shows user's interest in understanding the system's functions), d) what did it just do? (user's feeling of satisfaction at having achieved an understanding of how the system made a particular decision), and e) why didn't it do "z" instead of "x"? (shows user's resolution of curiosity at having achieved an understanding of the decision). HistoMapr xAI system can address explanation satisfaction criterion by answering users' questions through its explanation interface [52]. "Why?" button in the HistoMapr GUI is specifically designed to address these by providing explanation to why HistoMapr thinks an ROI is belonging to a specific type of lesion.

Curiosity metric is a very important criterion as explanations can suppress curiosity and reinforce flawed mental models. This can happen in a number of ways: a) an explanation might overwhelm people with details, b) the xAI system might not allow questions or might make it difficult for the user to pose questions, c) explanations might make people feel reticent because of their lack of knowledge, and d) explanations may include too many open variables and loose ends, and curiosity decreases when confusion and complexity increase. For these reasons, the assessment of users' feelings of curiosity might be informative in the evaluation of xAI systems. HistoMapr xAI system is designed to receive feedback from the end users by asking simple survey questions.

Finally, user performance, including measures of joint user-system performance, will improve as a result of being given satisfying explanations. A main aspect of user performance measurement is the quality of the performance of the user, such as the correctness of the user's predictions of what the AI will do. For these aspects of performance, just like performance of the HistoMapr, we will measure response speed and correctness (hits, errors, misses, false alarms), but in this case the user's predictions of the machine outputs [52]. Examination can be made for both typical and atypical cases/situations. Additionally, HistoMapr can measure the correctness and completeness of the user's explanation of the machine's output for cases that are rare, unusual, or anomalous.

5   Future Outlook

Computational pathology is poised to revolutionize digital pathology by delivering meaningful automation of anatomic pathology by augmenting pathologists. There are real concerns about such automation that revolve around trusting and validating computational pathology tools. Using xAI, HistoMapr is a type of platform that can move forward in a transparent fashion, by permitting pathologists to understand how it works and why a specific decision is made. It is anticipated that such an approach will also ease regulation of computational pathology software because transparency facilitates supervision and real-time monitoring in order to ensure safety. xAI guidance ensures that pathologists have all the necessary information to make the best diagnoses they can make.

The computer assisted diagnosis for pathologist approach is a powerful framework that lends itself to any type of pathology diagnosis work. Although the first application for breast core biopsies was estimated to potentially be 56% more efficient than manual microscopy, time savings for large resection specimens could be much higher. This approach is highly efficient because HistoMapr presents the most clinically impactful ROIs to the pathologist first; this guidance enables the pathologist to focus on the hardest decisions first. It also permits the pathologist to focus on the decisions that only they can make, while managing other, less important decisions or tasks (e.g., assembling the results report, counting, measuring, rare event detection, etc.).

As mentioned before, almost all AI centered software development in pathology is currently based on Deep Learning and it is not currently possible to ask a Deep Learning system, "why?". This is a crucial feature for early computational pathology systems, because it will be necessary for pioneer pathologists to begin building trust even with highly-validated intelligent software guides (Fig. 9) [40,41]. Pathology is often considered to be the gold standard for patient diagnosis, and therefore pathologists have been conservative in adopting digital pathology. We regard xAI as a critical feature that differentiates HistoMapr from other AI technologies. It is critical to emphasize that the purpose of the xAI in HistoMapr is not to make a diagnosis independent of the pathologist, but to assist the pathologist in a transparent fashion in being more accurate and efficient.

6   Funding Sources

Research reported in this publication was partly supported by NSF SBIR Phase I Award No. 1843825, NIH Grant No. U01CA204836, and UPMC Center for Commercial Applications of Healthcare Data Award No. 711077.

References

1. Food and Drug Administration, U.S.A.: Intellisite3 pathology solution (pips, Philips medical systems) (2017)

2. Food and Drug Administration, U.S.A.: Aperio AT2 DX system (2019)
3. Pantanowitz, L., Sharma, A., Carter, A.B., Kurc, T., Sussman, A., Saltz, J.: Twenty years of digital pathology: an overview of the road travelled, what is on the horizon, and the emergence of vendor-neutral archives. J. Pathol. Inf. **9** (2018, online)
4. Louis, D.N., et al.: Computational pathology: a path ahead. Arch. Pathol. Lab. Med. **140**(1), 41–50 (2016)
5. Fuchs, T.J., Buhmann, J.M.: Computational pathology: challenges and promises for tissue analysis. Comput. Med. Imaging Graph. **35**(7–8), 515–530 (2011)
6. Kumar, N., Verma, R., Sharma, S., Bhargava, S., Vahadane, A., Sethi, A.: A dataset and a technique for generalized nuclear segmentation for computational pathology. IEEE Trans. Med. Imaging **36**(7), 1550–1560 (2017)
7. Eisses, J.F., et al.: A computer-based automated algorithm for assessing acinar cell loss after experimental pancreatitis. PloS One **9**(10) (2014, online)
8. Mercan, E., Mehta, S., Bartlett, J., Shapiro, L.G., Weaver, D.L., Elmore, J.G.: Assessment of machine learning of breast pathology structures for automated differentiation of breast cancer and high-risk proliferative lesions. JAMA Netw. Open **2**(8), e198777 (2019)
9. Tosun, A.B., Sokmensuer, C., Gunduz-Demir, C.: Unsupervised tissue image segmentation through object-oriented texture. In: 2010 20th International Conference on Pattern Recognition, pp. 2516–2519. IEEE (2010)
10. Li, H., Whitney, J., Bera, K., Gilmore, H., Thorat, M.A., Badve, S., Madabhushi, A.: Quantitative nuclear histomorphometric features are predictive of oncotype DX risk categories in ductal carcinoma in situ: preliminary findings. Breast Cancer Res. **21**(1), 114 (2019)
11. Huang, H., et al.: Cancer diagnosis by nuclear morphometry using spatial information. Pattern Recogn. Lett. **42**, 115–121 (2014)
12. Dong, F., et al.: Computational pathology to discriminate benign from malignant intraductal proliferations of the breast. PloS One **9**(12) (2014, online)
13. Nawaz, S., Yuan, Y.: Computational pathology: exploring the spatial dimension of tumor ecology. Cancer Lett. **380**(1), 296–303 (2016)
14. Fuchs, T.J., Wild, P.J., Moch, H., Buhmann, J.M.: Computational pathology analysis of tissue microarrays predicts survival of renal clear cell carcinoma patients. In: Metaxas, D., Axel, L., Fichtinger, G., Székely, G. (eds.) MICCAI 2008. LNCS, vol. 5242, pp. 1–8. Springer, Heidelberg (2008). https://doi.org/10.1007/978-3-540-85990-1_1
15. Tosun, A.B., Yergiyev, O., Kolouri, S., Silverman, J.F., Rohde, G.K.: Detection of malignant mesothelioma using nuclear structure of mesothelial cells in effusion cytology specimens. Cytometry Part A **87**(4), 326–333 (2015)
16. Farahani, N., Liu, Z., Jutt, D., Fine, J.L.: Pathologists' computer-assisted diagnosis: a mock-up of a prototype information system to facilitate automation of pathology sign-out. Arch. Pathol. Lab. Med. **141**(10), 1413–1420 (2017)
17. Fine, J.L.: 21st century workflow: a proposal. J. Pathol. Inf. **5** (2014, online)
18. Tosun, A.B., et al.: Histological detection of high-risk benign breast lesions from whole slide images. In: Descoteaux, M., Maier-Hein, L., Franz, A., Jannin, P., Collins, D.L., Duchesne, S. (eds.) MICCAI 2017. LNCS, vol. 10434, pp. 144–152. Springer, Cham (2017). https://doi.org/10.1007/978-3-319-66185-8_17
19. Li, C., Wang, X., Liu, W., Latecki, L.J.: DeepMitosis: mitosis detection via deep detection, verification and segmentation networks. Med. Image Anal. **45**, 121–133 (2018)

20. Janowczyk, A., Madabhushi, A.: Deep learning for digital pathology image analysis: a comprehensive tutorial with selected use cases. J. Pathol. Inf. **7** (2016, online)
21. Aresta, G., et al.: BACH: grand challenge on breast cancer histology images. Med. Image Anal. **56**, 122–139 (2019)
22. Liu, Y., Gadepalli, K., et al.: Detecting cancer metastases on gigapixel pathology images. arXiv preprint arXiv:1703.02442 (2017)
23. Bejnordi, B.E., et al.: Context-aware stacked convolutional neural networks for classification of breast carcinomas in whole-slide histopathology images. J. Med. Imaging (Bellingham) **4**(4), 044504 (2017)
24. Rudin, C.: Stop explaining black box machine learning models for high stakes decisions and use interpretable models instead. Nat. Mach. Intell. **1**(5), 206–215 (2019)
25. Gunning, D.: Explainable artificial intelligence (xAI). Defense Advanced Research Projects Agency (DARPA), nd Web 2 (2017)
26. Gunning, D., Stefik, M., Choi, J., Miller, T., Stumpf, S., Yang, G.Z.: XAI–explainable artificial intelligence. Sci. Robot. **4**(37) (2019, online)
27. Hoffman, R.R., Mueller, S.T., Klein, G., Litman, J.: Metrics for explainable AI: challenges and prospects. arXiv preprint arXiv:1812.04608 (2018)
28. Samek, W., Wiegand, T., Müller, K.R.: Explainable artificial intelligence: understanding, visualizing and interpreting deep learning models. arXiv preprint arXiv:1708.08296 (2017)
29. Uttam, S., et al.: Spatial domain analysis predicts risk of colorectal cancer recurrence and infers associated tumor microenvironment networks. bioRxiv (2019)
30. USCAP: United States and Canadian academy of pathology (USCAP) annual meeting
31. DPA: Pathology visions conference
32. Elmore, J.G., et al.: Diagnostic concordance among pathologists interpreting breast biopsy specimens. JAMA **313**(11), 1122–1132 (2015)
33. Montalto, M.C.: An industry perspective: an update on the adoption of whole slide imaging. J. Pathol. Inf. **7** (2016, online)
34. Jones, T., Nguyen, L., Torun, A.B., Chennubhotla, S., Fine, J.L.: Computational pathology versus manual microscopy: comparison based on workflow simulations of breast core biopsies. In: Laboratory Investigation, vol. 97, Nature Publishing Group 75 Varick St, 9th Flr, New York, NY, 10013-1917 USA, pp. 398A–398A (2017)
35. Simpson, J.F., Boulos, F.I.: Differential diagnosis of proliferative breast lesions. Surg. Pathol. Clin. **2**(2), 235–246 (2009)
36. Onega, T., et al.: The diagnostic challenge of low-grade ductal carcinoma in situ. Eur. J. Cancer **80**, 39–47 (2017)
37. Nguyen, L., Tosun, A.B., Fine, J.L., Taylor, D.L., Chennubhotla, S.C.: Architectural patterns for differential diagnosis of proliferative breast lesions from histopathological images. In: IEEE 14th International Symposium on Biomedical Imaging (ISBI 2017), pp. 152–155. IEEE (2017)
38. Nguyen, L., Tosun, A.B., Fine, J.L., Lee, A.V., Taylor, D.L., Chennubhotla, S.C.: Spatial statistics for segmenting histological structures in H&E stained tissue images. IEEE Trans. Med. Imaging **36**(7), 1522–1532 (2017)
39. Nguyen, A., Yosinski, J., Clune, J.: Deep neural networks are easily fooled: high confidence predictions for unrecognizable images. In: Proceedings of the IEEE Conference on Computer Vision and Pattern Recognition, pp. 427–436 (2015)
40. Tizhoosh, H.R., Pantanowitz, L.: Artificial intelligence and digital pathology: challenges and opportunities. J. Pathol. Inf. **9** (2018, online)

41. Hudec, M., Bednárová, E., Holzinger, A.: Augmenting statistical data dissemination by short quantified sentences of natural language. J. Off. Stat. **34**(4), 981–1010 (2018)
42. European Commission: Ethics guidelines for trustworthy AI (European commission, 2019) (2019)
43. US: The white house, executive office of the president of the United States, national artificial intelligence research and development strategic plan (2019)
44. Holzinger, A., Biemann, C., Pattichis, C.S., Kell, D.B.: What do we need to build explainable AI systems for the medical domain? arXiv preprint arXiv:1712.09923 (2017)
45. Floridi, L.: Establishing the rules for building trustworthy AI. Nat. Mach. Intell. **1**(6), 261–262 (2019)
46. Evans, A.J., et al.: Us food and drug administration approval of whole slide imaging for primary diagnosis: a key milestone is reached and new questions are raised. Arch. Pathol. Lab. Med. **142**(11), 1383–1387 (2018)
47. Ribeiro, M.T., Singh, S., Guestrin, C.: Model-agnostic interpretability of machine learning. arXiv preprint arXiv:1606.05386 (2016)
48. Miller, T., Howe, P., Sonenberg, L.: Explainable AI: beware of inmates running the asylum or: how i learnt to stop worrying and love the social and behavioural sciences. arXiv preprint arXiv:1712.00547 (2017)
49. Montavon, G., Samek, W., Müller, K.R.: Methods for interpreting and understanding deep neural networks. Digit. Signal Proc. **73**, 1–15 (2018)
50. Core, M.G., Lane, H.C., Van Lent, M., Gomboc, D., Solomon, S., Rosenberg, M.: Building explainable artificial intelligence systems. In: AAAI, pp. 1766–1773 (2006)
51. Ribeiro, M.T., Singh, S., Guestrin, C.: "Why should i trust you?" Explaining the predictions of any classifier. In: Proceedings of the 22nd ACM SIGKDD International Conference on Knowledge Discovery and Data Mining, pp. 1135–1144 (2016)
52. Holzinger, A., Carrington, A., Müller, H.: Measuring the quality of explanations: the system causability scale (SCS). KI-Künstliche Intell. **34**(2), 193–198 (2020)

Extension of the Identity Management System Mainzelliste to Reduce Runtimes for Patient Registration in Large Datasets

Norman Zerbe[1,2(✉)], Christopher Hampf[2], and Peter Hufnagl[1,2,3]

[1] Charité - Universitätsmedizin Berlin, Corporate Member of Freie Universität Berlin, Humboldt-Universität zu Berlin, and Berlin Institute of Health, Institute of Pathology, Berlin, Germany
norman.zerbe@charite.de
[2] Charité - Universitätsmedizin Berlin, Corporate Member of Freie Universität Berlin, Humboldt-Universität zu Berlin, and Berlin Institute of Health, Central Biobank Charité, Berlin, Germany
[3] HTW University of Applied Sciences Berlin, Center for Biomedical Image and Information Processing (CBMI), Berlin, Germany

Abstract. Identity management is a central component of medical research, the management of medical samples and related biomaterial data and data protection requirements. For daily use, it is important to ensure that an identity management system is able to manage large datasets with several million records within a feasible time. The Central Biomaterial Bank Charité (ZeBanC) aimed to use Mainzelliste, for the purpose of externalization of the identity management of a running biobank system. The evaluation results showed that is was not possible to register new patients into a database with several hundred thousand datasets in feasible runtimes.

The aims of this project were an evaluation and optimization of the performance within an increasing dataset and the reduction of runtimes of patient registration in the Mainzelliste environment without negative impact on the accuracy of record linkage. The longest runtimes were identified and optimized so that only those data which are required during registration are loaded. To speed up record linkage, parts of the algorithm were optimized. The initial record linkage, with an extensive runtime also compared patients, which are completely different and are definitely not duplicates. Moreover, a pre-matcher was included which compares two patients based on their hashes before a detailed comparison based on every attribute is started.

All implemented optimizations have a positive impact on runtimes without decreasing the accuracy. The optimizations described in this paper have been integrated into the official repository of Mainzelliste and are available to the community.

Keywords: Biobank · Identity management · Pseudonymization · Performace optimization · Nilsimsa · Patient matching

© Springer Nature Switzerland AG 2020
A. Holzinger et al. (Eds.): AI & ML for Digital Pathology, LNAI 12090, pp. 228–245, 2020.
https://doi.org/10.1007/978-3-030-50402-1_14

1   Introduction

Identity management has a key role in the management of biological samples and related biomedical data. In each context, specific data becomes available, which will be collected and linked with patients across different contexts. The use of patient data from routine contexts in medical research is a change of the purpose and, respectively, a secondary use [1]. Thus, several ethical, legal and data security conditions have to be fulfilled. Most patient identifying information (PII) are not required in medical research [1], therefore the data can be hidden behind a pseudonym. In each context, the patient receives a different pseudonym, so that it is not possible by using a pseudonym from one context to refer to records in other contexts of a particular patient. The identity management enables first-layer pseudonyms where identifying patient data contains, for example the name, date of birth and gender of a patient. In certain contexts, it is required to use second-layer pseudonyms, therefore a pseudonymization service is required as a part of the identity management. This service converts a first-level pseudonym into a second-level pseudonym by cryptographical encoding. In the inverted case, a second-level pseudonym can be decoded into a first-level pseudonym.

An authorized user is allowed to request PII of a patient. For this purpose, the corresponding pseudonym is resolved within the identity management system and the associated hidden PII are returned. This makes it possible, for example, to notify a study participant about an incidental finding [1] or to contact a potentially suitable participant for a new study [1], and last but not least to merge the same patient originating from multiple studies or data sources.

In Germany, several identity management solutions have been developed. One of them is the Enterprise Patient Identifier Crossreferencing (E-PIX)[2] tool, which can generate first-level and second-level pseudonyms in connection with gPas [3]. Both have been released under the GNU Affero General Public License (AGPLv3) [4] and are available via GitHub. The Institute of Medical Biostatics, Epidemiology and Informatics (IMBEI) developed Mainzelliste, a first-level web-based pseudonymization service. Mainzelliste is also released under AGPLv3, therefore the source code is downloadable [5] and can be edited by the community. Mainzelliste and E-PIX contain a record linkage. This ensures that patients who are already registered do not receive several pseudonyms for the same context, when a patient is registered multiple times. Mainzelliste is a widespread patient list and first-level pseudonymization service in Germany. It is used in different systems and contexts [5,6], for example within the Deutsches Konsortium für Translationale Krebsforschung (DKTK) and in Open Source Registry System (OSSE) [7].

For the externalization of an existing identity management in the Central Biomaterial Bank Charité (ZeBanC), Mainzelliste was chosen due to its compatibility with the Biobank Information Management System. The main requirement for identity management is the robust and efficient storage of several million patients. Motivated by the missing information regarding a maximum or a tested number of patients to be managed, Mainzelliste was pre-evaluated previously.

The results implied that when storing collectives of several hundred thousand patients, the original Mainzelliste had an insufficient performance.

High performance is a central requirement of an ID management system. There are mainly two use cases in terms of patient registration. On the one hand new patients will be registered. On the other hand, data stocks of other systems or legacy data stocks have to be registered. The registration of one patient in a large dataset in Mainzelliste creates large runtimes. The registration of an entire stock of patients needs correspondingly much time.

The registration of a patient in Mainzelliste serves to store the identification data and to generate a pseudonym. The pseudonym can be resolved by Mainzelliste, so that the corresponding PII can be obtained. The user who registers a patient with a client must be authenticated and authorized prior to transferring PII. Mainzelliste cannot authenticate a user [8], thus it is possible and required to delegate this functionality to a different system [8]. In the following example, a user is authenticated by the medical data server (MDAT-Server) [8,9]. After that, the MDAT-Server calls Mainzelliste to generate a session that is represented by a session identifier. On this session, access tokens are generated, which authorize a user for a certain action, e.g. registration of a patient or resolution of a pseudonym. The client has to transfer the desired action to the MDAT-Server that subsequently requests Mainzelliste to generate an access token, based on the received action. The access token is represented by an identifier and will be transferred via the MDAT-Server to the client. Afterwards, the client can send a request directly to Mainzelliste. For the registration of a patient, the client has to transfer the access token and the PII of the patient to Mainzelliste. This executes the registration and returns one generated pseudonym for a particular

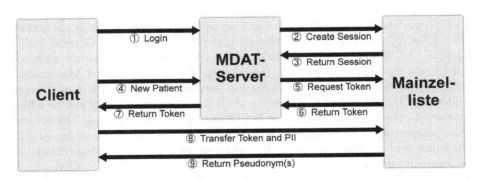

Fig. 1. Example of patient registration. The client logs on for authentication via the MDAT-Server (1). The MDAT-Server calls Mainzelliste to create and receive a session (2, 3). The client transfers the desired action, in this case a registration of a new patient (4). The MDAT-Sever requests a new access token (5, 6). The generated token is transferred to the client (7). The client requests Mainzelliste directly with the responded access token and the PII of the new patient (8). Mainzelliste performs the patient registration and returns the generated pseudonym back to the client (9). If the patient is already in the database, the existing pseudonym will be returned. The number of generated and returned pseudonyms is based on the specification in the configuration file 10.

patient. If several pseudonyms are defined, e.g. for various contexts, then these pseudonyms will also be returned. To resolve a pseudonym, the client transfers the access token and receives the PII of the patient. The entire process for a patient registration is illustrated in Fig. 1.

Mainzelliste uses a patient identifier (PID) of Faldum and Pommerening, which generate a string of eight characters [8, 11] as a pseudonym. Moreover, it is also possible to include a proprietary algorithm to generate pseudonyms.

2   Objectives

The main aim was to evaluate Mainzelliste regarding patient registrations into large data sets. For this purpose, the algorithms for record linkage, the database and the data transfer was analyzed. Here, the components that generate large runtimes were identified. Based on these identified components, several optimizations to increase the performance were implemented. The optimizations were tested stand-alone and combined with a large number of simulated patient data to reach the maximum performance. A requirement for the optimizations was that they should not influence the accuracy of record linkage in a negative manner. This paper presents optimizations for Mainzelliste which reduce the runtime for patient registration within large data sets.

3   Methods

To identify potential optimizations for the patient registration, the components of Mainzelliste have been analyzed and evaluated. For this purpose the patient registration was divided into several parts, as shown in Sect. 3.1. Thus, the components with the largest runtimes could be identified. Therefore, it was possible to optimize the components with the highest impact. The patient data that have been used were simulated with attributes similar to real first names, surnames etc. (see Sect. 3.2.).

3.1   Patient Registration

The process of patient registration was divided into several parts that for each of these the runtimes could be determined separately. Based on these measurements, it was possible to identify the sections with the biggest runtimes. The following subdivision was used:

– *Check Token*: Before the record linkage is called, the transmitted access token for the patient registration is checked for validity. If the token is valid, the process continues with the patient registration, otherwise the process is aborted and an error message is thrown.
– *Validation of Attributes*: If the token is valid, the transmitted PII were checked for validity. This is based on the regular expressions which are specified for certain attributes in the configuration file [10]. For example, numbers

in the first name are not allowed. Obligatory specified attributes may not contain empty values. If all attributes are valid, the process continues with the patient registration, otherwise the process is aborted and an error message is thrown.

- *Transformation of Attributes*: As a part of record linkage, the attributes are compared in normalized form. Here, for each attribute one or more transformations are configured. For example, all lower case letters are replaced with upper case letters, therefore a comparison is case-insensitive. The normalized attributes are stored in addition to the non-normalized attributes in the database, so they do not need to be recreated during the record linkage.
- *Retrieval of Patient Data*: The record linkage required all attributes of the registered patients for a comparison. Hence, all data for each patient are queried from the database. This data contains the normalized and non-normalized attributes of a patient.
- *Record Linkage*: The record linkage is implemented in the matcher component. The matcher compares the normalized, non-empty attributes of a patient to be registered to the already registered patients, depending on the used algorithm. Based on two thresholds in the configuration file [10], the similarity of two patient records that leads to identification as duplicate can be adjusted. For example, if two patients have a similarity equal to or higher than 95%, then it should be detected as a duplicate. If patient attributes show a similarity equal to or lower than 60%, then it should be detected as non-duplicate. Between these thresholds, the patients are detected as possible duplicates. Based on these thresholds, the matcher returns whether a duplicate is detected or not. If it is not sure, the matcher returns a possible duplicate. The method of record linkage used is "EpiLink" [12].
- *Evaluation of Matching*: If no duplicate is found, a new patient identifier (PID) is generated and the patient data are stored in the database. If a duplicate is detected, the existing PID is returned. If the system could not clearly determine whether a duplicate exists, the attributes have to be reviewed and resubmitted.
- *Response*: Depending on the result of the record linkage, a message is generated which contains the PID of the patient or an information that the attributes have to be checked manually.

3.2   Patient Data

The PII are transferred to Mainzelliste for a patient registration. These attributes are specified in the configuration file of Mainzelliste [10]. Here, in addition to the indication of the data type, also transformations and validators are specified, which define how incoming attributes are transformed and which values are valid for a comparison in the record linkage.

For the assessment of runtime, the attributes first name, surname, birth name, gender, birth date (separated into day, month and year), place of residence, postal code, street and house number were chosen. In real world environments, it may happen that certain attributes are not set, such as the birth name. However, to obtain comparable measurements, all attributes were set.

The patient datasets used are artificial. That means that the datasets do not represent real patients but are comparable based on their structure. The dataset is created by existing values, such as real first names, surnames, random birth dates and so on. The addresses are a combination of real street names, postal codes and places. However, the addresses do not really exist.

The process of patient registration will be aborted if an incorrect value of an attribute, e.g. a wrong birth date such as the 30th of February, is contained in a transferred patient data set. In this case, a patient will not be registered and no pseudonym is returned. For the runtime measurement and to receive comparable runtimes, it is important that the process is not aborted. Therefore, all attributes and access tokens which have been used were valid.

3.3 Runtime Measurements

The measurements of runtimes were conducted with several sizes of databases, so that the relationship between the runtime and the number of registered patients could be evaluated. Some program sections require more time with a larger database than others, as shown in Fig. 2 and Fig. 3. However, other sections need an almost constant runtime.

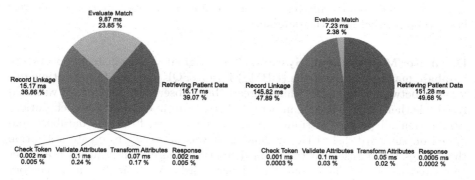

Fig. 2. Runtime measurement of a patient registration into a database with 1,000 patients. The runtime was mainly caused by the record linkage, retrieval of patient data and for the evaluation of the match.

Fig. 3. Runtime measurement of a patient registration into a database with 10,000 patients. The runtime was mainly caused by the record linkage and retrieval of patient data. All other parts of the program had an almost constant runtime.

3.4   Optimizations

As shown in Fig. 2 and Fig. 3, the record linkage, the retrieval of patient data and the evaluation of matches created the longest runtimes. The main potential for optimization was seen in these program sections, accordingly.

Several components with potential opportunities for optimization were analyzed. First, the persistence framework was examined. This has an influence on the data exchange between Mainzelliste and a database. Lazy Loading was implemented so that the transferred data could be reduced. Furthermore, the database was changed with an in-memory database. This increased the process of querying and storing patient records. For faster duplicate detection, parts of the record linkage algorithm have been optimized. A pre-matching was implemented since the record linkage needed most of the time to perform a registration. This method will be executed before the original algorithm of record linkage is applied. Thus, it is possible to exclude duplicates without performing the record linkage.

Persistence Framework. Prior to our optimization, a query to the database returned all patient data, such as normalized and non-normalized attributes. However, a comparison of two patients requires just the normalized attributes. Hence, all attributes, not required for record linkage, were forced to be lazy loaded. In this way, the values of the attributes were only loaded from the database when they were required. Therefore, those attributes that were not required in the record linkage, such as the non-normalized attributes, do not have to be queried from the database.

Database Management System. The original Mainzelliste supports the database management systems (DBMS) PostgreSQL and MySQL. Runtime differences between these DBMS have already been observed. Therefore, it was analyzed whether other DBMS can achieve better runtimes, since for each patient registration all patient attributes have been retrieved from the database and stored on the hard disk drive by default. It was necessary to create a solution that stores the datasets in the main memory because such requests are faster compared to access data from a hard drive disk. Accordingly, an in-memory database was used to store the data. This would introduce the disadvantage that in case of a system crash, all data would be lost. Therefore, a database which stored the data in main memory for requests and also persists on hard drive was the optimal solution. For this, the Hyper Structured Query Language Database (HSQLDB) was chosen. This database supports different modes, including the so-called In-Process (Stand-alone) Mode [13]. In this mode, the database is a part of Mainzelliste and both applications run in the same Java Virtual Machine. The main advantage of this solution is that requested datasets do not have to be converted and sent over the network. Moreover, the database in this mode is only accessible from Mainzelliste. However, Mainzelliste is the only application which generates requests in the database, accordingly this it is not scored as a disadvantage.

Mainzelliste was extended to support a HSQLDB, so it can easily used, without any adjustments.

Exchange Groups. Mainzelliste supports the definition of so-called exchange groups [10]. By default, the record linkage always compared the same attributes of two patients (for example, the place of residence). Attributes which are in an exchange group were compared in all possible permutations. The default configuration contains an exchange group with the attributes first name, surname and birth name. In this case, all duplicates were found, even when the attributes are swapped accidentially. This can happen, for example when a patient originates from a country where the surname is called before the first name.

In this case for example, not only are the first names of two datasets compared during the record linkage but the first name is also compared to the surname and the birth name. The permutation with the highest similarity will be used for the calculation of overall similarity.

Without exchange groups, three comparisons would be performed by using the example first name, surname and birth name. With exchange groups, eighteen comparisons will be performed, generating significantly longer runtimes. Nevertheless, exchange groups are an important component of the record linkage, thus they should be contained in Mainzelliste. Some comparisons are unnecessary, because attributes are double compared, although the similarity could be known if the same comparison was already executed. Double comparison happens because the permutations are considered independently. An approach for optimization was to assign the attributes with the highest similarity to reduce attribute comparisons. Tests of this optimization showed that the accuracy was in one particular case lower than the original implementation. Meanwhile, the developer of Mainzelliste implemented the Hungarian method for exchange group comparison. Thus, the assignment is correct and there are no unnecessary comparisons. The runtimes shown later are based on this implementation.

Nilsimsa-Hash. The record linkage required all normalized attributes of the patient to register and of all patients already registered. Loading the data and the comparison of attributes create large runtimes. This also happened if two patients have completely different values in attributes. Therefore, we were looking for an optimization that only compares two patients if they had at least one certain similarity. This reduced the number of comparisons of attributes in the record linkage significantly. All other patients will be considered to be non-duplicates.

For this purpose, every patient receives a generated hash, based on their attributes, which is stored in the database. All or only part of the attributes may be used as input data for the hash. The hash function has to fulfill certain properties. If the input data are similar, then the hashes have to be similar too. Hash functions like MD5 [14] or SHA-1 [15] are not suitable, because a change of one character in the input data results in completely different hashes. With the locality-sensitive hashing, it is possible to generate hashes which can be compared for similarity [16]. We applied the Nilsimsa method. Here, the result of a comparison of two hashes is a score between −127 and 128. If the score is 128, the hashes and the input data are the same. The lower the score, the more different were the hashes as well as the input data. With this method, a pre-matching was implemented. Before record linkage, the hashes of two patients are compared. If the resulting score is above a specified threshold, then the attributes of the patients have a certain similarity, the record linkage starts and compares all attributes. Otherwise, the patient will be considered as non-duplicate and record linkage is skipped.

The pre-matching is required for a comparison of the hashes only. Therefore, all other class attributes were annotated with the lazy loading property. So if two patients were identified as non-duplicate, the attributes of the patient already registered did not had to be requested from the database. The input data to be included and the threshold to be applied can be specified in the configuration file. In addition, the concatenation of attributes with constant strings can be also specified. This allows for formatting the input data before the hash is created.

Combinations of Optimizations. The shown improvements work independently of each other, therefore these can be combined. The lazy loading is always implemented, because it has no negative impact to the record linkage. The use of a HSQLDB, the optimized version of exchange groups and the pre-matching by the Nilsimsa hash may be used independently or combined. It is possible to enable or disable the optimization of exchange groups or pre-matching by using a configuration property, even if it was already enabled by the new revision of Mainzelliste.

Test Cases. An artificial patient data set was generated and used for testing the introduced optimizations (shown in Sect. 3.2). For the following tests, various errors were included into the dataset. For example, some characters in the first name, surname or birth name were swapped, changed or deleted. Moreover, these attributes were entirely swapped or the birth name was deleted. In the birth date, digits were swapped or changed. However, all values of the faulted datasets were valid in terms of their format, due to the pre-validation of attributes in advance of the record linkage. The attributes which are not used in the optimizations were free of errors since there would have been no impact on the optimized record linkage. For example, the first name, surname and birth name were changed for the exchange groups, other attributes such as the address were not used for generating hashes or in exchange groups.

Before the determination of whether an erroneous dataset generated a duplicate, a faultless dataset was registered. After that, the erroneous dataset was registered. If a duplicate was recognized, the same PID of the faultless dataset was returned. Otherwise a new PID was returned, so the duplicate was not recognized. Thus, it could be identified which kinds of errors generated duplicates for a certain optimization.

The tests were only performed for the optimization of the exchange groups and pre-matching with Nilsimsa hashing. The other optimizations such as the lazy loading or the changed DBMS have no impact on the accuracy of record linkage.

4   Results

The optimizations were performed on various hardware systems. The runtimes were dependent of the hardware used. Consequently, lower runtimes were achieved with more powerful processors. The number of possible patient registrations depends on the available memory, because this is the place where the patient data are stored, at least for the purpose of record linkage. With a HSQLDB, the patient data were stored in any case for entire runtime in memory. The larger the available memory, the more patients could be registered in Mainzelliste.

The runtimes shown here are based on measurements with 100,000 patients which were registered into Mainzelliste. Here, all datasets were free of errors, so 100,000 patients were stored in the database after this test.

Moreover, datasets with errors were generated to determine the impact on the accuracy of the record linkage. Here, 2,000 non-duplicate patient datasets were generated and registered in Mainzelliste. For testing purposes each dataset was registered an additional six times. Five of these contained errors. This resulted in a number of 12,000 registrations where 10,000 of these registrations were based on faulty datasets and should be recognized as duplicates.

The following results were determined on a system with two quad-core processors with 4.0 GHz and 16 GB of RAM.

In order to compare the runtimes with different combinations of optimizations (Table 1) for a patient registration, a pre-filled database with 100,000 patients was used. The runtimes presented in Figs. 4, 5, 6, 7 are the average of 100 registrations.

Table 1. Comparison of measured runtimes in milliseconds of a patient registration into a database with 100,000 patients with different optimization combinations. Only the program parts of receiving patient data, record linkage and evaluating match will be compared. The lowest runtimes were reached with the combination of all optimizations.

No.	Optimizations	Receiving patent data	Record linkage	Evaluate match
1	HSQLDB and Lazy Loading	109.59	1275.39	2.18
2	HSQLDB, Lazy Loading and Exchange Groups	111.61	810.01	3.08
3	HSQLDB, Lazy Loading and Hashing	104.43	174.06	2.71
4	HSQLDB, Lazy Loading, Exchange Groups and Hashing	101.13	106.71	2.42

4.1   Lazy Loading/DBMS Change

The lazy loading and the change of the DBMS has no impact on the accuracy of record linkage. However, with these optimizations reductions in runtimes could be archived. The runtimes of a record linkage with lazy loading and HSQLDB are shown in Fig. 4.

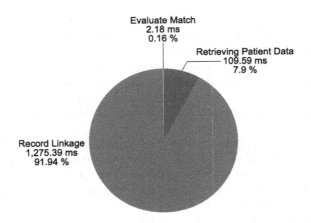

Fig. 4. Runtime measurement of a patient registration with lazy loading and a HSQLDB into a database with 100,000 patients.

The registration of 100,000 patients required 19 h and 18 min. A registration of one patient into a database with 100,000 datasets is shown in Fig. 4.

4.2   Exchange Groups

In the following representation of the optimization for exchange groups the test also contains the lazy loading and using of a HSQLDB. The runtimes of a registration are shown in Fig. 4.

Runtimes. The runtimes of a registration with optimized exchange groups are shown in Fig. 5. The registration of 100,000 patients required 12 h and 51 min.

Record Linkage. As shown in Table 2, the inclusion of the optimized exchange groups and simulated patient data generated slightly fewer duplicates, compared to the original version of Mainzelliste.

The duplicates in both variants were created only by changed, deleted and swapped characters in attributes. In particular, attributes with short length, such as a first name with three letters, are vulnerable. Deleted attributes, such as non-transferred birth name and swapped attributes do not create any duplicates.

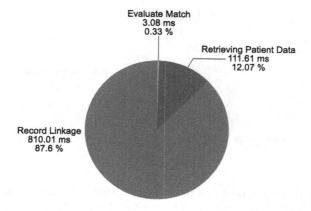

Fig. 5. Runtime measurement of a patient registration with lazy loading, a HSQLDB and optimized exchange groups into a database with 100,000 patients.

Table 2. Comparison of the number of created, possible and detected duplicates between the original Mainzelliste and optimized exchange groups.

Result	Optimized	Original
Duplicates created	649	651
Possible duplicates detected	1630	1630
Duplicates detected	9721	9719

4.3 Nilsimsa-Hash

The following tests of the optimization using a pre-matching with the Nilsimsa hashing also contains the lazy loading and the use of HSQLDB.

The creation of hashes was performed with various input data. On the one hand, the first name, surname and birth name were used, on the other hand the birth date was used. In the first variant, swapped attributes (for example first name and surname) resulted to very different hashes, which could not be used for the recognition of duplicates. The pre-matching is performed before the record linkage is executed, so that these errors could not be corrected with the exchange groups. Therefore, the following measurements with hashes are based on the birth date as input data. The threshold was determined by previous tests. This threshold is the highest one that generated the lowest possible runtime without duplicates.

Runtimes. Runtimes of registrations using Nilsimsa hashes are shown in Fig. 6. The registration of 100,000 patients required 3 h and 58 min.

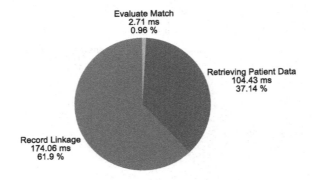

Fig. 6. Runtime measurement of a patient registration with lazy loading, a HSQLDB and use of Nilsimsa hashes into a database with 100,000 patients.

Record Linkage. To find an optimal threshold, the datasets were registered with different thresholds. The number of datasets which have to be compared by record linkage depends on a chosen threshold. A high threshold requires very similar input data to compare datasets by the record linkage. If a threshold is too high, errors such as swapped characters are not recognized. Therefore, a lower threshold is recommended, to find all duplicates. However, the more frequently a comparison is made by the record linkage, the higher the runtimes will be. For a possible low runtime, with possible low number of duplicates, the threshold should be set as high as possible, but as low as necessary.

As shown in Fig. 7, no duplicates have been generated at a threshold of 80, but the runtime was already reduced significantly. A lower threshold would result in a larger runtime, a higher threshold would produce more duplicates.

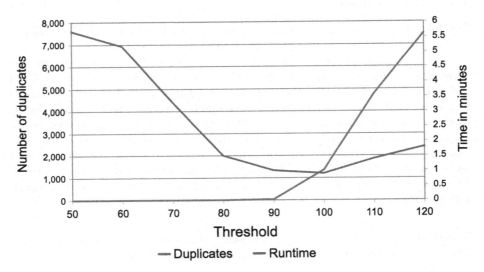

Fig. 7. Registration of 12,000 Patients with different thresholds. Based on the threshold used, the runtime and the number of created duplicates changed.

Duplicates must be stored in the database and have to be considered for any subsequent comparisons. Consequently, an increasing number of duplicates produces higher runtimes.

Restrictions of Attributes. To obtain optimal results with the help of pre-matching, certain restrictions on the input data must be observed. All attributes which serve as input data should meet the following requirements:

- *Constancy*: The attribute is never changed or only in exceptional cases. If an attribute is changed, the corresponding hash value of a patient needs to be updated. If a pre-matching is based on obsolete hashes, the probability is higher that existing duplicates will not be detected. The hash of a patient is automatically updated when the attributes are modified.
- *Obligatory*: The attribute is always given and is not simply optional. It always contains a non-empty value and is therefore a valid part of the hash.
- *Safe from exchange*: It is not suspected that an attribute is exchanged with another one, or that it can be prevented during validation. For example, it cannot be ensured that the first name and surname of a patient are not exchanged and thus should be included into hashing accordingly.

In addition, the input data should contain multiple attributes, so that a comparison is not depended on just one attribute.

Optimal attributes, for example, are the birth date consisting of day, month, year and the gender, or the place of birth, if it is obligatory to specify.

4.4   Combination of Optimizations

The combination of lazy loading, HSQLDB, optimized exchange groups and the use of Nilsimsa hashing was able to achieve the largest reduction of runtimes.

Runtimes. The runtime of registrations with a combination of all improvements is shown in Fig. 8. The registration of 100,000 patients required 2 h and 53 min.

Record Linkage. The combination of optimized exchange groups and Nilsimsa hash values reached the same accuracy as the only optimized exchange groups. With an optimal threshold, no duplicates were generated by using Nilsimsa hash values. The resulting accuracy in this case was dependent on the exchange groups.

4.5   Comparison of the Optimizations

In the following, all introduced optimizations are compared. The reduction of runtimes is illustrated by the registration of 10,000 patients. Therefore, Mainzelliste in the original version with a PostgreSQL database was compared to the combinations of optimizations discussed above.

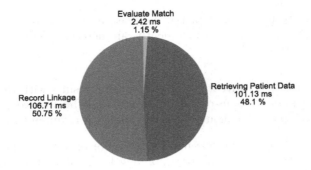

Fig. 8. Runtime measurement of a patient registration with lazy loading, a HSQLDB, optimized exchange groups and use of Nilsimsa hashes into a database with 100,000 patients.

As shown in Fig. 9, the combination of optimizations was significantly faster than the original version of Mainzelliste. The corresponding runtimes are illustrated in Table 3.

As shown in Table 3, the application of lazy loading and a HSQLDB led to a significant reduction of runtimes, without making any changes to the record linkage. A vastly better result could be reached with an optimization of the record linkage and the application of pre-matching with hashes. With all optimizations, the registration of 10,000 datasets requires only approximately 14.29% of the time, compared to the original version of Mainzelliste.

Table 3. Resulting runtimes of the original version of Mainzelliste and the different combinations of optimizations in a registration of 10,000 patient datasets.

No.	Optimizations	t in min
1	PostgreSQL (original Mainzelliste)	17:09
2	Lazy Loading, HSQLDB	11:56
3	Lazy Loading, HSQLDB, optimized exchange groups	08:11
4	Lazy Loading, HSQLDB, Hashing	2:56
5	Lazy Loading, HSQLDB, optimized exchange groups, Hashing	2:27

5   Discussion

The use of hashes require the use of an appropriate threshold. The lower this threshold, the higher the accuracy of the pre-matching will be. The threshold can be set to achieve a result that is equivalent to the original implementation of Mainzelliste. In this case, there is no reduction of runtimes. Moreover, it is also possible to deactivate the pre-matching in the configuration file completely.

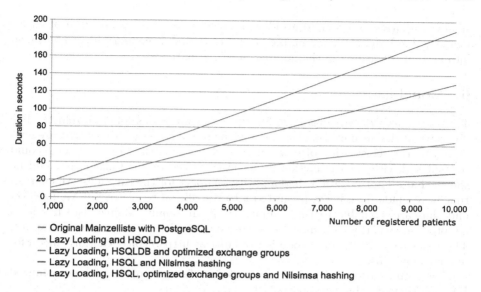

Fig. 9. Comparison of runtimes between the original Mainzelliste and various variants of the combination of optimizations. For every measurement, 10,000 patients with error-free data were registered.

To select the mentioned optimizations, corresponding components were implemented for record linkage. Each of them contains different combinations of the improvements introduced in this paper. The currently used method for record linkage in Mainzelliste was extended so that one variant contains the optimized exchange groups, another variant contains pre-matching with hashes and the last one contains both of these optimizations. Additionally, all variants are available in a version that is optimized for multi-core processors.

In the original Mainzelliste, one of the parts with the longest runtimes was requesting data from the database to fetch all patient data. A version of Mainzelliste was generated in which the record linkage is fully integrated into the database. Thus, the patient data do not have to be loaded into the application for every registration. However, the runtimes recorded for this case were higher than those of the original Mainzelliste. Another disadvantage of this solution is that it has to be implemented for every DBMS in a separate manner. This approach would reduce the compatibility of the existing record linkage and future extensions, and therefore it was discarded.

The patient data are stored permanently in the main memory using an in-memory database. If the data is to be stored on a hard drive disk, it needs to be loaded into the main memory again for every registration. It was observed that having a large number of datasets within a database resulted in a crash of Mainzelliste. This was because the data was too large for the available main memory and an appropriate exception handling was missing. In the future, an optimization is desired that will split the requests of all patient datasets into smaller packages, in order to avoid such crashes. With an application of an in-memory database, the maximum capacity of the main memory has to be taken into account regarding of the number of stored patients.

6   Conclusion

This paper introduced several performance optimizations for Mainzelliste. The objective of the optimization was mainly the reduction of runtimes that are generated by the registration of new patients in large existing datasets. This could be achieved without a reduction in accuracy of the record linkage. It could be shown that all optimizations had a positive impact for the runtimes. All changes that were made have been integrated into the official repository of Mainzelliste and thus are available to the community. Additionally, Mainzelliste has been adapted, so that these optimizations can be used with already existing systems. The repository with source code is available at https://bitbucket.org/medinfo_mainz/mainzelliste.

The optimized version provides a much more feasible solution for a centralized ID management solution, especially for large datasets.

Acknowledgments. We like to thank Mr. Andreas Borg for his input regarding certain implementation details. We also thank Dr. Martin Lablans for supporting this optimization.

References

1. Pommerening, K., Helbing, K., Ganslandt, T., Drepper, J.: Lecture Notes in Informatics. Bonn: Gesellschaft für Informatik; c2012. Chapter, Identitätsmanagement für Patienten in medizinischen Forschungsverbünden, p. 1520–1529
2. Bialke, M., et al.: MOSAIC - a modular approach to data management in epidemiological studies. Methods Inf. Med. **54**(4), 364–371 (2015). https://doi.org/10.3414/ME14-01-0133
3. Bialke, M., et al.: A workflow-driven approach to integrate generic software modules in a Trusted Third Party. J. Transl. Med. **13**(176), 1 (2015). https://doi.org/10.1186/s12967-015-0545-6
4. Gnu.org: GNU AFFERO GENERAL PUBLIC LICENSE; 2007. FREE SOFTWARE FOUNDATION, Inc. http://www.gnu.org/licenses/agpl-3.0.en.html. Accessed Nov 2019
5. Lablans, M., Borg, A.: Mainzelliste. https://bitbucket.org/medicalinformatics/mainzelliste. Accessed Nov 2019
6. IT-Reviewing-Board der TMF Technologie- und Methodenplattform für die vernetzte medizinische Forschung e. V.: IT-Infrastruktur in der patientenorientierten Forschung. Akademische Verlagsgesellschaft AKA GmbH (2014)
7. Unimedizin-Mainz.de: OSSE - Open Source Registry System for Rare Diseases in the EU; 2015. Johannes Gutenberg-Universität Mainz. https://www.unimedizin-mainz.de/imbei/informatik/ag-verbundforschung/osse.html. Accessed Nov 2019
8. Lablans, M., Borg, A., Ückert, F.: A RESTful interface to pseudonymization services in modern web applications. BMC Med. Inform. Decis. Mak. **15**, 2 (2015). https://doi.org/10.1186/s12911-014-0123-5

9. Lablans, M., Borg, A.: Schnittstelle der Mainzelliste. (2018). http:// www.unimedizin-mainz.de/typo3temp/secure_downloads/22397/0/ 2c87458bd4452fc79424886e199f11ed1f917bf6/Mainzelliste_Schnittstelle.pdf. Accessed Nov 2019

10. Lablans, M., Borg, A.: Mainzelliste - Konfigurationshandbuch. (2018). http:// www.unimedizin-mainz.de/typo3temp/secure_downloads/22397/0/2c87458bd445 2fc79424886e199f11ed1f917bf6/Mainzelliste_Konfigurationshandbuch.pdf. Accessed Nov 2019

11. Pommerening, K., Faldum, A.: Ein Algorithmus zur Erzeugung von pseudonymen Identifikatoren. Institut für Medizinische Statistik und Dokumentation der Johannes-Gutenberg-Universität Mainz. (2001). http://www.staff.uni-mainz.de/ pommeren/PID/Algorithmus.pdf. Accessed Nov 2019

12. Contiero, P., Tittarelli, A., Tagliabue, G., Maghini, A., Fabiano, S., Crosignani, P., et al.: The EpiLink record linkage software presentation and results of linkage test on cancer registry files. Methods Inf. Med. **44**(1), 66–71 (2005)

13. Toussi, F.: Chapter 1. Running and Using Hsqldb - Hsqldb Server; 2002– 2019. http://hsqldb.org/doc/guide/running-chapt.html#rgc_inprocess. Accessed Nov 2019

14. Turner, S., Chen, L.: Updated Security Considerations for the MD5 Message-Digest and the HMAC-MD5 Algorithms. (2011). RFC Editor http://www.rfc-editor.org/ rfc/rfc6151.txt. Accessed Nov 2019

15. Eastlake, D., Hansen, T.: US Secure Hash Algorithms (SHA and SHA-based HMAC and HKDF). (2011). RFC Editor. http://www.rfc-editor.org/rfc/rfc6234. txt. Accessed Nov 2019

16. Stein, B., Potthash, M.: Hashing-basierte Indizierung: Anwendungsszenarien, Theorie und Methoden. In: Proceedings 14th Workshop on Adaptivity and User Modeling in Interactive Systems (ABIS 2006), pp. 159–166. Hildesheim (2006)

Digital Image Analysis in Pathology Using DNA Stain: Contributions in Cancer Diagnostics and Development of Prognostic and Theranostic Biomarkers

Soufiane El Hallani[1]([⊠]), Calum MacAulay[2], and Martial Guillaud[2]

[1] Department of Laboratory Medicine and Pathology, University of Alberta, Edmonton, AB, Canada
elhallan@ualberta.ca
[2] British Columbia Cancer Research Centre, Integrative Oncology – Cancer Imaging Unit, Vancouver, BC, Canada

Abstract. Traditionally, histopathological evaluations of tissue sections are performed for the diagnosis and grading of cancers using subjective appraisal of the tissue and cell phenotypes. In the last decade, a combination of unprecedented advances in imaging and computing technologies and novel machine learning-based algorithms has driven the field of histopathology into a new dimension. Machine learning and deep learning methodologies applied on digitalized hematoxylin and eosin stained tissue sections have out-performed conventional methods to accurately identify cancer cells or classify tumors into prognostic groups. Nevertheless, we believe that a precise, standardized measurement of nuclear morphology and chromatin texture based on a DNA stain can further improve the diagnosis of cancers and identify patients with high-risk of recurrence, alone or in combination with other clinical, pathological or molecular information. Changes in the morphology of cell nuclei and tissue architecture are intrinsic characteristics and hallmarks of cancer. Nuclei from cancerous samples exhibit different morphological and chromatin texture than nuclei from normal cells, thus, reflecting the structural and molecular effects of genetic and epigenetic alterations driving cancer processes. By image analysis, the chromatin texture can be measured in high-resolution breaking down the components of the nuclear changes into multiple quantifiable units that can be studied independently and in combination using advanced machine learning methods. This allows the investigator to examine associations of such changes with cancer progression and clinical outcomes. There is now increasing interest in developing new algorithms and platforms to decipher spatial relationship between cell subpopulations in whole tissue sections.

Keywords: Digital pathology · Image analysis · Feulgen · Cancer screening · Cancer diagnosis · Prognostic biomarker · Predictive biomarker · Cell sociology

1 Introduction and Motivation

Traditionally, the histopathological diagnosis and grading of cancers are based on the appraisal of the changes in the morphology of the cells and tissue organization which

© Springer Nature Switzerland AG 2020
A. Holzinger et al. (Eds.): AI & ML for Digital Pathology, LNAI 12090, pp. 246–263, 2020.
https://doi.org/10.1007/978-3-030-50402-1_15

are the intrinsic hallmarks of cancers. Nuclei from cancerous samples exhibit different shapes and chromatin textures than nuclei from normal samples reflecting the structural and molecular effects of genetic and epigenetic alterations driving cancer processes [1–3]. For instance, increased proportion of heterochromatin condensation is a nuclear characteristic for high-risk cancer [4]. In the last two decades, advances in pathology slide scanning technologies and image processing algorithms have enabled the breakdown of the subjective and qualitative nuclear and architectural changes used by the pathologists into objective quantifiable units that can be studied independently and/or in combination using advanced statistical and machine learning methods [5]. In 2011, Beck et al. [6] developed an algorithm to quantify epithelial and stromal changes in H&E slides of more than 500 breast cancer patients and demonstrated that a scoring system based on these measurements was strongly associated with overall survival and was independent of clinical, pathological and molecular factors. After the first FDA approval of a slide scanner device for primary clinical diagnosis [7], the adoption of digital pathology has gained an exponential popularity in the community of pathologists and is expected to unlock a large number of research and development opportunities including digital applications for diagnosis, prognosis and prediction of treatment response in cancer diseases [8, 9]. While most of the digital pathology algorithms have been developed using the traditional H&E or Papanicolaou slides and artificial neural networks to assist pathologists in many tasks, alternative staining techniques and image analysis processing should not be disregarded, in particular if they can capture the changes in nuclear and chromatin features with improved performances [10], strong consistency [11] and have a proven track of diagnostic, prognostic and predictive clinical applications in a variety of cancer types [12–15]. In fact, the diversity of information (e.g. clinical, imaging and molecular data), high quality of data and integration of multiple machine learning approaches should be further encouraged for the success of artificial intelligence in oncology and other fields of medicine in general [16–18]. In this chapter, the authors review the use of Feulgen as the best stoichiometric stain for accurate quantification of DNA and better representation of the nuclear chromatin texture. Examples of successful applications of computer-assisted image analysis and machine learning in both cytology and histopathology specimens using Feulgen staining will be discussed regarding their accuracy and clinical utility.

2 Glossary

DNA Ploidy: DNA ploidy is a cytogenetic term describing the number of chromosome sets (n) or deviations from the normal number of chromosomes in a cell. In cytometry, the expression is used either to describe the DNA content in a cell or the total DNA distribution in a cell population.

Digital Image Analysis: Image analysis is the extraction of meaningful information from images using a computer device or electrical device combined to digital image processing techniques. It involves the fields of computer or machine vision, and medical imaging, and makes heavy use of pattern recognition, digital geometry, and signal processing.

Test Performance: Diagnostic test performance evaluates the ability of a qualitative or quantitative test to discriminate between two subclasses of subjects.

Test Accuracy: Diagnostic test accuracy measures the ability of a test to detect a condition when it is present and detect the absence of a condition when it is absent.

Screening: Screening is defined as the presumptive identification of unrecognized disease in an apparently healthy, asymptomatic population by means of tests, examinations or other procedures that can be applied rapidly and easily to the target population.

Diagnostic Biomarker: A diagnostic biomarker is used to confirm that a patient has a particular health disorder. Diagnostic biomarkers may facilitate earlier detection of a disorder than can be achieved by physical examination of a patient.

Prognostic Biomarker: A prognostic biomarker is a clinical or biological characteristic that provides information on the likely patient health outcome (e.g. disease recurrence) irrespective of the treatment.

Predictive Biomarker: A predictive biomarker indicates the likely benefit to the patient from the treatment compared to their condition at baseline.

3 State of the Art

3.1 Feulgen Stain and DNA-Based Image Analysis

The Feulgen technique is generally accepted as a stoichiometric DNA stain that is used to quantify the amount of DNA in cell nuclei in a reproducible and standardized manner [19]. Feulgen reaction allows the precise densitometric measurement of nuclear DNA because the amount of the dye bound per nucleus is proportional to its DNA content. Briefly, the DNA is submitted to mild acid hydrolysis to split off the purine bases from the double-stranded DNA. The result is an apurinic acid presenting aldehyde groups at the C1-position. A Schiff's base binds to these aldehyde groups and produces a blue-violet color with 545 nm maximum absorption wavelength [20]. The DNA image analysis is performed using a digital camera that captures images of Feulgen-stained individual nuclei in the specimen. The images are divided into image elements (picture elements - pixels). The gray tone value for each pixel represents the intensity of DNA specific staining. The value is saved in the computer which numerates between 0 (black) and 1023 (white). In-house image analysis software is used to measure the relative amount of DNA in each nucleus (DNA ploidy) by summing the optical density of all the pixels in the nucleus (Fig. 1).

In addition, due to the optimal object-to-background contrast of Feulgen stain, the software can measure the morphometric features including the size, shapes and border smoothness of nuclei. Changes in the nuclear chromatin appearance are common in dysplastic and cancer cell. Features describing the chromatin distribution pattern are referred to as chromatin texture features. Using Feulgen stain, they can be assessed by mathematical formulas that describe the distribution of gray levels in groups of pixels [21].

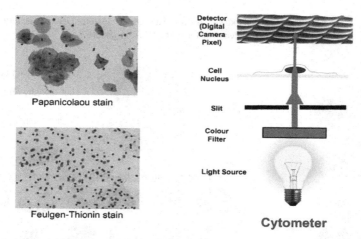

Fig. 1. Feulgen stain and ploidy measurement by image analysis.

For instance, Markovian texture features characterize gray-level correlation between adjacent pixels in the image. Non-Markovian texture features describe the local maxima and minima of gray-level differences in the object. Fractal texture features compare local differences integrated over the object at multiple resolutions. Run-length texture features measure the length of consecutive pixels with the same compressed gray-level value along different orientations (0°, 45°, 90°, 135°). Several studies investigated the suitability of Papanicolaou and hematoxylin staining, which are routinely used for daily cytopathology and histopathology, for DNA-based image analysis or ploidy measurement. Unfortunately, the coefficient of variation (CV) is broader in Papanicolaou and hematoxylin stains resulting in significant disproportionality and less reproducibility of the optical density and ploidy values [22, 23]. These studies confirmed that Feulgen remains the gold standard stain for the precise densitometric measurement of DNA content in nuclei [10] (Fig. 2).

The tissue sections are analyzed using in-house developed image analysis software (Getafics; BCCA, Vancouver, Canada). This software was specifically designed for semi-automatic analysis of DNA content, nuclear morphology, chromatin texture and tissue architecture. Briefly, after the Feulgen-stained tissue sections ae digitalized by a whole slide scanning system, the operator selects the region of interest by delineating the boundaries. A threshold algorithm is applied to the image, followed by a segmentation algorithm to separate touching and overlapping nuclei. Autofocusing and edge relocation algorithms are applied to the nuclei to locate the edge of the objects precisely and automatically segment the contour of the highest local gray-level gradient. The digital gray-level images of individual segmented nuclei are stored in a gallery and analyzed the nuclear or architecture features are extracted using computer calculations. The calculated values of these features are used as datasets that will be tested by multiple machine learning and classifier algorithms (Figs. 3 and 4).

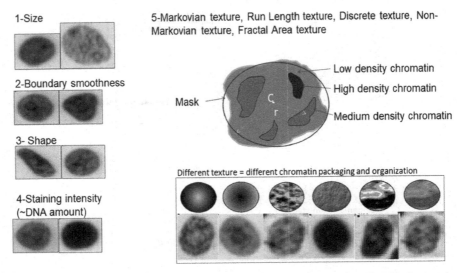

1-Size

2-Boundary smoothness

3- Shape

4-Staining intensity
(~DNA amount)

5-Markovian texture, Run Length texture, Discrete texture, Non-Markovian texture, Fractal Area texture

Mask

Low density chromatin

High density chromatin

Medium density chromatin

Different texture = different chromatin packaging and organization

Fig. 2. Measurement of morphometric and chromatin texture features based on Feulgen stain.

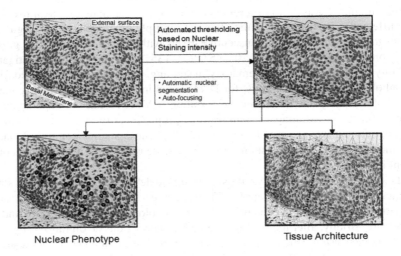

External surface

Automated thresholding based on Nuclear Staining intensity

Basal Membrane

• Automatic nuclear segmentation
• Auto-focusing

Nuclear Phenotype

Tissue Architecture

Fig. 3. In-house software for quantitative image analysis.

3.2   Cancer Screening

Population-based cervical cancer screening programs have been effective in reducing the incidence and mortality of cervical cancers [24]. Pap tests (liquid-based cytology or conventional smears) are widely adopted in developed countries as the gold standard screening method where cells are collected from the cervix to generate Papanicolaou-stained cytology slides for examination under the microscope [25]. However, there are many countries in the world where large scale screening programs have not yet been

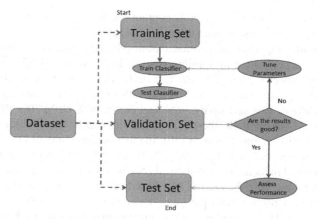

Fig. 4. Machine learning model using quantifiable features generated by image analysis software.

implemented due to several challenges including the shortage of cytopathologists and lack of skilled cytotechnologists who need to review high volumes of Papanicolaou-stained cytology slides. In addition, many cervical screening programs in resource-limited countries have a high false negative rate [26, 27]. Over the last decades, several automated imaging technologies were developed and clinically implemented to assist the cytotechnologists in reviewing the Pap slides review (i.e. BD FocalPoint Imaging System, ThinPrep Imaging System). Overall, the performance of the automated system has been well accepted and the list of benefits includes improved sensitivity in detection of squamous intraepithelial lesions and increased productivity compared to manual review of conventional Pap smears [28]. However, the adoption of the FDA-approved systems comes with increased costs (equipment and maintenance) and they may not be suitable for low-volume cytology laboratories. The British Columbia Cancer Agency group has developed a series of inexpensive fully automated systems combining point-of-care slide scanners with image analysis software that measures the ploidy of the cells to detect aneuploid cancerous cells based. Briefly, barcoded Feulgen-stained slides are placed in a slide loader and the operator initiates scanning on a supervisor computer. Although such machines can scan smears, liquid base cytology (LBC) slides are generally preferred to generate monolayers of cells simplifying the task of automated imaging. Autofocusing, image capture, segmentation of the nuclei, morphometric and ploidy measurements are all performed automatically without operator intervention. Reporting is done at the conclusion of an interactive review of the scan data for each slide which are comprised of stored images of the cell nuclei, counts of various cell types, and histograms and scatter plots of cell DNA index (calculated by the normalization of a cell DNA content to a population of normal diploid cells) and other morphometric features of the cell nuclei (i.e. nuclear size, smoothness of nuclear boundaries, etc.). The reviewer follows a very simple checklist procedure to systematically examine the data, looking: (a) first to check that the DNA scale (normalization) is valid, then; (b) checking the presence of aneuploid cell nuclei (DI > 2.5), then; (c) looking for aneuploid "stemlines", then; (d) assessing cell proliferation rate (proliferative cells contains between 2 to 4 copies of DNA); and (e) if none of these are present, then the case is negative.

Head-to-head comparison of automated ploidy-based cytometry versus conventional Pap cytology was performed in multiple studies. In a cohort of 1,555 patients seen in MD Anderson Cancer Center [29], the test performance of DNA-based ploidy (59% sensitivity, 93% specificity, 92% NPV, 63% PPV) was found equivalent to the local cytology laboratory (47% sensitivity, 96% specificity, 90% NPV, 70% PPV). In China, the studies found substantially increased sensitivity (up to the double). For instance, in a cohort of 9,950 screened women [30], the test performance of DNA-based ploidy was 54% sensitivity, 97% specificity, 92% NPV and 58% PPV while conventional Pap cytology performed in local hospital showed 25% sensitivity, 99% specificity, 85% NPV and 54% PPV. Since 2005, the use of DNA-based cytometers in China has continuously expanded to over 1 million tests per year. There are over 70 publications comparing the performance of DNA-based ploidy to conventional Pap smears; however, most of the studies published studies are observational and suffer from missing data or lack of follow-up cervical biopsies as the gold standard method to confirm the presence of high-grade dysplasia or malignancy when one or two tests are positive [31–33]. Overall, three conclusions can be drawn from these ground studies. First, the ploidy-based cytometry is a simple and reproducible technique. Second, it can be taught much more quickly than cytology. Records in China have demonstrated that it is routinely possible to teach the technology from slide preparation and staining, to operation of the cytometer, review of the DNA ploidy data and report generation in 10 working days. Third, the test performance of ploidy-based cytometry is comparable to conventional or liquid-based cytology performed by experienced and highly trained cytologists. The diffusion of the automated quantitative image cytometry is expected to expand as the various vendors continue to receive regulatory approvals [34, 35] and endorsement by medical societies and expert groups (Fig. 5).

3.3 Early Cancer Diagnostics

Although the importance of early diagnosis in improving the mortality and morbidity of cancer has long been recognized, the disease is still frequently diagnosed late and prognosis has not dramatically changed for the last decades. A major challenge for early diagnosis of epithelial cancers is our ability to recognize precursors or premalignant lesions at risk of progressing into invasive carcinomas. The progression appears to occur through a low-grade dysplasia (low risk of progression) to high-grade dysplasia (high risk of progression) to carcinoma sequence. One of the most significant challenges confronting the diagnosis of premalignant lesions is the poor agreement among pathologists in the histopathological diagnosis and grading of dysplasia. In Barrett's esophagus for instance, significant intra- and interobserver variability in the interpretation of biopsy specimens has been well documented, even between expert pathologists, especially at the lower end of the dysplasia spectrum (i.e. benign reactive cytologic atypia versus low-grade dysplasia) [36, 37]. In the context of digital pathology, there is an interest in developing tissue imaging biomarkers both to predict which patients may develop carcinoma (and therefore be offered surgical therapy with curative intent) and to aid guiding surveillance intervals following therapy. Using different image analysis and statistical

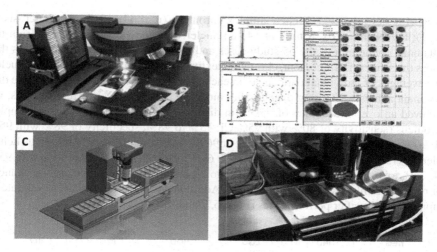

Fig. 5. Portable slide scanner for cervical cancer screening. (A) Microscope with slide loader and automated slide scanning, (B) Data review station, (C) and (D) Second generation slide scanner.

methods, the potential of image analysis to measure the grade of dysplastic lesions has been demonstrated in different tissues types, such as skin, ovary or prostate [38–40]. For instance, our group has previously shown that measuring the chromatin texture features alone can detect serial nuclear changes in the sequential progression of Barret's esophagus from normal epithelium to dysplastic epithelium to invasive carcinoma, and objectively distinguish reactive epithelial changes (indefinite for dysplasia) from low-grade dysplasia [12]. In addition, our results suggest that quantitative measurement of chromatin texture features has a better correlation with the class of dysplasia (low- versus high-grade). As opposed to morphologic features measuring changes in nuclear sizes and shapes, chromatin texture features are less sensitive to sectioning variation and could have a superior contribution in the differential diagnosis of Barrett's esophagus classification. We previously observed similar findings in multiple human epithelium sites, including the oral cavity [41], lung [42], cervix [43] and breast [44]. We believe that measurement of nuclear chromatin texture is significant because such changes are an indication of genetic or epigenetic changes that lead toward malignant transformation.

Another known problem in early cancer diagnosis is the difficulty to diagnose the well differentiated intraepithelial neoplasia based on traditional morphology. For instance, differentiated vulvar intraepithelial neoplasia (DVIN) possesses a high oncogenic potential but the high degree of differentiation often results in DVINs being mistakenly diagnosed as benign lesions (i.e. lichen simplex chronicus, lichen sclerosus). The p53 immunohistochemistry marker can be used to support the DVIN diagnosis; however, the characteristic suprabasal p53 overexpression can be encountered in any benign condition in which there is increased epithelial proliferation. The lack of p53 specificity encourages the development of alternative aid tools for DVIN diagnosis. We recently investigated the role of chromatin-based image analysis in distinguishing DVIN versus benign mimickers. Sixty-five vulva biopsy specimens with three major diagnosis categories were selected: Lichen simplex chronicus (n = 34); (2) Lichen sclerosis (n = 21); DVIN (n = 20). A total of 44,483 nuclei were individually captured from the squamous epithelium of the 65 study cases and analyzed for over 100 parameters that assess the shapes, DNA content, chromatin texture and overall architecture of the nuclei. The averages of individual parameters in each specimen are included in a stepwise discriminant analysis. Limiting the classifier model to only 2 nuclear texture features, we achieved an overall accuracy of 95.5% in distinguishing DVIN versus lichen simplex chronicus (sensitivity of 80% with 95% CI: 45% to 98%; specificity of 98% with 95% CI: 90% to 99.9%), and overall accuracy of 96.8% in distinguishing DVIN versus lichen sclerosus (sensitivity of 100% with 95% CI: 69% to 100%; specificity of 95% with 95% CI: 76% to 100%). Limiting the classifier to 2-parameters would increase the chances for reproducibility in independent cohorts. Additional test sets are needed to validate or improve the classifier performances (Figs. 6, 7 and 8).

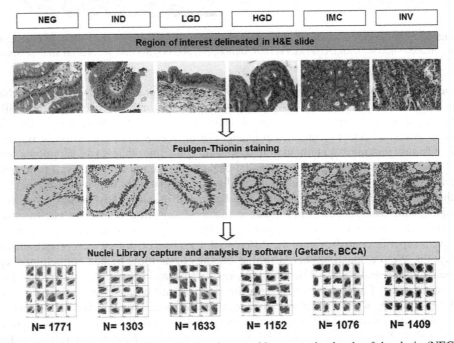

Fig. 6. Histological groups of Barrett's Esophagus with progressive levels of dysplasia (NEG: negative; IND: indefinite for dysplasia/reactive changes; LGD: low-grade dysplasia; HGD: high-grade dysplasia; IMC: intramucosal carcinoma; INV: invasive carcinoma).

3.4 Cancer Prognostics

Breast cancer is the leading cause of cancer-related deaths among women worldwide. Adjuvant systemic therapy, including hormonal and chemotherapy, has reduced mortality from breast cancer. As chemotherapy is toxic and has a negative impact on quality of

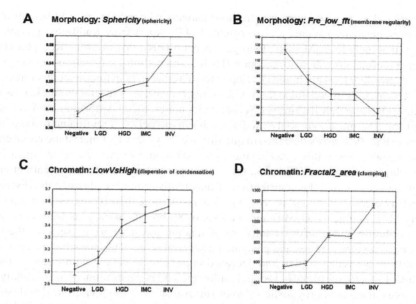

Fig. 7. Correlation of nuclear features with dysplasia progression in Barrett's Esophagus (A and B: examples of morphometric features; C and D: examples of chromatin texture features).

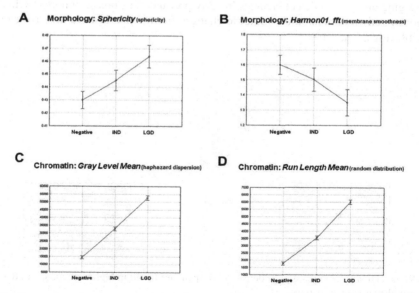

Fig. 8. Comparison between morphometric and chromatin texture features in distinguishing reactive changes (IND: indefinite for dysplasia) and low-grade dysplasia (LGD).

life, it should ideally be given only to those patients who gain significant benefit from it. At present, many patients are over-treated [45]. Apart from traditional prognostic markers that include TNM stage, Estrogen receptor (ER), Progesterone Receptor (PR), human epidermal growth factor receptor (HER2) and pathological features (grade), new genomic profiling tests are being developed to aid refinement in treatment recommendations. Recent recommendations from ASCO support the use of several biomarker assays, including OncotypeDX Recurrence Score (RS), EndoPredict, PAM50 and Breast Cancer Index [46]. The most commonly used assay is OncotypeDX, a multigene reverse transcriptase (RT)-PCR assay designed to quantify the 10-year risk of metastatic recurrence. The major obstacles of this assay are the high cost (about $4,000 per test) and the necessity to ship specimens to California for centralized testing which delays patient care. Our group investigated the contribution of quantitative image analysis in the discrimination between survivors and deceased patients with more than 10 years follow-up after surgery [14]. Feulgen-stained tissue sections of 80 breast carcinomas were processed by our in-house image analysis software. A random forest algorithm selected the best five nuclear texture features and generated a survival score. This classifier model could discriminate between survivor and deceased breast cancer patient with a sensitivity of 88% and a specificity of 85%. Using a multivariate Cox proportional hazards analysis, we assessed the added prognostic value of survival score with other clinical and pathological factors, such as age, lymph node status, tumor size and grade. The survival score was significantly associated with 10-year survival, independent of any tumor grade (1, 2 or 3) or other clinical factors (p = 0.005). In earlier studies, our group pioneered the use of imaging analysis to detect changes in early precancerous breast tumors (DCIS) and demonstrated continuous morphometric changes from hyperplasia to invasive cancers [47, 48] (Figs. 9 and 10).

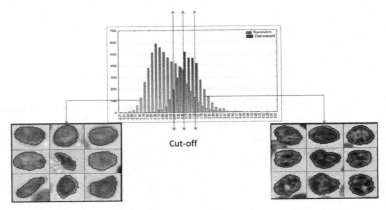

Fig. 9. Nuclei with clumps of high-density chromatin are found in higher frequency in tissue of deceased Breast cancer patients.

Low-risk patients   High-risk patients

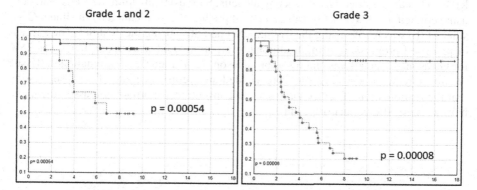

Fig. 10. Overall survival of low-grade (1 and 2) and high-grade (3) Breast cancers based on image analysis-based scoring system.

3.5 Cancer Theranostics

Prostate cancer is the most commonly diagnosed form of cancer in men worldwide. PSA screening has led to a steep increase in incidence of indolent PSA-detected cases, which ultimately do not contribute significantly to the overall mortality rates. Although some prostate cancers behave aggressively and will result in death, most of PSA detected cancers are non-aggressive, slow growing, and do not require immediate intervention. Active surveillance is a preferred approach for PSA detected early prostate cancer. Significantly, 5–10% of individuals with low-risk disease treated up-front with prostate brachytherapy or radical prostatectomy will experience poor outcomes. Additionally, >50% of active surveillance patients will progress, and will require treatment 5 years after initial diagnosis [49]. The effectiveness of active surveillance is limited without a tool to accurately provide prognostic information. Current treatment recommendations are based on PSA levels (iPSA), clinical staging, and Gleason score. Molecular assays are being proposed to predict the risk of clinical metastasis within 5 years of radical prostatectomy surgery; however, these molecular assays have financial and logistical limitations similar to those described in breast. We investigated whether image analysis of nuclear features and tissue architecture can distinguish patients with biochemical failure from biochemical non-evidence of disease (BNED) after radical prostatectomy (RP) for prostate cancer [15]. Of the 78 prostate cancer tissue cores collected from patients treated with RP, 16 who developed biochemical relapse (failure group) and 16 who were BNED patients (non-failure group) were included in the analyses (36 cores from 32 patients). A section from this TMA was stained stoichiometrically for DNA using the Feulgen methodology and stained slides were scanned. Prostate TMA core classification as biochemical failure or BNED after RP was conducted (a) based on cell type and cell position within the epithelium (all cells, all epithelial cells, epithelial >2 cell layers away from basement membrane) from all cores, and (b) based on epithelial cells more than two cell layers from the basement membrane using a Classifier trained on Gleason 6, 8, 9 (16 cores) only and applied to a Test set consisting of the Gleason 7 cores (20 cores). Successful core classification as biochemical failure or BNED after RP by a linear classifier was 75% using all cells, 83% using all epithelial cells, and 86% using epithelial >2 layers. Overall success of predicted classification by the linear Classifier of (b) was 87.5% using the Training Set and 80% using the Test Set. The success of predicted progression using traditional morphologic Gleason score alone was 75% for Gleason >7 as failures and 69% for Gleason >6 as failures. Combination of Tissue Architecture score and Gleason score yielded an overall accuracy of 89% suggesting that the combination of image analysis and conventional morphologic assessment can have a synergistic impact (Fig. 11).

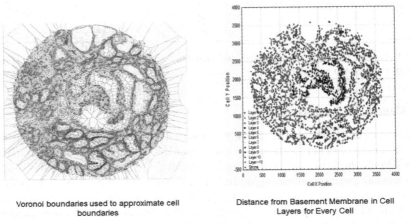

Voronoi boundaries used to approximate cell boundaries

Distance from Basement Membrane in Cell Layers for Every Cell

Fig. 11. Tissue Architecture analysis in Prostate cancers and assessment of nuclear features by epithelial layers.

4 Open Problems

So far, most of the image analysis algorithms applied to digital pathology are focused on the characterization of the tissue phenotype; however, cell proliferation, immune evasion, hypoxia and tumor heterogeneity are also important hallmarks of cancer. A better understanding of their individual role and of their mutual interactions is needed to unlock all the valuable information in the glass slide. Advances in optical imaging and immunohistochemistry technologies will allow us to decipher with unprecedented details, precision, and depth the individual expression and intensity of multiple markers as well as the spatial interaction of cell subpopulations ("cell sociology") in large histological images.

5 Future Outlook

The British Columbia Cancer Agency group developed several hyperspectral microscopy systems to rapidly collect 7–16 wavelength specific images (from 400 to 780 nm) across entire slides. These hyperspectral images can be used to spectrally un-mix the components within a slide that have unique features [50]. As an example, using the absorption spectra of each immunohistochemistry antibody, the stains are computationally unmixed to determine the concentration of each stain for every pixel in the selected area. Our program basically makes the assumption that every pixel in the recorded images (16 wavelengths) are a linear combination of the concentration of the individual stains occurring at that pixel weighted by the absorption characteristics of each of the stains occurring at that pixel. The method we used to separate these linear combinations of absorption stains with different concentration at each pixel was the Multivariate Curve Resolution – Alternating Least Squares algorithm. Different immunohistochemistry stains are available to assess each component of the tumor microenvironment. High expression of Ki-67 protein is known to be associated with aggressive cancers. Ki-67 is a robust marker due to the reproductive and strong signal of his antibody (Mib1). The tumor microenvironment is a complex mixture of tumor epithelium, stroma and immune cells, and the immune component of the tumor microenvironment is highly prognostic for tumour progression and patient outcome. The role of the immune evasion pathways (PD-1/PD-L1-CD8) and T lymphocytes (CD3-CD8) can be studied by immunohistochemistry markers which are currently being used to guide immunotherapy. Cell sociology approach may be critical to examine immune cell function, as anti-tumor immune activation depends on a complex network of interactions between antigen presenting cells, T cells, and target cells. Importantly, quantification via cell sociology has the potential to provide greater prognostic or predictive insight than cell density readings have historically provided. Recently, we showed that the characterization of the spatial tumor-immune cell interactions is associated with lung cancer recurrence [50]. The presence of poorly oxygenated (hypoxic) cells is associated with poor outcome after radiation, chemotherapy, and surgery in a wide range of solid tumors. Hypoxia can be measured by quantifying endogenous expression of hypoxia-induced proteins by immunohistochemistry (e.g., carbonic anhydrase-9; CA9 or glucose transporter-1; Glut-1).

Overall, we believe the application of hyperspectral imaging combined with cell sociology studies will significantly increase our understanding of cancer biological behavior and facilitate the development of robust imaging biomarkers to improve risk stratification and complement clinical prognostic factors. Moreover, hyperspectral imaging platform can also improve the ability of some nuclear morphometric and chromatin texture features to differentiate between cell groups. We discovered that diffraction effects in microscopy images can be readily separated from Feulgen stained material (sharp absorption max at 600 nm). Removal of these diffraction effects simplifies all downstream image analysis including segmentation and differentiation of overlapping cells (Fig. 12).

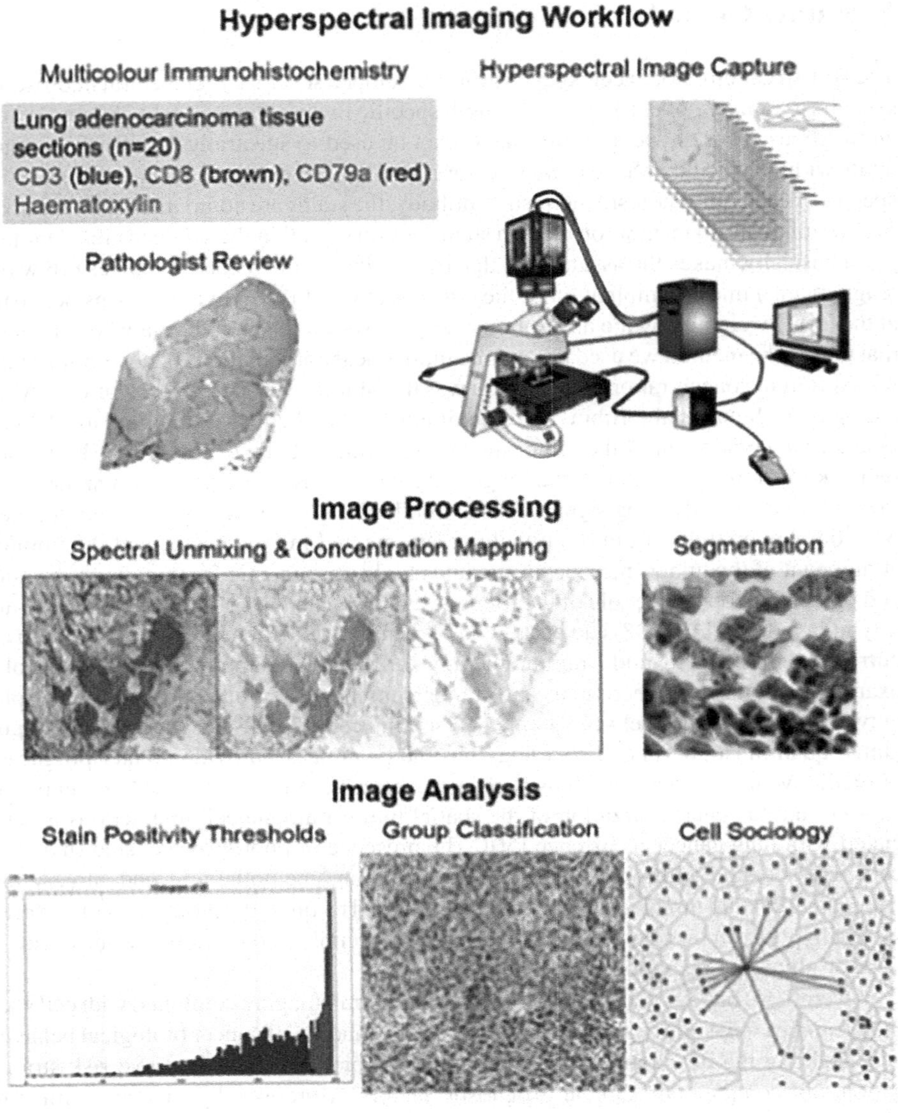

Fig. 12. Hyperspectral cell sociology platform (courtesy of Dr. Martial Guillaud).

References

1. Zink, D., Fischer, A.H., Nickerson, J.A.: Nuclear structure in cancer cells. Nat. Rev. Cancer **4**(9), 677–687 (2004)
2. Singh, H., Sekinger, E.A., Gross, D.S.: Chromatin and cancer: causes and consequences. J. Cell. Biochem. **79**(Suppl. 35), 61–68 (2000)

3. Almassalha, L.M., Tiwari, A., Ruhoff, P.T., et al.: The global relationship between chromatin physical topology, fractal structure, and gene expression. Sci. Rep. **7**, 41061 (2017)
4. Hveem, T.S., Njolstad, T.S., Nielsen, B., et al.: Changes in chromatin structure in curettage specimens identifies high-risk patients in endometrial cancer. Cancer Epidemiol. Biomarkers Prev. **26**(1), 61–67 (2017)
5. O'Connor, J.P., Aboagye, E.O., Adams, J.E., et al.: Imaging biomarker roadmap for cancer studies. Nat. Rev. Clin. Oncol. **14**(3), 169–186 (2016)
6. Beck, A.H., Sangoi, A.R., Leung, S., et al.: Systematic analysis of breast cancer morphology uncovers stromal features associated with survival. Sci. Transl. Med. **3**(108), 108ra113 (2011)
7. Mukhopadhyay, S., Feldman, M.D., Abels, E., et al.: Whole slide imaging versus microscopy for primary diagnosis in surgical pathology: a multicenter blinded randomized noninferiority study of 1992 cases (pivotal study). Am. J. Surg. Pathol. **42**(1), 39–52 (2018)
8. Tizhoosh, H.R., Pantanowitz, L.: Artificial intelligence and digital pathology: challenges and opportunities. J. Pathol. Inform. **9**, 38 (2018)
9. Bychkov, D., Linder, N., Turkki, R., et al.: Deep learning based tissue analysis predicts outcome in colorectal cancer. Sci. Rep. **8**(1), 3395 (2018)
10. Biesterfeld, S., Beckers, S., Del Carmen Villa Cadenas, M., et al.: Feulgen staining remains the gold standard for precise DNA image cytometry. Anticancer Res. **31**(1), 53–58 (2011)
11. Ghizoni, J.S., Sperandio, M., Lock, C., et al.: Image cytometry DNA ploidy analysis: correlation between two semi-automated methods. Oral Dis. **24**(7), 1204–1208 (2018)
12. Guillaud, M., Zhang, L., Poh, C., et al.: Potential use of quantitative tissue phenotype to predict malignant risk for oral premalignant lesions. Cancer Res. **68**(9), 3099–3107 (2008). PMID: 18451134
13. El Hallani, S., Guillaud, M., Korbelik, J., et al.: Evaluation of quantitative digital pathology in the assessment of barrett esophagus-associated dysplasia. Am. J. Clin. Pathol. **144**(1), 151–164 (2015)
14. Guillaud, M., Ye, Q., Leung, S., Carraro, A., et al.: Large-scale DNA organization is a prognostic marker of breast cancer survival. Med. Oncol. **35**(1), 9 (2017)
15. MacAulay, C., Keyes, M., Hayes, M., et al.: Quantification of large scale DNA organization for predicting prostate cancer recurrence. Cytometry A **91**(12), 1164–1174 (2017)
16. Holzinger, A., Haibe-Kains, B., Jurisica, I.: Why imaging data alone is not enough: AI-based integration of imaging, omics, and clinical data. Eur. J. Nucl. Med. Mol. Imaging **46**(13), 2722–2730 (2019)
17. Jean-Quartier, C., Jeanquartier, F., Jurisica, I., Holzinger, A.: In silico cancer research towards 3R. BMC Cancer **18**(1), 408 (2018)
18. O'Sullivan, S., Holzinger, A., Zatloukal, K., et al.: Machine learning enhanced virtual autopsy. Autops Case Rep. **7**(4), 3–7 (2017)
19. Chatelain, R., Willms, A., Biesterfeld, S., et al.: Automated Feulgen staining with a temperature controlled machine. Anal. Quant. Cytol. Histol. **11**, 211–217 (1989)
20. Haroske, G., Baak, J.P., Danielsen, H., et al.: Fourth updated ESACP consensus report on diagnostic DNA image cytometry. Anal. Cell. Pathol. **23**(2), 89–95 (2001)
21. Doudkine, A., Macaulay, C., Poulin, N., et al.: Nuclear texture measurements in image cytometry. Pathologica **87**(3), 286–299 (1995)
22. Bahr, G.F., Bartels, P.H., Bibbo, M., et al.: Evaluation of the Papanicolaou stain for computer-assisted cellular pattern recognition. Acta Cytol. **17**, 106–112 (1973)
23. Schulte, E.K.W., Fink, D.K.: Hematoxylin staining in quantitative DNA cytometry: an image analysis study. Anal. Cell. Pathol. **9**, 257–268 (1995)
24. Liu, S., Semenciw, R., Probert, A., et al.: Cervical cancer in Canada: changing patterns in incidence and mortality. Int. J. Gynecol. Cancer **11**, 24–31 (2001)
25. Guidozzi, F.: Screening for cervical cancer. Obstet. Gynecol. Surv. **51**, 247–252 (1996)

26. McCord, M.L., Stovall, T.G., Meric, J.L., et al.: Cervical cytology: a randomized comparison of four sampling methods. Am. J. Obstet. Cynecol. **166**, 1772–1779 (1992)

27. Stenkvist, B., Soderstrom, J.: Reasons for cervical cancer despite extensive screening. J. Med. Screen. **3**, 204–207 (1996)

28. Wilbur, D.C., Cibas, E.S., Merritt, S., et al.: ThinPrep processor: clinic trials demonstrate an increased detection rate of abnormal cervical cytologic specimens. Am. J. Clin. Pathol. **101**, 209–214 (1994)

29. Guillaud, M., Benedet, J.L., Cantor, S.B., et al.: DNA ploidy compared with human papilloma virus testing (Hybrid Capture II) and conventional cervical cytology as a primary screening test for cervical high-grade lesions and cancer in 1555 patients with biopsy confirmation. Cancer **107**(2), 309–318 (2006)

30. Sun, X.R., Wang, J., Garner, D., et al.: Detection of cervical cancer and high grade neoplastic lesions by a combination of liquid-based sampling preparation and DNA measurements using automated image cytometry. Cell Oncol. **27**(1), 33–41 (2005)

31. Xu, S., Mei, J.H., Han, Y.L., et al.: Quantitative analysis of cervical cell DNA and liquid-based cytology in cervical screening of early lesions comparison. Guangdong Yixue **34**, 1387–1390 (2013)

32. Tian, Y.W., Liu, G., Zhou, J., et al.: Application of DNA image cytometry in the cervical intraepithelial neoplasia and cervical cancer screening. Zhenduan Binglixue Zazhi **20**, 425–428 (2013)

33. Wei, L.F., Lin, H.M., Qin, Y.A.F.: Clinical research of cervical cell DNA quantitative analysis in opportunistic screening of cervical diseases among women in cities of Zhuang national minority regions. Huaxia Yixue **25**, 181–184 (2012)

34. Motic Regulatory. http://www.med.motic.com/Page.aspx?PageCategoryId=7&PageConte ntId=4&LangCode=zhcn

35. Landing Med Regulatory. http://landingmed.com/cn/

36. Reid, B.J., Haggitt, R.C., Rubin, C.E., et al.: Observer variation in the diagnosis of dysplasia in Barrett's esophagus. Hum. Pathol. **19**, 166–178 (1988)

37. Montgomery, E., Bronner, M.P., Goldblum, J.R., et al.: Reproducibility of the diagnosis of dysplasia in Barrett esophagus: a reaffirmation. Hum. Pathol. **32**, 368–378 (2001)

38. Glazer, E.S., Bartels, P.H., Prasad, A.R., et al.: Nuclear morphometry identifies a distinct aggressive cellular phenotype in cutaneous squamous cell carcinoma. Cancer Prev. Res. (Phila) **4**, 1770–1777 (2011)

39. Nielsen, B., Albregtsen, F., Kildal, W., et al.: The prognostic value of adaptive nuclear texture features from patient gray level entropy matrices in early stage ovarian cancer. Anal. Cell. Pathol. (Amst) **35**, 305–314 (2012)

40. Veltri, R.W., Khan, M.A., Miller, M.C., et al.: Ability to predict metastasis based on pathology findings and alterations in nuclear structure of normal-appearing and cancer peripheral zone epithelium in the prostate. Clin. Cancer Res. **10**, 3465–3473 (2004)

41. Guillaud, M., Zhang, L., Poh, C., et al.: Potential use of quantitative tissue phenotype to predict malignant risk for oral premalignant lesions. Cancer Res. **68**, 3099–3107 (2008)

42. Guillaud, M., le Riche, J.C., Dawe, C., et al.: Nuclear morphometry as a biomarker for bronchial intraepithelial neoplasia: correlation with genetic damage and cancer development. Cytometry A **63**, 34–40 (2005)

43. Swartz, R., West, L., Boiko, I., et al.: Use of nuclear morphometry characteristics to distinguish between normal and abnormal cervical glandular histologies. Anal. Cell. Pathol. **25**, 193–200 (2003)

44. Poulin, N., Frost, A., Carraro, A., et al.: Risk biomarker assessment for breast cancer progression: replication precision of nuclear morphometry. Anal. Cell. Pathol. **25**, 129–138 (2003)

45. Paik, S., Tang, G., Shak, S., et al.: Gene expression and benefit of chemotherapy in women with node-negative, estrogen receptor-positive breast cancer. J. Clin. Oncol. **24**(23), 3726–3734 (2006)
46. Harris, L.N., Ismaila, N., McShane, L.M., et al.: Use of biomarkers to guide decisions on adjuvant systemic therapy for women with early-stage invasive breast cancer: american society of clinical oncology clinical practice guideline. J. Clin. Oncol. **34**(10), 1134–1150 (2016)
47. Poulin, N., Susnik, B., Guillaud, M., et al.: Histometric texture analysis of DNA in thin sections from breast biopsies. Application to the detection of malignancy-associated changes in carcinoma in situ. Anal. Quant. Cytol. Histol. **17**(5), 291–299 (1995)
48. Susnik, B., Worth, A., Palcic, B., et al.: Differences in quantitative nuclear features between ductal carcinoma in situ (DCIS) with and without accompanying invasive carcinoma in the surrounding breast. Anal. Cell. Pathol. **8**(1), 39–52 (1995)
49. Grimm, P., Billiet, I., Bostwick, D., et al.: Comparative analysis of prostate-specific antigen free survival outcomes for patients with low, intermediate and high risk prostate cancer treatment by radical therapy. Results from the Prostate Cancer Results Study Group. BJU Int. **109**, 22–29 (2012)
50. Enfield, K.S.S., Martin, S.D., Marshall, E.A., et al.: Hyperspectral cell sociology reveals spatial tumor immune cell interactions associated with lung cancer recurrence. J. Immunother. Cancer **7**(1), 13 (2019)

Assessment and Comparison of Colour Fidelity of Whole Slide Imaging Scanners

Norman Zerbe[1(✉)], Alexander Alekseychuk[2], and Peter Hufnagl[1,3]

[1] Charité - Universitätsmedizin Berlin, Corporate Member of Freie Universität Berlin, Humboldt-Universität zu Berlin, and Berlin Institute of Health, Institute of Pathology, Berlin, Germany
norman.zerbe@charite.de
[2] Vision in X industrial imaging GmbH, Berlin, Germany
[3] Center for Biomedical Image and Information Processing (CBMI), HTW University of Applied Sciences Berlin, Berlin, Germany

Abstract. The aim of this work is to develop a colourimetrically justified method for determination of colour fidelity of WSI scanners. We measure the absolute accuracy of colour reproduction and assess the scanner's ability to resolve similar colours, which seems to be even more important for diagnostic and research tasks. Along this, some theoretical background is given which helps in understanding of common sources of failures in colour reproduction. The work was done in the framework of 2-nd and 3-rd International Scanner Contest. We hope this publication will be useful for scanner manufactures as well as for academical and clinical users.

Keywords: Whole slide imaging · Quality assurance · Color calibration · Digital pathology · Colour target

1 Introduction

A few researchers have concerned themselves with colour reproduction of WSI scanners [1,2]. They noticed the obvious differences in colour reproduction by WSI scanners and tried to calibrate them in order to improve their colour accuracy. Whether the calibration was really necessary, successful and sufficient was evaluated by colour difference measurements and by visual analysis, while the later method had been given greater value. Besides visual analysis is highly subjective by its nature and, thus, has to be done by the large number of (unbiased and healthy) persons to be representative, the procedures used have some conceptual flaws from our point of view. Namely, the spectral properties of the light sources were not considered and samples illuminated by incandescent bulbs were compared with images displayed on a computer monitor or the samples was even held and viewed against a computer monitor. In case if any measurements were done, they were done without chromatic adaptation of white point, which voids any relation of these numbers to the visual impression from the specimen.

A. Holzinger et al. (Eds.): AI & ML for Digital Pathology, LNAI 12090, pp. 264–278, 2020.
https://doi.org/10.1007/978-3-030-50402-1_16

In this work we address for the first time the colourimetrically justified and objective evaluation of colour fidelity of WSI scanners. This is done having in mind the particular application and meaning of colour in histological imagery. Thus, two criteria are proposed which allow to assess quality of a scanner with respect to colour fidelity.

This investigation was done in the framework of 2-nd and 3-rd International Scanner Contest [3]. Other researchers [4,5] applied and the resulting methods subsequently and also started to develop their own targets.

Before proceeding with description of our method, we would like to shed some light on caveats of colour reproduction and provide some background information on human perception of colour.

2   Basics of Colour Vision

There is no colour in nature. Electromagnetic radiation is emitted by light sources on different wavelengths or their mixtures, called spectra. These electromagnetic waves can be uniformly or selectively reflected by or transmitted through objects we see. Colour perception is a property of human visual system which is not able to discriminate individual wavelengths. Instead, humans feature a so-called trichromatic visual system. A human eye has tree types of colour sensitive receptors, called cones. Receptors of yet another, fourth, type are called rodes, but play no role in colour vision. Cones of each type are characterised by their spectral sensitivity, i.e. they are sensitive to different wavelengths at different extends. Their approximated spectral sensitivities are given on Fig. 1 [6]. Conventionally, the cones more sensitive to shorter waves are called S-type, to middle waves M-type and to long waves of visible part of light spectrum L-type. Neural outcome produced by a cone is a function of convolution between the spectral power distribution of light and the spectral sensitivity of the cone over the visible wavelengths range (about 380 to 780 nm). Neural outcomes of three cone types undergo further complex processing in visual cortex of human brain which then results in our *subjective perception of colour*.

One important consequence from this is that infinitely many different light spectra can cause subjective perception of the same colour. The phenomena is known under the name *metamerism*. It happens because the same integral value (cone response) can be produced by as little as a few spectral lines at different wavelengths, by a continuous spectrum and all cases in between these two extrema. The sensing instrument which aims to reproduce colour in the meaning as it is perceived by humans and is supposed to work for all variety of spectral compositions, must therefore be able either to acquire the complete visible spectra with sufficiently high spectral selectivity (then it is called multispectral imaging) or to resemble the spectral sensitivity of human cones as close as possible and properly encode their responses[1]. Clear enough the later way is technically more efficient and is the way most widely used in practical (cost-optimised) systems.

---

[1] Sensors sensitive to *reversible* linear combination of cone spectral sensitivities, i.e. with channels as weighted sums of cone spectral responses, will work too.

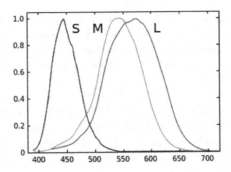

Fig. 1. Simplified spectral sensitivity of human cone cells of S, M and L types. Each curve is scaled on response axis to 0–1 range, i.e. relation of sensitivities between cones is not preserved.

3   Encoding of Colour

Cones of human visual system do not directly produce RGB values as we habit to think about colour. RGB triplet is just an encoding which allows to *reproduce* colour sensation, similar to the sensation caused by a given spectrum, by means of additive mixture of three colours, in this case approximately red, green and blue. Metamerism of human vision is utilised here. This three basic colours are called *primaries*. Primaries can have some complex spectra, but can be even monochromatic. Depending on the selection of primaries infinitely many encodings (colour spaces) are possible, albeit with varying degree of accuracy.

Along with physically implementable colour spaces, e.g. RGB, a bunch of abstract, so-called device independent, colour spaces exist, e.g. CIE XYZ or CIE L*a*b*. These abstract colour spaces are used due to historical reasons or because of a more efficient encoding and convenient representation. CIE XYZ, for example, is traditionally used as a reference and an intermediate space for colour space transformations. The conversion from XYZ to LMS is given in the CIE CAM02 model [7] by linear transformation

$$\begin{vmatrix} L \\ M \\ S \end{vmatrix} = \begin{vmatrix} 0.7328 & 0.4296 & -0.1624 \\ -0.7036 & 1.6975 & 0.0061 \\ 0.0030 & 0.0136 & 0.9834 \end{vmatrix} \begin{vmatrix} X \\ Y \\ Z \end{vmatrix} \tag{1}$$

and the corresponding reverse transformation by

$$\begin{vmatrix} L \\ M \\ S \end{vmatrix} = \begin{vmatrix} 1.0961 & -0.2789 & 0.1827 \\ 0.4544 & 0.4735 & 0.0721 \\ -0.0096 & -0.0057 & 1.0153 \end{vmatrix} \begin{vmatrix} X \\ Y \\ Z \end{vmatrix} \tag{2}$$

A representation in the widely used sRGB colour space can be derived from XYZ by

$$\begin{vmatrix} R_{lin} \\ G_{lin} \\ B_{lin} \end{vmatrix} = \begin{vmatrix} 3.2406 & -1.5372 & -0.4986 \\ -0.9689 & 1.8758 & 0.0415 \\ 0.0557 & -0.2040 & 1.0570 \end{vmatrix} \begin{vmatrix} X \\ Y \\ Z \end{vmatrix}$$

$$C_{srgb} = \begin{cases} 12.92\ C_{lin}, & C_{lin} \leq 0.0031308 \\ 1.055\ C_{lin}^{1/2.4} - 0.055, & C_{lin} > 0.0031308 \end{cases} \tag{3}$$

and converted back to XYZ by

$$C_{lin} = \begin{cases} C_{srgb}/12.92, & C_{srgb} \leq 0.04045 \\ ((C_{srgb} + 0.055)/1.055)^{2.4}, & C_{srgb} > 0.04045 \end{cases}$$

$$\begin{vmatrix} X \\ Y \\ Z \end{vmatrix} = \begin{vmatrix} 0.4124 & 0.3576 & 0.1805 \\ 0.2126 & 0.7152 & 0.0722 \\ 0.0193 & 0.1192 & 0.9505 \end{vmatrix} \begin{vmatrix} R_{lin} \\ G_{lin} \\ B_{lin} \end{vmatrix}, \tag{4}$$

where C has to be substituted each time with R, G and B, and all values have to be normalised to the [0,1] range prior usage in the formulae. The non-linear part of this transformation is called *gamma correction* and is to address the lightness-dependent ability of human vision to discriminate slightly different colours and, thus, to reduce the effective quantisation error of integer representation of RGB values [8]. The mean gamma of sRGB representation is 2.2.

The sRGB is one of the most popular colour space, and the *de facto* standard for consumer (i.e. less colour-critical) systems. The formulae above for sRGB conversion depend implicitly on the definition of sRGB primitives, i.e. precisely which shades of red, green and blue are used for the encoding. Conversion to/from an other RGB space will require knowledge of its primaries. The primaries, along with gamma, are stored in the colour profile of the imaging system. If no colour profile is specified, the usual practice is to assume sRGB.

In contrast to XYZ or RGB, the components of CIE L*a*b* are no longer a linear combination of cone responses LMS and separate the lightness (this is for what L* is in the word L*a*b*) and chromaticity (encoded by two other components a* and b*). In L*a*b* encoding the perceptual uniformity is aspired and even more care is taken to optimally utilize the available number of quantisation levels of digital signal by quantising with variable step according to variable ability of humans to discriminate subtle colour differences for different hues and different light intensities (lightnesses). The extensive description of L*a*b* colour space among with conversion formulae is given in [7] or the EN ISO 11664-4 standard.

4   The Importance of Illumination

Colour rendition of a reflective or transmissive sample depends severely on spectral properties of light source used for illumination. The spectrum reflected by or transmitted through the sample is product of the incident spectrum and the reflection or absorption spectrum of the sample. The reference illuminator here was historically daylight. It was recently substituted by the more reproducible black body irradiator running at the 5500 K temperature. Both of these sources produce continuous and nearly uniform spectrum (in its visible part).

In the trichromatic sensing model, convolution of the spectrum arriving the sensor with spectral sensitivity of individual channels has to be performed. It is important that in general case any non-uniformity in the spectrum of light source must be corrected by changing of the spectral sensitivity of sensor in order to get tristimulus values corresponding to daylight or 5500 K black body illuminator. It means that the sensor has to be designed having the particular source in mind. For almost all sensors this is not the case, i.e. the continuous uniform spectrum is assumed and no spectral correction for the source is made. Any light source different from the continuous uniform one will cause therefore colour distortions. It is not possible in general case to perform exact correction afterwards my changing of tristimulus values.

How significant is failure of colour reproduction will depend on the dissimilarity of light source to the daylight. Fluorescent (LID) lamps have usually only a few spectral lines, causing significant problems in colour reproduction, and LEDs are even fundamentally monochromatic. Manufacturers of such sources use secondary luminophors in order make emittance spectrum smoother (with different degree of success). In opposite to them, xenon arc lamps are nearly equal to daylight in visible range of wavelengths (e.g. see Fig. 2). Incandescent lamps (e.g. halogen) have inherently smooth spectrum but will require chromatic correction (see later).

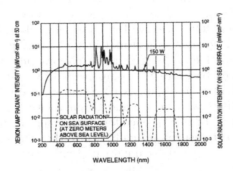

Fig. 2. Power spectrum of a short-arc xenon lamp in comparison to solar radiation. One may notice quite uniform power distribution in the visible range 380–780 nm, whereas quite non-uniform spiky behaviour in near-IR range.

Pronounced infrared (IR) component in the spectrum of light source causes usually an additional problem, especially for CCD sensors, because they are inherently IR-sensitive. The issue arises because the colour filters used in each channel usually cannot block IR sufficiently well and, thus, the tristimulus values become distorted. Therefore, additional measures (e.g. special filters) are required to reduce the influence of IR component.

5 Chromatic Adaptation

In case if tristimulus values were created without spectral correction of the source, any further correction can be only approximate. Still, such a correction is better than nothing and legitimated by the human vision. Namely, the human visual system is able to adaptively change its sensitivity to cone responses of different types, maintaining the (approximately) constant perceived appearance of white colour under different lightings.

The *von Kries transformation* [9] resembles this property of human vision and applies scaling to the LMS colour coordinates (i.e. responses of three cones) depending on the context, so that the adapted appearance of the white colour remains constant:

$$
C_{LMS}^{(2)} = C_{LMS}^{(1)} \begin{vmatrix} L_w^{(2)}/L_w^{(1)} & 0 & 0 \\ 0 & M_w^{(2)}/M_w^{(1)} & 0 \\ 0 & 0 & S_w^{(2)}/S_w^{(1)} \end{vmatrix}, \tag{5}
$$

where $C_{LMS}^{(1)}$ and $C_{LMS}^{(2)}$ are colours of the same object using illuminant 1 and 2, $(L_w^{(1)}, M_w^{(1)}, S_w^{(1)})$ and $(L_w^{(2)}, M_w^{(2)}, S_w^{(2)})$ are colours corresponding to white (or transparent) object under illumination 1 and 2 respectively.

The von Kries transform works in LMS colour space, thus colours expressed in other systems have to be transformed to LMS before correction and back to the source colour space after that. For example for sRGB we use Eq. 4 and 1 for the forward and Eq. 2 and 3 for the backward transformation.

While the primary purpose of the von Kries transformation is chromatic correction, it also ensures the same relative scaling of lightness. It means that all white points will have after transformation not only the same chroma and hue, but also the same lightness. However, the correction of the transfer function, for example for a non-standard gamma, is not addressed here at all - the proper transformation to XYZ is the task of the corresponding colour encoding system and its colour profile.

6 The Colour Difference

The notion of colour difference (dE) allows to quantitatively describe *how much* two colours differ. It does not say, however, *what* is particularly different.

The simplest way to find dE is to calculate the Euclidean distance between two colours in some colour space. Most colour spaces, however, are not particularly suitable for this purpose because they suffer from the so-called perceptual non-uniformity. It is because the human ability to distinguish different colours depends on the absolute value of the colour and the lightness. Figure 3 shows, for example, the contours of just noticeable colour differences on the CIE chromaticity diagram (in fact a slice in the Yxy colour space). Euclidean distance in the Yxy space is therefore not suitable.

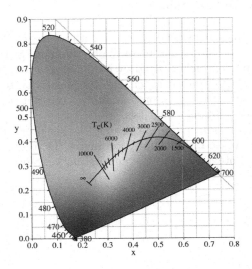

Fig. 3. Contours of just noticeable differences on CIExy chromaticity diagram. Orientation and size differ significantly depending on colour. (Color figure online)

This was one of the reasons for introduction of L*a*b* colour space. Euclidean distance in the L*a*b* colour space is known as CIE76 dE. It was however not perfect and improved two times by addition of correction terms leading to CIE94 and CIEDE2000 definitions. The later is believed to finally resolve the perceptual uniformity issue and is used therefore in our investigations. The formula for CIEDE2000 calculation, including all correction factors, is too large to be presented here, thus, we redirect interested reader to the original publication in [10].

Two colours with $dE <= 1$ are considered barely distinguishable, whereas $dE > 5$ corresponds to subjectively different colours.

7   Quality Criteria of Colour Reproduction of WSI Scanners

One option for the evaluation of colour reproduction qualities of WSI scanners is to use a colour difference formula together with reference objects whose colourimetric properties are known. The average difference dE_{mean}, found on a set of reference objects, i.e. average error, can serve as quantitative characteristic of accuracy of colour reproduction.

Additionally to mean error, dE's maximum dE_{max} and standard variance dE_{var} are of interest. dE_{max} is useful for detection of blindness to some colours in spite of sufficiently good average performance for all other test objects. dE_{var} may give an idea about random or systematic nature of colour shifts. The later is true particularly if one observes high dE_{mean} and low dE_{var}. This would indicate that all colours are off by some similar amount and probably because of some common systematic error.[2]

Accurate colour reproduction is fine and desired, however, it can be well possible to have an imaging system which offsets absolute values, but is still able to resolve small differences in colour. Even significant hue in reproduction, i.e. if all colours appear bluish or greenish, is probably not so dangerous as inability to distinguish slight shades of the same colour. Such inability may impair visibility of structures and, thus, in application to digital pathology we regard this as a greater failure.

Therefore we also test the scanner performance in this respect by measuring colour distances between similarly coloured reference objects. In this case, colour differences are calculated between pairs of scanned colours and not between the scanned and the reference value (as before). Instead, the differences in scanned colours are normalised by differences between reference colours corresponding to them:

$$dE_i^{rel} = \frac{dE2000(C_i^{meas}, C_{i+1}^{meas})}{dE2000(C_i^{ref}, C_{i+1}^{ref})}, \qquad (6)$$

where C_i^{meas} and C_{i+1}^{meas} are colour values measured for fields i and $i+1$ respectively and (C_i^{ref} and C_{i+1}^{ref}) are the corresponding reference values. The normalisation allows to directly see whether the colour differences present in reference objects are preserved in the digital image ($dE^{rel} \simeq 1$) or were diminished ($dE^{rel} \ll 1$). Values significantly greater than 1 are also not good because they suggest that some other colours (not presented on the test chart) could become merged. Ideally, all dE_i^{rel} have to be the same and equal to 1.

8   Test Method and Materials

A set of reference objects used for the assessment has to provide colour samples spread over the interesting colour range and their absorption spectra have to be reasonably filled. We use for this purpose the ANSI IT8.7/1 test target ("IT8 target") originally designed for graphic industry (Fig. 4). The IT8 target is commercially available in different dimensions and on different materials. It offers 264 colour samples representing different combinations of hue, saturation and lightness. Among them are six step wedges representing six most important colours in 12 different grades of lightness. Colourimetric characteristics of each field on the IT8 target are measured with high precision by the target's

---

[2] The opposite case, i.e. low dE_{mean} and high dE_{var}, is theoretically not possible because dE is always positive, thus, high dE_{var} will be accompanied with high dE_{mean} too.

Fig. 4. IT8.7/1 test target. Fields in columns 1–12 represent different combinations of hues, saturations and lightnesses. Columns 13–19 contain step wedges with different lightnesses of the same colour. Columns 20–22 are custom and not used in this study. (Color figure online)

manufacturer according to the requirements of ISO 13655 standard. These data supplement each physical copy of the target. They are used as references in our calculations. The target was cut to dimensions and mounted on a usual glass slide as shown on Fig. 5.

According to conventional practice, the sRGB colour space was assumed for scanned data in case if no colour profile was provided by the WSI scanner manufacturer[3].

The testing is performed as follows:

- The reference slide is scanned by each WSI scanner. Average colours of each test field are calculated by averaging of pixels in the middle 50% of each field.
- The chromatic correction of all scanned targets is performed as described in chromatic adaptation section above, i.e. their whites are adjusted to the same common chroma and hue corresponding to 5000 K black body and the same relative lightness.
- Colour differences are calculated according to CIEDE2000 formula for each of test fields. dE is calculated between values produced by the WSI scanner (chromatically adjusted on the previous step) and the reference values provided by the test target manufacturer for the D50 illuminant.
- dE's maximum (dE_{max}), average (dE_{mean}) and standard variance (dE_{var}) are calculated for each scanner over the whole test set. These results constitute *accuracy test*.

---

[3] As in 2012 and 2016, none of scanner manufacturers have provided colour profiles for their WSI scanners.

- Relative normalised colour differences dE^{rel} are calculated between similarly coloured fields in IT8 target according to Eq. 6. Colour step wedges in columns 13–19 are used for this purpose. Only pairs of neighbouring fields from the same step wedge are evaluated. No chromatic correction was done for dE^{rel} calculation, since it is the way how users observe the colours on WSI. i.e. uncorrected. Thus, average measured colours of each test field are directly used.
- Minimum and mean values of dE_i^{rel} over the whole test set are indicative to the ability of scanner to resolve similar colours. They constitute *resolution test*.

Fig. 5. IT8.7/1 target mounted on a glass slide.

9 Experimental Results and Discussion

Results of testing and comparison between different scanner models cannot be made public due to ISC policies. We provide here only an anonymized example of the evaluation results of some devices. Table 1 and Table 3 show detailed and summarised results of the accuracy test. Table 2 and Table 4 shows results of the colour resolution test. Analysis of these numbers shows that maximum colour errors dE_{max} for these devices are significantly larger than their mean errors dE_{mean}. This indicates that the devices does not perform uniformly and has pronounced problems with reproduction of some colours. They can be due to the non-uniform or even sparse power spectrum of light source, due to camera sensor or encoding in RGB - the exact reason is not possible to derive from these data. Non-uniform performance of this particular devices also leads to problems with correct resolution of slightly different colours. One can see from Table 2 that some colours will be difficult to distinguish on WSIs created by these devices, thus their applicability for diagnostic or education can be impaired.

Table 1. Experimental results for the colour accuracy evaluation. CIE dE2000 colour difference to reference values are given for columns 1–12 of the scanned and chromatic corrected IT8.7/1 test target for 4 vendors (A–D).

Ven.A	1	2	3	4	5	6	7	8	9	10	11	12
A	7,17	2,85	17,54	19,97	8,67	6,65	5,42	3,86	11,56	10,41	9,73	9,25
B	9,08	6,72	11,31	11,03	10,43	8,66	7,03	6,71	12,96	11,99	11,55	10,91
C	11,78	9,54	7,10	6,42	12,59	9,78	8,02	7,83	14,33	13,79	11,58	9,81
D	12,76	7,88	6,71	5,58	12,11	7,37	5,42	5,56	9,42	6,30	5,42	7,17
E	11,39	7,80	6,32	6,16	11,33	7,91	7,20	7,13	14,07	9,59	7,91	6,75
F	12,30	10,09	9,63	9,80	11,61	9,66	8,07	9,25	13,16	11,75	10,24	8,37
G	12,28	12,20	12,76	15,89	11,26	11,05	12,13	15,15	12,09	11,32	10,59	11,66
H	11,44	11,81	11,77	14,77	9,51	8,33	10,30	13,74	10,59	9,79	9,06	5,80
I	6,29	3,44	4,35	9,00	7,96	4,30	2,72	1,62	10,05	8,56	7,28	4,31
J	24,60	22,02	0,75	2,05	6,96	5,19	3,76	3,65	9,59	8,88	8,36	4,91
K	6,26	3,48	2,58	4,57	6,25	4,53	3,40	4,31	8,77	7,88	7,18	6,35
L	6,86	3,35	1,43	4,31	6,95	4,73	3,19	3,42	9,76	8,76	8,04	7,49

Ven.B	1	2	3	4	5	6	7	8	9	10	11	12
A	7,26	12,50	15,66	22,98	13,33	12,55	10,95	8,77	19,09	18,26	17,29	13,72
B	8,74	16,59	22,69	15,48	14,69	14,24	13,03	7,88	17,49	17,11	16,46	13,82
C	11,49	14,06	12,50	12,50	18,52	19,20	21,25	24,07	14,24	14,40	14,73	14,85
D	15,10	11,21	9,36	8,86	17,53	19,04	21,13	23,52	11,64	12,78	14,59	21,15
E	11,10	13,07	13,97	13,17	19,12	19,43	20,13	22,67	11,35	11,35	11,73	12,57
F	10,59	12,90	21,12	22,34	15,64	15,69	16,10	16,77	16,40	15,40	13,54	10,85
G	23,46	20,59	17,92	17,27	15,71	15,91	16,52	17,36	16,19	14,17	12,49	10,95
H	8,11	11,32	13,85	15,99	14,14	14,98	15,38	16,37	16,37	15,01	13,75	10,71
I	10,44	11,80	12,61	14,64	15,72	15,25	14,90	13,55	16,86	16,57	15,51	13,67
J	9,53	13,10	11,86	19,82	13,33	13,44	12,78	9,18	18,66	18,57	18,11	16,40
K	9,23	19,29	14,44	10,35	12,42	13,28	13,15	12,44	18,11	17,59	16,44	10,35
L	8,00	12,41	14,98	12,33	12,40	12,75	12,54	14,04	18,34	17,50	16,45	13,67

Ven.C	1	2	3	4	5	6	7	8	9	10	11	12
A	8,89	15,08	17,97	18,24	15,72	16,79	16,56	14,85	22,80	22,22	22,24	20,31
B	10,57	15,41	18,02	19,47	17,64	18,82	18,72	16,96	21,85	21,24	21,39	19,34
C	14,16	14,65	13,82	14,26	22,10	22,74	24,13	26,11	18,14	17,75	17,72	17,53
D	12,57	14,33	17,18	18,57	20,76	21,73	22,91	24,46	13,51	13,37	13,76	16,05
E	14,82	16,83	15,83	15,46	22,32	21,86	21,98	21,84	13,13	12,62	11,98	10,91
F	24,52	17,94	19,95	12,72	19,92	20,15	20,58	21,16	20,59	20,03	17,99	14,71
G	12,24	15,95	18,29	24,50	20,35	20,93	21,84	22,03	21,03	19,70	17,80	15,02
H	17,05	15,43	15,21	16,28	18,67	20,56	22,17	24,67	21,84	21,27	20,78	19,41
I	29,71	32,80	15,79	17,95	19,27	18,84	19,05	19,14	22,05	21,86	21,21	19,62
J	9,56	13,34	11,83	12,61	14,54	14,76	14,70	11,28	22,58	22,35	22,16	20,81
K	9,97	21,41	22,59	23,73	13,56	14,93	15,53	15,66	21,65	21,20	20,77	17,65
L	9,12	13,91	17,12	17,90	13,99	15,68	16,13	15,98	21,61	21,11	20,59	18,73

(*continued*)

Table 1. (*continued*)

Ven.A	1	2	3	4	5	6	7	8	9	10	11	12
A	9,20	14,52	15,94	13,62	18,69	15,97	11,81	8,68	26,48	24,82	22,34	14,91
B	12,54	16,11	16,95	17,38	21,98	20,39	16,31	5,87	25,88	25,17	23,91	18,10
C	31,38	20,78	21,91	39,39	29,02	27,72	25,36	24,32	24,12	24,32	24,18	22,24
D	17,64	18,87	19,21	19,37	28,94	25,45	24,37	20,99	18,18	15,27	14,39	18,01
E	33,30	21,91	20,64	19,87	27,33	24,69	21,80	16,92	18,41	16,84	15,16	11,87
F	27,51	30,63	23,71	21,30	26,03	23,30	19,83	16,97	24,31	21,34	16,84	7,34
G	15,42	18,81	22,04	27,45	25,79	24,86	24,00	22,59	24,24	20,28	16,43	9,46
H	13,57	17,07	17,13	18,76	23,28	23,28	24,84	26,02	24,84	21,95	20,29	13,90
I	15,68	13,53	12,12	40,24	22,03	20,13	19,94	21,10	23,97	22,42	21,52	20,42
J	9,58	15,53	16,95	12,45	17,53	16,74	16,53	17,95	25,55	24,55	23,67	22,51
K	9,46	14,67	17,91	21,80	26,32	22,22	15,83	29,63	24,15	22,44	20,51	17,30
L	8,98	13,90	16,41	15,96	27,04	21,38	13,29	18,89	24,92	22,25	19,20	13,90

Table 2. Experimental results for the colour resolution evaluation. dE^{rel} values for vertically-adjacent fields in columns 13–19 of IT8.7/1 test target for vendors A–D.

Ven.A	13	14	15	16	17	18	19
A–B	1,18	1,29	0,46	1,39	1,35	1,18	1,11
B–C	1,13	0,89	1,73	0,71	1,09	1,53	0,81
C–D	0,86	0,73	1,35	0,95	0,84	1,12	0,92
D–E	0,81	0,81	0,97	0,97	0,90	0,89	1,18
E–F	0,69	0,91	1,11	1,23	0,96	0,89	1,20
F–G	0,81	1,00	1,00	1,27	1,05	0,83	1,21
G–H	0,54	1,01	1,07	1,24	1,28	0,90	1,26
H–I	0,68	1,15	0,96	1,04	1,33	0,94	1,11
I–J	0,77	1,32	0,79	1,13	1,37	0,99	0,96
J–K	0,49	1,34	0,51	1,35	1,18	1,10	0,87
K–L	0,91	1,13	0,77	1,15	3,19	1,08	0,85
min	0,49	0,73	0,46	0,71	0,84	0,83	0,81
perfRes	0,78	0,94	0,86	0,97	0,97	0,95	0,95
Ven.B	**13**	**14**	**15**	**16**	**17**	**18**	**19**
A–B	1,31	1,23	1,45	1,98	1,60	1,35	1,34
B–C	0,97	1,14	1,09	1,88	1,34	1,14	1,25
C–D	0,79	1,08	0,98	1,75	1,24	1,11	1,35
D–E	0,59	1,01	0,82	1,17	1,07	0,99	1,17
E–F	0,63	0,92	0,90	0,81	0,70	1,06	0,88
F–G	0,67	0,81	0,94	0,63	0,55	1,02	0,68
G–H	1,01	0,66	0,96	0,61	0,46	1,36	0,67

(continued)

Table 2. (*continued*)

Ven.B	13	14	15	16	17	18	19
H–I	0,42	0,64	1,85	0,47	0,52	1,33	0,59
I–J	0,96	0,61	1,51	0,56	0,54	1,49	0,51
J–K	1,23	0,90	1,54	0,22	0,77	1,61	0,51
K–L	0,91	0,92	2,24	0,44	2,89	1,43	0,55
min	0,42	0,61	0,82	0,22	0,46	0,99	0,51
perfRes	0,81	0,86	0,96	0,70	0,78	1,00	0,76
Ven.C	**13**	**14**	**15**	**16**	**17**	**18**	**19**
A–B	1,28	1,37	1,42	2,10	1,57	1,35	1,49
B–C	0,91	1,29	1,03	2,08	1,53	1,07	1,53
C–D	0,90	1,36	0,91	1,79	1,44	1,08	1,53
D–E	0,82	1,20	0,76	1,10	1,11	1,03	1,15
E–F	0,85	1,04	0,61	0,79	0,76	1,07	0,80
F–G	1,17	0,77	0,56	0,60	0,63	1,15	0,60
G–H	0,96	0,64	0,95	0,55	0,52	1,19	0,52
H–I	1,13	0,61	0,94	2,74	0,47	1,50	0,52
I–J	1,82	0,61	1,04	3,14	0,54	1,36	0,35
J–K	1,30	0,62	1,40	0,11	4,95	1,63	0,45
K–L	1,36	0,80	1,60	0,06	0,88	1,43	0,58
min	0,82	0,61	0,56	0,06	0,47	1,03	0,35
perfRes	0,95	0,82	0,88	0,74	0,80	1,00	0,71
Ven.D	**13**	**14**	**15**	**16**	**17**	**18**	**19**
A–B	1,33	1,37	0,84	2,16	1,61	1,24	1,33
B–C	0,90	1,34	0,84	2,38	1,53	0,86	1,67
C–D	0,70	1,20	1,06	1,84	1,27	1,08	1,67
D–E	0,65	1,08	1,00	1,14	1,04	1,05	1,15
E–F	0,57	0,82	1,01	0,87	0,79	1,11	0,90
F–G	0,75	0,81	1,15	0,69	0,70	1,20	0,73
G–H	0,89	0,70	0,97	3,88	0,72	1,19	0,67
H–I	0,24	0,84	1,24	5,85	0,53	1,23	0,58
I–J	1,56	0,87	1,42	3,57	0,59	1,59	4,97
J–K	1,24	1,02	1,33	0,50	0,71	1,41	0,40
K–L	0,97	1,23	1,66	0,29	2,87	1,30	3,08
min	0,24	0,70	0,84	0,29	0,53	0,86	0,40
perfRes	0,79	0,91	0,97	0,85	0,82	0,99	0,84

Table 3. Summary of experimental results for the colour accuracy evaluation for columns 1–12 of the scanned and chromatic corrected IT8.7/1 test target for 4 vendors (A–D).

Vendor	dE_{mean}	dE_{min}	dE_{max}	dE_{var}
A	8,70	0,75	24,60	14,81
B	14,85	7,26	24,07	12,91
C	18,23	8,89	32,80	16,46
D	20,20	5,87	40,24	32,91

Table 4. Summary for experimental results for vertically-adjacent fields in columns 13–19 of IT8.7/1 test target for vendors A–D.

Vendor	dE_{min}^{rel}	dE_{mean}^{rel}
A	0,78	0,92
B	0,79	0,88
C	0,71	0,84
D	0,70	0,84

10   Conclusions and Outlook

The intend of this publication is to provide necessary background information relevant to correct reproduction of colours in histological samples by WSI scanners and to explain testing methodology applied during 2-nd and 3-rd International Scanner Contest. This publication is proved to be necessary because no of five scanners, which took place in the contest, did perform sufficiently well in this discipline. We hope the testing procedure will help scanner manufacturers to improve their products in respect to colour fidelity.

Although we evaluated "out of the box" data produced by WSI scanners, the same testing method can be applied by users doing custom calibration for the evaluation of their results. In this case it is suggested to use different reference sets (colour targets) for the calibration and the evaluation to eliminate possible bias.

The proposed procedure can be further refined by creation of specialised reference targets using specific set of histological stains. Then the evaluation of scanner performance can be done for narrower set of sample classes, for example "H&E-only performance". The presented method was used in [11] and implemented for public use in [12] .

References

1. Baxi, V.: Color Calibration on Whole Slide Imaging Scanners. Pathology Visions (2011)
2. Bautista, P.A., Hashimoto, N., Yagi, Y.: Color standardization in whole slide imaging using a color calibration slide. J. Pathol. Inform. 5(1), 4 (2014). https://doi.org/10.4103/2153-3539.126153
3. The International Scanner Contest. http://scanner-contest.charite.de/en/
4. Shrestha, P., Hulsken, B.: Color accuracy and reproducibility in whole slide imaging scanners. J. Med. Imaging (Bellingham) 1(2), 027501 (2014). https://doi.org/10.1117/1.JMI.1.2.027501
5. Clarke, E.L., Treanor, D.: Colour in digital pathology: a review. Histopathology 70(2), 153–163 (2017). https://doi.org/10.1111/his.13079
6. Stockman, A., MacLeod, D.I.A., Johnson, N.E.: Spectral sensitivities of the human cones. J. Opt. Soc. Am. A 10(12), 2491–2520 (1993)
7. Fairchild, M.D.: Color Appearance Models. The Wiley-IS & T Series in Imaging Science and Technology. Wiley, New York (2005)
8. Poynton, C.: The rehabilitation of gamma. In: Human Vision and Electronic Imaging III, pp. 232–249 (1998). http://www.poynton.com/PDFs/Rehabilitation_of_gamma.pdf
9. Brill, M.H., Michael, H.: The relation between the color of the illuminant and the color of the illuminated object. Color Res. Appl. 20, 70–76 (1995)
10. Sharma, G., Wu, W., Dalal, E.N.: The CIEDE2000 color-difference formula: implementation notes, supplementary test data, and mathematical observations. Color Res. Appl. 30, 21–30 (2005)
11. Haroske, G., Zwönitzer, R., Hufnagl, P.: Leitfaden "Digitale Pathologie in der Diagnostik". Pathologe 39(3), 216–221 (2018). https://doi.org/10.1007/s00292-018-0433-y
12. Hufnagl, P., Lohmann, S., Schlüns, K., Zerbe, N.: Implementation of the "Digital Pathology in Diagnostics" guideline: support systems and their functionality. Pathologe 39(3), 222–227 (2018). https://doi.org/10.1007/s00292-018-0436-8

Deep Learning Methods for Mitosis Detection in Breast Cancer Histopathological Images: A Comprehensive Review

Nassima Dif$^{(\boxtimes)}$ (ID) and Zakaria Elberrichi (ID)

EEDIS Laboratory, Djillali Liabes University, Sidi Bel Abbes, Algeria
difnassima05@gmail.com, elberrichi@gmail.com

Abstract. In breast cancer histology, there are three important features for tumor grading, where the proliferation score presents a key component. The mitotic count strategy is among the used methods to predict this score. However, this task is tedious and time consuming for pathologists. To simplify their work, there is a recognized need for computer-aided diagnostic systems (CADs). Several attempts have been made to automate the mitosis detection based on both machine and deep learning (DL) methods. This study aims to provide the readers with a medical knowledge on mitosis detection and DL methods, review and compare the relevant literature on DL methods for mitosis detection on H&E histopathological images, and finally discuss the remaining challenges and some of the perspectives.

Keywords: Mitosis detection · Deep Learning · Breast Cancer · Convolutional Neural Networks · Computer Aided Diagnostic Systems

1 Introduction and Motivation

Breast cancer (BC) is considered as the most diagnosed cancer among women [12]. In histopathology, the pathologist observes stained BC biopsies with hematoxylin and eosin (H&E) under a microscope for grading. With the availability of whole slide scanners, the glass slides are digitized as whole slide images (WSIs). Their analysis is important for tumor assessment, diagnosis, and treatment.

The proliferative activity is one of the three prognostic parameters in BC, where the mitotic index is among the used methods to measure it [10]. Usually, the pathologist counts manually mitoses on the selected high power fields (HPFs) from WSIs. Though, this task is tedious, time-consuming and prone to subjectivity and inter-variability between pathologists. To reduce their workload, computer-aided diagnostic systems (CADs) are proposed. These systems are based on machine [84] and deep learning [18] methods.

The first automated experimental study on H&E tissue sections was reported by Kaman et al. in 1984 [81] for mitosis count. In 1993, Kate et al. [42] have

© Springer Nature Switzerland AG 2020
A. Holzinger et al. (Eds.): AI & ML for Digital Pathology, LNAI 12090, pp. 279–306, 2020.
https://doi.org/10.1007/978-3-030-50402-1_17

computerized this task on stained specimens by Feulgen owing to its capacity to highlight the DNA content. Traditionally, researchers have used machine learning (ML) to automate the mitosis detection task [84]. However, these methods suffer from some serious drawbacks related to their dependency on data representation. Since 2012, the interesting obtained error rate in the ImageNet large scale visual recognition challenge (ILSVRC) has encouraged the image vision community to exploit deep learning (DL) methods due to their capacity to learn data representation. In most recent studies, a considerable literature has been published on DL techniques for mitosis detection. Where, a significant number of published papers is based on convolutional neural networks (CNNs) [6, 79].

In recent years, there has been an increasing amount of relevant review papers on the exploitation of DL methods in biomedicine [14], healthcare [59,65], medical [55], and histopathological [82] image analysis. Specifically, the analysis of breast cancer images got a significant interest in different reviews: mammography and MRI [13], breast histology [6] and nuclei detection [39,95].

The paper on deep learning in mammography and breast histology [33] details 10 relevant papers on the mitosis detection by DL methods. However, since 2018, researchers have shown an increased interest in DL strategies for mitosis detection. Despite this concern, no one as far as we know has published a related review paper. The purpose of this contribution is to provide a comprehensive review on the proposed DL methods for the mitosis detection task. The mitosis detection can be carried out on time-lapse phase-contrast microscopy images [76] and stained images by PHH3 [80] or H&E [15]. In this review, we were interested in DL mitosis detection methods on H&E stained images due to their extensive use and availability.

In this review, 28 publications have been collected from the literature review papers on DL methods for medical image analysis and Google Scholar. We used the following keywords to search for publications: 'mitosis detection', 'deep learning', 'breast cancer', 'convolutional neural networks'. First, we selected the period 2012–2019, then 2018–2019 for a maximum of recent investigations. The second strategy was to filter the concerned researches among all works that cited ICPR12 [69], AMIDA13 [86], MITOSIS-ATYPIA-14 [68], and TAUPAC16 [83] papers.

The remaining part of this chapter proceeds as follows: Sect. 2 defines the used terms in this review. Section 3 explains the background of mitosis detection and deep learning, and the related works on DL methods. The purpose of this section is to provide the DL experts with sufficient medical knowledge on breast cancer, in particular, the mitosis detection task, and to detail the DL methods to the medical image analysis community. Section 4 details the open problems and discuses some future outlook. Finally, the last section concludes this work.

1.1 Glossary

– **Breast Cancer (BC).** An uncontrolled proliferation of cells in the breast.

- **Hematoxylin and Eosin (H&E).** Staining procedure that helps to highlight the structural morphology of cells and the other features under the microscope.
- **Histopathology.** A branch of pathology, where changes in tissues are studied.
- **Mitotic Index.** An index that reveals the number of cells undergoing nuclear divisions (mitosis).
- **Whole Slide Images (WSIs).** High resolution images that represent a complete microscope slide.
- **Whole Slide Digital Scanners (WSD).** A scanner that digitizes glass slides into virtual slides, presented as whole slide images (WSIs).
- **Computer Aided Diagnostic Systems (CAD).** Systems that assist specialists in their diagnostic process and help them to make more robust decisions.
- **Machine Learning (ML).** A branch of artificial intelligence, this field helps to extract exploitable and relevant knowledge from big volumes of data.
- **Deep Learning (DL).** A branch of machine learning, based essentially on neural networks.
- **Convolutional Neural Network (CNN).** A deep learning network, inspired by the visual cortex and composed of three types of layers: convolutional layers, pooling layers, and fully connected layers.
- **Fully Convolutional Network (FCN).** A CNN variant, composed of convolutional, pooling and upsampling layers.

2 State of the Art

2.1 Deep Learning

2.1.1 Convolutional Neural Networks (CNN)

Convolutional neural networks are inspired by the visual cortex. In 1962, Hubel et al. [38] proposed a hierarchical model based on complex (C) and simple (S) neuronal cells. According to their observations, Fukushima et al. [28] have developed a deep neural network for pattern recognition. This architecture was particularly useful in Lecun et al. [47] investigation, where they demonstrated the efficiency of CNN networks (LeNet) for supervised learning.

The impressive obtained error rate in the ILSVRC by the AlexNet network [46] has encouraged the computer vision community to propose more optimized architectures. Overfitting is one of the most challenging drawbacks in this field. To solve this issue, the main inspiration was to highlight the role of parameter reduction techniques. In the VGGNet architecture [75], the size of filters has been reduced to F = 3 to propose deeper configurations with a small number of parameters. While the Inception network [78] has assessed the significance of inception blocks. ResNet [34] has considered the use of residual blocks to prevent the vanishing gradient problem. Inception-ResNet [77] has examined the implication of residual connections in inception blocks. These findings contributed to a better exploitation of deep neural networks for medical image analysis.

2.1.2   Fully Convolutional Network (FCN)

The fully convolutional network (FCN) is a CNN variant, composed of convolutional, pooling and upsampling layers. This network was largely exploited within the semantic segmentation [52] due to its capacity to perform pixel-wise prediction. Upsampling layers play an important role in semantic segmentation, their purpose is to upsample the output of convolutional layers to obtain the same input size.

2.1.3   Region Convolutional Neural Network (R-CNN)

The region convolutional neural network (R-CNN) [31] is a CNN variant, designed for object detection. This architecture has proved its efficiency compared to the pixel-wise CNN classification method in terms of computational complexity. First, this method performs a selective search on the input image to propose the candidate regions. Then, the CNN is used as a feature extractor. Finally, the generated feature vectors are used to train the bounding box regressor based on the SVM classifier.

To speed up the R-CNN training and the prediction run time, the Fast-RCNN [30] architecture was proposed. Despite R-CNN, this architecture performs end-to-end learning, where the feature vectors are supplied to the region of interest pooling layer. Then, the obtained vector is used for classification and bounding box prediction. The faster R-CNN [67] proposes the exploitation of a separated network for the candidate regions selection instead of the selective search method to reduce the fast R-CNN computational complexity.

2.2   Generalities on Breast Cancer and Mitotic Count

The cancer is defined as an uncontrolled proliferation of cells, the most commonly diagnosed cancer among women is breast cancer (BC) with 11.6% of total cancers death [12]. For BC detection, screening tests are employed such as mammography [41,72], ultrasound [98], and MRI [20]. The ultrasound has proved its efficiency compared to the mammography test in the diagnosis of solid breast lesions [102]. These tests help for earlier detection and therefore improve the chance for surviving.

After an abnormal screening test, a breast biopsy is recommended for tumor assessment, diagnosis, and treatment. There are different types of breast biopsies: fine-needle aspiration (FNA), core needle biopsy (CNB) and excision biopsy (EB). The CNB is known as the preferred technique for histological evaluation and surgical management [91]. Since it is less expensive than the EB, and in contrast to FNA, it highlights the overall histological structure [61]. During the CNB process, a core tissue is extracted by the expert. To extract accurately the tissue from the region of interest, the ultrasound-guided core needle biopsy strategy is used [26]. Then, the tissue is sent to the pathologist for examination.

The pathologist prepares the specimens by formalin fixation and embedding in paraffin then cuts paraffin sections at 3–5 μm thickness [1]. The staining helps to highlight the structural morphology of cells and the other features under the microscope. There are different types of staining protocols, where the hematoxylin and eosin (H&E) is the most used staining protocol, H stains the cell nuclei with blue-black and E stains the other structures with various degrees of pink [25].

The pathologist observes the stained biopsies under a brightfield microscope or a whole slide digital scanner. The scanner digitizes glass slides into virtual slides, presented as whole slide images (WSIs), under a specific magnification. Then, the pathologist selects regions of interest (ROIS) from these WSIs and analyses them based on specialized software [24]. Figure 1 highlights the difference between WSI and ROI[1].

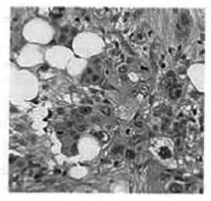

Fig. 1. The difference between a whole slide image and a region of interest from the TAUPAC16 dataset. (Color figure online)

The analysis of the stained specimens helps the pathologist to verify the presence of breast cancer. When the BC is detected, the pathologist performs a histological classification and checks the extent of cancer (in situ or invasive). The BC can be developed in epithelial (carcinoma) or stromal tissues (sarcomas), and carcinomas can be located in milk ducts or milk-producing glands, referred as ductal carcinoma (DC) or lobular carcinoma (LC) respectively [56]. The ductal carcinoma in situ is the most diagnosed cancer among women with 83% of cases [90].

The pathologist uses the grading and the staging systems as prognostic factors to assess the cell's appearance, size of the tumor and its proliferative behavior. Nowadays, the Nottingham grading system [27] is used for breast cancer grading.

The Nottingham histological system [27] is based on three morphological features: tubule formation, nuclear pleomorphism, and mitotic count. These features are scored from 1 to 3. The tubule formation score presents an indicator

---

[1] http://tupac.tue-image.nl/node/3.

of the percentage of tubular structures in the tumor area, nuclear pleomorphism indicates the degree of variability of nuclei compared to normal cell nuclei, and the mitotic count specifies the number of mitotic in the tumor and its proliferative behavior [8].

The proliferative activity presents an important prognostic parameter in the BC, it is related to the aggressiveness of cancer, where the high proliferative activity is associated with an uncontrolled cell division and therefore reveals a high risk. This activity can be measured by various methods including S-phase fraction, immuno-histochemistry of proliferation-associated to antibodies (Ki-67) and mitotic activity [10].

In oncology, the mitotic index reveals the number of cells undergoing nuclear divisions (mitosis). In the mitosis process, there are four basic phases: prophase, metaphase, anaphase, and telophase. The mitotic nucleus appears denser compared to the normal ones at the beginning of mitosis and transforms into a cell with two nuclei in telophase.

To compute the mitotic index, the pathologist identifies the representative regions of interest (ROIs) at a low magnification since the WSI may contain tens of thousands of HPFs. Each ROI corresponds to 2 mm^2 or 10 high power fields (HPFs). Then mitoses are counted manually under ×40 magnification to score ROIs from 1 to 3 according to the number of mitotic per region. The mitotic count process is tedious, time-consuming (from 5 to 10 min per ROI [29]) and suffers from inter and intra-variability between pathologists [60]. This variability is related to several factors: (a) the subjective selection of the most mitotically active ROIs [11], (b) the various morphology of mitosis within its transformation process, (c) its similar appearance to other structures such as necrotic nuclei and compressed nuclei which can result a high false-positive rate, (d) the small number of mitosis compared to the normal cells nuclei. Hence, to enhance the detection task, a strict protocol must be followed [22]. As a solution to these limitations and to reduce the pathologist's workload, computer-aided diagnostic systems are proposed to automate the mitosis detection task.

2.3   Computer Aided Diagnostic Systems (CAD)

Computer-aided diagnostic (CAD) systems assist specialists in their diagnostic process and help them to make more robust decisions. CADs are based on machine (ML) [50] and deep learning (DL) methods [65].

Machine learning methods (ML) rely on data representation. Where the feature extraction process is required before the training task. These features are extracted according to the field of application and described as handcrafted features. The extraction process requires prior knowledge in the area of interest, especially in case of medical data. In computer vision, the majority of previous studies on CAD systems have emphasized the use of ML methods, due to their limited requirements in terms of computational resources and volume of data.

Deep learning (DL) is defined as a multi-level representation learning and based mainly on deep neural networks such as convolutional neural networks (CNN) and recurrent neural networks (RNN). In recent years, there has been an increasing amount of literature on deep learning methods in different domains [32,35,45,50,100]. These rapid developments were influenced by various factors related to (a) the remarkable obtained error rate on the ImageNet dataset [46], (b) the availability of the powerful graphics processing units (GPUs), and (c) the massive available volumes of data.

One major important advantage of using DL methods is their capacity to learn data representation from raw data, which involves less human intervention compared to the traditional ML algorithms. However, despite their efficiency, DL algorithms suffer from major drawbacks: the overfitting problem on a limited volume of data, their high computational complexity, and memory requirements.

The main challenge of DL algorithms for medical image analysis is the limited number of accessible medical images. Moreover, the manual annotation of thousands of images for training requires a considerable effort by experts. On the other hand, the high resolution of histopathological images can cover these limitations by generating a large volume of patches form one digital image based on data augmentation techniques. A considerable amount of literature has been published on the application of DL methods for histopathological image analysis [82]. In the breast cancer histology, the exploitation of DL algorithms has covered several applications such as invasive breast cancer detection [19], epithelial and stromal regions segmentation [96], nuclear atypia scoring [97], and mitosis detection [18].

Several attempts have been made to propose automated methods for the mitosis detection task, in both machine [51] and deep learning [18] fields. The purpose of these studies was to resolve the different obstacles related to this automation. The mitosis has highly variable biological structures, and a similar appearance to other structures and artifacts, which can lead to a high false-positive rate. For example, in telophase, the cell contains two separated nuclei and highlights the presence of one mitosis. Furthermore, their low frequency and the limited number of cells undergoing mitotic compared to the normal nuclei cells are leading causes to the data unbalancing problem. Moreover, biopsies preparation, staining, and digitization are key issues in the generation of non-uniform histological images.

The following part reviews the proposed automatic deep learning methods for mitotic figures detection.

2.4 Datasets

The main obstacle faced by many researchers for histopathology images analysis was the availability of public big data, this issue is related to several restrictions: (a) privacy, (b) the extensive time and effort for their annotation, and (c) the variability of staining and digitization methods and scanners between laboratories.

To promote the development of robust frameworks for breast cancer histopathological image analysis, many challenges have been organized. Their purpose was to improve the performance on open access and high quality annotated datasets, where different tasks have been covered: metastasis detection in lymph nodes (CAMELYON16, CAMELYON17), mitosis detection (ICPR12 [69], AMIDA13 [86], MITOS-ATYPIA-14 [68])), nuclear atypia scoring (MITOS-ATYPIA-14 [68]) and tumor proliferation scoring (TUPAC16 [83]).

Table 1 compares between the proposed datasets for the mitosis detection task.

Table 1. Publicly available datasets for mitosis detection.

Dataset		ICPR12	AMIDA13	MITOS-ATYPIA-14	TUPAC16	TUPAC16 auxiliary
Scanners		Aperio (A) Hamamatsu (H) Microscope (M)	Aperio (A)	Aperio (A) Hamamatsu (H)	Aperio (A)	Aperio (A) Leica SCN400 scanner (L)
WSI	Total	5	23	–	821	73
	Dimension	–	–	–	50000 × 50000	–
HPF	Total	50	596	136	–	656
	Dimension A	2084 × 2084	2000 × 2000	1539 × 1376	–	2000 × 2000
	Dimension H	2252 × 2250	–	1539 × 1376		L: 5657 × 5657
	Dimension M	2767 × 2767		–		–
Mitoses	Train	226	550	–	–	1552
	Test	100	533	–	–	
Pathologists		1	2	3	–	3
Winner		IDSIA [18]	IDSIA [86]	CUHK team	LUNIT [62]	LUNIT [62]

The (a) ICPR 2012 is a small size dataset composed of 5 WSIs, which have been collected from one laboratory and annotated by one pathologist. This dataset has not considered the problem of inter variability between pathologists and laboratories, which limits the power of the trained models in terms of generalization. To improve the proposed systems, more challenging datasets have been published: AMIDA13 and MITOS-ATYPIA-14. The (b) AMIDA13 has been collected at different time points and contains a considerable number of annotated HPFs (596) by 2 pathologists. The MITOS-ATYPIA-14 is a larger dataset composed of 1136 HPFs and annotated by 3 pathologists. However, these datasets have not automated the full grading task, since, the ROIs were selected manually by pathologists. Moreover, the pathologist computes manually the proliferation score according to the detected mitosis by the automatic system. For a fully automatic workflow, the TUPAC16 dataset addresses the possibility to predict automatically the tumor proliferation score from the WSI, where two auxiliary datasets have been provided: TUPAC16 auxiliary for mitosis detection and regions of interest for the automatic selection of ROIs. TUPAC16 auxiliary is an extension of the AMIDA13 dataset with 50 supplementary WSIs.

2.5   Deep Learning Methods for Mitosis Detection

Figure 2 displays the distribution of the 28 selected papers per year. It highlights a considerable amount of researches in 2018 including January 2019. The first contribution was published in 2008, most studies in this period have emphasized the use of machine learning approaches because of: their large exploitation in computer vision, the lack of powerful resources and publicly available mitosis detection datasets. Since 2012, there has been a growing interest in deep learning methods due to the availability of datasets, the optimization of DL architectures, open-source libraries and pre-trained models.

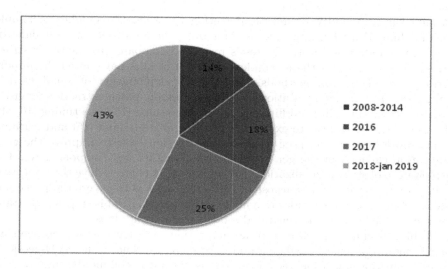

Fig. 2. The distribution of mitosis detection papers per year.

The mitosis detection task with DL methods has several drawbacks related to:

- The limited number of medical data.
- The limited number of mitotic figures because of their low frequency.
- The high false positive rate.
- The high variance between the digitized histopathological images under different conditions.
- Overfitting problems.
- The required computational resources and memory storage.

To solve these limitations, several attempts have been made in the state of the art, where different strategies have been exploited, such as:

- Regularization strategies to reduce overfitting problems.
- Transfer learning, fine tuning, and the exploitation of CNN as a feature extractor to reduce the training run time complexity and overfitting problems.
- FCN and deep detection methods to enhance the precision and to reduce the computational complexity.
- Regression networks to reduce the inference time.

- Multi-scale learning to exploit the contextual information and to enhance the detection task.
- Two stages learning methods to solve the high false positive rate problem.

2.5.1   Regularization Methods

Despite the availability of mitosis detection datasets, the number of simple remains limited for DL applications. Moreover, these datasets are unbalanced, since, the number of mitotic figures is restricted compared to the other structures. Thus, to address these complexities, prior studies have noted the importance of regularization methods, such as: the exploitation of small models [18,21,88], the data augmentation techniques (random patch extraction, translation, rotation, mirroring and flipping), transfer learning [15], fine-tuning [16,94], the use of CNNs as feature extractors [5], ensemble learning [15] and learning from crowds [4]. The purpose of these investigations was to improve the generalization capacity of the generated models. Another key component was the exploitation of stain normalization techniques [44,54,66] to reduce the inter variability between labs. The purpose of these strategies is to covert the processed slides under various conditions to a normalized space [54]. This step is important for the exploitation of the generated models within other labs.

Table 2 resumes the used stain normalization techniques as a preprocessing before the application of DL methods. As far as we know, the SVD-geodesic based stain normalization technique [54] is the most commonly employed in the automatic mitosis detection field [4,21,62,64,85,99]. For more information, Saafin et al. [70] reviewed the relevant literature on stain normalization methods for digital pathology image analysis. Despite the importance of this preprocessing, many significant papers have ignored this step [15,18]. However, the stain normalization is not required when training and testing a model on generated images under common conditions, but it helps to exploit this model within heterogeneous labs.

Table 2. The used stain normalization techniques in the proposed mitosis detection methods.

Reference	Stain normalization method
(Albarqouni et al.) [4]	SVD-geodesic based stain normalization technique [54]
(Das et al.) [21]	
(Veta et al.) [85]	
(Paeng et al.) [62]	
(Zerhouni et al.) [99]	
(Rao et al.) [64]	
(Wu et al.) [94]	Color transfer between images [66]
(Kausar et al.) [43]	
(Akram et al.) [2]	
(Beevi et al.) [7]	A nonlinear mapping approach using image-specific color deconvolution [44]
(Shah et al.) [74]	Stain specific standardization method [9]

2.5.2   Pixel-Wise and Patch-Wise Classification Strategies

Many recent papers have used DL methods for mitosis counting on the H&E stained slides. To the best of our knowledge, Malon et al. [57] have made the first attempt to automate this task based on convolutional neural networks. They used a set of 728 images at ×400 magnification, then the SVM classifier was trained on the obtained results to automate the grading process. Tables 3 and 4 present the proposed deep learning methods for mitosis detection.

The proposed DL methods for automatic mitosis detection are categorized into pixel [4,18,85,99] and patch wise classification [40,94] strategies. The pixel-wise classification method is considered as a semantic segmentation, where each pixel is labeled separately as mitosis or non-mitosis. Cireşan et al. [18] proposed a max-pooling CNN as a pixel-wise classifier for mitosis detection, where they averaged the output of three classifiers to improve the generalization capacity. The best-obtained results in both ICPR and AMIDA challenges provide strong evidence on the efficiency of this method. However, one major drawback of this approach is its high inference time: 8 min per HPF. Moreover, the pathologist selects many ROIs (HPFs) from the same WSI for analysis. This makes this method time consuming and not feasible for clinical use.

To reduce the time complexity, the patch wise classification strategies have been widely considered. First, patches or mitosis candidates are generated and subsequently, trained as mitosis or not mitosis. In the patch generalization process, the images are converted to blue ratio to highlight the candidate nuclei, due to their high blue intensity in the stained digital slides. Then a segmentation method is performed based on different mechanisms: globally fixed and local dynamic thresholding [88], k-means clustering algorithm [5], aggressive and weaker color threshold and grid search [58], krill held algorithm (KHA) [7], otsu's thresholding method [21,62], globally binary thresholding [87].

The related literature to the classification of mitosis candidates has highlighted several use cases of DL methods: training a network from scratch [21,40], transfer learning [15] or fine tuning [43,94], the use of CNNs as feature extractors [5,7] and the combination between handcrafted and CNN features [58,71,88].

2.5.3   Training from Scratch and Fine-Tuning

Janowczyk et al. [40] trained the cifar-10 AlexNet network to classify the mitosis candidates, based on extracted patches at x20 magnification. However, this low magnification can be a major source of uncertainty for CNN. In another study, Das et al. [21] have evaluated the effectiveness of a shallower CNN on the decomposed sub-patches by the Haar wavelet decomposition method. These methods proved their efficiency for mitosis classification. On the other hand, training a network from scratch is time-consuming and can lead to an overfitting problem due to the limited amount of data. To overcome these limitations, transfer learning and fine-tuning methods have been explored in several studies [43,94]. In these methods, pre-trained models are adapted to the new classification task,

Table 3. Deep learning methods for mitosis detection (1).

Method	Segmentation	Classification	Training	Dataset
[57]	Color histogram	CNN SVM	From scratch	A set of 728 images at 400X magnification
IDSIA [18]	Max pooling CNN		From scratch	ICPR12
[40]	Blue-ratio	CNN: cifar-10 AlexNet network	From scratch	–
[21]	Blue-ratio + Otsu's thresholding	CNN	From scratch	ICPR12 MITOS-ATYPIA-14
FF-CNN [94]	Blue-ratio	FF-CNN	Fine tuning: AlexNet model	MITOS-ATYPIA-14
[5]	K-means clustering	CNN for feature extraction SVM for classification	From scratch	MITOS-ATYPIA-14
[7]	Krill Held Algorithm (KHA)	CNN for feature extraction Softmax for classification	Fine tuning: caffe VGGNet model	MITOS-ATYPIA-14 Regional Cancer Centre (RCC)
HC + CNN [88]	Blue-ratio images + laplacian of Gausian + globally fixed and local dynamic thresholdings	Logistic regression model on CNN features Random forest classifier on handcrafted features	From scratch	ICPR12
[58]	Aggressive and weaker color threshold and grid search	CNN (LeNet) for feature extraction SVM for classification	From scratch	ICPR12
[71]	Blue-ratio images + morphological erosion and dilation operations	CNN	From scratch	ICPR12 MITOS-ATYPIA-14 AMIDA13
CasNN [15]	FCN	CNN	Fine tuning (CNN)	ICPR12 MITOS-ATYPIA-14
DeepMitosis [48]	Segmentation: FCN Detection: faster R-CNN Verification: CNN (ResNet50)		–Fine tuning (FCN) from VGGNet16– Transfer learning (R-CNN) from VGG_CNN_M_1024 –From scratch (CNN)	ICPR12 MITOS-ATYPIA-14
MITOS-RCNN [64]	MITOS-RCNN based on faster-RCNN		Fine tuning VGG-16 layers	ICPR12 MITOS-ATYPIA-14 AMIDA13
[49]	Lightweight R-CNN		From scratch	ICPR12 MITOS-ATYPIA-14
[16]	DRN		Fine Tuning from [17]	ICPR12
[93]	DRN + Hough voting		From scratch	AMIDA13
AggNet [4]	–	Multi-scale CNN	From scratch	AMIDA13
MFF-CNN [43]	Blue-ratio	MFF-CNN	Fine tuning from a caffeNet model	MITOS-ATYPIA-14
[87]	Blue ratio + global binary thresholding	CNN	From scratch	ICPR12 TAUPAC16

(continued)

Table 3. (*continued*)

Method	Segmentation	Classification	Training	Dataset
MSSN [53]	–	CNN	From scratch	ICPR12 MITOS-ATYPIA-14
[2]	–	CNN	From scratch	MITOS-ATYPIA-14 TAUPAC16
Wide resNet [99]	CNN (wide ResNet)		From scratch	ICPR12 MITOS-ATYPIA-14 TAUPAC16
L-view [62]	Otsu's method + binary dilatation	–CNN (L-view based on residual blocks) –SVM for tumor scoring	From scratch	TAUPAC16
[92]	Blue-ration + thresholding methods	– DRN + Hough transform –Decision tree for tumor scoring	From scratch	TAUPAC16

Table 4. Deep learning methods for mitosis detection (2).

Method	Segmentation	Classification	Training	Dataset
[85]	Max pooling CNN		From scratch	AMIDA13 Dataset from two pathology labs in the Netherlands [3]
[63]	Max pooling CNN with one dropped fully connected layer		From scratch	AMIDA13
[80]	Brown and blue cannels	CNN	From scratch	TAUPAC16 Dataset from three different hospitals in the Netherlands
[74]	Otsu's method + binary dilatation	MitosNet (CNN variant)	From scratch	Dataset from three international pathology centers

where the weights are transferred to another target network, then a subset of layers is retrained according to the new classification problem.

Wu et al. [94] fine-tuned their deep fully fused convolutional neural network (FF-CNN) based on the AlexNet model. The FF-CNN fuses multi-level features by linking the output of Conv3 and Conv4 to the fully connected layer. Their application has outperformed the winner of the ICPR2014 challenge, which proves the capacity of fine-tuning in the mitosis detection task. One additional

advantage of using fine-tuning strategies is their limited computational requirements in terms of GPU's capacity, where a standard CPU is enough to complete
this task.

2.5.4   Feature Extraction with CNN

In other investigations, CNNs have been used as feature extractors. Albayrak
et al. [5] employed the CNN network for feature extraction, LDA and PCA
methods for feature reduction and the SVM algorithm for classification. For
a more optimized run-time complexity in the feature extraction phase, other
studies [7] suggest the use of fine-tuned models as feature extractors, where the
last four convolutional layers of the Caffe VGGNet model have been retrained.

Both machine and deep learning strategies proved their efficiency in the mitosis detection task. ML methods are based on handcrafted or DL based features.
Thus, to take advantage of these two techniques, several studies have addressed
the hybridization between both handcrafted and DL features. Wang et al. [88]
proposed a cascade approach (HC + CNN), where they trained separately classifiers with CNN-based features and handcrafted features, followed by a third
classifier in case of confusion between the decision of the two classifiers. The
final class was computed based on an averaging between the generated models.
In further studies, Malon et al. [58] combined nuclear features (texture, color,
and shape) and CNN features (LeNet 5 [47]), and Saha et al. [71] incorporated 24
handcrafted feature in the first fully connected layer of the CNN. These investigations highlight the efficiency of the hybridization compared to the handcrafted
or CNN features when employed separately.

2.5.5   FCN and Deep Detection Methods

To reduce the considerable inference time for the mitosis detection process, other
researches have suggested the exploitation of the fully convolutional network
(FCN) as a coarse retrieval. Chen et al. [15] proposed a hybrid method based
on the FCN to retrieve mitosis candidates and a fine-tuned CaffeNet model for
classification. This method has reduced the inference time from 8 min [18] to
0.5 s per HPF. Other investigations suggest converting the obtained DL models
into FCNs to speed up the detection process [2, 62, 94].

Nevertheless, Li et al. [48] have critiqued the use of the FCN to infer the
location of mitosis, since, it ignores the regional information. To enhance this
process, they showed for the first time the role of deep detection methods for
mitosis detection. Their hybrid framework (Deepmitosis) is composed of deep
detection (DeepDet), verification (DeepVer) and segmentation (DeepSeg) networks. The main component is the DeepDet network, which localizes mitosis based on the faster R-CNN [67]. Another earlier study by Rao et al.
[64] proposed a novel variant of the faster R-CNN (MITOS-RCNN) for small
object detection. In another research, Li et al. [49] developed a lightweight

region-based CNN inspired by the RCNN [31], their main purpose was to propose a fast system on CPU computers.

2.5.6 Regression Networks

Another strategy to adjust the inference time for the clinical use was to formulate the mitosis detection task as a regression problem [16,92,93]. Chen et al. [16] proposed a method based on the deep regression network (DRN) with fully convolutional kernels. This network is composed of convolutional (CLs) and deconvolutional layers (DLs). The CLs perform the down-sampling phase for feature extraction, whereas DLs are used to restore the original input size. To prevent overfitting, they fine-tuned the off-the-self deepLab model [23]. Wollmann et al. [93] combined between the deep residual network and the hough voting method. The architecture of this network is composed of three parts: downsampling, factor disentangling part and a pixel-wise classification. The pixel-wise classification provides two branches, which are combined based on the hough voting layer. This method reduces the computational time compared to the other ensemble learning methods due to its single training process.

2.5.7 Multi-scale Learning

The previous studies have suggested training DL methods on a single scale image. On the other hand, the contextual information is important, since the pathologist can observe digital slides from different scales. For an accurate detection task, other studies have been interested in multi-scale learning. Albarqouni et al. [4] proposed an augmented architecture (AggNet), based on a multi-scale CNN and an aggregation layer. To improve the generalization, this network was retrained based on the crowd's annotation labels. This study has been the first attempt to thoroughly examine the CNN networks for generating ground truth labeling from non-expert crowd annotations, in the biomedical context. In another paper, Kausar et al. [43] developed a multi-scale FCNN model (MFF-CNN) based on two different scales FF-CNNs [94] and a fusion layer.

2.5.8 Two Stages Learning Methods

The mitoses are characterized by their low frequency, which can bias the nature of the generated dataset for classification. For example, Cireşan et al. [18] have generated a training set that includes only 6.6% of mitosis pixels. Hence, this may cause a serious class unbalancing and a high false-negative (FN) rate issues. Various approaches have been proposed to solve these limitations [2,40,48,53,87] by exploring the advantages of the two stages learning methods.

Wahab et al. [87] proposed a method based on a two-phase CNNs. In the first stage, the CNN classifies mitosis into easy, normal and hard non-mitosis, the mitosis candidates and the hard non-mitosis are augmented by both rotations and flipping, while the easy non-mitoses are under-sampled by the blue ratio histogram-based clustering. Then, the generated dataset is retrained by the second phase CNN. In another research, Ma et al. [53] proposed a two-stage deep method. First, a multi-scale and similarity learning convnets (MSSN) was used to treat the FN problem. Subsequently, a similarity prediction model was trained to reduce the high false-positive rate. Akram et al. [2] proposed a deep learning-based self-supervised algorithm. First, CNN was trained on the two sets: BG-rand and FG-Lab which contains the background samples and the centred patches on mitosis. Then, the false-positive detected samples noted as BG-hard were exploited with FG-WSI for retraining the CNN model. This work has analyzed the effect of semi-supervised learning through the use of the extracted mitosis patches from the unlabelled dataset (FG-WSI). Li et al. [48] developed a DeepVer to verify the false positives that have been provided by the Deep-Det network. Even though the efficiency of these hybrid systems, the obtained results reveal that the DeepVer model did not improve the performance on the ICPR12 dataset. Another strategy to reduce the FP rate was the exploration of a weighted fitness function [99]. Zerhouni et al. [99] exploited the wide residual network in a pixel-wise classification strategy. To strengthen their training set, they fused between three heterogeneous datasets: ICPR12, MITOS-ATYPIA-14 and the auxiliary mitosis detection dataset in the TAUPAC16 challenge.

2.5.9   Detection from WSI

The previously cited studies are restricted to the detection of mitosis from HPFs. Nevertheless, the pathologist must select manually HPFs from the WSI. Thus, to automate the full detection task, the manual selection of ROIs should be automated. In construct to ICPR12, AMIDA13 and MITOS-ATYPIA-14 challenges, the TUPAC16 has explored the prediction of the proliferation score directly from WSIs. The availability of this dataset has encouraged many researchers to propose frameworks for tumor proliferation score prediction [62, 92]. These methods are composed of three main steps: HPFs extraction, mitosis detection, and tumor proliferation score prediction.

Paeng et al. [62] used Otsu's method and the binary dilatation to extract tissue blobs. The extracted patches represent a square of 10 consecutive HPFs. Then, the L-view network was trained on the associated regions to a high cell density. Finally, the tumor proliferation score was predicted based on the number of detected mitosis, 21 handcrafted features, and the SVM classifier. The best results in the TAUPAC16 challenge provide strong evidence about the efficiency of this method. Wollman et al. [92] exploited the threshold-based attention mechanism for the ROI extraction. Then, a DNN network with the Hough transform method was employed for mitosis detection. Finally, the decision tree classifier was trained on the obtained results for the mitosis count.

2.6   Results

Table 5 compares the obtained results by the proposed methods for the mitosis detection task in terms of recall (R), precision (P) and f-measure or accuracy (F1/Acc).

Figure 3 highlights the obtained results on the ICPR12 dataset. These results indicate the efficiency of the faster RCNN for detection [48]. Furthermore, CNNs [21] tend to perform better than their hybridization with handcrafted features

Table 5. The obtained results by the deep learning methods for mitosis detection.

Dataset	Method	Precision	Recall	F-measure/ Accuracy
ICPR12	[21]	0.845	0.837	0.841
	DeepMitosis [48]	0.854	0.812	0.832
	[87]	0.83	0.76	0.79
	[16]	0.779	0.802	0.79
	[49]	0.78	0.79	0.784
	IDSIA [18]	0.88	0.70	0.782
	MSSN [53]	0.776	0.787	0.781
	HC + CNN [88]	0.84	0.65	0.7345
	[58]	0.747	0.590	0.659
	CasNN [15]	0.460	0.507	0.482
AMIDA13	[18]	0.610	0.612	0.611
	[93]	0.547	0.686	0.609
	AggNet [4]	0.441	0.424	0.433
MITOS-ATYPIA-14	[21]	0.996	0.987	0.981
	[5]	–	–	Acc 0.968
	[7]	0.874	0.901	0.886
	CasNN [15]	0.804	0.772	0.788
	MSSN [53]	0.379	0.617	0.470
	DeepMitosis [48]	0.431	0.443	0.437
	MFF-CNN [43]	0.405	0.453	0.428
	[49]	0.40	0.45	0.427
	FF-CNN [94]	–	–	0.393
TUPAC16 auxiliary	[87]	0.57	0.53	0.55
	[62]	–	–	0.652
	[80]	–	–	0.480
ICPR12 + MITOS-ATYPIA-14 + AMIDA13	[71]	0.92	0.88	0.90
	MITOS-RCNN [64]	–	–	0.955
ICPR12 + MITOS-ATYPIA-14 + TAUPAC16 auxiliary	[99]	–	–	0.648
MITOS-ATYPIA-14 + TAUPAC16 auxiliary	[2]	0.613	0.671	0.640

[88], or their exploitation as features extractors [58]. However, their use in a pixel-wise strategy is too expensive for inference. Thus, the key aspect figures into gathering the appropriate selection among various parameters: architecture, strategy, and the network's hyper-parameters. Despite the fast inference time of CasNN [15], this method is less accurate compared to the other approaches, which can be justified by the limits of the FCN for mitosis location inference.

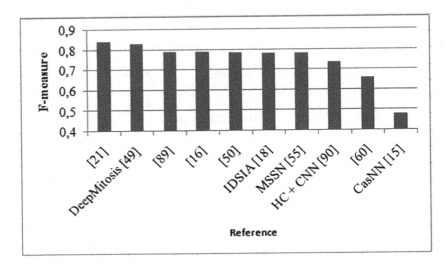

Fig. 3. The obtained results on the ICPR2012 dataset.

Few studies have examined the DL methods on the AMIDA13 dataset. The best results were obtained by the max pooling CNN in terms of f-measure value [18], whereas the proposed method by Wollmann et al. [93] yields the best recall rate. The AggNet [4] reported significantly a lower level of f-measure compared to the previous results. This can be explained by the noisy annotations by non-experts in the crowd.

Despite the ICPR12 dataset, the results on the MITOS-ATYPIA-14 dataset (Fig. 4) highlight the effectiveness of the exploited DL methods as a feature extractors [5,7] and the cascade method CasNN [15] compared to the other approaches [43,48,49,53,94]. The reported results by Albayrak et al. [5] reveal the effectiveness of this approach, where the results have been improved from 0.786 to 0.969 by the feature selection strategy. However, the number of selected features (10) to distinguish the complex morphology of mitosis may be reviewed.

The obtained results on the ICPR12, AMIDA13 and TUPAC16 auxiliary datasets provide additional evidence on the problem of inter variability between pathologists and laboratories. Hence, the annotation of the AMIDA13 by various pathologists, and collecting the TUPAC16 auxiliary dataset from diverse laboratories can justify their low accuracy compared to the ICPR12.

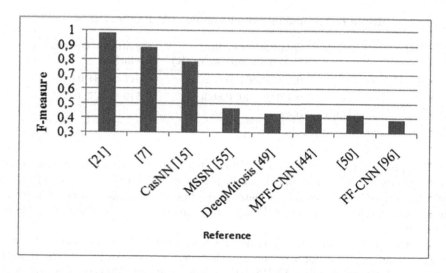

Fig. 4. The obtained results on the MITOS-ATYPIA-14 dataset.

To prevent overfitting, other studies [2,64,99] combined between different datasets for training and testing. Considerable results were obtained by Saha et al. [71] and Rao et al. [64] by combining the ICPR12, MITOS-ATYPIA-14, and AMIDA13 datasets. Saha et al. [71] improved the performance of their deep learning framework with 14% by including 24 significant handcrafted features from a total of 55. However, the importance of handcrafted features is not validated in other studies, this could be attributed to the nature of the selected features and the deep learning architectures.

Table 6 compares between obtained results by the proposed methods for the automated tumor proliferation scoring (TAUPAC16 dataset). The best results have been achieved by Paeng et al. [62] in terms of quadratic weighted cohen's kappa score.

2.7   Computational Time and Materiel

Table 7 resumes the capacity of the exploited GPUs and the processing time of the DL methods for mitosis detection. Powerful GPUs were employed [16,48] and parallelized [64,94] to accelerate the training and the inference time.

The results emphasize the high computational time of the pixel-wise method [18] compared to the other approaches [15]. For a fair comparison, we regrouped these methods by GPU type. Some investigations depend on CPUs [87,88] owing to their restricted requirements related to the shallower CNNs and the small datasets (ICPR12). However, the achieved inference time by Wang et al. [88] (1.5 min per HPF) is not feasible for clinical use, which points out the importance of GPUs.

Table 6. The obtained results on the TAUPAC16 dataset.

Dataset	Method	Quadratic weighted Cohen's kappa score (K)	Spearmans correlation coefficient
TAUPAC16	[62]	0.567 [0.464, 0.671]	0.617 [0.581 0.651]
	[80]	0.471 [0.340, 0.603]	0.519 [0.477, 0.559]
	[92]	0.42	–

The proposed DRN network by Chen et al. [16] is 6 times slower compared to its use by Wollmann et al. [93] on a less powerful GPU as it was influenced by other parameters such as the patch size. The most optimized computational time was obtained on parallel GPUs (<0.5 s) due to their distributed treatment [43,64,94].

Another important parameter is the complexity of the dataset, where we observe a noticeable difference between the inference time in [93] on the ICPR12 dataset and the challenging TUPAC16 auxiliary dataset. The considerable inference time obtained by Wollmann et al. [92] is explained by the end to end classification on the WSIs (50000 px × 50000 px) instead of HPFs.

Table 7. Computational time and the used materiel in the proposed methods for mitosis detection.

GPU	Reference	Training time	Inference time
GPU	[18]	One day for each network	8 min
	[49]	–	6.93 s
Without GPU computation	[88]	11.4 h	1.5 min
	ICPR12 [87]	15 h	48 s
Nvidia GeForce GTX 750M	[4]	–	–
Nvidia Getforce GTX 970	[93]	2.5 days	2.5 s
Nvidia GeForce GTX titan X	[16]	-	15 s
	[48]	–	0.4 s to 0.7 s
	[15]	–	0.5 s 0.3 s
	TAUPAC16 [87]	30 h	1 min
Nvidia Quadro K4200 graphics processor	[21]	–	16 s
4 Nvidia Tesla M40 GPUs	[94]	–	0.375 s
	[43]	–	0.388 s
5 NVIDIA tesla K80 GPUs for training AND a single GPU for testing	[64]		0.5 s
–	[92]	–	5 min (WSI)
–	[71]	–	0.3 s

3   Open Problems and Future Outlook

As discussed in the previous section, different DL methods have been proposed to solve various problems related to the mitosis detection task, where a variety of datasets have been published (ICPR12, AMIDA13, MITOS-ATYPIA-14, TAU-PAC16) to encourage the research within the mitosis detection task. Although, the main problem lies in the limited number of mitotic figures (1552 as a maximum), which restricts the capacity of the trained DL models to distinguish between the complex morphology of mitosis and other structures. Moreover, these datasets are collected from a maximum of three different pathology centers. Therefore, this limits the generalization ability of the generated models. The solution is to enhance the model's capacity by learning the whole variance. Some studies have suggested the use of stain standardization techniques, whereas many others have ignored this important step on multi-center datasets [87,92]. The main reason of the restricted number of samples in the medical image datasets is not related to their availability, but rather to the considerable workload by expert pathologists for their annotation.

The crowdsourcing is among the proposed solutions to the lack of annotated data. The study presented by Albarqouni et al. [4] is one of the first investigations to the exploitation of crowdsourcing in the mitosis detection task. Despite the efficiency of these techniques in the other domains, their use in the medical field is critical because of the noisy labels by non-expert participants. More researches using controlled and validated labels by experts is needed to obtain more robust results.

Another solution to the lack of annotated data is semi-supervised learning, which has been previously used to train models on both labeled and unlabelled samples. This technique presents an alternative method to supervised learning in case of a limited amount of labeled data. Up to now, the research has tended to focus on supervised rather than semi-supervised learning for mitosis classification by DL techniques [2]. Therefore, the exploitation of these methods for future works can present a good perspective.

Fine-tuning and transfer learning techniques have been proposed to overcome the overfitting problem related to the lack of annotated data. These techniques present 21% of the selected papers, where the trained models on the ImageNet dataset have been reused and fine-tuned on the mitosis datasets. This is explained by the similarity of low-level features (edges and corners). However, there is no theoretically principles and much uncertainty still exists about the relationship between these two heterogeneous domains. Consequently, sharing models within the same domain could be more helpful due to the similar appearance of the histopathological images compared to the other fields.

Other investigations propose the exploitation of shallower networks to prevent overfitting. These networks are characterized by a limited number of layers, whereas there has been no research based on deep architectures with parameters reduction techniques such as inceptions [78], MobileNet [37,73], and suffleNet [101].

The literature has highlighted the importance of the obtained results especially on the ICPR12 and MITOS-ATYPIA-14 datasets. Where several samples from training and testing sets have been collected from the same source. Thus, the efficiency of the generated models on different sourced samples is not guaranteed. The analysis by Kaman et al. [85] provides important insights on the worst agreement between the automated method and pathologists when evaluated on a new dataset from two pathology labs. Consequently, those models must be validated on new samples and accepted by pathologists. The effectiveness of the pathologist's results was justified by their top-down analysis strategy to include the contextual information, which is related to the size of the patch in the automated methods. The multi-scale learning was employed to solve the lack of sufficient context [94], whereas the majority of studies are based on a single scale learning. Hence, the exploitation of multi-scale contextual networks [89] could be promising in future works.

In the majority of the proposed DL methods, the architectures were presented as a black box, where there has been no clear strategy on the choice of layers and hyperparameters. The progressive visual analytic system (Deepeyes) [63] reveals the importance of visualization to identify unnecessary filters or layers, which can present a good tool to analyze the future proposed architectures for the mitosis detection task. Moreover, more attention is needed to make solutions comprehensible and understandable. In this context, explainable AI [36] helps to make results interpretable by medical experts by creating cooperation between humans and algorithms.

4   Conclusion

The developments in computer vision and digital pathology encouraged the proposition of computerized methods to automate several challenging tasks in the medical domain. Mitosis detection is among the laborious tasks for an expert pathologist, which suffers from inter variability and subjectivity. To solve these shortcomings, DL methods are used due to their capacity to learn data representation. However, their main obstacles are resumed in the required computational resources, the limited amount of data and their unbalanced nature in the medical domain.

To conclude, the literature identifies the strength of DL methods for mitosis detection. Nevertheless, they still suffer from several shortcomings, which support their use as a second tool to aid pathologists rather than their direct exploitation for clinical use.

References

1. Agoff, S.N., Lawton, T.J.: Papillary lesions of the breast with and without atypical ductal hyperplasia: can we accurately predict benign behavior from core needle biopsy? Am. J. Clin. Pathol. **122**(3), 440–443 (2004)

2. Akram, S.U., Qaiser, T., Graham, S., Kannala, J., Heikkilä, J., Rajpoot, N.: Leveraging unlabeled whole-slide-images for mitosis detection. In: Stoyanov, D., et al. (eds.) OMIA/COMPAY -2018. LNCS, vol. 11039, pp. 69–77. Springer, Cham (2018). https://doi.org/10.1007/978-3-030-00949-6_9

3. Al-Janabi, S., van Slooten, H.J., Visser, M., Van Der Ploeg, T., Van Diest, P.J., Jiwa, M.: Evaluation of mitotic activity index in breast cancer using whole slide digital images. PLoS One 8(12), e82576 (2013)

4. Albarqouni, S., Baur, C., Achilles, F., Belagiannis, V., Demirci, S., Navab, N.: AggNet: deep learning from crowds for mitosis detection in breast cancer histology images. IEEE Trans. Med. Imaging 35(5), 1313–1321 (2016)

5. Albayrak, A., Bilgin, G.: Mitosis detection using convolutional neural network based features. In: IEEE 17th International Symposium on Computational Intelligence and Informatics (CINTI), pp. 000335–000340. IEEE (2016)

6. Anwar, S.M., Majid, M., Qayyum, A., Awais, M., Alnowami, M., Khan, M.K.: Medical image analysis using convolutional neural networks: a review. J. Med. Syst. 42(11), 226 (2018)

7. Beevi, K.S., Nair, M.S., Bindu, G.: Automatic mitosis detection in breast histopathology images using convolutional neural network based deep transfer learning. Biocybern. Biomed. Eng. 39(1), 214–223 (2019)

8. Beikman, S., Gordon, P., Ferrari, S., Siegel, M., Zalewski, M.A., Rosenzweig, M.Q.: Understanding the implications of the breast cancer pathology report: a case study. J. Adv. Pract. Oncol. 4(3), 176 (2013)

9. Bejnordi, B.E., et al.: Stain specific standardization of whole-slide histopathological images. IEEE Trans. Med. Imaging 35(2), 404–415 (2015)

10. Beresford, M.J., Wilson, G.D., Makris, A.: Measuring proliferation in breast cancer: practicalities and applications. Breast Cancer Res. 8(6), 216 (2006)

11. Bonert, M., Tate, A.J.: Mitotic counts in breast cancer should be standardized with a uniform sample area. Biomed. Eng. Online 16(1), 28 (2017)

12. Bray, F., Ferlay, J., Soerjomataram, I., Siegel, R.L., Torre, L.A., Jemal, A.: Global cancer statistics 2018: globocan estimates of incidence and mortality worldwide for 36 cancers in 185 countries. CA Cancer J. Clin. 68(6), 394–424 (2018)

13. Burt, J.R., Torosdagli, N., Khosravan, N., RaviPrakash, H., Mortazi, A., Tissavirasingham, F., Hussein, S., Bagci, U.: Deep learning beyond cats and dogs: recent advances in diagnosing breast cancer with deep neural networks. Br. J. Radiol. 91(1089), 20170545 (2018)

14. Cao, C., et al.: Deep learning and its applications in biomedicine. Genom. Proteom. Bioinf. 16(1), 17–32 (2018)

15. Chen, H., Dou, Q., Wang, X., Qin, J., Heng, P.A.: Mitosis detection in breast cancer histology images via deep cascaded networks. In: Thirtieth AAAI Conference on Artificial Intelligence (2016)

16. Chen, H., Wang, X., Heng, P.A.: Automated mitosis detection with deep regression networks. In: IEEE 13th International Symposium on Biomedical Imaging (ISBI), pp. 1204–1207. IEEE (2016)

17. Chen, L.C., Papandreou, G., Kokkinos, I., Murphy, K., Yuille, A.L.: Semantic image segmentation with deep convolutional nets and fully connected CRFs. arXiv preprint arXiv:1412.7062 (2014)

18. Cireşan, D.C., Giusti, A., Gambardella, L.M., Schmidhuber, J.: Mitosis detection in breast cancer histology images with deep neural networks. In: Mori, K., Sakuma, I., Sato, Y., Barillot, C., Navab, N. (eds.) MICCAI 2013. LNCS, vol. 8150, pp. 411–418. Springer, Heidelberg (2013). https://doi.org/10.1007/978-3-642-40763-5_51

19. Cruz-Roa, A., et al.: High-throughput adaptive sampling for whole-slide histopathology image analysis (HASHI) via convolutional neural networks: application to invasive breast cancer detection. PLoS One 13(5), e0196828 (2018)

20. Dalmış, M.U., et al.: Using deep learning to segment breast and fibroglandular tissue in MRI volumes. Med. Phys. 44(2), 533–546 (2017)

21. Das, D.K., Dutta, P.K.: Efficient automated detection of mitotic cells from breast histological images using deep convolution neutral network with wavelet decomposed patches. Comput. Biol. Med. 104, 29–42 (2019)

22. van Diest, P.J., et al.: Reproducibility of mitosis counting in 2,469 breast cancer specimens: results from the multicenter morphometric mammary carcinoma project. Hum. Pathol. 23(6), 603–607 (1992)

23. Everingham, M., Van Gool, L., Williams, C.K., Winn, J., Zisserman, A.: The pascal visual object classes (VOC) challenge. Int. J. Comput. Vision 88(2), 303–338 (2010)

24. Farahani, N., Parwani, A.V., Pantanowitz, L.: Whole slide imaging in pathology: advantages, limitations, and emerging perspectives. Pathol. Lab. Med. Int. 7, 23–33 (2015)

25. Fischer, A.H., Jacobson, K.A., Rose, J., Zeller, R.: Hematoxylin and eosin staining of tissue and cell sections. Cold Spring Harbor Protoc. 2008(5), pdb-prot4986 (2008)

26. Fishman, J.E., Milikowski, C., Ramsinghani, R., Velasquez, M.V., Aviram, G.: US-guided core-needle biopsy of the breast: how many specimens are necessary? Radiology 226(3), 779–782 (2003)

27. Frierson Jr., H.F., et al.: Interobserver reproducibility of the nottingham modification of the bloom and richardson histologic grading scheme for infiltrating ductal carcinoma. Am. J. Clin. Pathol. 103(2), 195–198 (1995)

28. Fukushima, K., Miyake, S.: Neocognitron: a self-organizing neural network model for a mechanism of visual pattern recognition. In: Amari, S., Arbib, M.A. (eds.) Competition and Cooperation in Neural Nets. Lecture Notes in Biomathematics, vol. 45, pp. 267–285. Springer, Heidelberg (1982)

29. Gal, R., Rath-Wolfson, L., Rosenblatt, Y., Halpern, M., Schwartz, A., Koren, R.: An improved technique for mitosis counting. Int. J. Surg. Pathol. 13(2), 161–165 (2005)

30. Girshick, R.: Fast R-CNN. In: Proceedings of the IEEE International Conference on Computer Vision, pp. 1440–1448 (2015)

31. Girshick, R., Donahue, J., Darrell, T., Malik, J.: Region-based convolutional networks for accurate object detection and segmentation. IEEE Trans. Pattern Anal. Mach. Intell. 38(1), 142–158 (2015)

32. Hadsell, R., et al.: Learning long-range vision for autonomous off-road driving. J. Field Robot. 26(2), 120–144 (2009)

33. Hamidinekoo, A., Denton, E., Rampun, A., Honnor, K., Zwiggelaar, R.: Deep learning in mammography and breast histology, an overview and future trends. Med. Image Anal. 47, 45–67 (2018)

34. He, K., Zhang, X., Ren, S., Sun, J.: Deep residual learning for image recognition. In: Proceedings of the IEEE Conference on Computer Vision and Pattern Recognition, pp. 770–778 (2016)

35. He, X., Deng, L.: Deep learning for image-to-text generation: a technical overview. IEEE Signal Process. Mag. 34(6), 109–116 (2017)

36. Holzinger, A., Langs, G., Denk, H., Zatloukal, K., Müller, H.: Causability and explainabilty of artificial intelligence in medicine. Wiley Interdisc. Rev. Data Min. Knowl. Disc. 9, e1312 (2019)

37. Howard, A.G., et al.: MobileNets: efficient convolutional neural networks for mobile vision applications. arXiv preprint arXiv:1704.04861 (2017)
38. Humphrey, A., Sur, M., Ulrich, D., Sherman, S.: Receptive fields, binocular interaction, and functional architecture in the cat's visual cortex. J. Comp. Neurol. **233**, 159–189 (1985)
39. Irshad, H., Veillard, A., Roux, L., Racoceanu, D.: Methods for nuclei detection, segmentation, and classification in digital histopathology: a review–current status and future potential. IEEE Rev. Biomed. Eng. **7**, 97–114 (2013)
40. Janowczyk, A., Madabhushi, A.: Deep learning for digital pathology image analysis: a comprehensive tutorial with selected use cases. J. Pathol. Inf. **7**, 29 (2016)
41. Kallenberg, M., et al.: Unsupervised deep learning applied to breast density segmentation and mammographic risk scoring. IEEE Trans. Med. Imaging **35**(5), 1322–1331 (2016)
42. Kaman, E., Smeulders, A., Verbeek, P., Young, I., Baak, J.: Image processing for mitoses in sections of breast cancer: a feasibility study. Cytometry J. Int. Soc. Anal. Cytol. **5**(3), 244–249 (1984)
43. Kausar, T., Wang, M., Wu, B., Idrees, M., Kanwal, B.: Multi-scale deep neural network for mitosis detection in histological images. In: International Conference on Intelligent Informatics and Biomedical Sciences (ICIIBMS), vol. 3, pp. 47–51. IEEE (2018)
44. Khan, A.M., Rajpoot, N., Treanor, D., Magee, D.: A nonlinear mapping approach to stain normalization in digital histopathology images using image-specific color deconvolution. IEEE Trans. Biomed. Eng. **61**(6), 1729–1738 (2014)
45. Klein, G., Kim, Y., Deng, Y., Senellart, J., Rush, A.M.: OpenNMT: open-source toolkit for neural machine translation. arXiv preprint arXiv:1701.02810 (2017)
46. Krizhevsky, A., Sutskever, I., Hinton, G.E.: ImageNet classification with deep convolutional neural networks. In: Advances in neural information processing systems, pp. 1097–1105 (2012)
47. LeCun, Y., Bottou, L., Bengio, Y., Haffner, P., et al.: Gradient-based learning applied to document recognition. Proc. IEEE **86**(11), 2278–2324 (1998)
48. Li, C., Wang, X., Liu, W., Latecki, L.J.: Deepmitosis: mitosis detection via deep detection, verification and segmentation networks. Med. Image Anal. **45**, 121–133 (2018)
49. Li, Y., Mercan, E., Knezevitch, S., Elmore, J.G., Shapiro, L.G.: Efficient and accurate mitosis detection-a lightweight RCNN approach. In: ICPRAM, pp. 69–77 (2018)
50. Litjens, G., et al.: A survey on deep learning in medical image analysis. Med. Image Anal. **42**, 60–88 (2017)
51. Liu, A., Li, K., Kanade, T.: Mitosis sequence detection using hidden conditional random fields. In: IEEE International Symposium on Biomedical Imaging: From Nano to Macro, pp. 580–583. IEEE (2010)
52. Long, J., Shelhamer, E., Darrell, T.: Fully convolutional networks for semantic segmentation. In: Proceedings of the IEEE Conference on Computer Vision and Pattern Recognition, pp. 3431–3440 (2015)
53. Ma, M., Shi, Y., Li, W., Gao, Y., Xu, J.: A novel two-stage deep method for mitosis detection in breast cancer histology images. In: 24th International Conference on Pattern Recognition (ICPR), pp. 3892–3897. IEEE (2018)
54. Macenko, M., et al.: A method for normalizing histology slides for quantitative analysis. In: IEEE International Symposium on Biomedical Imaging: From Nano to Macro, pp. 1107–1110. IEEE (2009)

55. Madabhushi, A., Lee, G.: Image analysis and machine learning in digital pathology: challenges and opportunities. Med. Image Anal. **33**, 170–175 (2016)
56. Makki, J.: Diversity of breast carcinoma: histological subtypes and clinical relevance. Clin. Med. Insights Pathol. **8**, 23–31 (2015). CPath-S31563
57. Malon, C., Miller, M., Burger, H.C., Cosatto, E., Graf, H.P.: Identifying histological elements with convolutional neural networks. In: Proceedings of the 5th International Conference on Soft Computing as Transdisciplinary Science and Technology, pp. 450–456. ACM (2008)
58. Malon, C.D., Cosatto, E.: Classification of mitotic figures with convolutional neural networks and seeded blob features. J. Pathol. Inform. **4**, 9 (2013)
59. Miotto, R., Wang, F., Wang, S., Jiang, X., Dudley, J.T.: Deep learning for healthcare: review, opportunities and challenges. Briefings Bioinform. **19**(6), 1236–1246 (2017)
60. Orchid, N.N., Puthanpurayil, S.: Factors affecting the assessment of mitotic count in histopathological sections of tumors: a study of interobserver and intraobserver variability. Int. J. Res. Med. Sci. **4**(3), 762 (2016)
61. Oyama, T., Koibuchi, Y., McKee, G.: Core needle biopsy (CNB) as a diagnostic method for breast lesions: comparison with fine needle aspiration cytology (FNA). Breast Cancer **11**(4), 339–342 (2004)
62. Paeng, K., Hwang, S., Park, S., Kim, M.: A unified framework for tumor proliferation score prediction in breast histopathology. In: Cardoso, M.J., et al. (eds.) DLMIA/ML-CDS -2017. LNCS, vol. 10553, pp. 231–239. Springer, Cham (2017). https://doi.org/10.1007/978-3-319-67558-9_27
63. Pezzotti, N., Höllt, T., Van Gemert, J., Lelieveldt, B.P., Eisemann, E., Vilanova, A.: DeepEyes: progressive visual analytics for designing deep neural networks. IEEE Trans. Visual Comput. Graphics **24**(1), 98–108 (2017)
64. Rao, S.: MITOS-RCNN: a novel approach to mitotic figure detection in breast cancer histopathology images using region based convolutional neural networks. arXiv preprint arXiv:1807.01788 (2018)
65. Ravì, D., et al.: Deep learning for health informatics. IEEE J. Biomed. Health Inform. **21**(1), 4–21 (2016)
66. Reinhard, E., Adhikhmin, M., Gooch, B., Shirley, P.: Color transfer between images. IEEE Comput. Graphics Appl. **21**(5), 34–41 (2001)
67. Ren, S., He, K., Girshick, R., Sun, J.: Faster R-CNN: towards real-time object detection with region proposal networks. In: Advances in Neural Information Processing Systems, pp. 91–99 (2015)
68. Roux, L., et al.: Mitos & atypia. Image Pervasive Access Lab (IPAL), Agency for Science and Technology & Research Institute for Infocom Research, Singapore, Technical report, vol. 1, pp. 1–8 (2014)
69. Roux, L., et al.: Mitosis detection in breast cancer histological images an ICPR 2012 contest. J. Pathol. Inform. **4**, 8 (2013)
70. Saafin, W., Schaefer, G.: Pre-processing techniques for colour digital pathology image analysis. In: Valdés Hernández, M., González-Castro, V. (eds.) MIUA 2017. CCIS, vol. 723, pp. 551–560. Springer, Cham (2017). https://doi.org/10.1007/978-3-319-60964-5_48
71. Saha, M., Chakraborty, C., Racoceanu, D.: Efficient deep learning model for mitosis detection using breast histopathology images. Comput. Med. Imaging Graph. **64**, 29–40 (2018)
72. Samala, R.K., Chan, H.P., Hadjiiski, L., Helvie, M.A., Wei, J., Cha, K.: Mass detection in digital breast tomosynthesis: deep convolutional neural network with transfer learning from mammography. Med. Phys. **43**(12), 6654–6666 (2016)

73. Sandler, M., Howard, A., Zhu, M., Zhmoginov, A., Chen, L.C.: MobileNetV2: inverted residuals and linear bottlenecks. In: Proceedings of the IEEE Conference on Computer Vision and Pattern Recognition, pp. 4510–4520 (2018)
74. Shah, M., Wang, D., Rubadue, C., Suster, D., Beck, A.: Deep learning assessment of tumor proliferation in breast cancer histological images. In: IEEE International Conference on Bioinformatics and Biomedicine (BIBM), pp. 600–603. IEEE (2017)
75. Simonyan, K., Zisserman, A.: Very deep convolutional networks for large-scale image recognition. arXiv preprint arXiv:1409.1556 (2014)
76. Su, Y.T., Lu, Y., Chen, M., Liu, A.A.: Spatiotemporal joint mitosis detection using CNN-LSTM network in time-lapse phase contrast microscopy images. IEEE Access **5**, 18033–18041 (2017)
77. Szegedy, C., Ioffe, S., Vanhoucke, V., Alemi, A.A.: Inception-v4, Inception-ResNet and the impact of residual connections on learning. In: Thirty-First AAAI Conference on Artificial Intelligence (2017)
78. Szegedy, C., et al.: Going deeper with convolutions. In: Proceedings of the IEEE Conference on Computer Vision and Pattern Recognition, pp. 1–9 (2015)
79. Tajbakhsh, N., et al.: Convolutional neural networks for medical image analysis: full training or fine tuning? IEEE Trans. Med. Imaging **35**(5), 1299–1312 (2016)
80. Tellez, D., et al.: Whole-slide mitosis detection in H&E breast histology using PHH3 as a reference to train distilled stain-invariant convolutional networks. IEEE Trans. Med. Imaging **37**(9), 2126–2136 (2018)
81. Ten Kate, T., Belien, J., Smeulders, A., Baak, J.: Method for counting mitoses by image processing in Feulgen stained breast cancer sections. Cytometry J. Int. Soc. Anal. Cytol. **14**(3), 241–250 (1993)
82. Jimenez-del Toro, O., et al.: Analysis of histopathology images: from traditional machine learning to deep learning. In: Biomedical Texture Analysis, pp. 281–314. Elsevier (2017)
83. Veta, M., et al.: Predicting breast tumor proliferation from whole-slide images: the TUPAC16 challenge. Med. Image Anal. **54**, 111–121 (2019)
84. Veta, M., Pluim, J.P., Van Diest, P.J., Viergever, M.A.: Breast cancer histopathology image analysis: a review. IEEE Trans. Biomed. Eng. **61**(5), 1400–1411 (2014)
85. Veta, M., Van Diest, P.J., Jiwa, M., Al-Janabi, S., Pluim, J.P.: Mitosis counting in breast cancer: object-level interobserver agreement and comparison to an automatic method. PLoS One **11**(8), e0161286 (2016)
86. Veta, M., et al.: Assessment of algorithms for mitosis detection in breast cancer histopathology images. Med. Image Anal. **20**(1), 237–248 (2015)
87. Wahab, N., Khan, A., Lee, Y.S.: Two-phase deep convolutional neural network for reducing class skewness in histopathological images based breast cancer detection. Comput. Biol. Med. **85**, 86–97 (2017)
88. Wang, H., et al.: Mitosis detection in breast cancer pathology images by combining handcrafted and convolutional neural network features. J. Med. Imaging **1**(3), 034003 (2014)
89. Wang, X., Ma, H., Chen, X., You, S.: Edge preserving and multi-scale contextual neural network for salient object detection. IEEE Trans. Image Process. **27**(1), 121–134 (2017)
90. Ward, E.M., et al.: Cancer statistics: breast cancer in situ. CA Cancer J. Clin. **65**(6), 481–495 (2015)
91. Willems, S.M., Van Deurzen, C., Van Diest, P.: Diagnosis of breast lesions: fine-needle aspiration cytology or core needle biopsy? A review. J. Clin. Pathol. **65**(4), 287–292 (2012)

92. Wollmann, T., Rohr, K.: Automatic grading of breast cancer whole-slide histopathology images. Bildverarbeitung für die Medizin 2017. I, pp. 249–253. Springer, Heidelberg (2017). https://doi.org/10.1007/978-3-662-54345-0_56

93. Wollmann, T., Rohr, K.: Deep residual Hough voting for mitotic cell detection in histopathology images. In: IEEE 14th International Symposium on Biomedical Imaging (ISBI 2017), pp. 341–344. IEEE (2017)

94. Wu, B., et al.: FF-CNN: an efficient deep neural network for mitosis detection in breast cancer histological images. In: Valdés Hernández, M., González-Castro, V. (eds.) MIUA 2017. CCIS, vol. 723, pp. 249–260. Springer, Cham (2017). https://doi.org/10.1007/978-3-319-60964-5_22

95. Xing, F., Yang, L.: Robust nucleus/cell detection and segmentation in digital pathology and microscopy images: a comprehensive review. IEEE Rev. Biomed. Eng. **9**, 234–263 (2016)

96. Xu, J., Luo, X., Wang, G., Gilmore, H., Madabhushi, A.: A deep convolutional neural network for segmenting and classifying epithelial and stromal regions in histopathological images. Neurocomputing **191**, 214–223 (2016)

97. Xu, J., Zhou, C., Lang, B., Liu, Q.: Deep learning for histopathological image analysis: towards computerized diagnosis on cancers. In: Lu, L., Zheng, Y., Carneiro, G., Yang, L. (eds.) Deep Learning and Convolutional Neural Networks for Medical Image Computing. ACVPR, pp. 73–95. Springer, Cham (2017). https://doi.org/10.1007/978-3-319-42999-1_6

98. Yap, M.H., et al.: End-to-end breast ultrasound lesions recognition with a deep learning approach. In: Medical Imaging 2018: Biomedical Applications in Molecular, Structural, and Functional Imaging, vol. 10578, p. 1057819. International Society for Optics and Photonics (2018)

99. Zerhouni, E., Lányi, D., Viana, M., Gabrani, M.: Wide residual networks for mitosis detection. In: IEEE 14th International Symposium on Biomedical Imaging (ISBI 2017), pp. 924–928. IEEE (2017)

100. Zhang, R., et al.: Real-time user-guided image colorization with learned deep priors. arXiv preprint arXiv:1705.02999 (2017)

101. Zhang, X., Zhou, X., Lin, M., Sun, J.: ShuffleNet: an extremely efficient convolutional neural network for mobile devices. In: Proceedings of the IEEE Conference on Computer Vision and Pattern Recognition, pp. 6848–6856 (2018)

102. Zhi, H., Ou, B., Luo, B.M., Feng, X., Wen, Y.L., Yang, H.Y.: Comparison of ultrasound elastography, mammography, and sonography in the diagnosis of solid breast lesions. J. Ultrasound Med. **26**(6), 807–815 (2007)

Developments in AI and Machine Learning for Neuroimaging

Shane O'Sullivan[1]([⊠])(iD), Fleur Jeanquartier[2](iD), Claire Jean-Quartier[2](iD),
Andreas Holzinger[2](iD), Dan Shiebler[3], Pradip Moon[4](iD),
and Claudio Angione[4,5](iD)

[1] Department of Pathology, Faculdade de Medicina Universidade de Sao Paulo,
São Paulo, Brazil
doctorshaneosullivan@gmail.com
[2] HCI-KDD, Holzinger Group, Institute for Medical Informatics and Statistics,
Medical University of Graz, Graz, Austria
{f.jeanquartier,c.jeanquartier}@hci-kdd.org
[3] Department of Cognitive Linguistic and Psychological Sciences, Carney Institute
for Brain Science, Brown University, Providence, RI, USA
danshiebler@gmail.com
[4] Department of Computer Science and Information Systems, Teesside University,
Middlesbrough, UK
{P.Moon,C.Angione}@tees.ac.uk
[5] Healthcare Innovation Centre, Teesside University, Middlesbrough, UK

Abstract. This paper reviews guidelines on how medical imaging analysis can be enhanced by Artificial Intelligence (AI) and Machine Learning (ML). In addition to outlining current and potential future developments, we also provide background information on chemical imaging and discuss the advantages of Explainable AI. We hypothesize that it is a matter of AI to find an invariably recurring parameter that has escaped human attention (e.g. due to noisy data). There is great potential in AI to illuminate the feature space of successful models.

Keywords: Explainable AI · Stereology · Neurodegenerative diseases · Neuroimaging · Disector · 7 T post-mortem MRI · Brain mapping

1 Introduction and Motivation

In this paper, our approach is to discriminate between: general challenges to AI/ML image analysis (irrespective of the specific approach); challenges specific to Black Box methods; challenges that Explainable AI alone can help to overcome; and challenges that Black Box methods together with Explainable AI can help to overcome. In addition to outlining the challenges and our hypotheses, we also include an extensive review to assess the use of AI and ML-enhanced

We thank the organization CNPQ (Brazilian National Council for Scientific and Technological Development). This entity provided support that was invaluable to our research.

© Springer Nature Switzerland AG 2020
A. Holzinger et al. (Eds.): AI & ML for Digital Pathology, LNAI 12090, pp. 307–320, 2020.
https://doi.org/10.1007/978-3-030-50402-1_18

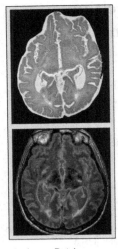

	MRI, Volumetry Contrasts, Architectonics Multi-modal Deep Learning (Multi-modal Medical Image Fusion & Image Segmentation) Explainable AI (Layer-wise Relevance Propagation & Local Interpretable Model-Agnostic Explanations)	→ Find recurring patterns → Correlate diseases → Validate diagnosis → Dealing with increasing amount of data → Identify different image attributes → Locate and correlate brain regions → Filter out noise → Find new feature spaces
Image Databases	Utilize different AI & ML methods	Opportunities

Fig. 1. Graphical abstract (brain images from [52])

magnetic resonance imaging (MRI) for the evaluation of neurodegenerative diseases in comparison to the use of histological information (Fig. 1).

2   Glossary

The following abbreviations and terms are used in this manuscript:

AD	Alzheimer Disease
AI	Artificial Intelligence
CAG	Cytosine-adenine-guanine
CV	Cross Validation
DL	Deep Learning
Explainable AI	Explaining the behavior of otherwise black-box models
fMRI	functional Magnetic Resonance Imaging
HD	Huntington's Disease
LDA	Linear Discriminant Analysis
ML	Machine Learning
MRA	Magnetic Resonance Angiography
MRI	Magnetic Resonance Imaging
Neurodegenerative diseases	Diseases caused by the death of neurons and/or other cells in the brain
NMR	Nuclear Magnetic Resonance
PCA	Principal Component Analysis
PD	Parkinson's disease
RF	Random Forests

RFDA   Regularized Fisher Discriminant Analysis
SC-CNN   Spatially Constrained Convolutional Neural Network
SPECT   Single Photon Emission Computed Tomography
Virtual Autopsy The use of imaging to diagnose cause of death
USG   Ultrasonography

3   State-of-the-Art

3.1   Role of AI/ML

We define AI as the whole field working on understanding intelligence towards context-adaptive systems; the backbone, however, is ML as a methodological subset of AI, whilst e.g. Deep Learning (DL) is just one specific methodological subset of ML [24]. In the following we only briefly point to some of the manifold possibilities which AI/ML offer for the topic of this paper. The most important methods for classification of brain states include Linear Discriminant Analysis (LDA) and regularized Fisher Discriminant analysis (RFDA) to get a classifier, Independent Component Analysis (ICA) and Principal Component Analysis (PCA) for dimensionality reduction of the input data, several cross-validation (CV) schemes for model evaluation/selection, however, keeping potential pitfalls in mind [35,52].

The human brain has a significantly high individual variability with substantial amount of information that needs to be analysed. To count neurons manually can be an extremely time-consuming process to perform by human eye observations alone. Non-homogeneous brain shrinkage is one major challenge where, in combination, imaging and AI/ML may be effective. By providing a huge amount of information for histology, several ML methods can help to validate in vivo MRI findings and MRI limitations. This leads to improving and enhancing the capabilities of MRI through the identification of even more alterations. Moreover, in brain informatics problems include the detection and interpretation of volume changes in neurodegenerative diseases and more global aspects such as brain volume, gyration, cortical thickness, hippocampal shape changes and allometric studies correlating, for example, cortical volume with hippocampal and subcortical nuclear volume in schizophrenics.

As a first step, by using different contrasts in MRI, one can obtain more information, not only regarding volume quantification, but also iron deposition, myelin quantification and brain parcellation with myeloarchitectonics [39] and other sequences. Architectonics is considered to reflect the functional properties of the brain and its surface. The manifold problems with such approaches include the high-dimensionality of the data, which would make standard approaches of AI awkward, yet impossible to use, therefore, it is necessary to harness the full potential of current AI/ML. As a next step, one can attempt to quantify the architectonics, the size of defined fields, and correlate with their normative data for different diseases and normal ageing. Due to the high individual variability of the brain, these studies will require investigating extensive data. For this step, accessing and analysing the large database using simple methods will most likely lead to a null finding. We hypothesize that this is a matter of AI to find an invariably recurring parameter that has escaped human attention (e.g. due to noisy data).

However, one must take care when discussing AI in the context of initial/early stages of neurodegenerative or neuropsychiatric diseases. It is necessary to perform both MRI and volumetry when there is no access to the tissue. It is also important to take into consideration that changes other than visible changes (e.g. volume) are causing symptoms in the early and later stages of schizophrenia or depression. In addition, from a clinical and neuropsychiatric view, schizophrenia itself is very challenging and complicated. It is the same matter as assessing proficiency based on the size of the brain. Many would assume that bigger brains are more proficient than smaller brains, however, the contrary can be true because one can find small brains in highly intelligent people and vice versa.

Generally, next to imaging there are genetic biomarkers for disease classification but these are applicable only in specific cases. Established biomarkers for Alzheimer's disease (AD), Parkinson's disease (PD) and Huntington's disease (HD) are based on visual analysis including MRI. Genetic variants of apolipoprotein E, tau as well as amyloid precursor protein or presenilin 1 and 2 are significant for AD, however, they are not imperative for the development of the disease, thus, are not reliably applicable for diagnosis. So far, AD is diagnosed clinically by a patient's detailed history and mental state and finally determined pathologically by brain autopsy [10,70].

The use of imaging to to diagnose the cause of death (virtual autopsy) has already proven its value, although it has limitations, especially regarding microscopic changes [52]. The possibility of having postmortem MRI in a high number of cases, with histology included, is an invaluable combination to validate the usefulness of MRI in this setting. This is in regards to, not only cases, but also healthy controls, and it provides more understanding to populational variability. Imaging yields an immense number of data and data needs to be interpreted. There is a region of transition between pure statistical analysis of data and interpretation by AI. One strategy is the investigation of brains from persons with well-characterized disabilities. A good example is Alzheimer's Disease, where the visual inspection of neuroimagery is susceptible to limitations of human vision; here AI methods have shown to be equally or even more effective than human clinicians in diagnosing dementia from neuroimages [16].

Pathognonomic indicators include cerebral atrophy and neurofibrillary tangle and amyloid plaque pathology. The likelihood and/or course of HD can be genetically tested by the determination of the number of cytosine-adenine-guanine (CAG)-repeats [12] of Huntingtin; the gene product of the affected gene on chromosome 4. The neuropathological interaction between early striatal and cortical atrophy proved to be puzzling [17] and imaging of prodromal cerebral cortical changes is difficult to detect [48]. An exemplary novel approach of disease characterization has been recently described for AD. The technique is based on imaging of brain structural connectivity atrophy in combination with a multiplex network for generating a classification score [1]. Automated differentiation of PD has been described also based on various ML derived classification algorithms using quantitative MRI data [19].

3.2 AI/ML Methods

A myriad of different AI and ML methods exist, so we scratch the surface here and focus our description only on Deep Learning (DL), which we recommend for these particular studies. We refer the reader to [21] for an overview of ML in general, and to [6,14,20] for more specific details. AI-aided diagnosis has been used as a supporting tool for physicians for a long time [5,63]. Due to the increasing computational power and available storage capacities, many methods, which proved to be computationally-demanding in the past, can now sufficiently be used in daily routine. Standard examples of state-of-the-art methods today, include not only DL [2], but also Support Vector Machines (SVM) [11] and Random Forests (RF) [7].

Among these methods, DL is rapidly proving to be the state-of-the-art foundation, leading to improved accuracy. It has also opened up new frontiers in biomedical data analysis generally, and in clinical medicine specifically, with astonishing rates of progress [15]. In favour of AI-aided diagnosis, quantitative changes could be evaluated in combination with functional neuroimaging and interpretation of big data in a longitudinal setting.

Recent work has been performed relating to automatic detection and classification of cell nuclei in histopathological images of cancerous tissue [61]. The authors applied DL [33] and produced encouraging results by applying a so-called Spatially Constrained Convolutional Neural Network (SC-CNN) [53] to perform nucleus detection. SC-CNN regresses the likelihood of a pixel being the centre of a nucleus, where high probability values are spatially constrained to locate in the vicinity of the centers of nuclei.

However, the current approaches in ML and neuroimaging do not facilitate essential mechanistic investigations validation by way of histology. Rather than only showing the ability to detect patterns of brain alterations, ML can also benefit from improving knowledge about algorithm choices and particular characteristics of precision power related to specific disease mechanisms.

3.3 Multimodal Deep Learning in Medical Imaging

In the machine learning context, algorithms dealing with data from multiple heterogeneous sources are referred to as "multimodal" or "multi-view" learning algorithms [47]. The advantages of using multimodal deep learning in the biomedical context are: (i) they require little or no pre-processing input data, because both features and fused representations are learned from data; (ii) they perform implicit dimensionality reduction within the architecture, which is a desired property in feature-rich biomedical datasets; (iii) they support early, late, or intermediate fusion [69]. However, they usually require powerful graphics processing units (GPUs) for reasonable training time.

Multimodal deep learning can be used to solve complex machine learning problems in areas of high dimensional unstructured data like computer vision, speech and natural language processing. The main advantage of deep learning is that, it automatically learns hierarchical representation for each modality instead of manually designing modality-specific features that are then fed with machine learning algorithm. In medical image analysis, the medical expert can use multiple image modalities information, e.g. computed tomography (CT), magnetic resonance imaging (MRI), and ultrasound imaging for diagnosis and treatment. Therefore, multimodal deep learning is suitable for medical applications issues like tissue and segmentation, multimodal medical image retrieval and computer-aided diagnosis. There are however two significant challenges faced by the medical applications community when using multimodal deep learning, namely the difficulty in obtaining sufficient labelled data, and class imbalance [57].

Multimodal deep learning is widely used for brain imaging studies. Collecting data of magnetic resonance imaging (MRI) of multiple modalities of the same individual is popular in brain imaging studies. Multimodal brain imaging study can provide a more comprehensive understanding of the brain and its disorders. For instance, it can inform us about how brain structure shapes brain function, in which way they are impacted by psychopathology, and which structural aspects of physiology could drive human behaviour and cognition [9].

Multimodal medical image fusion techniques are the most significant methods to identify and investigate disease to provide complementary information from different multimodalities. Multimodal medical images can be categorized into several types, which include computed tomography (CT), magnetic resonance angiography (MRA), magnetic resonance imaging (MRI), positron emission tomography (PET), ultra sonography (USG), nuclear magnetic resonance (NMR) spectroscopy, single photon emission computed tomography (SPECT), X-rays, visible, infrared and ultraviolet. Structural therapeutic images are MRI, CT, USG and MRA, which provide high-resolution images. Functional therapeutic images are PET, SPECT and functional MRI (fMRI) which provide low-spatial resolution images with useful information.

Multimodal medical image fusion increases the effectiveness of image-guided disease analysis, diagnosis and assessment of medical problems. Image fusion has several applications like medical imaging, biometrics, automatic change detection, machine vision, navigation aid, military applications, remote sensing, digital imaging, aerial and satellite imaging, robot vision, multi focus imaging, microscopic imaging, digital photography and concealed weapon detection [55]. Due to their versatility, multimodal algorithms can be used in wider biomedical applications involving genomics, proteomics, metabolomics and other types of omics data. Interestingly, they have been successfully used when the features originate from different domains, and some of them are generated by mechanistic models [67]. In this case, preprocessing of the features, coupled with late or intermediate fusion should be preferred to early fusion. This approach, based on computational systems biology and machine learning, could provide key mechanistic insights into neurological disorders [60].

Medical image segmentation is a challenging task in medical image analysis. Multimodal deep learning has been used in medical imaging, especially for providing multi-information about the target (tumour, organ or tissue). Segmentation using multimodal has been implemented as a fusion of multi-information to improve segmentation [36]. Deep learning provides state-of-the-art performance in image classification, segmentation, object detection and tracking tasks. Recently, deep learning has gained interest in multimodal image segmentation because of its self-learning and simplification ability over a large amount of data [71].

3.4   Databases for AI/ML

Reproducibility, validation and prediction benefit from existing imaging data and related information. There already exist some databases that provide open data for modeling, testing and inferring [28,41,54]. Thereupon these web resources, some information is provided about AI or ML approaches. However, both reliable data containing patient data as well as ML performance depend largely on the studied disease and its features. Some example of data from animal models include the Cambridge MRI database (this provides open phenotypic data for animal models of HD [59]), and the Mouse Tumor Biology Database (this provides different kinds of information on tumors in mice [8]). Moreover, the project BRAINS provides anonymised images and related clinical information from healthy subjects across human life span via data request and access agreement [29]. The Open Access Series of Imaging Studies provides MRI data sets of subjects clinically diagnosed with Alzheimer's disease [37]. Functional MRI data from subjects with Huntington's disease can be found within Track-HD study [64]. The Parkinson's Disease Biomarkers Program provides access to brain scans and related information for researchers [49].

Classification of disease subtypes, subjects, brain regions, and gradings are often based on ML approaches via automatically segmenting brain MRI data [23]. Making use of such databases, ML not only helps in (semi-)automatically segmenting images, but it is also a tool for trying to answer several research questions, for example predicting tumor growth [27] or investigating minimal tumor burden and therapy resistance by cancer patients [50,51]. Some case reports also show AI outperforming human domain experts [18,31,56]. Recent advances already try to bridge imaging and genetic studies. Imaging genetic studies combine investigations of genotype and imaging phenotype to better understand brain structure, function and the further cause and effects of a specific disease. Imaging genetics studies improve our understanding of pathways that are related to the cause or effect in cerebral disorders [30]. Genome-wide association studies suggest genetic relationships for structural as well as functional measures among family members [65].

3.5   AI-Aided Disease Classification Using Chemical Imaging

Further use of chemicals, such as metabolic biomarkers, on imaging basis could be included, for example, in therapy monitoring on a cellular basis [46]. AI-aided diagnosis for clinical purposes and computational models for prediction could involve quantitative changes next to functional imaging built upon brain MRI data. In this regard, molecular fMRI techniques exhibit the specificity for neural pathways or signaling components at cellular-level specificity [4]. The method of fMRI has been used to study time-resolved volumetric measurements of dopamine release [34]. Chemical exchange saturation transfer allows for signal-amplification of, for example, deoxyglucose and its phosphorylated metabolite in order to image glucose uptake [45]. This technique of MR imaging has been used to image glucose uptake in head and neck cancer [66]. Proton MRS is commonly used for studies on brain metabolites, including the marker of neuroaxonal integrity N-acetylaspartate, cholin for membrane turnovers, (phospho) creatine for energy metabolism and myo-inositol for astroglial activation [44].

MR techniques for imaging brain metabolism can assist in the studying of brain disorders, in aid of novel MRI contrasts for visualizing neuronal firing across brain regions, pH imaging of glioma and both glutamatergic neurotransmission and cell-specific energetics [26]. The understanding of oxidative metabolism plays a fundamental role in many diseases, which supports demand for the development of non-invasive methods for routine analyses [42].

3.6   Explainable AI

There are several methods which are relevant for further studies and for testing whether and to what extent they can be useful to contribute towards the aforementioned use-cases. Six of the most relevant include: BETA, LRP, LIME as well as GAMs, Bayesian Rule Lists and Hybrid Models, particularly with a human-in-the-loop. BETA (Black Box Explanations through Transparent Approximations) is a model-agnostic framework for explaining the behavior of black-box classifiers by instantaneously optimizing for fidelity to the original model and interpretability of the explanation [32]. There is also a more general solution to the problem of understanding classification decisions by pixel-wise decomposition of nonlinear classifiers which allows visualizing the contributions of single pixels to predictions for kernel-based classifiers over bag of words features and for multilayered neural networks [3].

LRP (Layer-Wise Relevance Propagation) is another general solution for understanding classification decisions via pixel decomposition of nonlinear classifiers, which allows running the "thought processes" backwards [3,43]. This enables to retrace which input had which influence on the respective result. In individual cases, this lets us understand how a deep learning method has come to a certain medical diagnosis or a risk assessment. LIME (Local Interpretable Model-Agnostic Explanations) developed by Ribeiro, Singh and Guestrin [58] is a model-agnostic system, where $x \in \mathbb{R}^d$ is the original representation of an instance being explained, and $x' \in \mathbb{R}^{d'}$ is used to denote a vector for its interpretable representation (e.g. x' may be a feature vector containing word embeddings, with x' being the bag of words). The goal is to identify an interpretable model over the interpretable representation that is locally faithful to the classifier, i.e.

$$g : \mathbb{R}^{d'} \to \mathbb{R}, g \in G,$$

where G is a class of potentially interpretable models, such as linear models, decision trees, or rule lists etc.; given a model $g \in G$, it can be visualized as an explanation to the human expert in $\mathbb{R}^{\chi}$. LIME works separately with each instance, they are permuted and a measure of similarity to the original instances is calculated. Consequently, the complex model provides predictions for each of these permutated instances and the influences of the alterations can be understood for each instance. In this way, for example, a medical doctor can check whether and to what extent results can be realistic. All these models cannot explain why a certain decision has been made, which is a goal of current research to find out in the context of the aforementioned use cases.

In medical domains, the explainability and interpretability of algorithms are as critical as their performances [25]. It can be nearly impossible for a doctor or medical professional to effectively integrate their expert knowledge with a model's output unless they can interpret why that model made the decision that it did [22]. Over the past several decades, AI researchers have developed a wide range of techniques for interpretable and explainable classification. These techniques fall into four general categories: sensitivity analysis, linear approximation, rule-based decompositions, and models of causality.

Sensitivity analysis techniques attempt to model which regions of the input space are most important for the classification decision. For a neural network, the simplest sensitivity analysis technique is the "input gradient technique," which involves taking the (smoothed) gradient of the input features with respect to the model loss function [62]. Several sensitivity analysis techniques, including the above-mentioned LRP [43] and LIME [13,58] use a linear model to (locally) approximate a complex classifier, since linear models can be easily interpreted based on feature weights. LRP directly decomposes the model output on any training sample into the weighted sum of the model features, and LIME builds a linear classifier to approximate model behavior in the region of a particular training sample.

Rule-based algorithms represent a classification problem as a set of rules on the input features. These include algorithms like Decision Trees and Bayesian Rule Lists [68]. The most straightforward way to build these algorithms is to assemble them directly from the training data, but this approach can have extremely high variance and is often insufficient for modern applications. A more modern approach is to use rule-based algorithms to approximate pre-trained classifiers, similarly to how LIME and LRP approximate complex algorithms with linear functions. One example of this is the above-mentioned BETA algorithm, which builds a rule set to approximate a black box classifier [32]. The most direct way to build an explainable classifier is to directly model the causal relationships between the features and the classification output. The classic way to do this is to use a Bayesian Network [38] to model the conditional independences of features and latent factors, but this approach can be challenging to scale to the size of modern datasets and feature spaces.

4   Open Problems and Future Outlook

This paper entails exploring an intriguing subject. Our understanding of brain disease comes from different sources, but pathology remains to be one of the most important. However, it is a very time-consuming process because it requires manually performed tasks. On the other hand, MRI provides a lot of information on a larger scale, and has already seen major transformations with its use of AI. For cerebral disorders, we discussed in what way can AI generally, and ML specifically, contribute.

We hypothesized that AI can help to find invariably recurring parameters that have escaped human attention (e.g. due to noisy data) to validate diagnosis. In addition, AI helps to deal with an ever increasing amount of data that would take much longer to be analyzed manually. Several ML methods can help to identify and provide more meaningful information regarding the signals of different contrasts, location (with high resolution 7 T MRI), texture, size, dimension, patient information and specific patterns. Moreover, AI could be used to locate, correlate and compare all brain regions, in order to study the high individual variability of human gyri and sulci, signal variability, normal ageing process, clinical records and neurodegenerative diseases.

AI has the potential to go beyond helping filter out noise. One reason humans may be limited is not only due to the noise, but also due to wrong decisions on the feature space wrong. For example, in structural MRI, we automatically make the feature space a voxel. However, that unit results from the measurement technique, rather than any hypothesis or regularity about the brain or disease. There is great potential for AI to reveal other meaningful feature spaces, such as volume, heterogeneity, variability. It is possible that a meaningful feature space involves voxel-to-voxel relationships, or interdependencies, for example. Therefore, AI can help us elucidate the right feature spaces, eliminating or reducing human bias.

References

1. Amoroso, N., et al.: Brain structural connectivity atrophy in Alzheimer's disease. arXiv (2017)
2. Arel, I., Rose, D.C., Karnowski, T.P.: Deep machine learning - a new frontier in artificial intelligence research - research frontier. IEEE Comput. Intell. Mag. **5**, 4 (2010). https://doi.org/10.1109/MCI.2010.938364
3. Bach, S., Binder, A., Montavon, G., Klauschen, F., Müller, K.R., Samek, W.: On pixel-wise explanations for non-linear classifier decisions by layer-wise relevance propagation. PloS one **10**(7), e0130140 (2015)

4. Bartelle, B.B., Barandov, A., Jasanoff, A.: Molecular fMRI. J. Neurosci. **36**(15), 4139–4148 (2016)
5. Baxt, W.G.: Use of an artificial neural network for the diagnosis of myocardial infarction. Ann. Intern. Med. **115**, 11 (1991)
6. Bishop, C.M.: Pattern Recognition and Machine Learning. Springer, Heidelberg (2006)
7. Breiman, L.: Random forests. Mach. Learn. **45**, 1 (2001). https://doi.org/10.1023/A:1010933404324
8. Bult, C.J.: Mouse tumor biology (MTB): a database of mouse models for human cancer. Nucleic Acids Res. **43**, D818–D824 (2014). https://doi.org/10.1093/nar/gku987
9. Calhoun, V.D., Sui, J.: Multimodal fusion of brain imaging data: a key to finding the missing link(s) in complex mental illness. Biol. Psychiatry Cogn. Neurosci. Neuroimaging **1**(3), 230–244 (2016)
10. Daffner, K.: Current approaches to the clinical diagnosis of Alzheimer's disease. In: Scinto, L.F.M., Daffner, K.R. (eds.) Early Diagnosis of Alzheimer's Disease. Current Clinical Neurology, pp. 29–64. Humana Press, Totowa (2000). https://doi.org/10.1007/978-1-59259-005-6_2
11. Furey, T.S., Cristianini, N., Duffy, N., Bednarski, D.W., Schummer, M., Haussler, D.: Support vector machine classification and validation of cancer tissue samples using microarray expression data. Bioinformatics **16**, 10 (2000)
12. Gardiner, S.L., van Belzen, M.J., Boogaard, M.W., et al.: Huntingtin gene repeat size variations affect risk of lifetime depression. Transl. Psychiatry **7**, 1277 (2017). https://doi.org/10.1038/s41398-017-0042-1
13. Gilpin, L.H., Bau, D., Yuan, B.Z., Bajwa, A., Specter, M., Kagal, L.: Explaining explanations: an overview of interpretability of machine learning. arXiv preprint arXiv:1806.00069 (2018)
14. Goodfellow, I., Bengio, Y., Courville, A.: Deep Learning. MIT Press, Cambridge (2016)
15. Greenspan, H., Van Ginneken, B., Summers, R.M.: Guest editorial deep learning in medical imaging: overview and future promise of an exciting new technique. IEEE Trans. Med. Imaging **35**, 5 (2016)
16. Gupta, A., Ayhan, M., Maida, A.: In natural image bases to represent neuroimaging data. In: International Conference on Machine Learning, pp. 987–994 (2013)
17. Hadzi, T.C., et al.: Assessment of cortical and striatal involvement in 523 Huntington disease brains. Neurology **79**, 1708–1715 (2012)
18. He, K., Zhang, X., Ren, S., Sun, J.: Delving deep into rectifiers: surpassing human-level performance on ImageNet classification. In: Proceedings of the IEEE International Conference on Computer Vision, pp. 1026–1034 (2015)
19. Heim, B., et al.: Magnetic resonance imaging for the diagnosis of Parkinson's disease. J. Neural Transm. **124**, 8 (2017)
20. Holzinger, A.: Introduction to machine learning and knowledge extraction (make). Mach. Learn. Knowl. Extr. **1**(1), 1–20 (2017)
21. Holzinger, A., et al.: Machine learning and knowledge extraction in digital pathology needs an integrative approach. In: Holzinger, A., Goebel, R., Ferri, M., Palade, V. (eds.) Towards Integrative Machine Learning and Knowledge Extraction. LNCS (LNAI), vol. 10344, pp. 13–50. Springer, Cham (2017). https://doi.org/10.1007/978-3-319-69775-8_2
22. Holzinger, A., Carrington, A., Müller, H.: Measuring the quality of explanations: The system causability scale (scs). Comparing human and machine explanations.

KI - Künstliche Intelligenz (German J. Artif. Intell.). Special Issue on Interactive Machine Learning, Edited by Kristian Kersting, TU Darmstadt **34**(2) (2020). https://doi.org/10.1007/s13218-020-00636-z

23. Holzinger, A., Goebel, R., Palade, V., Ferri, M.: Towards integrative machine learning and knowledge extraction. In: Holzinger, A., Goebel, R., Ferri, M., Palade, V. (eds.) Towards Integrative Machine Learning and Knowledge Extraction. LNCS (LNAI), vol. 10344, pp. 1–12. Springer, Cham (2017). https://doi.org/10.1007/978-3-319-69775-8_1

24. Holzinger, A., Kieseberg, P., Weippl, E., Tjoa, A.M.: Current advances, trends and challenges of machine learning and knowledge extraction: from machine learning to explainable AI. In: Holzinger, A., Kieseberg, P., Tjoa, A.M., Weippl, E. (eds.) CD-MAKE 2018. LNCS, vol. 11015, pp. 1–8. Springer, Cham (2018). https://doi.org/10.1007/978-3-319-99740-7_1

25. Holzinger, A., Langs, G., Denk, H., Zatloukal, K., Mueller, H.: Causability and explainability of artificial intelligence in medicine. Wiley Interdisc. Rev. Data Min. Knowl. Disc. **9**(4), e1312 (2019). https://doi.org/10.1002/widm.1312

26. Hyder, F., Rothman, D.: Advances in imaging brain metabolism. Ann. Rev. Biomed. Eng. **19**, 485–515 (2017)

27. Jeanquartier, F., et al.: Machine learning for *in silico* modeling of tumor growth. In: Holzinger, A. (ed.) Machine Learning for Health Informatics. LNCS (LNAI), vol. 9605, pp. 415–434. Springer, Cham (2016). https://doi.org/10.1007/978-3-319-50478-0_21

28. Jeanquartier, F., Jean-Quartier, C., Schreck, T., Cemernek, D., Holzinger, A.: Integrating open data on cancer in support to tumor growth analysis. In: Renda, M.E., Bursa, M., Holzinger, A., Khuri, S. (eds.) ITBAM 2016. LNCS, vol. 9832, pp. 49–66. Springer, Cham (2016). https://doi.org/10.1007/978-3-319-43949-5_4

29. Job, D.E., et al.: A brain imaging repository of normal structural MRI across the life course: brain images of normal subjects (brains). NeuroImage **144**, 299–304 (2017)

30. Klein, M., et al.: Brain imaging genetics in ADHD and beyond- mapping pathways from gene to disorder at different levels of complexity. Neurosci. Biobehav. Rev. **80**, 115–155 (2017). https://doi.org/10.1016/j.neubiorev.2017.01.013

31. Klöppel, S., Abdulkadir, A., Jack, C.R., Koutsouleris, N., Mourão-Miranda, J., Vemuri, P.: Diagnostic neuroimaging across diseases. Neuroimage **61**(2), 457–463 (2012)

32. Lakkaraju, H., Kamar, E., Caruana, R., Leskovec, J.: Interpretable and explorable approximations of black box models. arXiv preprint arXiv:1707.01154 (2017)

33. Lecun, Y., Bengio, Y., Hinton, G.: Deep learning. Nature **521**, 7553 (2015). https://doi.org/10.1038/nature14539

34. Lee, T., Cai, L.X., Lelyveld, V.S., Hai, A., Jasanoff, A.: Molecular-level functional magnetic resonance imaging of dopaminergic signaling. Science **344**(6183), 533–535 (2014)

35. Lemm, S., Blankertz, B., Dickhaus, T., Mueller, K.R.: Introduction to machine learning for brain imaging. Neuroimage **10**(1016), 387–399 (2011)

36. Li, C., Sun, H., Liu, Z., Wang, M., Zheng, H., Wang, S.: Learning cross-modal deep representations for multi-modal MR image segmentation. In: Shen, D., et al. (eds.) MICCAI 2019. LNCS, vol. 11765, pp. 57–65. Springer, Cham (2019). https://doi.org/10.1007/978-3-030-32245-8_7

37. Marcus, D.S., Wang, T.H., Parker, J., Csernansky, J.G., Morris, J.C., Buckner, R.L.: Open access series of imaging studies (OASIS): cross-sectional mri data in young, middle aged, nondemented, and demented older adults. J. Cogn. Neurosci. **19**(9), 1498–1507 (2007)
38. Margaritis, D.: Learning Bayesian network model structure from data. Ph.D. thesis, Carnegie-Mellon University Pittsburgh PA School Of Computer Science (2003)
39. Marques, J.P., et al.: Studying cyto and myeloarchitecture of the human cortex at ultra-high field with quantitative imaging: R1, R2(*) and magnetic susceptibility. Neuroimage **147**, 152 (2017)
40. Martino, D., et al.: The differential diagnosis of Huntington's disease-like syndromes: 'red flags' for the clinician. J. Neurol. Neurosurg. Psychiatry **84**, 650–656 (2013)
41. Di Martino, A., et al.: The autism brain imaging data exchange: towards a large-scale evaluation of the intrinsic brain architecture in autism. Mol. Psychiatry **19**(6), 659–667 (2014)
42. Mellon, E.A., Beesam, R.S., Elliott, M.A., Reddy, R.: Mapping of cerebral oxidative metabolism with MRI. Proc. Nat. Acad. Sci. **107**(26), 11787–11792 (2010)
43. Montavon, G., Binder, A., Lapuschkin, S., Samek, W., Müller, K.-R.: Layer-wise relevance propagation: an overview. In: Samek, W., Montavon, G., Vedaldi, A., Hansen, L.K., Müller, K.-R. (eds.) Explainable AI: Interpreting, Explaining and Visualizing Deep Learning. LNCS (LNAI), vol. 11700, pp. 193–209. Springer, Cham (2019). https://doi.org/10.1007/978-3-030-28954-6_10
44. Mormina, E., et al.: Cerebellum and neurodegenerative diseases: beyond conventional magnetic resonance imaging. World J. Radiol. **9**(10), 371–388 (2017). https://doi.org/10.4329/wjr.v9.i10.371
45. Nasrallah, F.A.: Imaging brain deoxyglucose uptake and metabolism by gluco-CEST MRI. J. Cereb. Blood Flow Metab. **33**(8), 1270–1278 (2013)
46. Ngen, E.J., Artemov, D.: Advances in monitoring cell-based therapies with magnetic resonance imaging: future perspectives. Int. J. Mol. Sci. **18**, 1 (2017)
47. Ngiam, J., Khosla, A., Kim, M., Nam, J., Lee, H., Ng, A.Y.: Multimodal deep learning. In: Proceedings of the 28th International Conference on Machine Learning (ICML-2011), pp. 689–696 (2011)
48. Nopoulos, P.C., et al.: Cerebral cortex structure in prodromal Huntington disease. Neurobiol. Dis. **40**, 544–554 (2010). https://doi.org/10.4322/acr.2018.003
49. Ofori, E., Du, G., Babcock, D., Huang, X., Vaillancourt, D.E.: Parkinson's disease biomarkers program brain imaging repository. Neuroimage **124**, 1120–1124 (2016). https://doi.org/10.1186/s40708-019-0096-3
50. O'Sullivan, S., Holzinger, A., Zatloukal, K., Saldiva, P., Sajid, M.I., Wichmann, D.: Machine learning enhanced virtual autopsy. Autops. Case Rep. **7**(4), 3–7 (2017). https://doi.org/10.4322/acr.2017.037
51. O'Sullivan, S., Holzinger, A., Wichmann, D., Saldiva, P., Sajid, M., Zatloukal, K.: Virtual autopsy: machine learning and artificial intelligence provide new opportunities for investigating minimal tumor burden and therapy resistance by cancer patients. Autops. Case Rep. **8**, 1 (2018). https://doi.org/10.4322/acr.2018.003
52. O'Sullivan, S., et al.: The role of artificial intelligence and machine learning in harmonization of high-resolution post-mortem MRI (virtopsy) with respect to brain microstructure. Brain Inform. **6**(1), 3 (2019). https://doi.org/10.1186/s40708-019-0096-3
53. Pathak, D., Krahenbuhl, P., Darrell, T.: Constrained convolutional neural networks for weakly supervised segmentation. In: Proceedings of the IEEE International Conference on Computer Vision, pp. 1796–1804 (2015)

54. Poldrack, R.A., Gorgolewski, K.J.: Making big data open: data sharing in neuroimaging. Nature Neurosci. **17**(11), 1510–1517 (2014)

55. Rajalingam, B., Priya, R.: Multimodal medical image fusion based on deep learning neural network for clinical treatment analysis. Int. J. Chem. Tech. Res. CODEN (USA) IJCRGG **11**, 0974–4290 (2018). ISSN

56. Rajpurkar, P., et al.: Chexnet: radiologist-level pneumonia detection on chest x-rays with deep learning. arXiv preprint arXiv:1711.05225 (2017)

57. Ramachandram, D., Taylor, G.W.: Deep multimodal learning: a survey on recent advances and trends. IEEE Signal Process. Mag. **34**(6), 96–108 (2017)

58. Ribeiro, M.T., Singh, S., Guestrin, C.: Why should i trust you?: Explaining the predictions of any classifier. In: Proceedings of the 22nd ACM SIGKDD International Conference on Knowledge Discovery and Data Mining, pp. 1135–1144. ACM (2016)

59. Sawiak, S.J., Morton, A.J.: The cambridge MRI database for animal models of Huntington disease. NeuroImage **124**, 1260–1262 (2016)

60. Sertbas, M., Ulgen, K.O.: Unlocking human brain metabolism by genome-scale and multiomics metabolic models: relevance for neurology research, health, and disease. OMICS **22**(7), 455–467 (2018)

61. Sirinukunwattana, K., Raza, S.E.A., Tsang, Y.W., Snead, D.R., Cree, I.A., Rajpoot, N.M.: Locality sensitive deep learning for detection and classification of nuclei in routine colon cancer histology images. IEEE Trans. Med. Imaging **35**, 5 (2016)

62. Smilkov, D., Thorat, N., Kim, B., Viégas, F., Wattenberg, M.: SmoothGrad: removing noise by adding noise. arXiv preprint arXiv:1706.03825 (2017)

63. Szolovits, P., Patil, R.S., Schwartz, W.B.: Artificial intelligence in medical diagnosis. Ann. Intern. Med. **108**, 1 (1988)

64. Tabrizi, S.J., et al.: Biological and clinical manifestations of Huntington's disease in the longitudinal TRACK-HD study: cross-sectional analysis of baseline data. Lancet Neurol. **8**(9), 791–801 (2009). https://doi.org/10.1016/S1474-4422(09)70170-X

65. Thompson, P.M., et al.: The enigma consortium: large-scale collaborative analyses of neuroimaging and genetic data. Brain Imaging Behav. **8**(2), 153–182 (2014)

66. Wang, J., et al.: Magnetic resonance imaging of glucose uptake and metabolism in patients with head and neck cancer. Sci. Rep. **6**, 30618 (2016)

67. Yaneske, E., Angione, C.: The poly-omics of ageing through individual-based metabolic modelling. BMC Bioinform. **19**(14), 415 (2018)

68. Yang, H., Rudin, C., Seltzer, M.: Scalable Bayesian rule lists. arXiv preprint arXiv:1602.08610 (2016)

69. Zampieri, G., Vijayakumar, S., Yaneske, E., Angione, C.: Machine and deep learning meet genome-scale metabolic modeling. PLoS Comput. Biol. **15**(7), e1007084 (2019)

70. Zhang, X., et al.: PET/MR imaging: new frontier in Alzheimer's disease and other dementias. Front. Mol. Neurosci. **10**, 343 (2017)

71. Zhou, T., Ruan, S., Canu, S.: A review: deep learning for medical image segmentation using multi-modality fusion. Array **3–4**, 100004 (2019)

Fuzzy Image Processing and Deep Learning for Microaneurysms Detection

Sarni Suhaila Rahim[1,2(✉)], Vasile Palade[1], Ibrahim Almakky[1], and Andreas Holzinger[3]

[1] Faculty of Engineering, Environment and Computing, Coventry University, Priory Street, Coventry CV1 5FB, UK
{ad0490,ab5839,ab8961}@coventry.ac.uk

[2] Faculty of Information and Communication Technology, Universiti Teknikal Malaysia Melaka, Hang Tuah Jaya, 76100 Durian Tunggal, Melaka, Malaysia
sarni@utem.edu.my

[3] Institute for Medical Informatics, Statistics and Documentation, Medical University Graz, Graz, Austria
andreas.holzinger@medunigraz.at

Abstract. Diabetic retinopathy is an eye disease generated by long-standing diabetes, and it is one of the main causes of vision loss if not diagnosed and treated properly. Diabetic retinopathy consists of several types of lesions found in the retina of diabetic individuals. One of the important lesions of diabetic retinopathy is microaneurysms, which are small red dots that appear due to the local weakness of the capillary walls. This paper presents a novel automatic microaneurysms detection method, in retinal images by employing fuzzy image processing and deep learning. Firstly, the paper explores the existing systems of diabetic retinopathy screening, with a focus on the microaneurysms detection methods and deep learning classification. The proposed system consists of two parts, namely: image preprocessing with a combination of fuzzy image processing techniques, and also the microaneurysms classification using deep neural networks. This paper investigates the capability of a combination of different fuzzy image preprocessing techniques for the detection of microaneurysms in eye fundus images. In addition to the proposed microaneurysms detection system, the paper also highlights a novel dataset for the microaneurysms detection that includes the ground truth data. The purpose of the proposed automated microaneurysm detection with digital analysis of eye fundus images is to substitute current practice that is based on manual diagnosis and visual inspection, and eventually to contribute to producing a more reliable diabetic retinopathy screening system.

Keywords: Diabetic Retinopathy · Microaneurysms · Fuzzy image processing · Deep learning · Colour fundus images · Eye screening

1 Introduction

Diabetic Retinopathy (DR) is one of the major complications of diabetes mellitus, which causes blindness. In the early phases of the disease, diabetic retinopathy is asymptomatic,

© Springer Nature Switzerland AG 2020
A. Holzinger et al. (Eds.): AI & ML for Digital Pathology, LNAI 12090, pp. 321–339, 2020.
https://doi.org/10.1007/978-3-030-50402-1_19

where diabetic patients are unaware of their diabetes condition and the retinopathy changes. Therefore, screening is necessary for an early detection of DR and to identify the group at risk of losing vision.

Diabetes mellitus is a growing problem, with high numbers of diabetics reported each year all over the world. A user/patient friendly and cost effective screening tool is required to take care of such large number of individuals at risk, without compromising the care standard. Early detection through the screening and effective risk management would help avoid complications of diabetes and eventually reduce the mortality. According to Mathers and Loncar [1], in the year of 2014, the number of diabetic people was 422 million. World Health Organization (WHO) reveals that diabetes is one of the major causes of blindness, in addition to heart attack, kidney failure, stroke and also lower limb amputation [2]. In addition, it is claimed in [2] that, recently, approximately 1.3 billion people live with vision impairment worldwide. Furthermore, people over 50 years form the majority with vision impairment and it is considered that 80% of all vision impairment cases are preventable [2]. Diabetic retinopathy is one of the leading reasons of vision impairment [2], besides glaucoma, cataract, uncorrected refractive errors, age-related macular degeneration, corneal opacity and trachoma.

Screening of diabetic retinopathy is one of the primary and important ways for preventing loss of vision. Cunha-Vaz [3] reports that there is an urgent need to create software with automatic methods to detect retinopathy, mainly by digital analysis of the retinal photographs. Therefore, the proposed image processing based system aims to be able to detect the presence of early stage diabetic retinopathy signs, which is microaneurysms, and direct those patients for further management, i.e., follow-up and appropriate treatment.

This paper focuses on the microaneurysms detection, one of the earliest and important features of diabetic retinopathy. Microaneurysms are small dots found on the retina, resulted from the ballooning out process of a weak capillary wall. Microaneurysms initially appear as small red dots, which may later become yellowish due to the related leakage, and which finally occlude [3]. According to Taylor and Batey [4], in a small number of cases, microaneurysms which are found outside the macular region should not disturb the sight of the patient, and they are detectable only via photography. However, the microaneurysms detection at an initial phase is vital, and it is the first step towards the diabetic retinopathy prevention. Figure 1 shows the fundus photograph image of a diabetic retinopathy eye showing microaneurysms signs.

The detection of microaneurysms is considered a challenging task. According to the medical expert from the Department of Ophthalmology, Melaka Hospital, Malaysia, the counting of microaneurysms is very difficult because of the following issues: (a) In the case microaneurysms are present, there will be many of them indeed and this will produce an inaccurate counting. The counting process becomes even more complicated in the case of overlapping microaneurysms (b) Microaneurysms could be simply confused with blot haemorrhages, as they have almost the same size. Therefore, this chapter proposes a novel development of a microaneurysms detection system, by introducing fuzzy image processing approaches to overcome those challenges. The developed methodology uses a novel dataset collected from the Melaka Hospital, Malaysia.

This chapter is structured as follows. Section 2 presents some previous related research work on automatic methods for diabetic retinopathy detection, focusing on detection methods for microaneurysms. The section is divided into two sub-sections for better understanding, comprising the developed microaneurysms detection system and deep learning methods. Meanwhile, Sect. 3 defines in detail the newly developed dataset, which highlights the microaneurysms ground truth. Section 4 explains the proposed system for the detection of microaneurysms in eye fundus images by implementing fuzzy image processing techniques and deep learning. Finally, Sect. 5 concludes the proposed work and presents some future work.

2 Related Work

There are several previously developed systems reported in the literature that aimed for automatic diabetic retinopathy detection and diagnosis. Some are general detection systems for diabetic retinopathy, which classify the fundus image into two general detection classes, i.e., retinopathy absence and retinopathy presence [28–35]. Moreover, some other systems focus on the diabetic retinopathy features' detection, namely microaneurysms, haemorrhages, exudates and others [6–22, 36–43]. The automatic localisation of microaneurysms is still considered as a very challenging task, and, thus, further study is required in order to find appropriate methods for this purpose.

2.1 Microaneurysms Detection

Automatic detection methods aim to highlight the issues of manual screening, such as time consuming, low sensitivity, high cost and, most importantly, low human detection ability. Several systems for the detection of microaneurysms have been reported in the literature [6–22], where various techniques and methods were proposed, which aim to create a reliable system. However, the reported microaneurysms detection systems have not implemented fuzzy processing during the preprocessing stage and deep learning for the classification.

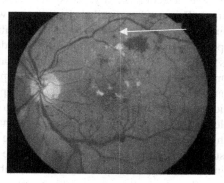

Fig. 1. Microaneurysm representation [5]

In our earlier work, a basic system for general diabetic retinopathy detection has been proposed by implementing a combination of non-fuzzy techniques [23]. In addition, several individual systems for the automatic detection of microaneurysms in colour eye fundus images have also been reported in [24]. The first system proposed the automatic localisation of microaneurysms in colour eye fundus images using segmentation of blood vessels and extraction of some related features. The second system highlights an image processing techniques combination and circular Hough transform, while the third system performed the microaneurysms detection by implementing fuzzy image processing. The third developed system proposed the use of a method called circular Hough transform for the microaneurysms localisation, due to the ability of this method in detecting circular shapes. The third system which consists of two subsystems, where the first subsystem proposed image processing techniques combination and also circular Hough transform method, while the second system variant presented fuzzy image processing techniques for the detection of microaneurysms. Both systems were compared to investigate the ability of implemented fuzzy image processing techniques. From the obtained results, it was summarised that the fuzzy preprocessing techniques implementation enable improved contrast enhancement for eye fundus images, and it greatly supports in the detection of the microaneurysms. The development of the microaneurysms detection system was enhanced in the fourth developed system, based on the promising results of the fuzzy histogram equalisation technique implementation to detect microaneurysms in the third developed system. The implementation of fuzzy filtering and also fuzzy edge detection, individually, besides the fuzzy histogram equalisation for the automatic localisation of microaneurysms was proposed in [25]. The reported analysis shows that the fuzzy pre-processing techniques implementation enhanced the contrast as well as other improvements, like better segmentation and brightness for fundus images. It also indicates that the use of fuzzy image processing techniques plays a significant part in generating a better image quality and performance.

The capability of a combination of different fuzzy image processing techniques has been investigated later, for the detection of diabetic retinopathy and maculopathy in eye fundus images, in [26]. This time, the proposed system implements fuzzy techniques in the image pre-processing part, by using fuzzy filtering, followed by the fuzzy histogram equalisation and fuzzy edge detection. Firstly, the system classified images into two classes (DR present or not). Then, a more detailed classification was done by classifying into ten classes of retinopathy, which provides more details about the disease stage. In addition to the proposed system, we also proposed a new dataset, which contains 600 colour eye fundus images [27]. We enhanced the combination of different fuzzy image processing techniques capability for the diabetic retinopathy and maculopathy detection with the retinal structures segmentation in [27]. This paper presented a novel combination of diabetic retinopathy detection as well as maculopathy detection in eye fundus images by implementing fuzzy image processing. The maculopathy detection is vital, since maculopathy will eventually cause vision loss if the affected macula is not timely treated. The results showed that employing fuzzy image processing in addition to the extraction of retinal structures can help create a more reliable diabetic retinopathy screening system. Hence, the proposed system in this chapter continues our previous work and implements a fuzzy techniques combination for the image pre-processing part for the detection of microaneurysms.

2.2 Microaneurysms Detection

Deep learning is a popular area of machine learning, where a model learns to perform classification tasks directly from images, texts or sound. A traditional machine learning classification workflow starts with manually extracting relevant features from the input data and uses them for classification. On the other hand deep learning automatically extracts the necessary features from the input data, which eliminates the need for feature engineering. Deep neural networks utilise multiple nonlinear processing layers to learn a nested hierarchy of representations. However, deep learning models require large amounts of training data that is usually costly to acquire, especially in the medical field.

The most popular deep learning approach to image classification is deep convolutional neural networks (DCNNs). The DCNN architecture is well suited to process two-dimensional data, such as images, as it utilizes the convolution operation. Recently deep learning has been gaining a lot of attention, where the recent advances in deep learning help meet user expectations, which is crucial for some applications. Deep learning have been used extensively in many application areas, such as automated driving, aerospace and defense, industrial automation, text processing, and others. For example, in medical research, deep learning has been used to automatically detect cancer cells [46, 47] and in other medical image processing tasks.

Deep learning has been previously implemented in the screening of diabetic retinopathy [28–43]. Automated diabetic retinopathy detection in eye fundus images employing deep learning have been proposed in [28–35]. These research works demonstrated and implemented different methods and structures, neural networks architectures, used different datasets, training and testing methods and grading, with various results and performances. In addition, some researchers proposed some image pre-processing techniques aiming to improve the quality of image and also the recognition of subtle features and, eventually, targeting to increase the classification accuracy. Among the pre-processing techniques proposed were resizing, normalisation, denoising, scaling, center, cropping, extraction of green channel and contrast enhancement, such as histogram equalisation and contrast limited adaptive histogram equalisation (CLAHE).

The research works demonstrated in [36–43] focus on a more specific detection of diabetic retinopathy signs, which is the detection of microneurysms. These research works presented the microaneurysms detection through the integration of a deep learning classification framework. Chudzik et al. [36] proposed a patch-based CNN for microaneurysms detection, with a network fine-tuning scheme called Interleaved Freezing. During the preprocessing phase, the green plane of the images are extracted followed by the application of the Otsu thresholding. Lam et al. [37] developed an automated method of localising microaneurysms and exudates with a limited number of training data, using five CNN models, i.e., AlexNet, VGG16, GoogleNet, ResNet and Inception-v3. The original images were cropped, normalised and classified using patch-based sliding-window approach.

Meanwhile, Hatanaka et al. [38] proposed the combination of three types of detectors, i.e., the double-ring filter, shape index based on the Hessian matrix and Gabor filter to conduct automated microaneurysms detection using deep CNNs. Dai et al. [39] developed an interleaved deep mining technique to cope with the unbalanced microaneurysms detection. Harangi et al. [40] proposed a deep learning-based approach for the detection of microaneurysms, with fusion of different individual deep CNN architectures. Shan and Li [41] implemented a Stacked Sparse Autoencoder (SSAE), as the automatic feature extractor, to learn from the image patches, and later fed into a Softmax Classifier (SMC) to categorize a patch into two classes, which are microaneurysms present or microaneurysms not present. In addition, microaneurysms detection in colour fundus images using a deep neural network with a dropout training procedure, using maxout activation function without preprocessing techniques or feature extraction, is presented by Haloi [42]. Tan and colleagues [43] proposed a 10-layer CNN to automatically segment and discriminate the diabetic retinopathy signs, such as exudates, haemorrhages and microaneurysms. The colour input image is normalised, and resulting areas that receive no light or little light will appear grey. Although the study shows that it is possible to get a single CNN to segment these diabetic retinopathy features on a wide range of fundus images with reasonable accuracy, however, the results show lower sensitivity for microaneurysms compared to the other two signs. This shows that the detection of microaneurysms is more difficult than the detection of other diabetic retinopathy signs.

It can be concluded that various approaches and different deep learning classifiers have been introduced to detect the microaneurysms. However, further study is required to find suitable techniques for the detection of microaneurysms, as the automated microaneurysms detection is still considered as a very challenging task. It can be concluded that within these previously reported diabetic retinopathy and microaneurysms detection systems using deep learning classification, fuzzy processing has not been implemented during the pre-processing stage. Therefore, the main impact of this chapter is proposing a combination of fuzzy image pre-processing techniques in detecting the microaneurysms with a deep learning classifier. The proposed developed approaches are evaluated with a new data set, and it offers an understanding into the appropriateness for utilisation in an automatic screening system for diabetic retinopathy.

3   Experimental Dataset

The newly developed dataset consists of a total of 600 colour fundus images from a 300 patient's folder collected from the Eye Clinic, Department of Ophthalmology, Melaka Hospital, Malaysia. The original images, which are sized 3872×2592 pixels stored in JPEG format, provide high-quality details. The information of the developed dataset are presented in [26], in Sect. 3-"Proposed System" and in [27], in Sect. 3-"Experimental Datasets". Initially, the 600 colour fundus images were classified by three experts from the Department of Ophthalmology, Melaka Hospital, Malaysia into ten retinopathy stages: No Diabetic Retinopathy (DR), Mild DR without maculopathy, Mild DR with maculopathy, Moderate DR without maculopathy, Moderate DR with maculopathy, Severe DR without maculopathy, Severe DR with maculopathy, Proliferative DR without maculopathy, Proliferative DR with maculopathy and Advanced Diabetic Eye Disease.

However, the mentioned dataset in [27] is focusing on the ten retinopathy classification of diabetic retinopathy and maculopathy detection. By using the same 600

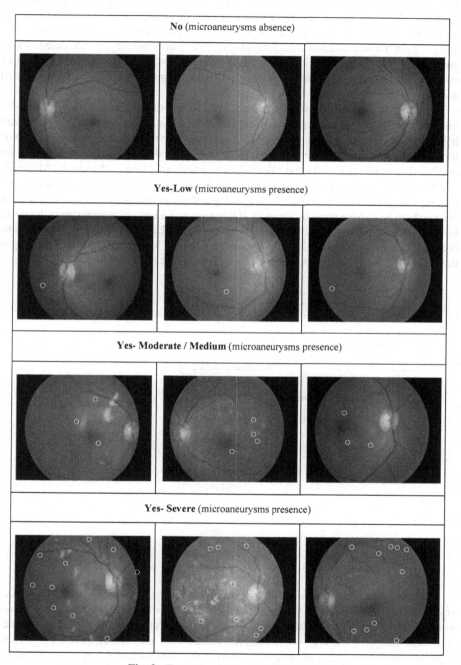

Fig. 2. Example of images in the dataset

images, the manual diagnosis was extended and it focused on the diagnosis of microaneurysms by the Consultant Ophthalmologists, Department of Ophthalmologist, Melaka
Hospital, Malaysia. This is another contribution, as this research provides another novel
dataset that focuses on the important sign of diabetic retinopathy, microaneurysms. The
images have been classified into four stages: "No" microaneurysms detected, "Yes-
mild" microaneurysms detected, "Yes-moderate/medium" and "Yes-severe" number of
microaneurysms detected. Some examples of the images from the newly developed
microaneurysms data set are shown in Fig. 2.

For the manual grading process, an excel file comprising the link to each eye fundus
image and the microaneurysms classes, as presented in Fig. 3, was provided. As presented
in Fig. 3, the microaneurysms presence first concerns two main classifications, i.e., "No"
for microaneurysms not detected, and "Yes" for microaneurysms detected. There are
another three sub-choices for the "Yes" choice, which are "Low", "Moderate/Medium"
and Severe", according to an approximate number of microaneurysms estimated by the
expert. The choice of these three cases is dependent on the threshold values for each
class, which have been fixed in advance. If there are just a few microaneurysms detected,
i.e., between one to ten, then the image is classified as "Low". If more microaneurysms
are detected, i.e., between 11 to 20, it is classified as "Moderate/Medium". Finally if
there are even more, i.e., more than 20, then the classification will be "Severe".

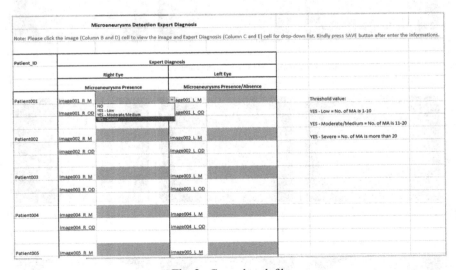

Fig. 3. Ground truth file

The findings of the microaneurysms expert diagnosis are presented in Fig. 4. As a
result of the expert grading, the total number of images in each class was as follows:
not detected ("No") class with 379 images, while the detected ("Yes") can be divided
into three categories: low (104), moderate/medium (62) and, finally, severe (49). There
were six images unclassified and excluded from the expert manual diagnosis, due to the
poor quality, and it resulted in a total of 594, instead of 600 images. Microaneurysms

Patient028	image028_R_M	YES - Low	image028_L_M	YES - Low
	image028_R_OD		image028_L_OD	
Patient029	image029_R_M	YES - Moderate/Medium	image029_L_M	YES - Moderate/Medium
	image029_R_OD		image029_L_OD	
Patient030	image030_R_M	YES - Moderate/Medium	image030_L_M	YES - Moderate/Medium
	image030_R_OD		image030_L_OD	
Patient031	image031_R_M	YES - Severe	image031_L_M	YES - Severe
Patient032	image032_R_M	YES - Moderate/Medium	image032_L_M	YES - Low
Patient033	image033_R_M	NO	image033_L_M	NO
Patient034	image034_R_M	YES - Low	image034_L_M	YES - Low
Patient035	image035_R_M	YES - Low	image035_L_M	YES - Moderate/Medium
Patient036	image036_R_M	YES - Moderate/Medium	image036_L_M	YES - Moderate/Medium

Fig. 4. Expert microaneurysm diagnosis file

Table 1. Expert diagnosis summary (Categorisation I)

Microaneurysms presence stage	No. of images
No	379
Yes - Low	104
- Moderate/Medium	62
- Severe	49
Total	594

detection is challenging due to the small size of microaneurysms, therefore high quality images are required to ensure an accurate diagnosis. The ground truth delivered by the expert can be placed into two categories. Table 1 shows the original classification made by the expert, which is divided into four classes of microaneurysms detection.

Table 2. Expert diagnosis summary (Categorisation II)

Microaneurysms detection stage	No. of images
No (microaneursysms absence)	379
Yes (microaneurysms presence)	215
Total	594

The second categorisation divides into two cases, which are microaneurysms absence "No" and microaneurysms presence ("Yes"), as presented in Table 2.

4 Proposed System

The proposed system implements a combination of fuzzy techniques for image pre-processing, such as fuzzy filtering and fuzzy histogram equalisation. In addition, the system implements the classification stage using deep learning. These techniques are implemented using the newly developed dataset for microaneurysms detection.

The proposed microaneurysms detection system has been developed using the Matlab R2018b environment. The system starts with the image acquisition process, where the system selects images from the folder for further processing. Next, the image pre-processing task takes place in order to improve the image quality. This task includes the implementation of the fuzzy image pre-processing techniques. Finally, in the classification phase, a deep learning classifier is trained using the generated features, in order to classify the images into their respective classes. Figure 5 shows the block diagram of the proposed system for automatic detection of microaneurysms for diabetic retinopathy screening and classification. The individual stages are discussed in more detail in the following sections.

4.1 Image Preprocessing

Image preprocessing takes place after the image acquisition process in order to improve the quality of the image. The present system utilizes the following image pre-processing techniques: resizing, greyscale, green channel extraction, fuzzy filtering, fuzzy histogram equalisation and fuzzy edge detection. Figure 6 shows the output image for different colour channels, meanwhile Fig. 7 shows the output image after fuzzy filtering, fuzzy histogram equalisation and the fuzzy edge detection process are performed.

4.1.1 Resizing

The original colour fundus images from the newly dataset were resized. The original images, which are of size 3872×2592 in JPEG format, provide high quality and good details. The resizing is performed for convenient use of the CNN. Most of previous research suggested that the images are cropped and resized to square number of pixels. However, in this proposed work, the fundus images are downsized proportional to the original image size, the new size being 242×162, in order to preserve the details of the original images.

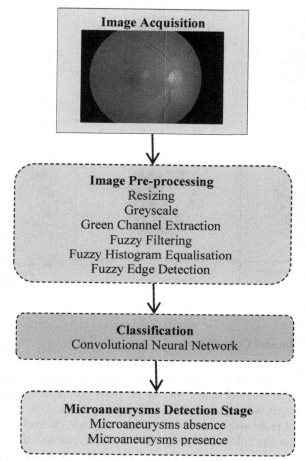

Fig. 5. Block diagram of the proposed automatic detection of microaneurysms using fuzzy image processing and deep learning

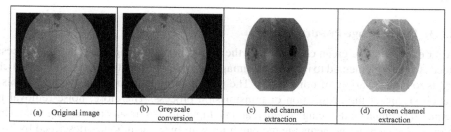

Fig. 6. Greyscale, red and green channel extracted image (Color figure online)

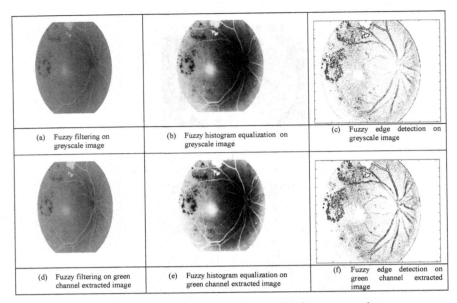

(a) Fuzzy filtering on greyscale image	(b) Fuzzy histogram equalization on greyscale image	(c) Fuzzy edge detection on greyscale image
(d) Fuzzy filtering on green channel extracted image	(e) Fuzzy histogram equalization on green channel extracted image	(f) Fuzzy edge detection on green channel extracted image

Fig. 7. Pre-processing the output image with fuzzy approaches

4.1.2 Colour Channel Conversion

The second preprocessing technique is the conversion of the colour fundus image, which consists of the red, green and blue channels. The colour input images are converted into greyscale and green channel image. In our previous proposed systems [23–26], the colour fundus images were converted into a greyscale image. Due to the capability of the green channel previously presented in [27], the green channel extraction is used rather than other image colour conversion formats. The reason of the extraction of the green channel from the colour fundus images has been explained in [27]. The next pre-processing techniques are performed on the greyscale and green channel inverted images. Figure 6 shows the output image obtained after the different conversions are applied, i.e., greyscale conversion, red channel, and green channel, for comparison.

4.1.3 Fuzzy Image Pre-processing

After extracting the green channel from the original colour image, the filtering process needs to be implemented to improve the image quality or restore the digital image, which tends to have a variety of noise types. The poor photo quality may be due to the noise acquired during the acquisition or transmission process. Therefore, noise removal is required to enhance the image quality, and is important before any processing task. The proposed system implements the median filter with fuzzy techniques, described by Toh et al. [44], called the Fuzzy Switching Median (FSM) filter. The proposed technique was working well in removing noise. The technique has been used in [26, 27] for the diabetic retinopathy and maculopathy detection. The detailed explanations about the FSM filter implementation are presented in [25, 44].

Next, after filtering the image from noise, the fuzzy histogram equalisation is performed on the images, which aims to improve the image's contrast. The colour fundus images are more challenging compared to the other types of fundus photography examination, which are angiography and red-free. Therefore, the implementation of the histogram equalisation by employing fuzzy techniques helps to enhance the contrast of the fundus images for better visualisation and detection. The technique called Brightness Preserving Dynamic Fuzzy Histogram Equalisation (BPDFHE) proposed by Sheet et al. [45] was found to work well on colour fundus images in [24–27], and has been chosen as a preprocessing technique in this proposed system as well. Detailed explanation about the proposed fuzzy histogram equalisation, including the comparison implementation with other histogram equalisation techniques, can be found in [24, 25].

The final fuzzy image processing technique performed is the fuzzy edge detection. By using membership functions, we are able to overcome the small intensity differences between two neighbouring pixels problem, by defining the degree with which the pixel belongs to an edge or a uniform region. A detailed explanation about the proposed fuzzy edge detection, including the membership functions for the inputs and outputs, is presented in [25].

4.2 Classification

A Deep CNN model is used for the classification phase. Figure 8 shows the structure of the proposed network architecture for the microaneurysms detection. The CNN architecture starts with an image input layer of the size ($162 \times 242 \times 1$), where the resized preprocessed images are inputted. Following that, the model has four convolutional layers, each followed by a rectified linear unit (ReLU), batch normalization and max pooling layers. The output of the final max pooling layer is then flattened before being inputted into the output layer which has two neurons. The final layer implements a Softmax function that is tasked with outputting the probabilities of the input image belonging to either of the two classes, microaneurysms presence or microaneurysms absence.

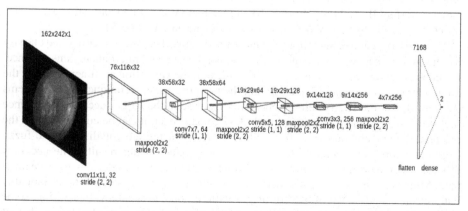

Fig. 8. Proposed deep convolutional neural network structure

The final error for the model is calculated using the cross entropy function (C):

$$C = \sum_{i=1}^{N} \sum_{j=1}^{K} t_{ij} \ln y_{ij} \qquad (1)$$

where N is the total number of images, K is 2 (the number of classes), t_{ij} is the indicator that sample i belongs to class j, and y_{ij} is the model's output for sample i for class j. Stochastic gradient descent with momentum (SGDM) was used to train the model with an initial learning rate of 0.0001. 70% of the samples in the dataset are selected randomly to form the training set, while the remaining 30% is used for testing. Each of the models was trained for 100 epochs with a batch size of 128.

4.3 Results

The performance analysis summary of the proposed system, which employs different techniques (System Variants I-V), is presented in Table 3. For System Variant I, there is no image processing implemented, except the input image resizing process, while System Variant II proposed the implementation of fuzzy image processing techniques, such as fuzzy filtering and fuzzy histogram equalisation, besides the greyscale conversion. System Variant III implemented greyscale conversion, fuzzy filtering, fuzzy histogram equalisation and fuzzy edge detection. The extraction of green channel, fuzzy filtering and fuzzy histogram equalisation are implemented in System Variant IV. System Variant V proposed the fuzzy filtering, fuzzy histogram equalisation and fuzzy edge detection including the green channel extraction. A total of 594 images, which consist of 379 images from the "microaneurysms not detected" class and 215 images from the "microaneurysms detected" class are involved in the classification stage. For the validation phase, the network is trained to predict the labels of the validation data and the final validation accuracy is calculated. Accuracy means the fraction of examples that the network predicts correctly. All systems are trained and validated on the same neural network architecture. The validation accuracy for System I is 66.29%, and the validation accuracy for System II is 69.66%. System III and System IV generated validation accuracies of 69.10%, while System V obtained a validation accuracy of 68.54%.

The experimental results show that the trained network is able to identify and classify for the two classes, which are microaneurysms presence and microaneurysms absence. It can be observed that there is a small increment in the validation accuracy between the no image pre-processsing (System I) and the pre-processing techniques-based systems (System II, System III, System IV, System V), although the largest accuracy difference (between 66.29% and 69.66%) is small (3.37%). However, it can be concluded that the pre-processing techniques, i.e., fuzzy filtering, fuzzy histogram equalisation and fuzzy edge detection, help increase the accuracy and produce better results. The accuracy difference could be higher if the proposed system is trained and validated with more input data. Moreover, the results show that it is possible to segment the diabetic retinopathy features on a small range of fundus images with reasonable accuracy. In addition, some changes and improvements on the network architecture, for example, the number of layers and the layer parameters, have been performed in order to produce better results.

Table 3. Summary of results

	System I	System II	System III	System IV	System V
Techniques	Resizing	Resizing, greyscale, fuzzy filtering, fuzzy histogram equalisation	Resizing, greyscale, fuzzy filtering, fuzzy histogram equalization, fuzzy edge detection	Resizing, green channel extraction, fuzzy filtering, fuzzy histogram equalization	Resizing, green channel extraction, fuzzy filtering, fuzzy histogram equalization, fuzzy edge detection
Number of images	594 images				
Number of classes	2 classes				
Expert grading					
No (Microaneurysms not detected)	379 images				
Yes (Microaneurysms detected)	215 images				
Training data	70%				
Validation data	30%				
Training options					
Optimization algorithm	Stochastic gradient descent with momentum (SGDM)				
Learning rate	0.0001				
Maximum epochs	100				
Validation frequency	1				
Validation accuracy	66.29%	69.66%	69.10%	69.10%	68.54%

Although the accuracy generated is in the medium range (i.e., not that good), it is considered acceptable due to some limitations, including the total number of images available.

5   Conclusions and Future Work

An automatic system for the detection of microaneurysms in colour fundus images using fuzzy image pre-processing techniques and deep learning has been developed in this paper. Although the detection of microneurysms is challenging due to the special characteristics of the microaneurysms, it can be concluded that the proposed techniques were able to improve to some degree the contrast and eventually improve the system performance for the automated microaneurysms detection system.

The system can be enhanced by implementing different other combinations of preprocessing techniques including those based on fuzzy approaches. The system can be further extended by implementing retinal structures extraction, such as optic disc and vessel segmentation for image preprocessing to produce a more reliable microaneurysms detection system. The system will also be extended to get more details on the microaneurysms classification, as proposed by the first categorisation of the novel dataset (Table 1), namely to classify into no microaneurysms presence, low, moderate/medium and severe cases. Further explorations on deep learning architectures for classification will be performed in order to increase the microaneurysms detection accuracy. Deep learning implementations are considered challenging when dealing with small or medium size datasets, as it is our case. Other convolutional neural networks, such as AlexNet, GoogLeNet, ResNet VCG16, VCG19, Inception-v3 and Inceptionrestnet-v2, could be used and validated with the proposed system. An accurate system could be used to help the diabetic retinopathy screening team to perform better and more efficient screening. The proposed developed system could be a benchmark for the development of other retinopathy signs' detection system, such as for exudates, haemorrhages and neovascularisation. Besides presenting the novel development of an automatic detection for microaneurysms, this paper also introducing a new dataset of microaneurysms, which would be useful to researchers and practitioners working in the diabetic retinopathy screening field.

Deep Learning approaches have great potential for automatic detection of diabetic retinopathy, but the limitations of such approaches are exactly in the "automatic" thus "black-box" behaviour. Due to raising legal issues such automatic approaches become difficult to use in the future, consequently the field of explainable AI [48] becomes more and more important. Explainable AI develops methods for making such deep learning approaches transparent. However, for diagnostic and educational purposes there is a need to go beyond explainable AI; For example, to reach a level of explainable medicine there is a crucial need for causability. Causability [49] is different from Causality [50] but closely connected. Causability provides measurements for the quality of explanations produced by explainable AI methods and to enable the medical professional to understand why an algorithm came up with a certain result, or why a result had a certain error rate. This calls for contextual understanding which can be fostered by bringing a human-in-the-loop [51], which adds the component of human expertise to AI processes.

Acknowledgements. This project is part of a postdoctoral research currently being carried out at the Faculty of Engineering, Environment and Computing, Coventry University, United Kingdom. The deepest gratitude and thanks go to the Universiti Teknikal Malaysia Melaka (UTeM) for sponsoring this postdoctoral research. The authors are thankful to the Ministry of Health Malaysia and the Melaka Hospital, Malaysia, for providing the database of retinal images and also for the manual grading done by the experts.

References

1. Mathers, C.D., Loncar, D.: Projections of global mortality and burden of disease from 2002 to 2030. PLoS Med. **3**(11), e442 (2006)
2. World of Organization. http://www.who.int/en/news-room/fact-sheets/detail/blindness-and-visual-impairment. Accessed 20 Mar 2019
3. Cunha-vaz, J.: Diabetic Retinopathy. World Scientific Publishing Co Pte Ltd, Singapore (2010)
4. Taylor, R., Batey, D.: Handbook of Retinal Screening in Diabetes: Diagnosis and Management. Wiley, Chichester (2012)
5. Ministry of Health Malaysia Diabetic Retinopathy Screening Team: Handbook guide to diabetic retinopathy screening-Module 5-2012. Ministry of Health Malaysia, Putrajaya (2012)
6. Adal, K.M., Ali, S., Sidibe, D., Karnowski, T., Chaum, E., Meriaudeau, F.: Automated detection of microaneurysms using robust blob descriptors. SPIE Medical Imaging-Computer Aided Diagnosis, 8670-22 (2013)
7. Adal, K.M., Sidibe, D., Ali, S., Chaum, E., Karnowski, T.P., Meriaudeau, F.: Automated detection of microaneurysms using scale-adapted blob analysis and semi-supervised learning. Comput. Methods Programs Biomed. **114**, 1–10 (2014)
8. Akram, M.U., Khalid, S., Tariq, A., Khan, S.A., Azam, F.: Detection and classification of retinal lesions for grading of diabetic retinopathy. Comput. Biol. Med. **45**, 161–171 (2014)
9. Akram, M.U., Khalid, S., Khan, S.A.: Identification and classification of microaneurysms for aerly detection of diabetic retinopathy. Pattern Recogn. **46**, 107–116 (2012)
10. Alipour, S.H., Rabbani, H., Akhlaghi, M.R.: Diabetic retinopathy grading by digital curvelet transform. Comput. Math. Med. **2020** (2012). Article 761901. https://doi.org/10.1155/2012/761901
11. Antal, B., Hajdu, A.: Improving microaneurysm detection in color fundus images by using context-aware approaches. Comput. Med. Imaging Graph. **37**, 403–408 (2013)
12. Aravind, C., Ponnibala, M., Vijayachitra, S.: Automatic detection of microaneurysms and classification of diabetic retinopathy images using SVM technique. In: IJCA Proceedings on International Conference on Innovations in Intelligent Instrumentation, Optimization and Electrical Sciences ICIIIOES, vol. 11, pp. 18–22 (2013)
13. Hatanaka, Y., Inoue, T., Okumura, S., Muramatsu, C., Fujita, H.: Automated microaneurysm detection method based on double-ring filter and feature analysis in retinal fundus images. In: Soda, P. (eds.) Proceedings of the 25th International Symposium on Computer-Based Medical Systems, CBMS, USA, pp. 1–4. IEEE (2012)
14. Kose, C., Sevik, U., Ikibas, C., Erdol, H.: Simple methods for segmentation and measurement of diabetic retinopathy lesions in retinal fundus images. Comput. Methods Programs Biomed. **107**, 274–293 (2012)
15. Lichode, R.V., Kulkarni, P.S.: Automatic diagnosis of diabetic retinopathy by hybrid multi-layer feed forward neural network. Int. J. Sci. Eng. Technol. Res. (IJSETR) **2**(9), 1727–1733 (2013)
16. Prakash, J., Sumanthi, K.: Detection and classification of microaneurysms for diabetic retinopathy. Int. J. Eng. Res. Appl. **4**, 31–36 (2013)
17. Punnolil, A.: A novel approach for diagnosis and severity grading of diabetic maculopathy. In: Proceedings of the 2013 International Conference on Advances in Computing, Communications and Informatics, New York, pp. 1230–1235. IEEE (2013)
18. Saleh, M.D., Eswaran, C.: An automated decision-support system for non-proliferative diabetic retinopathy disease based on Mas and HAs detection. Comput. Methods Programs Biomed. **108**, 186–196 (2012)

19. Selvathi, D., Prakash, N.B., Balagopal, N.: Automated detection of diabetic retinopathy for early diagnosis using feature extraction and support vector machine. Int. J. Emerg. Technol. Adv. Eng. **2**(11), 762–767 (2012)

20. Sopharak, A., Uyyanonvara, B., Barman, S.: Automated microaneurysm detection algorithms applied to diabetic retinopathy retinal images. Maejo Int. J. Sci. Technol. **7**(2), 294–314 (2013)

21. Sujithkumar, S.B., Vipula, S.: Automatic detection of diabetic retinopathy in non-dilated RGB retinal fundus images. Int. J. Comput. Appl. **47**(19), 26–32 (2012)

22. Sundhar, C., Archana, D.: Automatic screening of fundus images for detection of diabetic retinopathy. Int. J. Commun. Comput. Technol. **2**(1), 100–105 (2014)

23. Rahim, S.S., Palade, V., Shuttleworth, J., Jayne, C.: Automatic screening and classification of diabetic retinopathy fundus images. In: Mladenov, V., Jayne, C., Iliadis, L. (eds.) EANN 2014. CCIS, vol. 459, pp. 113–122. Springer, Cham (2014). https://doi.org/10.1007/978-3-319-11071-4_11

24. Rahim, S.S., Jayne, C., Palade, V., Shuttleworth, J.: Automatic detection of microaneurysms in colour fundus images for diabetic retinopathy screening. J. Neural Comput. Appl. **521**, 1–16 (2015)

25. Rahim, S.S., Palade, V., Shuttleworth, J., Jayne, C., Omar, R.N.R.: Automatic detection of microaneurysms for diabetic retinopathy screening using fuzzy image processing. In: Iliadis, L., Jayne, C. (eds.) EANN 2015. CCIS, vol. 517, pp. 69–79. Springer, Cham (2015). https://doi.org/10.1007/978-3-319-23983-5_7

26. Rahim, S.S., Palade, V., Jayne, C., Holzinger, A., Shuttleworth, J.: Detection of diabetic retinopathy and maculopathy in eye fundus images using fuzzy image processing. In: Guo, Y., Friston, K., Aldo, F., Hill, S., Peng, H. (eds.) BIH 2015. LNCS (LNAI), vol. 9250, pp. 379–388. Springer, Cham (2015). https://doi.org/10.1007/978-3-319-23344-4_37

27. Rahim, S.S., Palade, V., Shuttleworth, J., Jayne, C.: Automatic screening and classification of diabetic retinopathy and maculopathy using fuzzy image processing. Brain Inf. **3**(4), 249–267 (2016). https://doi.org/10.1007/s40708-016-0045-3

28. Lam, C., Yi, D., Guo, M., Lindsey, T.: Automated detection of diabetic retinopathy using deep learning. In: AMIA Joint Summits on Translational Science Proceedings. AMIA Joint Summits on Translational Science 2017, pp. 147–155 (2018)

29. Voets, M., Mollersen, K., Bongo, L.A.: Replication study: development and validation of a deep learning algorithm for detection of diabetic retinopathy in retinal fundus photographs (2018). https://arxiv.org/pdf/1803.04337.pdf

30. Xu, K., Feng, D., Mi, H.: Deep convolutional neural network-based early automated detection of diabetic retinopathy using fundus image. Molecules **22**(12), 1–7 (2017)

31. Rakhlin, A.: Diabetic retinopathy detection through integration of deep learning classification framework (2017). https://www.biorxiv.org/content/biorxiv/early/2018/06/19/225508.full.pdf

32. Gulshan, V., Peng, L., Coram, M., et al.: Development and validation of a deep learning algorithm for detection of diabetic retinopathy in retinal fundus photographs. JAMA **316**, 1–9 (2016)

33. Rajanna, A.R., Aryafar, K., Ramchandran, R., Sisson, C., Shokoufandeh, A., Ptucha, R.: Neural networks with manifold learning for diabetic retinopathy detection. In: Proceedings of IEEE Western NY Image & Signal Processing Workshop (2016). https://arxiv.org/pdf/1612.03961.pdf

34. Pratt, H., Coenen, F., Broadbent, D.M., Harding, S.P., Zheng, Y.: Convolutional neural networks for diabetic retinopathy. Procedia Comput. Sci. **90**, 1–6 (2016)

35. Ghosh, R., Ghosh, K., Maitra, S.: Automatic detection and classification of diabetic retinopathy stages using CNN. In: 4th International Conference on Signal Processing and Integrated Networks (SPIN), USA, pp. 550–554. IEEE (2017)

36. Chudzik, P., Majumdar, S., Caliva, F., Al-Diri, B., Hunter, A.: Microaneurysm detection using deep learning and interleaved freezing. In: Proceedings of SPIE 10574, Medical Imaging 2018: Image Processing 1057411, pp. 1–9 (2018)

37. Lam, C., Yu, C., Huang, L., Rubin, D.: Retinal lesion detection with deep learning using image patches. Invest. Ophthalmol. Vis. Sci. **59**(1), 590–596 (2018)

38. Hatanaka, Y., Ogohara, K., Sunayama, W., Miyashita, M., Muramatsu, C., Fujita, H.: Automatic microaneurysms detection on retinal images using deep convolution neural network. In: International Workshop on Advanced Image Technology (IWAIT), pp. 1–2 (2018)

39. Dai, L., et al.: Clinical report guided retinal microaneurysm detection with multi-sieving deep learning. IEEE Trans. Med. Imaging **37**(5), 1149–1161 (2018)

40. Harangi, B., Toth, J., Hajdu, A.: Fusion of deep convolutional neural networks for microaneurysm detection in color fundus images. In: 2018 40th Annual International Conference of the IEEE Engineering in Medicine and Biology Society (EMBC), pp. 3705–3708 (2018)

41. Shan, J., Li, L.: A deep learning method for microaneurysm detection in fundus images. In: 2016 IEEE First International Conference on Connected Health: Applications, Systems and Engineering Technologies (CHASE), pp. 357–358 (2016)

42. Haloi, M.: Improved microaneurysm detection using deep neural network (2016). https://arxiv.org/pdf/1505.04424.pdf

43. Tan, J.H., et al.: Automated segmentation of exudates, haemorrhages, microaneurysms using single convolutional neural network. Inf. Sci. **420**, 66–76 (2017)

44. Toh, K.K.V., Mat Isa, N.A.: Noise adaptive fuzzy switching median filter for salt-and-pepper noise reduction. IEEE Signal Process. Lett. **17**(3), 281–284 (2010)

45. Sheet, D., Garud, H., Suveer, A., Mahadevappa, M., Chatterjee, J.: Brightness preserving dynamic fuzzy histogram equalization. IEEE Trans. Consum. Electron. **56**(4), 2475–2480 (2010)

46. Hu, Z., Tan, J., Wang, Z., Zhang, K., Zhang, L., Sun, Q.: Deep learning for image-based cancer detection and diagnosis – a survey. Pattern Recogn. **83**, 134–149 (2018)

47. Couture, H.D., et al.: Image analysis with deep learning to predict breast cancer grade, ER status, histologic subtype, and intrinsic subtype. NPJ Breast Cancer **30**, 1–8 (2018)

48. Holzinger, A., Kieseberg, P., Weippl, E., Tjoa A.M.: Current advances, trends and challenges of machine learning and knowledge extraction: from machine learning to explainable AI. In: Holzinger, A., Kieseberg, P., Tjoa A., Weippl E. (eds) Machine Learning and Knowledge Extraction, CD-MAKE 2018. LNCS, vol. 11015, pp. 1–8. Springer, Cham (2018). https://doi.org/10.1007/978-3-319-99740-7_1

49. Holzinger, A., Langs, G., Denk, H., Zatloukal, K., Mueller, H.: causability and explainability of artificial intelligence in medicine. Wiley Interdisc. Rev. Data Min. Knowl. Discovery, **9**(4) (2019). https://doi.org/10.1002/widm.1312

50. Pearl, J.: Causality: Models, Reasoning, and Inference (2nd Ed.). Cambridge, Cambridge University Press (2009)

51. Holzinger, A.: Interactive machine learning for health informatics: when do we need the human-in-the-loop?. Brain Inf. **3**(2), 119–131. https://doi.org/10.1007/s40708-016-0042-6. Springer Nature

Author Index

Printed in the United States
By Bookmasters